P9-CKF-999

This book is an essential resource for new and seasoned practitioners alike, containing both practical advice and an excellent compilation of hard-to-access resources and guidelines.

—*Ronald F. Levant, EdD, ABPP, President, 2005, American Psychological Association; Dean and Professor, Nova Southeastern University, Fort Lauderdale, FL*

This is an outstanding "professional practice guide" that is destined to find a large audience of aspiring and current therapists who hunger for the real-life 'nuts and bolts' about how to conduct a successful practice.

—*Derald Wing Sue, PhD, Department of Counseling and Clinical Psychology, Teachers College, Columbia University, New York*

A compact gem of a book. A wise guide for how to think about the kind of resources you will need, along with a comprehensive library of essential American Psychological Association practice guidelines.

—*Ronald E. Fox, PhD, former President, American Psychological Association; The Consulting Group of HRC, Chapel Hill, NC*

Practical, accessible and comprehensive! A must-have that is useful for students and professionals.

—*Beverly Greene, PhD, ABPP; Professor of Psychology, St. John's University, Jamaica, NY*

Simply excellent—the authors have blended years of experience to concisely provide a wealth of information on every topic needed to thrive in psychological practice today. A "must have" for students and veterans alike. Bravo!!

—*P. Paul Heppner, PhD, President, American Psychological Association Division 17 (Society for Counseling Psychology); Department of Educational, School, and Counseling Psychology, University of Missouri—Columbia*

Drs. Pope and Vasquez provide new (and not so new) independent practitioners with vital practical and business information that their graduate schools should have provided but probably didn't.

—*Dorothy W. Cantor, PsyD, former President, American Psychological Association; private practice, Westfield, NJ*

Pope and Vasquez raise important questions and provide solid, practical advice about how to be successful in practice. This book could save you a lot of wasted time, money, and grief.

—*Tommy T. Stigall, PhD, private practice, Baton Rouge, LA*

Pope and Vasquez have done it again! This well-constructed, comprehensive, and practical resource provides the perfect "how-to" guide in a clear, engaging, and readable format; this book packs in everything the young (and many older) practitioners will need without bogging down or becoming overwhelming and contains all the essential, realistic, hands-on, no-nonsense details they never taught you in graduate school.

—*Gerald P. Koocher, PhD, ABPP, School for Health Studies, Simmons College, Boston, MA*

A "must read" resource for those in independent practice. This book teaches the business of a psychology practice—balancing financial success and a meaningful life.

—*Jean Lau Chin, EdD, ABPP; Systemwide Dean, California School of Professional Psychology, Alliant International University, San Francisco, CA*

Drs. Pope and Vasquez have created a valuable and easy to read guidebook that provides the practical, nuts-and-bolts information and resources needed for success in practice. This book is required reading for all practitioners and practitioners-in-training.

—*Jeffrey E. Barnett, PsyD, President, American Psychological Association Division 42 (Psychologists in Independent Practice)*

This book should be mandatory reading for any psychologist interested in independent practice. The contents contain invaluable information and resources in an easy-to-read format. I wish this book had been available to me when I first started my practice!

—*Lisa Grossman, JD, PhD, independent practice, Chicago, IL*

From ethics to logistics, Pope and Vasquez cover the practice landscape with skill and depth. This is an invaluable resource for seasoned practitioners and early career psychologists alike.

—*Douglas C. Haldeman, PhD, President, Association of Practicing Psychologists, Seattle, WA*

Reads like a novel, informs like an encyclopedia. This book is a virtual template for developing and maintaining a successful practice . . . enlightening for all experiential levels—graduate student to retiree.

—*Josephine D. Johnson, PhD, former President, Michigan Psychological Association; private practice, Farmington Hills, MI*

Starting a practice? Retooling an established practice? This book's for you!...an invaluable resource with all the nuts and bolts you need to build the practice that is right for you.

—*Katherine C. Nordal, PhD, Chair, American Psychological Association Committee for the Advancement of Professional Practice, 2005*

This fascinating book provides a range and depth of proactive information, from the pragmatic (including appendixes relevant to psychologists across North America) to the philosophical. It offers strategies that are broadly applicable and asks questions that invite attention to each practitioner's unique circumstance.

—*Kate F. Hays, PhD, CPsych, founder, The Performing Edge, a Toronto-based consulting practice devoted to sport and performance psychology*

This is a CrackerJack of a book for professionals, with a prize in every chapter and appendix. . . . the authors have put together a very useful book. I wish I had had something like this when I started in practice.

—*Jack G. Wiggins, PhD, former President, American Psychological Association; Missouri Institute of Mental Health, St. Louis, MO*

I highly recommend this easy-to-read book that offers a wealth of information and resources for both the beginning and seasoned practitioner. It will provide you with the tools and strategies that you need for a truly successful practice.

—*Lisa Porche-Burke, PhD, President, Phillips Graduate Institute, Encino,CA*

Ken Pope and Melba Vasquez bring a wonderful combination of personal and professional perspectives to this extraordinarily helpful hands-on resource. It should be a must-read for all beginning practitioners and a continuing resource for those more seasoned.

—*Jean Carter, Past President, American Psychological Association Division 42 (Psychologists in Independent Practice)*

What graduate school did not teach you, Pope and Vasquez have. They bridge the gap between graduate school education and professional psychology. This book is an essential read for all student/early career psychologists in need of truly understanding the intricacies of graduating and practicing in a field where one must learn how to create opportunities and begin to meet the needs of a more diverse client population. An invaluable resource!

—Miguel E. Gallardo, PsyD, Board of Directors, American Psychological Association Division 42 (Psychologists in Independent Practice); President, California Latino Psychological Association; Counseling Center, University of California, Irvine

How did I survive 46 years as a therapist without this book? It is chock full of essential information and advice that will help me thrive for the next 46 years.

—Thomas Greening, PhD, ABPP, independent practice; Editor, Journal of Humanistic Psychology

An invaluable, reassuring guide in today's world of constant change, this unique blend of thoughtful wisdom, practical steps, and diverse resources is a welcome addition for all practitioners, from those just beginning to those who have decades of experience.

—Pat DeLeon, former President, American Psychological Association

How to Survive and Thrive as a Therapist is a treasure trove of practical tips to ensure success for the early career professional and for the seasoned therapist who wants to branch out and grow. The authors offer straight talk on all the key aspects of a rewarding practice: from money to ethical development to self-care to marketing and beyond. Ken Pope and Melba Vasquez offer wisdom and hard-won experience of a kind practitioners will find nowhere else.

—Carol D. Goodheart, EdD; Treasurer, American Psychological Association; private practice, Princeton, NJ

How to Survive and Thrive as a Therapist

How to Survive and Thrive as a Therapist

INFORMATION, IDEAS, AND RESOURCES FOR PSYCHOLOGISTS IN PRACTICE

KENNETH S. POPE
AND MELBA J. T. VASQUEZ

American Psychological Association • Washington, DC

First Printing, December 2004
Second Printing, December 2005
Third Printing, May 2010
Published by
American Psychological Association
750 First Street, NE
Washington, DC 20002
www.apa.org

To order
APA Order Department
P.O. Box 92984
Washington, DC 20090-2984
Tel: (800) 374-2721; Direct: (202) 336-5510
Fax: (202) 336-5502; TDD/TTY: (202) 336-6123
Online: www.apa.org/books/
E-mail: order@apa.org

In the U.K., Europe, Africa, and the Middle East, copies may be ordered from
American Psychological Association
3 Henrietta Street
Covent Garden, London
WC2E 8LU England

Typeset in Goudy by MacAllister Publishing Services, Indianapolis, IN

Printer: Maple-Vail Book Manufacturing Group, York, PA
Cover Designer: Berg Design, Albany, NY
Project Manager: MacAllister Publishing Services, Indianapolis, IN

The opinions and statements published are the responsibility of the authors, and such opinions and statements do not necessarily represent the policies of the American Psychological Association.

Library of Congress Cataloging-in-Publication Data

Pope, Kenneth S.
　How to survive and thrive as a therapist : information, ideas, and resources for psychologists in practice / Kenneth S. Pope and Melba J. T. Vasquez.—1st ed.
　　p. cm.
　Includes bibliographical references and index.
　ISBN 1-59147-231-8 (alk. paper)
　1. Psychology—Practice. I. Vasquez, Melba Jean Trinidad. II. Title.

BF75.P66 2005
　150'.68—dc22

　　　　　　　　　　　　　　　　　　　　　　　　　　　　2004023318

British Library Cataloguing-in-Publication Data
A CIP record is available from the British Library.

Printed in the United States of America

CONTENTS

ABOUT THIS BOOK

We wrote this book as a resource for starting, growing, or improving a psychology practice. It's for psychologists (and other mental health professionals) who are just starting out—and may be unsure about what steps to take to open a practice—as well as for those who have been in practice for many years and are looking for ways to expand, strengthen, rethink, redirect, or improve their practice.

Graduate programs and internships offer a wealth of strategies for responding to those who are hurting and come to us for help. We learn theory, research, and interventions. We gain skills in assessment and therapy. Training in business principles and the other practicalities of practice tends to be much less extensive.

Most of us end up with far more knowledge and skill in responding to people in pain, in conflict, and in crisis than to our own critical needs for a successful business plan, productive marketing strategies, an office well suited to our practice, sound policies and procedures, ways to meet legal requirements, an attorney and professional liability policy we can count on, methods of self-care, a secure use of computers in our practice, and the other nuts and bolts of a psychology practice.

This book presents in a concise format information, ideas, and resources for the practicalities of practice; most chapters are almost in the form of bulleted lists. This book is *not* about assessment and therapeutic theory or technique. It is *not* a review of assessment instruments or therapy research.

Chapters on what some therapists choose to attend to only after they are well into practice appear early in the book, reflecting our belief that these are best addressed before opening the doors to a practice. For example, the chapter, "Creating Strategies for Self-Care," appears before the chapter, "Finding an Office," and "Finding an Attorney" appears before "Finding Clients and Referral Sources." Some therapists begin thinking about self-care only when their practice has left them frustrated, depleted, and depressed. They may begin the search for a skilled, experienced, trustworthy attorney only when they face a fast-approaching deadline for responding to a subpoena, a complex crisis involving questions of mandatory reporting, a licensing board investigation, or an ethics complaint.

In addition to the 14 chapters, 15 appendixes present resources that we believe can be invaluable for the practitioner:

> Contact Information for Psychology Licensing Boards in Canada and the United States
>
> APA Ethical Principles of Psychologists and Code of Conduct
>
> Canadian Code of Ethics for Psychologists, Third Edition
>
> APA Record Keeping Guidelines
>
> APA Guidelines for Child Custody Evaluations in Divorce Proceedings
>
> APA Guidelines for Psychological Evaluations in Child Protection Matters
>
> APA Guidelines for Psychological Practice With Older Adults
>
> APA Guidelines for the Evaluation of Dementia and Age-Related Cognitive Decline
>
> APA Guidelines for Providers of Psychological Services to Ethnic, Linguistic, and Culturally Diverse Populations
>
> APA Guidelines on Multicultural Education, Training, Research, Practice, and Organizational Change for Psychologists (Abridged Version)
>
> APA Guidelines for Psychotherapy With Lesbian, Gay, and Bisexual Clients
>
> APA Rights and Responsibilities of Test-Takers: Guidelines and Expectations
>
> APA Statement on Services by Telephone, Teleconferencing, and Internet
>
> Specialty Guidelines for Forensic Psychologists
>
> APA Strategies for Private Practitioners Coping With Subpoenas or Compelled Testimony for Client Records or Test Data

In our experience, many psychologists in practice do not have convenient access to the material in these appendixes. We wanted to gather them into one volume that practitioners could keep handy on the shelf or desk and take with them to consultations or court.

One of the many aspects of psychology practice that make it fascinating, challenging, and fulfilling is that it can't be done in a rote, one-size-fits-all, by the number, routine way. There's no best or guaranteed path, and no single approach works for every psychologist in every time and place. One of the challenges is to create a practice that is right for you and your community. This means in part that it responds in effective ways to the needs of the people it serves, it lets your potential clients know that you're there and available, and it is financially successful, however you define that term. Just as important, it is consistent with who you are as an individual and the values that are most important to you and is a source of meaning and fulfillment in your life. This challenge is the focus of chapter 1.

How to Survive and Thrive as a Therapist

1

WHO ARE YOU AND WHAT
IS IMPORTANT TO YOU?

The answers to those questions are the key to creating a meaningful psychology practice. They are also the key to the resources in this book.

However excellent our training, many of us leave graduate school uncertain about how to start, nurture, and guide an independent practice. Finding what you need to do—and *avoid* doing—can be a challenge because there is no *one* way to do it, no *best* way, no way that works for every individual in every community and every situation.

In this book we've tried to draw together information, ideas, and resources from a few basic areas for creating a practice that is right for you and your community. This means in part that the practice is a sound business and a financial success (however you define that term). Equally important, the practice must be consistent with your deepest values and who you are, is part of a meaningful life, and brings you joy (at least some of the time) and fulfillment.

It is easy to let our choices be guided more by our fears or our urgency for something-right-now than by our informed judgment, especially when we are anxious and uncertain about how to begin a venture like a psychology practice. In a market of few vacancies, we may be tempted to take the first office that seems halfway decent. After days spent searching for an office, once we find one we like, we may rush to sign the lease without questioning the fine print that will affect us for years to come. If we're lucky enough to know referral sources who will send us an endless stream of clients with problems in a particular area, we may breathe a sigh of relief that we can easily build an almost ready-made financially successful practice around these clients, not realizing until years pass that this kind of practice is not an area we find very interesting, challenging, or fulfilling.

Anxiety-driven choices, particularly made in the absence of adequate information, can send even the most promising practice careening in the wrong direction. The initial excitement—whatever it was that made us choose psychology as a career in the first place—never fulfills its promise but fades and dies until showing up for work each day becomes a drain, an obligation in which we are counting down the hours until the day is finally over, counting the days until the week comes to an end, counting the weeks until . . . .

Our hope is that the information, ideas, and resources in this book will reassure and support practitioners, enable more informed choices, and result in better practices. Unfortunately, there seems to be no shortage of practitioners who—because of anxiety, lack of support, or other factors—accept too quickly what a community seems ready to offer them instead of considering the opportunities they themselves might create in that community. Some work hard building a practice without asking whether the practice is right for the practitioner as well as for the community. Too many seem to end up burdened rather than enlivened by work that they would never choose to do if they could start over again. Even if financially rewarding, the practice takes from their lives more than it gives back, and the practitioners channel their time and energy into work they don't believe is ultimately very important. They set out to build a practice but instead construct a prison in which they waste their lives.

As you choose the steps, resources, and recommendations in the following chapters that are right for you and that can be helpful in creating a practice that is right for you, consider making this evaluative process a regular and integral part of your practice. At least once a year, assess each aspect of your practice. Was the practice a good choice for you and is it *still* a good choice for you? Are the different parts of your practice working together not only as a sound and financially successful business but also as a fulfilling career? Is *this* how you want to spend your time? Do you still like what you're doing? Is the income stream what you want it to be? Can you tolerate the ebb and flow of income and the financial uncertainties? Are you working with populations and on problems that are meaningful and rewarding for you? Does your practice allow you the right balance in such areas as autonomy, control, and connectedness with others? Do you want more or less leisure time? If not, how can you change your practice? What can you do differently? What additional support do you need to move in a different direction? What opportunities can you identify or create to enable your practice to reflect more directly who you are and what is important to you?

2

INCOME, EXPENSES,
AND A BUSINESS PLAN

Maybe you're independently wealthy or you have friends or family who'll support you. Or maybe you'll win a record lottery your first few weeks in practice.

Otherwise, your practice revenue will have to cover your practice expenses if you're not going to go bankrupt.

And if you look to your practice to support you (and perhaps some loved ones), you'll need to do far more than break even. Your profits will need to cover your daily living expenses and those of any dependents.

Unless you want to go through your career without the ability to take a break, you'll need enough profits to fund the days, weeks, or months you take off each year and whatever your vacations cost. Being self-employed means that no one will pay you for your sick days, vacation, or maternity and family leave.

If you want to cut back on your work at some point in your career, entering a partial or complete retirement, you'll also have to fund your own retirement and invest enough along the way so that your income continues even when you stop working.

Because your ability to support yourself in the style to which you'd like to become accustomed and the survival of your practice depend on all this working out, this challenge can be a source of anxiety for many psychologists and all but overwhelm someone just starting out.

It makes sense to prepare a 3- to 5-year (or longer term) business plan. This approach calls for you to write down your financial goals and how you're going to try to get there (i.e., the specific action steps you need to take) in light of financial realities. How much growth do you want to see in your practice each year? Will your annual expenses be relatively fixed (allowing for inflation, etc.), will they increase as you take on more work, or will they decrease as your practice becomes more efficient? How many hours a week do you want—or are you able—to work? What are your investment goals? How much do you want to invest each year in the practice itself, in your retirement fund, or in other ventures?

The plan needs to be flexible, of course. It should be adaptable to the anticipated and unanticipated fluctuations of the national economy, the lean years and feast years of your own practice's income, your multitude of expenses, and the other factors that can affect your bottom line.

If you're just starting out, it may help to go through the following list of 30 possible expenses. Choose those that are relevant for your practice, and do some research so that you can estimate what your expenses will be in these areas (and any other expenses you anticipate that are not included in this list):

- Professional license
- Professional association memberships
- Federal and state taxes
- City business license/tax
- Professional liability insurance
- Premises liability insurance
- Insurance for office equipment in the event it is lost in a fire or flood, stolen, and so on
- Medical insurance and costs for illnesses not covered by medical insurance
- Disability insurance (which may include the coverage of office rent and similar expenses, as well as income protection in the event you are unable to practice)
- Assessment supplies
- Advertising, marketing, and practice-building (includes business cards, brochures, Yellow Pages listing, etc.)
- Office deposit and office rent
- Office furniture for consulting room, waiting room, and so on
- Office electricity, heating, and cooling
- Office-cleaning service
- Prints or other artwork, plants, flowers, and other expenses for office ambiance

- Office coffee, tea, water service, and so on (Some therapists have these just for their own use; others offer them to clients.)
- Phone charges, including office phone systems or individual lines, long-distance service, cell phones, and so on
- Postage
- Attorneys and other legal fees
- Accountants
- Professional workshops, continuing education courses, and conferences, including registration fees, materials, and—if the event takes place out of town—transportation, lodging, and other expenses related to travel
- Professional books and journals
- Computers (hardware, software, Internet access, technical support, etc.), faxes, and other electronics or office machines
- Receptionist, secretary, or clerical help
- Answering service
- Billing service (or if you do your own billing, the cost of billing forms, HCFA forms, etc.)
- Transportation (to and from your office and other places that you work as a professional) and parking
- Lost revenue through unpaid bills (Unless you collect all fees in advance of providing the service, some of those to whom you submit bills may end up not paying and you'll encounter the expenses of unpaid-for services. Practitioners vary widely in their experiences of bad debt.)
- Expenses due to involuntary loans and cash flow difficulties. Some clients, insurance companies, managed care organizations, law firms, and so on, may take weeks or months to pay for your clinical, forensic, consulting, or other psychological services. Unless you charge a late-payment fee, you are giving them interest-free loans. Even if you do not have to take a loan to cover the gap until you're paid, this money is unavailable for you to invest in growing and maintaining your practice.

It's helpful to write down on a spreadsheet or similar format the anticipated expense of each area for each month for at least a 3-year period. Once you've filled in the best possible estimate of your necessary expenses, you'll have a sense of how much it may cost just to keep the doors of your practice open. (To get a better feel for anticipated expenses, it may be helpful to use this estimate to calculate your average weekly and daily expenses.) It also shows the patterns of expenses. Some of the fundamental costs are for start-up items (e.g., chairs and other furniture for the office). If you don't have enough savings to cover a "getting started" period when your income can't keep up with your expenses, and if taking out a loan is either unwise or impossible (i.e., the bank won't lend you the money), it may make sense to consider taking a "day job" with a hospital, clinic, or other employer while you build up a practice gradually. You could begin seeing patients on your day off or during evening or early morning hours whenever you aren't at work, or subletting space on a "per hour" or "per day" basis from a colleague who is not using his or her office during that time. Check your "day job" contract to see if it has any "no compete" clauses. (Some employment contracts include a section prohibiting the employee from engaging in similar work—such as providing therapy—within a certain geographic area for a specified time after leaving the company. If a "no compete" clause would prohibit you from starting a practice, you might find it helpful to consult an employment attorney about whether the clause is enforceable.)

Once you figure out how to cover your startup costs, you can examine each month's anticipated expenses to figure out how much revenue you must bring in not only to cover those expenses but also to meet your financial goals. This month-by-month plan will help you monitor and manage your cash flow so that you don't get caught short on certain months when your expenses spike (e.g., the 4 months of the year when you pay your quarterly estimated federal and, if relevant, state taxes or the month each year when your professional liability coverage premium is due). If your only source of revenue is fees for psychological services you provide in your office, you can figure out how many clients you need to see at what fee to cover your expenses and provide an adequate income. Remember that if you are not paid at the time of service (i.e., if you send bills to your clients, an insurance company, or managed care organization), you can't count on receiving the revenue in the same month in which you provided the service.

As you map out the first several years of your practice using the best possible estimates you can come up with, it is worth asking, what happens if things don't work out according to plan? Your actual expenses may be higher than anticipated and your hoped-for clientele may not show up on schedule. It's wise to have a "Plan B" (and perhaps a Plan C, Plan D, etc., as well) to cope with unexpected expenses, revenue shortfalls, and other challenges.

As you begin your practice, keep careful records—on paper, using computer software, or through a bookkeeper or accountant—of all financial data related to your practice. These records—in addition to being helpful for preparing your tax forms—will form an empirical basis for making future estimates of income and expenses and for revising your business plan.

Psychologists learn how to analyze data, and your financial records are a gold mine of data you can examine to learn about your practice. As with virtually any research project, you can look at the data in many ways depending on what you find useful and relevant to your concerns. Here are a few analyses you might consider.

What is your net profit (revenue minus expenses) each month, and what are the patterns across time? For example, are there particular months each year—months that you need to plan for—when your net profit shrinks, perhaps moving over into the negative numbers (e.g., a summer month when you take your vacation, your revenue drops to zero, and many of your expenses continue)? Is there an overall upward trend in your net profit?

What are your sources of expenses each month, and what percentage of your total expenses does each source account for? Do the patterns suggest any ways that you can spend more effectively? Effective spending does not always mean cutting expenses. Is each source of expense positively or negatively correlated with your revenue? For example, are increases in advertising expenses related to more people seeking services from you, resulting in greater revenue? The analysis takes into account that an increase in advertising one month may not produce results until the following months.

What are your sources of revenue each month, and what percentage of your total revenue does each source account for? What patterns emerge over time and what changes do they suggest you might make in your practice? Imagine a scenario in which you see a mix of direct-pay, insurance, and managed care clients. You notice that your revenue has steadily declined on Thursdays over the course of a year. Looking closer at your records, you see that as older direct-pay clients whom you've been seeing on Thursdays have terminated, you've accepted more managed care clients on that day until now all eight clients you see on Thursday are managed care clients. The managed care company pays you half your customary fee. It might be worth exploring the possibility of replacing these clients, as they terminate, with direct-pay clients at your customary fee. Filling only half of your eight Thursday openings with direct-pay clients at your customary fee would produce the same revenue as filling all eight openings with managed care clients. You could consider whether to leave the office a half-day early each Thursday as a self-care strategy or fill all eight openings with direct-pay clients.

What is your total indebtedness (if any), your sources of debt, the amount it is costing you to service the debt (e.g., interest charges), and your patterns of debt over time? Aside from formal business loans and unpaid balances on their student loans, many psychologists carry debt in the form of credit cards. Are there cards available or are there other sources of borrowing (such as home equity loans) that offer low interest rates? If you are borrowing to make ends meet, what percentage of the money you take in is accounted for by the money you borrow each month? (If you earn $6,300 and need to borrow an additional $700 each month, your borrowing accounts for 10% of the money you take in.) What percentage of your monthly expenses does repayment of the principle and interest constitute?

If you bill for your services rather than collecting the fee at the time of service, what is the total of uncollected money each month? What is the average number of days (or weeks, months, years, or lifetimes) between the time you provide a service and the time you have the fee in hand? (Even when you receive a check for payment, an additional lag may take place before the check is deposited in your account and clears.) What opportunities can you identify or create to shorten the time between providing the service and having the fee for your service in hand?

What do you do with your revenue each month? What percentage is allocated to the expenses of keeping your practice running? What percentage is allocated to attempts to expand your practice? What percentage do you put aside or invest solely for your retirement? What percentage do you invest for other purposes? What percentage do you spend for your personal needs? What percentage do you use for other purposes? Do these percentages change in any systematic patterns over time? What improvements could you make in what you use your revenue for each month?

What is the total value of all that you have put aside to date in your retirement, including all holdings, investments, government retirement plans, and savings earmarked exclusively for retirement? Is this total growing significantly month to month, or at least year to year? If you continue at this rate, what kind of retirement will you be able to afford?

How much money do you have available for "uh-oh" situations or true emergencies? "Uh-oh" situations are the unpleasant surprises that tend to occur from time to time in any practice. Suddenly, the car you rely on to get you to and from work needs several thousand dollars of repairs to get it running again. Or your office is broken into, and your extensive battery of psychological and neuropsychological tests worth in excess of $10,000 gets stolen. You then discover that your theft insurance will cover only a small portion of the replacement costs. How much cash do you have on hand or available each month to meet these financial challenges? An example of an emergency is one of your loved ones falling seriously ill and needing major medical care running in the tens or hundreds of thousands of dollars, and you finding out that your health insurance leaves significant gaps in coverage. What is the total amount of money you could secure through cash on hand, liquidating assets, and borrowing if it were important to you to raise as much money as possible?

Again, these are just some possible ways to look at the financial data of your practice. You may want to adapt some of them or create others that better fit your practice, needs, and concerns.

Earlier in this chapter we said it "makes sense" to prepare a business plan, mapping out how you want your business to grow, the specific goals and objectives for the next 3 to 5 years or so, and how you believe (or hope) you can get from here to there. It's hard to argue with the potential value of a good business plan based on realistic estimates of expenses and income, and it seems foolish, perhaps even dangerous, to run a business without one. We strongly recommend that everyone take the time to create a business plan. Part of its value for those who are just about to open a practice is that the information you gather about the actual costs of professional liability insurance, premises liability insurance, dues for professional organizations, and so on can help make your expectations and decisions much more realistic. Part of its value for those who are already in practice is that it can be a real eye-opener about overlooked and excessive expenses that can be trimmed or reallocated.

Although we *strongly* recommend a business plan and emphasize the potential risks and wastes of working without one, it's important to note—psychology being an empirical as well as a rational discipline—that in our experience some psychologists seem to create and maintain successful, thriving, fulfilling practices without making a formal business plan. They seem to operate spontaneously or intuitively without a net, taking advantage of opportunities as they appear. And that's a point that's worth taking seriously: Every psychologist is unique in some ways and works in a community and environment that differs from all others in some ways. What works for one may be a disaster for another. The purpose of this book is to provide some information, ideas, approaches, and resources that we believe are helpful. But with each item, it is important for you to weigh it carefully to see if it fits you, your values, your strengths and weaknesses, and who you want to be as a psychologist.

3

CREATING STRATEGIES
FOR SELF-CARE

We strongly recommend creating strategies for self-care *before* opening a practice, using them as a basis for professional planning, and making them a fundamental part of the professional life. If planning for self-care is neglected at the start of a practice, it can drain the enthusiasm, joy, resilience, caring, and meaning out of a career, sometimes interfering with the practitioner's ability to do good work. Self-neglect can lead to depletion, discouragement, and burnout.

WHAT HAPPENS WHEN SELF-CARE
IS NEGLECTED? SEVEN THEMES

Neglecting self-care often has corrosive consequences for the therapist and his or her work. Every psychologist is unique in important ways, does work that is unique in important ways, and experiences the effects of neglecting self-care in a personal way. Yet some themes seem to arise frequently. Each of the following may be a consequence of, intensified by, or a reflection of neglecting self-care, though each, of course, may have other causes.

Disrespecting Clients

Therapists who have become overwhelmed by their work may begin disrespecting their clients, talking about them to others in ways that are demeaning and lack fundamental respect. They may begin to spend time complaining about how unmotivated, ungrateful, selfish, insensitive, dishonest, lazy, and generally undesirable their clients are. They may become judgmental and critical toward their clients, losing empathy and kindness. They may begin dehumanizing their clients, referring to them only by labels (e.g., "that schizo" or "that borderline"). They may begin telling jokes at their clients' expense and ridiculing them in other ways.

Disrespecting Work

Therapists who become depleted and discouraged through a lack of self-care may begin trivializing, ridiculing, or becoming overly self-critical about what they do. They may begin speaking of therapy as a charade, a fraud, or a joke. They may view their work as empty, ineffective, and meaningless. Such therapists may begin showing up late for sessions, deciding to skip some scheduled sessions altogether, or failing to return clients' phone calls.

Making More Mistakes

Except for the therapists who are not human, all therapists make mistakes. Monitoring, acknowledging, accepting responsibility for, and attempting to address the consequences of our mistakes is one of our fundamental responsibilities as psychologists. But self-neglect can lead to impaired ability to attend to work. We may begin making more and more mistakes. We find ourselves scheduling two clients at the same time, forgetting to show up for an appointment, calling a client by the wrong name, misplacing a client's chart, or locking ourselves out of our own office.

Lacking Energy

Therapists who do not take care of themselves may run out of energy and find themselves without adequate sources of rest and renewal. They may wake up tired, barely find the will to drag themselves out of bed and to work, fight to stay awake and alert during a session, wonder how they're ever going to make it through the rest of the work day, leave work—*FINALLY*—too exhausted to socialize or do anything fun, and face the prospect of going to bed only to begin the grueling process again.

Becoming Anxious and Afraid

If we fail to care for ourselves, we can begin to feel that we are no longer up for the uncertainties, challenges, demands, and stresses of practice. What if our referral sources all dry up and our current clients terminate? Did we bungle that last assessment, wind up with the wrong diagnosis, and miss crucial aspects of what is going on with the client? Did we say the wrong thing when responding to a suicidal crisis, and will that person commit suicide before the next session? What if that agitated client becomes violent during a session? What if someone files a malpractice suit and a licensing complaint?

Using Work to Block Out Unhappiness, Pain, and Discontent

If our self-care has been neglected and work doesn't bring meaning or satisfaction to our lives, one self-defeating response is to try to lose ourselves and our uncomfortable feelings in wall-to-wall work. More and more clients, projects, and responsibilities are taken on until little if any free time is available to reflect on our lives, to spend time alone apart from work, or to become aware of how empty, demoralized, or miserable we are. Some psychologists work long hours and revel in it, deriving great joy and fulfillment, but the pattern here is different: Filling the time with work brings little that is positive to the self, except for its ability to distract attention from an unfulfilling life. Work is only one of the resources, such as food, alcohol, and drugs, that people may use to block out the results of neglected self-care.

Losing Interest

Neglecting self-care may lead to an empty professional life that is no longer a source of excitement, joy, growth, meaning, and fulfillment, and as a consequence, we may lose interest in it. We no longer feel the investment in the work and the connection to our clients. We go numb and try to function as much as possible on automatic pilot. We go through the motions, forcing ourselves to do as good a job as we can, but our heart is no longer in it. Lack of self-care can lead to a lack of caring.

MAKING SURE THE STRATEGIES FIT

Goodness of fit is as important in self-care strategies as it is in clothes. Making or buying clothes that fit our friends, that fit the "average" person, or are the most popular sizes is unlikely be a good approach to finding clothes that fit us. Using self-care strategies that are lifesavers for our colleagues may make us miserable. What sustains, replenishes, and gives meaning to an individual may flow far from the mainstream. Few of us would consider advising a person who has found happiness, significance, and contentment in a solitary monastic life with vows of silence and poverty, "You know, you really ought to get out and socialize more, and find ways to earn some money so that you'll have a nest egg you could rely on. I know you'd feel better about yourself and have a better life!"

Listening to ourselves, experimenting, and being honest with ourselves about what works and what doesn't are part of creating self-care strategies that fit us as individuals. Although no one-size-fits-all plan exists for any self-care strategy, the following are a few of the challenging areas that many psychologists contend with in making sure they are taking good care of themselves.

Isolation

A solo practice can be isolating by its very nature. We spend our days in our own office, seeing client after client. We can lose touch with our friends, colleagues, and the world beyond our office building, especially if we work long hours. Even during those times when we do not have a patient scheduled, charts must be updated, bills must be prepared, work-related phone calls must be made, and so on. Some psychologists find it helpful to place strict limits on the time they spend in their office and formally schedule activities that bring them out of isolation. Creating ways to stay in connection with others seems to be one of the most basic, important, and helpful self-care strategies for many psychologists.

Monotony

Even when we limit our time with clients to, say, 30 to 35 hours a week, spending so much time seeing clients can be too much for some psychologists. Some may begin to seek out other kinds of work—teaching a course; consulting; leading a supervision group; getting active in local, state, regional, or national professional organizations; and so on, to break up their days and provide variety.

Fatigue

How much time do you need between clients? Are 5, 10, or 15 minutes enough? How many clients can you see in a row without needing a longer break of at least an hour or more? How many clients can you see in the course of a day without feeling so depleted that the quality of your work falls toward the end of the day? Psychologists differ *greatly* in these areas. Some psychologists can work four consecutive 50-minute sessions with a 10-minute break between each, take an hour off for lunch, and return for another four consecutive sessions without any significant lapse in their enthusiasm or competence. Others may find that they can provide adequate services to no more than five clients each day. It's important to consider what a full-time practice will be for you. Some consider 25 to 30 client hours a week to be a full-time practice because of the additional hours needed to run a practice (keeping clinical records, bookkeeping, returning phone calls, etc.).

Part of self-care in this area is being realistic about the workload we can handle well and creating a schedule that accommodates our capacities. The focus must remain on the amount of work we can actually do well and not the amount that we feel we should do, or used to be able to do, or that some of our colleagues can do. Sometimes a conflict arises between the number of hours in which we can do good work and the number of hours we believe we must spend with clients to pay the bills or grow our practice. Effective self-care strategies not only influence our break patterns, such as the breaks we take between sessions or our vacations but they also emphasize activities, attitudes, and approaches that help us recover from fatigue and that replenish and renew us.

The Sedentary Life

Psychological assessment and therapy are usually—but not always—done while the client is sitting (or lying down) and the psychologist is sitting, neither moving around much. For many psychologists, self-care includes creating opportunities during the day for moving, stretching, and physical exercise. Physical exercise is a major self-care strategy for many psychologists not only for its physical benefits and its contrast with the sedentary nature of their work but also for its psychological benefits (see clinical and sport psychologist Kate Hays's book, *Move Your Body, Tone Your Mood* [New Harbinger, 2002]).

The Dispirited Life

If a psychology practice per se doesn't automatically provide enough physical movement and exercise for many psychologists, it may also fail for many to nurture adequately the life of the spirit. Setting aside adequate time and opportunities for meditation, prayer, and other spiritual or religious practices can be an important aspect of self-care for some psychologists. Some psychologists find that such diverse activities as reading or writing poetry, hiking through the woods, playing or listening to music, sitting on a river bank or hillside, acting in or viewing a play, or watching a sunset help nourish their spiritual lives.

The Unsupported Life

Network of Support

Graduate schools and internships place us in a network of professors, supervisors, administrators, and other students. Facing a challenge, we can talk it over with teachers and classmates. Our clinical work is closely monitored, and we receive positive and negative feedback, ideas, suggestions, and guidance. When we start an independent practice, the responsibility to create that network of support falls to us. What are some important components of a support network? Chapter 5 discusses finding an attorney who can provide key support before you open the doors of your practice by reviewing your forms, policies, and procedures.

Supervision, Consultation, and Additional Training

Identify or create resources for talking over your work, expanding your knowledge and skills, and continuing to grow as a psychologist. Is there someone you'd like to hire to provide you with supervision or consultation? Would you like to create a peer-supervision group that meets on a regular basis? What continuing education courses, workshops, and other activities would you find helpful in updating and expanding your knowledge and improving your skills? Consider what other sources of support you'll need to practice effectively.

Accountant

We recommend that each practitioner find and begin working with an accountant you can trust who will review your business plan, look at your current financial resources, and advise you on tax matters. The accountant will be able to discuss issues such as the pros and cons of incorporation, what expenses will be deductible, procedures for keeping records and receipts for tax purposes, and comparing the relative financial merits of a home office and a separate office.

Billing and Bookkeeping

Many practitioners choose to do their own billing and bookkeeping. If you choose this route, you might look into software programs that can help with these tasks (see chap. 10). However, some clinicians prefer not to take on this additional administrative task. Instead, they hire an individual or company to do their bookkeeping and billing. Some businesses specialize in this service for psychotherapists or for health care providers more generally. You can check with your colleagues to see whom they use and recommend.

You'll need to ensure that the services are compliant with the Health Insurance Portability Accountability Act (HIPAA) regulations. The U.S.

government's HIPAA sets requirements for psychologists (and other health professionals) who transmit health information in an electronic form (e.g., electronically submitting a claim for reimbursement). Subsequent sections provide the addresses of web sites where you can find detailed guidance for complying with HIPAA from the APA Practice Organization, the U.S. Department of Health and Human Services, and the U.S. Department of Civil Rights.

Psychopharmacologist

Unless you're able to prescribe medications, find someone skilled in psychopharmacology who will work collaboratively with you and your patients. Some patients, of course, do not need psychotropic medications and others may come to you already taking medications prescribed by someone else, but you may want to refer some patients to a psychopharmacologist with prescription authority for an evaluation to see if medication might be helpful.

Emergency and Hospitalization Resources

What are the emergency, inpatient, day-treatment, and similar mental health services available in your community? How much do they cost, and what are their admission criteria? Visit them and introduce yourself to the staff and administration. Find out what their policies and procedures are and if you are eligible for staff privileges. If one of your clients needs hospitalization or other crisis services, you'll be familiar with what options are available and what steps need to be taken. Some clinicians include a phone number for emergency services on their answering machine's outgoing message; others include it on their informed consent form.

Mandatory and Discretionary Reporting Resources

Find the contact information for the agencies to which you'd file mandatory or discretionary reports of suspected child abuse, elder abuse, and so on. There may be times when you are unsure of whether you are obligated to file a report. One of the sources you can consult at such times is the agency to whom you would file the report. You can call them up and, without providing any identifying information about the actual people involved, provide the agency with a hypothetical and ask if such a situation falls under the duty to report (and then document that consultation as one of the steps you took to decide whether to report). You may also call your attorney or your professional liability carrier for guidance.

Neglected Health

Moving from a graduate school environment that often includes a student health service and at least some health coverage to being suddenly out on our own in independent practice makes it easy to neglect our health and medical needs. It becomes our responsibility to find affordable health care coverage that fits our individual needs and a competent physician whom we can trust. Medical insurance can be obtained from a variety of sources, including professional organizations, self-employment associations (e.g., National Association for the Self-Employed), and some local associations such as the local chamber of commerce. Colleagues and local insurance brokers may be good sources of information.

The Stressed or Distressed Life

Therapists may experience periods of extreme unhappiness and distress. In one national study of therapists' accounts of their own experiences as therapy patients,[1] 84% of them had previously been in therapy. Within this group, 61% reported experiencing at least one episode of what they termed clinical depression, 29% reported having felt suicidal, and 4% reported having attempted suicide.

Practice itself may be stressful. In another national study of practicing psychologists,[2] 97% reported fearing that a client would commit suicide, 91% reported fearing that a client would get worse, 86% reported fearing that a client would need clinical resources that are unavailable, 89% reported fearing that client would attack a third party, 88% reported fearing that colleagues would be critical of their work with a patient, 83% reported fearing being attacked by a patient, and 18% reported having been attacked by a patient. Over half reported having been so afraid about a client that it affected their eating, sleeping, or concentration. About 12% reported that a client had filed a formal complaint (e.g., malpractice or licensing) against them. Over 3% had obtained a weapon to protect themselves from a patient.

Anger was another major theme of the study. For example, 81% reported anger at a client who was verbally abusive, 83% reported anger at a client because of unpaid bills, and 46% reported having become so angry at a patient that they did something they later regretted.

Effective self-care strategies take realistic account of both how stressful a psychology practice can be and how distressed we can become. What resources can we develop *and use* to cope with the stress of our work? How

---

[1]Pope, K. S., & Tabachnick, B. G. (1993). Therapists as patients: A national survey of psychologists' experiences, problems, and beliefs. *Professional Psychology: Research & Practice, 25*, 247–258. This article is available at http://kspope.com

[2]Pope, K. S., & Tabachnick, B. G. (1993). Therapists' anger, hate, fear, and sexual feelings: National survey of therapist responses, client characteristics, critical events, formal complaints, and training. *Professional Psychology: Research and Practice, 24*, 142–152. This article is available at http://kspope.com

can we address our own distress, seek professional help if we need it, and become aware if we reach a point of being too distressed or impaired to work effectively?

The Need for Change

Self-care strategies that support, strengthen, deepen, replenish, and enliven may, less than a year later, become a senseless obligation, distraction, and waste of time. Psychologists who focus on the subtle, sweeping, and profound changes in their clients' lives may sometimes overlook changes in their own lives and how these changes affect their self-care needs and strategies. Effective self-care includes monitoring how our self-care needs can change over time, calling us to create new strategies.

4

FINDING AN OFFICE

Having a safe, suitable, comfortable place to work can be crucial. The search for such an ideal can be demanding and tiring. The frustration of spending time and energy looking, looking, looking can cause the weary searcher to give up and take what's immediately available, having the length of the lease to regret all the ways that the office was a terrible choice.

As with so many of the issues in this book, there is no "right" or "perfect" office in the abstract. The ideal office for one practitioner and practice can be a disaster for others. The following set of questions can help you identify the office that meets your needs and wants, as well as help you avoid overlooking potential problems that tend to show themselves only after the lease has been signed.

Are you ready for your own office?

If you can afford it, leasing an entire office suite (with a waiting room, consulting room, group room, work room, store room, etc.) has the advantage that you can set it up any way you like, use it any time you like, and not worry about having to move your practice at least until the lease is up. But professionals just starting out may find it more affordable to rent an established office part-time during the hours when a colleague is not using it. You can agree on a set fee per week or month or an hourly fee can be assessed on a "per use" basis. You'll avoid the long-term obligations of a lease and the substantial startup costs of buying furniture and so on. One potential problem to anticipate if you sublease someone else's office part-time is having to suddenly schedule an emergency appointment (e.g., a client is in crisis) when someone else is using the office.

Is it the right building and locale for you and your practice?

Some practitioners prefer a contemporary office in a large, modern building such as a high-rise. It may suit their personal taste and they may believe it presents a business-like image for their corporate and forensic clients. Others may enjoy working in a bungalow or small, one-story building that houses a limited number of offices and believe it presents a more casual, warmer, more inviting setting.

Is it the right size for you?

The compact office that looks so engagingly warm and cozy during the walk-through may turn out to be too small to accommodate family meetings, group therapy, or even having several of your colleagues over for a weekly peer-review session. Even if there is enough room to move extra chairs into the consulting room for a therapy group, is there a convenient place to store the chairs when the group is not in session? Which brings us to . . .

Is there enough storage space?

Some clinicians will bring extra chairs and other furnishings into the office during a session with more than one client. Some will have extensive assessment instruments that may take up considerable space and are to be stored away when not in use. Some will have toys for play-therapy and other equipment for children that are best stored out of the way when the client is not a child. Try to imagine the various kinds of equipment you'll need—not just now but during the years specified by the lease as your practice evolves —and see if adequate, secure, and convenient storage is available (i.e., not in storage lockers located five floors below your office in the building's basement). As your practice grows and the years pass, you'll need a secure area in which to store an increasing number of charts for former clients. Make sure you'll have adequate, secure space in which to store these charts.

Where (and how) are the restrooms?

Some therapists like to have a private restroom that they alone—or they and their clients—can use. Others use the restrooms available in the office building. Part of this decision is based on preferences for privacy and convenience.

If the therapist and clients are to use the office building's restrooms, how convenient are they to your office? Some two- or three-floor buildings may have restrooms only on one floor. If the restrooms are on a different floor from your office and on the other side of the building, a "quick trip" may end up being just the opposite. If the restrooms can be locked from the inside, the therapist who makes an urgent trip between sessions only to find the restroom "occupied" may regret not having an emergency contingency plan.

How well are the office building's restrooms maintained? Where do they fall on the continuum that runs from "spotless" to "I don't care how desperate I am, I'll find somewhere else"?

Is the layout right for your practice?

Some practitioners just want an office in which to work and a waiting room. Clients may enter the waiting room from the building's hallway, then enter the clinician's office from the waiting room, and then exit when the session is over back through the waiting room and out into the hall. Other practitioners may want a different path for clients to exit from the consulting room so that one client doesn't encounter the next in the waiting room. Still other practitioners may want an "exit room" that is separate from the waiting room so that clients need not step directly from the consulting room into the public hallway but rather have a private place where they can spend a few minutes composing themselves (e.g., if they're crying).

How good is the sound proofing?

It's useful to assess the sound properties of the office as realistically as possible. You might have a colleague or two come with you to test them. One person, for example, might sit in the waiting room while one or more colleagues go to the consulting room to (a) talk at what they would consider a "normal" level, (b) talk, as some folks do, somewhat loudly, (c) laugh, (d) cry, or (e) shout in anger. Can the person in the waiting room hear any of this? You can try this test by yourself if you bring along a tape player or radio, but you'll probably get more accurate (and useful) results if other people are present to help you carry out the experiment.

If the office is not soundproofed and your prospective landlord agrees to make changes, make sure the criteria for adequate soundproofing are clearly defined in your lease, that a deadline has been created for meeting the criteria, and that the lease specifies what happens if the deadline is not met by the time you are scheduled to occupy the office.

Music, water fountains, and "white noise" can give an extra level of insurance to the soundproofing.

How difficult will it be for people to get to your office?

Anticipating the areas in which your clientele will tend to live and work, how easy will this office be for them to find? If many of them rely on public transportation, is it convenient to the subway, bus line, or similar forms of transportation? If you plan to work in the evenings and on weekends, will the transportation be available? (Public transportation on some routes may be scaled back or eliminated entirely on evenings, nights, weekends, and holidays.) If many of your clients drive to your office, do the freeways and surface streets provide reasonably easy access? How bad and how often are the traffic jams in this area? How's the parking around your office? Is the on-street parking so grim that clients will likely have to park blocks away? If parking lots are close by, do they tend to have spaces available and how much do they charge? How easy is it to get from the bus or subway stop or the parking spaces to your office if it is pouring rain, snowing, 104 degrees, or otherwise challenging weather?

Is your office accessible to people with disabilities?

What obstacles, if any, would a person in a wheelchair encounter when entering your building and going to your office? If the building has steps, are there also ramps or elevators? Are the restrooms equipped for use by people who use wheelchairs? If a client or colleague meeting you at your office is blind, is there a Braille guide to the elevator buttons and other information necessary to navigate your building? If the front door of your building is routinely locked and clients use an intercom to identify themselves before being "buzzed in," would someone who is deaf be able to use that system? If not, is there a reasonable alternative? (For additional information and resources on this topic, please see the Web site *Accessibility & Disability Information & Resources in Psychology Training & Practice* at http://kpope.com.)

How safe is the area?

What is the crime rate in the immediate area? What are the chances that you or someone else making the trip from a parking place, bus stop, or subway station to your office building will be safe from robbery, rape, beatings, or other forms of assault? What are the chances that you or anyone else will be safe once inside the office building itself—in the elevator or stairwell, in the restroom, or in your waiting room? Is your office building, parking area, or any area in between safe after dark?

What is your office like during the hours you'll be using it?

A realtor or the building manager may show you the office early on a Saturday or Sunday morning. You take your time examining every aspect, asking every question you can think of, and it just seems perfect for you—the ideal office at a reasonable price. You sign the lease, move in, and begin scheduling clients. But it's only when you're there during the weekdays—not early on a quiet weekend—that you discover that into your ideal third-floor office waft the chemical smells from a hair salon, the unappetizing food smells from a restaurant, and the exhaust from the traffic below. The office seems to vibrate because the people in the office right above yours are . . . what *are* they doing? Practicing the shot put? Trying to open a safe by repeatedly lifting it and dropping it? Testing the durability of sledgehammers by striking them full force against the floor?

During which hours is the office building open?

Some office buildings may shut down and lock their doors at night or on weekends. Those who lease the office will have keys, but it may make it difficult to see clients outside weekday business hours. Ask when, if at all, the office building's doors are locked and unlocked, the elevators are shut down and resume service, the hallway lights are shut off and turned back on, the heating and air-conditioning are stopped and started, and so on.

When (and how) is your office cleaned?

Some office buildings supply office cleaning and maintenance services; others leave this up to the tenant. If these services come as part of the lease, what services are included? Is it just emptying the wastebaskets, or are the floors swept and the furniture dusted? How often is the service provided— daily, weekly, or on some vague schedule no one has figured out?

When will your office be cleaned? Some office buildings, for example, clean offices after business hours, say, at 6, 7, or 8 p.m. If this is when you might be seeing clients, that might be a problem. It's hard to overestimate the difficulties of doing effective psychotherapy when a worker is asking you and the client to lift your feet so that the vacuum cleaner can get to the rug under-neath your chairs.

If you're responsible for cleaning your own office and waiting room, find out just how long the trek is going to be when you empty your wastebasket. Give some thought as to whether this is a good use of your time and whether your schedule will even give you the time to do this task.

What sort of climate control is there for the building and your office?

Is the heating or cooling system for your office separate from the rest of the building (e.g., the lobby and hallways)? What sorts of controls are there for heating and cooling your office? Is there one control for both your office and the waiting room? Sometimes the lack of differential controls for indi-vidual rooms can be a significant problem. A setting that is just right for the consulting room may leave the waiting room like a sauna or a polar ice cap.

What kinds of ventilation are there in your office and waiting room?

Some rooms in office buildings (especially waiting rooms) lack windows and are completely dependent on the ventilation system. In some high-rise office buildings, the windows will not open but are sealed shut. Not being able to open a window to let in fresh air, enjoy a mild breeze, or air out a room that has somehow acquired an "interesting" odor can be a real disadvantage. The available methods of ventilation may become quite important in regard to smoking, the topic of the next question.

What is the building's smoking policy and how is it enforced?

Some buildings may attempt to establish and enforce a "no smoking" policy throughout the building. Some will leave it up to those who lease individual offices to set the smoking policy for their individual space. Some accept that at least some people will likely smoke in the building's restrooms.

Those who value a smoke-free environment—and who may be allergic to tobacco smoke or have health problems aggravated by exposure to tobacco smoke—may find that smoke from the building's restrooms or other offices— even offices on other floors—may make it through the building's ventilation ducts to their own office.

What do the other tenants say?

After the realtor or building manager has shown you the building and office, drop back by later that day or the next, introduce yourself to people in the other offices, and ask about the building and its services. What do they like and dislike about the building? What did they learn about after they'd moved in? Those who have been in the building for a while can be sources of useful information. Is the elevator often out of order? Does the cleaning crew tend to be less than helpful (e.g., break coffee mugs, scratch computer screens during cleaning, throw away papers that were left on a desk, leave the door unlocked when they leave)? Are serious problems in the lobby or hallways often left unaddressed? Does smoking occur in the building regardless of what the smoking policy is? Other tenants are often good sources of information about how effective and reliable the building's heating and cooling systems are, parking availability, how swiftly and completely repairs are made, and safety issues.

What is—and isn't—in the lease?

The leases presented by many landlords—particularly if the landlord is a large corporation—will enumerate in detail the landlord's rights and the tenant's responsibilities. Receiving *much* less space and emphasis in the typical lease are the landlord's responsibilities and the tenant's rights.

The landlord almost certainly had the lease prepared, or at least reviewed, by a real estate attorney, someone familiar with the legislation and case law, as well as the common practice and pitfalls in this area, and who has been paid to look after the interests of the landlord. Consequently, leases may be difficult to decipher by a layperson. The legally accepted meaning of some elements of the lease may not become apparent until it is too late for the tenant who does not have training as a real estate attorney. Our recommendation is that hiring an attorney who is skilled and experienced in this area of law to review the contents and wording of the lease *from the perspective of your interests* is money well spent. The attorney's fee will be a relatively small fraction of the total sum you'll be paying for the office over the course of the lease and may pay for itself by preventing disasters many times over.

Make sure all your concerns are addressed in the lease. Don't rely on oral agreements; use the contract to clarify every aspect that is important to you. Make sure you understand everything in the contract, why it is in there, and what the implications are.

What period does the lease cover? What renewal options does the lease offer? If another office in the building becomes vacant, do you have the right of first refusal if you want to move to a different office within the building or expand your office space by leasing additional offices? Can you sublet your office to someone else when you aren't using it?

Pay particular attention to cost of living and any other increases in rent, fees, or assessments over the term of the lease. Are there any additional fees or assessments of any kind? For example, if building repairs are necessary because of water damage to the lobby, if the central heating system is broken, or snow needs to be cleared from the parking lot, are these expenses assessed from the building's tenants?

Under what conditions can the lease be terminated, and what notice or procedures are involved?

When are your rent payments due? What are the penalties for late payments, and is there any grace period?

Under what conditions can the landlord enter the office once you have leased it? Must he or she give you any notice or obtain your permission? Can he or she enter your office when you are not there?

Will you need a satellite office?

Some practitioners maintain satellite offices so that they are available in two or more locations. One option is to switch offices with other therapists who also want to practice in additional locations. Two practitioners may have their own personal offices in which they practice most of the week, but one or two days a week they go to the other person's office to practice. Often the therapists who maintain a satellite office have been in practice for a while and have found that they can increase their clientele by being available to see clients in a different geographic area.

Lease or buy?

For those who can afford it, buying an office can be a good investment. The monthly payments you make will not disappear as "rent" but will go toward your mortgage, build equity, and eventually result in your owning the structure. You may be able to sublet the office when you're not using it, using the rent you take in to help pay the mortgage.

One of the interesting aspects of buying your own office is that you get to discover what kind of a landlord you are. The responsibilities fall to you. If a pipe bursts in the ceiling while you're having a session with a suicidal client in crisis, if the air conditioner quits working while the temperature outside is 102, or if the lock on the bathroom door jams and a client is unable to come out, *you* get to solve the problem. Quickly. In your spare time.

A home office?

This chapter has focused on renting or buying an office that is separate from your residence. Some clinicians, however, choose to start or to continue a practice in a home office. Using a home office can be a little more challenging for the beginning therapist who lacks the experience and confidence that come later in a career.

Home offices and separate offices both have potential strengths and weaknesses. Some clinicians are reluctant to use a home office because of their loss of privacy, personal preferences, theoretical orientations, or other factors. They prefer that their patients not know where they live. Sometimes this is a safety consideration. Sometimes it is wish to avoid dealing with patients who make a mistake about the appointment schedule and show up on the wrong day (which may be the therapist's day off). They may show up at the therapist's home in the middle of the night in crisis, or they may become curious or obsessed with the therapist and park down the street to watch his or her house or "hang out" in the neighborhood. Some clinicians prefer not to use a home office as a way to have a clear separation between home and work. This is done either as a way to help contain their work time (leaving an office that is geographically separated from your home helps provide a clear boundary between work and family, social, or leisure activities; otherwise it may be easier to stay or return to work with your office in your home) or perhaps the change in location helps make it easier for them to leave their work behind at the end of the day.

Some clinicians, on the other hand, enjoy the convenience of working out of their home. They have no transportation expenses, they spend no time traveling to and from the office, they don't have to cope with traffic, and they don't have to search for a parking space or paying a parking fee. If their car breaks down, they don't have to make alternate arrangements to get to the office and back home. They may enjoy being able to spend their breaks between clients, lunchtimes, and unexpected free time (e.g., when a client cancels at the last minute) "at home." They may also find out, through discussions with their accountant, that a home office offers some financial advantages in terms of potential write-offs and so on.

When deciding whether a home office is right for you and your practice, it's useful to consider the following issues:

- Are there any zoning regulations in your neighborhood that would prohibit you from operating this business in your home or that would affect your practice in any way?
- Does your residence have a private entrance that patients can use? If not, does this pose any potential difficulties? For example, if others live in your home, would clients encounter them and would this have any risks or downsides?
- Do you have rooms in your home that are appropriate to serve as a consultation office and a waiting room?
- Is there a bathroom that clients can use?

- Would your home office be accessible to people with disabilities, including people who use wheelchairs?
- Is your office conveniently located in relation to your potential clients, and can it be reached easily by car or public transportation?
- Are there any clients whom you would consider seeing in a separate office but might not feel comfortable or safe seeing in a home office?
- If you have a partner, children, or share your home with others, how will they feel about your seeing patients in your home office and how will this affect your practice? For example, is there any chance that one of your young children would interrupt your therapy sessions?

FORM FOR OFFICE HUNTING

When visiting potential offices, it may be helpful to carry along the following structured form, which covers this chapter's major points.

Style and size of building _____

Size of office _____

Amount, location, and security of storage space _____

_____

Location and condition of restrooms _____

_____

Layout of consulting room, waiting room, and so on _____

_____

Soundproofing _____

Accessibility in terms of freeways, surface streets, public transportation,

traffic jams, and so on _____

_____

Parking _____

Accessibility for people with disabilities _____

_____

Safety issues _____

Office conditions during the hours you'll be using it _____

_____

Hours the building is open (including weekends and holidays) _____

_____

When (and how) the office is cleaned _____

_____

Climate control for the building and for your office (separate controls

for each room?) _____

Ventilation in office and waiting room _____

_____

Building's no smoking policy and enforcement _____

_____

Comments from other tenants _____

_____

Lease provisions _____

_____

5

FINDING AN ATTORNEY

When psychologists encounter a difficult legal problem, they may begin asking around for a "really good" attorney. This is often a good way but not a good time to find an attorney.

We recommend finding and consulting an attorney *before* you're out practicing and get hit with a problem. Locating the right attorney—right for you and your practice—early in the process is a form of primary prevention that can avoid all sorts of shocks, missteps, and crises.

The downside of consulting an attorney before you open your practice, of course, is that you pay for several hours of the attorney's time when it doesn't seem absolutely necessary. But the potential benefits can far outweigh the costs.

If you start looking for an attorney before you open your practice—or at least before you encounter a legal problem—your search can be unhurried, free from pressure, and careful. You won't be searching desperately with the clock ticking as you wonder how to respond to a suicidal client's ominous message on your answering machine, a threatening note from a potentially violent client, or a subpoena demanding materials you believe you shouldn't turn over (see Appendix O).

You can also take your time to find out which attorneys your colleagues recommend, what their strengths and weaknesses are, and what their fees are. If you need more initial information, you can check out the cases they've handled. Finding the attorney's range of experience is important. Some attorneys, for example, specialize in representing psychologists and other mental health professionals in malpractice suits, but not in licensing board hearings or vice versa.

In addition to seeing who your colleagues recommend (or warn against), you might check to see if your state or local psychological association offers legal consultant services to its members. Typically, the attorney who provides the services will review legal documents and provide information about the relevant legislation and case law for basic practice issues, but he or she would not provide representation in more serious matters such as a malpractice suit.

You can take your time setting up an initial appointment with the best candidate emerging from your search. When you make your initial call to set up the appointment, the attorney may be in the midst of a trial and unavailable for nonurgent matters. Because you're not facing an imminent crisis, you can schedule a time convenient for both of you for your first meeting.

The first part of the initial appointment can focus on whether this is the right attorney for you and your practice. This is your opportunity to interview the person on whom you'll depend for legal guidance and in whose hands your career may rest if you're the object of a licensing complaint or malpractice suit. Is there anything about the way the attorney answers your questions that gives you serious pause? Is there anything about him or her that makes you question whether you can trust, confide in, or work with this person? If the attorney is part of a large firm, what is his or her relation to the firm—partner, associate, "of counsel," or some other role? Will decisions about the services provided to you (e.g., how to handle a case should you be sued for malpractice) be made solely by this attorney or will others in the firm have a role?

One important issue that can be addressed in the interview—and also with other psychologists who have been represented by the attorney—is the attorney's availability. Some attorneys are excellent in representing psychologists but may limit their availability. They may go for long periods without returning calls, but this relative unresponsiveness may be temporary. Some attorneys may not return nonurgent calls while they are in trial. They may want to concentrate all their attention and work on the trial at hand. Psychologists may not appreciate this approach until they themselves are the defendant.

Some attorneys may fail to respond promptly on a more consistent basis because they are chronically overscheduled. A brilliant attorney may build an impressive reputation and begin taking on too many clients. Unfortunately, important details, deadlines, and whole cases may get lost in the crowd.

Still other attorneys may decline to return many calls because they do not want to engage in what they call "client hand-holding." They want to spend their energy on the legal matters and minimize the time spent updating, reassuring, comforting, empathizing with, soothing, and "handling" the client.

As with so many other factors, there is no "right" way for attorneys to handle their availability (at least in our opinion). What is crucial is finding an attorney whose approach matches your needs and, if possible, wants.

It's worth asking if the attorney does work for your malpractice carrier. Each carrier tends to have certain attorneys that it works with in each geographic area. If your attorney is one that your carrier routinely assigns to represent psychologists in your area, it may simplify things if you're sued for malpractice. Even if the attorney does not customarily handle cases for the carrier, the carrier may allow him or her to defend you against a suit. When sued, some psychologists and their attorneys have made compelling arguments to the carrier that the psychologist's "regular" attorney is in the best position to defend against the suit. The carrier, however, may or may not be persuaded by the argument. Our view is that it makes sense to choose the attorney that best matches the needs of you and your practice, even if that person does not routinely work for your malpractice carrier and even if that means that another attorney may represent you should you be sued.

What should the attorney do for you at this point, just as you're starting out? Skilled and experienced attorneys can spot potential problems in psychologists' policies and procedures in such areas as how they set and collect fees, how they handle "no show" appointments and dropouts, how they respond to emergencies, and the other aspects of a practice. Chapter 7 discusses thinking through policies and procedures.

Attorneys can also identify difficulties in your forms and documents. We recommend that you have copies of all your forms on your computer and that you print out a specific form only when you need it. Such documents include intake forms and informed consent forms for assessment, therapy, consultation, audiotaping or videotaping sessions, and release of information. This approach has three main advantages. First, it makes it easy to update the forms when there are changes in the relevant legislation, case law, professional standards, or your practice. Second, you can fill in the blanks (e.g., the client's name, date, and other details) before the form is printed out and signed. Third, it makes it easy to make any ad hoc changes in the form, adapting it to any particular use.

Often it seems easier to use a form that someone else has already developed. Starting with such a form can save considerable time and effort, but two significant potential pitfalls are possible. First, because someone else developed the form for a different practice, there is little chance that it will magically fit your unique practice. Whenever you borrow a form from another source, study it carefully to see how you can adapt it to the best possible fit with your own practice. How can it communicate most effectively with your clients? If it is an informed consent form for assessment or therapy, how can it most clearly convey your approach and what's involved in the assessment or therapy you provide? Does it explain what the client needs to know about the nature, purposes, costs, and implications of assessment or therapy in order to make an adequately informed consent to or refusal of services?

Second, unless the form was developed specifically for the state in which you practice, it needs to be reviewed and, if necessary, adapted to comply with relevant state legislation and case law. This is a valuable service your attorney can provide in reviewing your forms. The state may, for example, require that an informed consent for release of information form be in type at least as large as a specific standard (to ensure readability and avoid important information becoming lost in the "fine print"), must include the specific purpose and recipient of the release, and must include a date on which the consent to release expires (which must not exceed a certain duration).

Where can psychologists who are just starting out obtain forms they can adapt to their own practice as well as to state legislation and case law? One good source is colleagues, clinics, and hospitals in your community. Again, any form you find from another source will almost certainly need to be adapted to your practice and should be reviewed by your attorney. The American Psychological Association Insurance Trust has placed a sample informed consent form for therapy online at http://www.apait.org/resources/risk management/inf.htm and a sample informed consent form for forensic services at www.apait.org/resources/riskmanagement/finf.asp. Other sample forms can be found in *Articles, Research, & Resources in Psychology* at http://kspope.com; *Ethics in Psychotherapy and Counseling: A Practical Guide, Second Edition* by Kenneth S. Pope and Melba Vasquez (Jossey–Bass, 1998); *MMPI, MMPI-2, & MMPI-A in Court: A Practical Guide for Expert Witnesses and Attorneys, Second Edition,* by Kenneth S. Pope, James N. Butcher, and Joyce Seelen (American Psychological Association, 2001); *Promoting Practice Health: Documentation For a Risk Managed Clinical Practice* by Ed Nottingham and Gordon Herz (in preparation); and *The Paper Office, Third Edition* by Edward L. Zuckerman (Guilford, 2003).

The U.S. government's Health Insurance Portability Accountability Act (HIPAA) requires that psychologists (and other health professionals) who transmit health information in electronic form (e.g., electronically submitting a claim for reimbursement) must use forms and procedures that comply with certain criteria. Extensive information is available online through the Department of Health and Human Services at http://www.cms.hhs.gov/ hipaa and the Office of Civil Rights at http://www.hhs.gov/ocr/hipaa.

The American Psychological Association's Practice Organization and the American Psychological Association's Insurance Trust have developed a HIPAA course that includes step-by-step strategies for compliance and an array of HIPAA-compliant forms for each of the states (i.e., the forms developed for each state were designed to comply with that state's relevant legislation and case law). Information about the course and about related HIPAA materials is available at http://www.apapractice.org.

Finally, you and the attorney can make a list of "When this happens, I call the attorney" items. One mistake that new clinicians can make is not contacting their attorney the first few times they receive a subpoena for records (see Appendix O). Being served with this legal document can be intimidating and some clinicians may assume that they can't go wrong by doing what the form says (e.g., turn over a client's records). As emphasized throughout this book, legislation and case law about responding to subpoenas differ from state to state. However, in many instances, despite receiving a valid subpoena for client records, it may be your legal obligation to claim privilege on behalf of the client and refuse to turn over the records pending further developments (e.g., the client formally waives the privilege; the psychologist receives a court order to turn over the records). Knowing when to contact your attorney—for example, about a subpoena, a lease agreement, a contract for group practice, an ethics complaint, or a requirement to report child abuse—when you are just starting out can be an essential element in surviving and thriving in practice.

6

FINDING PROFESSIONAL
LIABILITY COVERAGE

It will come as no big surprise that we believe there is no single best form or provider of professional liability coverage, just as there is no one "best office" or "best attorney." The challenge is to find the coverage that best fits you and your practice.

Here are some questions to ask and issues to consider as you investigate the policies offered by various carriers.[1]

Can you understand the written policy?

It's important to obtain a sample or specimen policy from each company and read it carefully. Can you understand it? Does it clearly state who is covered in what ways under what circumstances? If you are sued and you have any doubt or dispute about whether you are covered, the determination will most likely turn on the exact wording of the policy. Abstraction, vagueness, ambiguity, and terms that don't quite fit are unlikely to be helpful when you are facing a suit. If the policy seems full of loopholes—whether intentional or unintended—either seek written clarification from the company or look for another carrier.

---

[1]This is obviously not a comprehensive list of all the questions and issues that may be relevant to you. We've tried to identify some of the most useful questions and most important issues for many psychologists.

Does the policy as written cover what you actually do?

The policy will define a scope of coverage along with a list of specific exclusions (i.e., acts that are not covered). Policies for psychologists will almost certainly cover traditional forms of assessment and therapy, but consider what else you might be doing as part of your practice. For example, what would happen in the following scenarios?

- You and some colleagues form a "peer supervision" group so that you can discuss your work and get feedback and suggestions. A client of one of the other therapists in the group commits suicide and you are one of the named defendants in the subsequent malpractice suit on the basis of you supposedly providing supervision to the therapist. Does this fall under your professional liability coverage?
- You write an article on mental health trends for your local newspaper and are sued for plagiarism and copyright infringement. It's a bogus complaint, but you'll still have to defend against it. Does the carrier defend you against this complaint?
- One of your clients claims to have slipped on a wet spot ("Someone must have spilled a cup of coffee there or something") on your waiting room floor, injured a vertebra, and suffered major medical bills. Does the policy include premises liability?
- You're at a movie and someone in the audience experiences a psychotic episode and begins threatening people. You try to help talk the person down, but during the outburst an attack occurs and someone is killed. You are one of the named defendants in a wrongful death suit. Are you covered?
- One of your clients is on vacation in another state (where you are not licensed), calls you in crisis, and talks with you during a brief phone session.[2] Later the client sues you for malpractice, filing the suit in the other state. Do the facts that the client received service and filed the suit in a state where you are not licensed affect your coverage?
- You're traveling abroad and respond by phone to a client in crisis. The client later sues you for malpractice on the basis of this phone session. Does the policy cover you for acts performed while you were in another country where you are not licensed?
- You give a talk on self-help at the local library. Someone in the audience later claims to have followed your advice and suffered psychological harm as a result of your talk at the library. When

---

[2] Please see Appendix M.

the audience member sues you, does the professional liability carrier provide the attorney and defense?

- You carry your client notes on a laptop that is unfortunately stolen. The thief anonymously publicizes your notes and several patients sue, including you as a defendant. Are you covered?
- You decide to hire a secretary to help you with all the paperwork, scheduling, and so on. One of the people you interviewed for the job but did not hire sues you for discrimination. Does your professional liability policy apply?

Policies tend to avoid long lists of every possible professional activity, situation, and event. However, if the wording of the policy leaves you or your attorney in any doubt that you will be covered for what you do as a psychologist, we recommend that you seek written clarification from the carrier *before* you encounter trouble.

Does the company have an adequate track record?

If a company has been providing professional liability coverage to psychologists for a number of years, this may reflect a commitment to providing this service not only through periods that are good in terms of the professional liability insurance business but also the times that are unfavorable, lean, or downright brutal. At the very least, it shows that the company has managed to keep enough customers sufficiently satisfied to stay in this branch of the business over the long haul. Take a look at the track record. Have premiums stayed relatively steady, increased gradually, or soared over the years? What kind of reputation does the company have among your colleagues? Have psychologists who are covered by the company and been sued wound up being thankful and enthusiastic fans of the company?

Is the company financially sound?

Find out if the policy is issued through an *admitted carrier*. An admitted carrier participates in the state's Guarantee Fund. If any admitted carrier goes out of business, policy holders may seek protection through the Guarantee Fund. Holders of policies issued through a nonadmitted carrier (also called a surplus lines carrier) cannot seek protection through the Guarantee Fund.

Take a look at the company's financial rating as reported by A. M. Best. These ratings are online at http://www.ambest.com. A carrier might have a rating of A+ or A++. If the company does not have a high rating (i.e., if the company falls below A or A− or is not rated at all), consider looking elsewhere. Don't entrust the defense of your reputation and career to a company that may not have the financial resources to back you in the event that you are sued.

Is the policy claims-made or occurrence-based?

Assume that you buy a professional liability policy from a company for 1 year and then renew it twice so that you have the policy from that company for a total of 3 years. If it is an occurrence-based policy and you're sued *for something that happened during those 3 years,* the policy will be in force regardless of whether you are sued during those 3 years or at any time after the policy has expired. The policy will be valid as long as the claim concerns an event that took place during the policy's 3-year span.

If it is a claims-made policy, however, the policy will be in force only if the suit is for something that happened during those 3 years *and* if the suit itself (i.e., the "claim") is filed during those 3 years. If you want to be covered under this policy for future claims about something that happened during those 3 years, you would need to buy an additional endorsement known as a "tail."

In summary, an occurrence policy applies to events that occur during the years specified by the policy. (In the example above, it was a 3-year period.) A claims-made policy applies to events that occur during the years the policy was purchased for only if the claim (i.e., the malpractice suit) for those events is also filed during those same years.

Understandably, purchasing a 1-year occurrence policy tends to cost more than a 1-year claims-made policy. To compare the two forms of coverage meaningfully requires looking at the accumulated costs over your lifetime. If you have a 25-year career and buy an occurrence policy for each of the 25 years (all from the same company or changing companies from time to time), you're covered for the quarter century that you practice and for the subsequent retirement years. But if you buy claims-made coverage, what happens if you change companies after, say, 10 years, and someone sues you 5 years later for something you allegedly did during those 10 years? To obtain claims-made coverage for those claims that are filed later, you'll either buy a "tail" from the company that you are leaving or a "nose" from the new company. A tail extends the time that your former company will cover claims for something that happened during the years when you bought the policy. A nose shifts the responsibility to your new company to cover claims for something that happened during the years when you bought a policy from the old company.

As if all this were not complicated enough, the premiums for claims-made policies tend to pattern their rates in a stepwise manner. Assume hypothetically that you're destined to be sued for something you've done in the first year of your claims-made policy. It is actuarially less likely that the suit will be filed that same year than filed in some subsequent year. As a result, the premiums for a claims-made professional liability policy tend to rise systematically toward a plateau.

Making informed choices about claims-made policies—and how they may compare financially to occurrence policies—involves obtaining clear information. We recommend that you gather the necessary details from the companies about their patterns of stepwise increases in premiums, the length and costs of their tails, the costs of their noses, and the conditions under which the fees for tails are reduced or waived (e.g., the psychologist becomes disabled and unable to work).

An additional factor making it harder to compare the costs of the various claims-made policies (or to compare them with occurrence policies) is that each company may offer contingent discounts. The discounts may be contingent on completion of a certain number and kind of continuing education courses, the amount of time devoted to psychological practice (e.g., a steep discount may be offered to someone who practices 10 or fewer hours per week), particular kinds of credentials such as a diplomate from the American Board of Professional Psychology, and so on.

Is the company offering the policy easy to reach and responsive to your questions?

You'll likely have a lot of questions about each policy you review. You'll want to know how well it fits your practice, whether it makes sense for you financially, and whether the company will justify your trust in it should you ever have to rely on it to defend against a formal complaint. How easy or hard does the company make it for you to find clear, accurate answers to your questions? When you call, does an automated system put barriers between you and an actual human being? Are you put on hold for extended periods of time? Once you reach a receptionist, are you connected rapidly with someone both qualified and authorized to answer your questions? If you ask a question that they have to do some research on to answer, do they call you back reasonably quickly or weeks after you've already made a decision? Or perhaps not at all? If you ask them to e-mail, fax, or mail you a sample policy, do you receive it promptly? In other words, when you phone them, do they come across as competent, consumer-friendly, and responsive or more like an "I don't care" computer company with the world's worst tech support?

If you're sued, what happens if the company wants to settle and you object?

An insurance carrier's decision to settle a case can have enormous consequences for you. It can affect your reputation and career. Some of your colleagues, clients, and friends may assume that you must have done something wrong. They may view it as similar to a plea bargain in a criminal trial. If you testify as an expert witness, you may be cross-examined on the fact that you were sued for malpractice, did not mount a defense, and paid the plaintiff at least some of the money demanded in the suit. The attorney conducting the deposition or cross-examination may ask if part of the money that you or your insurance company paid was to "gag" the plaintiff to prevent others from learning about the matter. (Some settlements include a stipulation preventing one or both parties from discussing the case.)

Find out from each company what happens if you object to a settlement offer that the company wants to accept. In some instances, the company may decline to continue to defend you so that if you want to continue the fees for your attorney for pretrial discovery and preparation and for trying the case itself will come out of your pocket. If you subsequently lose the case and the plaintiff is awarded a larger sum than the settlement offer, you may have to pay the difference.

What rights, if any, do you have if you find your attorney or defense to be unacceptable?

You may be assigned an attorney who you do not believe is qualified or well prepared to defend your particular case. It may be that the attorney has never previously tried a case involving this area of malpractice law and seems to have difficulty grasping the concepts. The attorney may not return your calls, subpoena the records that are basic to discovery, prepare you for your deposition, or seem prepared in conducting a deposition. What procedures does the company use in evaluating complaints about the attorneys it assigns? Do you have any recourse if you have reason to believe you're not receiving an adequate defense?

What dollar limits does each company offer?

The dollar limits are usually expressed as the total limit per claim and the total limit for the policy. You might choose a policy that has a $250,000 limit per claim and a $500,000 limit for the policy. If you're sued, the most the company will pay for that claim is $250,000, but it will cover any number of claims (limiting each to $250,000) until the $500,000 limit has been reached. As with most other forms of insurance, the higher the limits, the larger the premiums. Some managed care companies require a $1,000,000 limit per claim and a $3,000,000 limit for the policy year. They may also require an annual confirmation that your policy is in force.

Do the dollar limits include or exclude the attorney's fees and expenses?

The attorney fees and expenses for any given trial can be unpredictable. When an attorney begins putting in a lot of time on a case, securing and reading records, interviewing fact witnesses, hiring expert witnesses, conducting depositions, submitting briefs, arguing pretrial motions, and doing the other important work of trial preparation, the expenses can mount up fast. And this is before the trial itself. We strongly advise that you consider a policy in which such expenses *are not counted* as part of the dollar limits.

Does the policy cover some of the income you lose while defending against this complaint?

You may spend days away from your office being deposed and testifying during the trial. This is time when presumably you would be seeing clients and earning the money it takes to put a roof over your head and food on the table. Find out the degree to which the policy reimburses you for this lost income.

Does the policy provide coverage for a licensing board complaint?

Although licensing boards, unlike malpractice courts, do not award monetary damages, their actions can affect your reputation and career. They have the power to revoke your license. Because defending a formal complaint to a licensing board can be expensive, we recommend choosing a policy that includes coverage of the legal expenses for responding to licensing complaints.

7

THINKING THROUGH YOUR POLICIES AND PROCEDURES

One key aspect of independent practice is that you don't report to any CEO, supervisor, or boss who tells you what to do. You're not handed a booklet of the organization's policies and procedures. If there's something you want to do—attend a convention perhaps or move your summer vacation from August up to July—you don't have to seek approval from the board of directors.

In other words, you're on your own.

This is a wonderful freedom, but it also presents a set of complex responsibilities. You will need to create, implement, evaluate, and revise your own policies and procedures.

As with so many other issues in this book, your policies and procedures need to fit who you are and what's important to you. We strongly recommend that you do not adopt a policy or procedure simply because someone else uses it, it comes highly recommended, or most therapists in your community use it. Find out as many ways of doing things from as many sources—colleagues, books, the Internet, and so on—as possible, but use these examples only to inform—not replace—your own thinking. Try to create each policy and procedure so that it best fits your values, approaches, and goals.

We also recommend that you write down each policy and procedure you develop *before* opening your practice. Writing them down can help clarify them. You may want to give some of these policies and procedures to your clients in written form as part of the process of informed consent. A written handout can ensure that clients understand their obligations regarding such matters as fees and appointment cancellations. This will help prevent misunderstandings regarding what you expect of them and what they can expect of you. Section 3.10d of the APA Ethical Principles of Psychologists and Code of Conduct (see Appendix B) states, "Psychologists appropriately document written or oral consent, permission, and assent."

In the rest of this chapter we list some of the most basic questions you'll need to answer when developing policies and procedures that fit what's important to you.

How do you handle an initial session with someone seeking therapy? Some therapists start with the assumption that this is the first session of therapy. The therapist or client—or both—may discover that they are not a good match, that the client would work better with another therapist, but the provisional assumption from the first meeting onward is that therapy has begun. Other therapists explicitly delay starting therapy until after the first session. For some, the first session is described as a consultation, an opportunity for both the therapist and prospective client to learn something about each other, to evaluate whether they think they can work well together and whether they would make a good match. Only if both agree that working together makes sense would they agree to begin therapy. However, the therapist might recommend other therapists or interventions. Some therapists do not charge a full fee for this initial session; others charge a higher fee because they are conducting a psychological assessment.

How long is your "typical" session of individual psychotherapy (or whatever type of therapy—couple, group, family, etc.—you specialize in)? An hour? Fifty, 45, or 40 minutes? How long is the break you typically take between sessions? Do you ever offer "double" sessions, running twice as long, for any reason, or offer sessions of a different length? How firmly or flexibly do you manage time boundaries at the end of sessions? Do you always end the session on time—to the minute—or do you bring the session to a close within a few minutes of the scheduled end time? Are there any circumstances in which you would extend a session (e.g., if a client is overwhelmed and in crisis)? Are you willing to see some clients two or three or more times a week for emergency sessions?

What is your standard fee for a session of individual psychotherapy or for whatever type of psychological service you specialize in? For what reasons, if any, do you ever reduce your fee for a client who has been paying a full fee? When you first begin working with a client, what do you tell him or her about the possibility of increases in your fees? Do you increase them according to a set schedule? If not, how do you decide whether and when to increase your fees, by how much, and with whom (i.e., all clients or only some)? Do you ever accept people into therapy who are unable to pay the full fee? If so, how do you decide what to charge them? Do you have a formal sliding scale and, if so, what factors determine where a client's fee falls on the scale? Do you ever provide therapy for no fee? Some therapists are strongly opposed to providing free therapy for a variety of reasons, including their own experiences. Others routinely offer free therapy to those in financial need and report good results. Arguments between the two groups tend to be not much more successful in changing anyone's mind than arguments between psychoanalysts and behaviorists.

When do you collect your fees? Do you ask for a session fee at the beginning of that session (i.e., in advance of service), at the end (i.e., as soon as you have provided the service), on a weekly or monthly basis? Do you send out bills?

What forms of payment do you accept? Cash only? Personal checks? Third-party checks? Credit cards? What is your policy on bounced checks?

What sources of payment do you accept? Only direct payments from the client? Insurance coverage? Managed care? If you accept payment from insurance companies, contact the company to find out what they require in terms of the content of the records you keep (i.e., what elements you need to include) and record review. Some companies may require that sessions be approved or authorized in advance, a process often called *precertification*. Some require that you file periodic reports (e.g., every six sessions) that you will have to fill out for review and they will supply the form to use. You'll need to obtain the client's informed consent for this release of information. If you bill insurance companies, will you require that the client pay you your complete fee at the time of the session (so that the insurance payment goes directly to the client), or are you willing to accept the copayment from the client and wait for the insurance company to pay you the rest?

If you plan to provide services to managed care patients, you'll need to fill out their application forms and allow time for the process of becoming an authorized provider under each managed care plan. Talking with colleagues in your area may be one of the best sources of information on this topic. Different communities have different arrays of managed care companies, and the same managed care company may have very different track records in different states. Colleagues will be able to tell you their experiences with each company they've worked for, how reliable and responsive the company is, how promptly bills are paid, how difficult it is to gain authorization for various services, whether paperwork is routinely lost, how much time you'll likely spend "on hold" while checking about a particular client or claim, and so on. Some therapists decline to be paid directly by any third-party source; however, they may offer to prepare a statement that the client can submit to the insurance company.

What is your policy when a fee is not paid on time? If you ask for the fee at the time of service (e.g., at the beginning of a session), what do you do if the client does not bring the money or a checkbook to the session? What do you do if a check bounces? If you bill for your services, how many days or weeks does the client have to pay? Are there specific financial penalties for late payment? How large a debt, if any, do you allow a client to accumulate? At what point, if any, do you discontinue therapy because a client is not paying the bill? Do you ever use a collection agency? If not, how do you handle unpaid bills? What if a client or former client with a large outstanding balance requests a copy of his or her records or requests that you send a report to someone?

What methods do you make available to clients for contacting you—e.g., to reschedule—between sessions? Does your office phone have an answering machine or an answering service? If you use an answering machine, does anyone else have the code to play back the messages, and when you play back messages, can anyone overhear? If a client leaves a message (about a crisis, rescheduling an appointment, etc.), how promptly do you return the call? The same day? Within 24 hours? Do you have a beeper? Do you communicate with your clients via e-mail?

What is your policy regarding talking with clients between sessions at your office? Aside from rescheduling the next session or similar business that can be handled quickly, do you make yourself available to talk with your clients by phone? Are you available just during weekday business hours? What about evenings, weekends, and holidays? Are there any limits to how long you will talk? Do you charge for this time? If someone cannot come in for their regularly scheduled session, are you available to have a phone session with the client during that same time?

What are your policies regarding cancellations and missed appointments? Do you charge a full fee for all missed appointments and for appointments not cancelled with at least 24 hours' notice? If not, can you specify clearly what exceptions you make?

How do you handle informed consent? As we discussed in more detail in a previous book,[1] informed consent cannot be reduced to a written form or confined to a static moment. It is a process that involves the therapist's ability to communicate with a unique person and make an informed judgment that he or she is in a good position to decide whether to consent to or decline specific psychological services. The information provided and the way it is provided depend on what kind of service (e.g., assessment or therapy) is under consideration, but the adequacy of the consent process can be assessed in terms of how well it addresses the following questions (which are adapted from our previous book):

- Does the person understand who will be providing the service and the psychologist's qualifications (e.g., license status)? If the

---

[1]Pope, K. S., & Vasquez, M. J. T. (1998). *Ethics in Psychotherapy and Counseling: A Practical Guide* (2nd ed.). San Francisco, CA: Jossey–Bass.

service will be provided under supervision, with consultation, or other arrangements involving more than the individual psychologist, does the person understand the arrangement and its implications (e.g., for privacy, confidentiality, privilege, and record-keeping)?

- Does the person understand the reason for meeting with the psychologist? Most people consulting an independent practitioner will have scheduled their own appointment on their own initiative, but some may show up because they were told to by an internist, an attorney, or a court and have no clear idea why they are there.
- Does the person understand what services the psychologist will be offering and what the effects of these services may be?
- Does the person understand the factors that may limit or significantly affect the services (e.g., the managed care coverage only authorizing five sessions of therapy)?
- Does the person understand the relevant fee policies, including those for unpaid bills and for missed or canceled appointments?
- Does the person understand the limitations to privacy, confidentiality, or privilege (e.g., conditions under which the psychologist either must or may disclose information to a third party)?
- Does the person understand his or her rights under the Health Insurance Portability Accountability Act (HIPAA)?
- Does the person understand the degree to which the clinician is or is not available by phone between scheduled sessions?

Do you acknowledge or express appreciation for specific referrals (e.g., thank a colleague for referring a client to you)? If so, how do you ensure that your communication with the referral sources is consistent with the client's rights to privacy, confidentiality, and informed consent for the release of information?

What is your policy about recording information about therapy sessions in the patient's chart? Some psychologists keep the most minimal records possible within the framework of the APA Record Keeping Guidelines (see Appendix D), any relevant state laws and regulations, and any relevant requirements imposed by third-party payment sources (e.g., managed care organizations, insurance companies, or employee assistance programs). Others keep exceptionally detailed and comprehensive records. Our suggestion is that the record of each therapy session should make clear, at a minimum: (a) the date, time, and duration of the session; (b) the basics of what happened during the session; (c) the evolving assessment (including whether the client is in crisis or at risk for suffering or inflicting serious harm); (d) current interventions (including any adjunctive therapies, medications, and actions to be taken by the client or therapist before the next session); (e) progress or setbacks, if any; (f) any changes in the treatment plan; and (g) when the next appointment is scheduled.

Good records, in our opinion, distinguish between material that is important and helpful and material that is misleading, excessive, or problematic. Consider the following chart entry describing a session:

> Met with Lilly for a 4th therapy session from 9:00 to 9:45 a.m. [today's date] focusing mainly on her suicidal impulses. Continues to feel that what she calls the "aftershocks" of her rape 2 months ago are "unbearable." Cried during much of the session. Said tensions and turmoil among her coworkers at the office make her feel worse. Is continuing the meditation and self-talk, which she says are beginning to help. Believes she is almost ready to join the support group for rape survivors that we discussed last week. As noted previously, she meets the criteria for PTSD, which seems the most appropriate diagnosis. Has not developed a suicide plan and we both agreed that she was not at risk to take her life at this time. Next session scheduled at the same time next week. She will call if she begins to feel in danger of taking her life. Reviewed steps she could take if I were not available by phone and she were in serious crisis.

Now consider another chart entry describing the same session:

> Lilly is proving to be the typical "difficult client": self-dramatizing with her talk of suicide to get my attention. Arrived dressed very seductively today, obviously hoping to turn me on. Wonder if this is a central dynamic with her, maybe having something to do with her rape. Talked about how her boss at work, [first and last name], is cheating on his wife with his secretary, [first and last name]. (Is Lilly secretly jealous?) Also thinks the comptroller, [first and last name], may be embezzling funds. Is it possible that she's lying about this to keep me interested? Next session will press her more to take a good, hard look at herself.

The second note provides little, if any, information about what brought the client to seek help and the specific means the therapist is using to provide that help. The description of the client's supposed "central dynamic" provides no information about what the client was actually wearing but may reflect only the therapist's strong reaction to it. Third parties are named needlessly in a way that may be harmful to them should the records become part of a legal action.

Will you see a client who is working with another therapist for adjunctive therapy (e.g., phobia desensitization or hypnosis to stop smoking)?

What is your policy about meeting clients outside your office? Do you ever schedule sessions (e.g., for *in vivo* desensitization) in public places outside your office, make a hospital visit to a client facing surgery, or meet with clients in their homes if they are homebound due to a disability or fatal disease? Would you accept a client's invitation to a party, or attend a client's graduation or wedding ceremony? How do you handle unexpected meetings with clients, such as discovering that a client is sitting next to you and your partner in a crowded movie theater, is a member of a board or committee you've just joined, has signed up for a seminar you're teaching, is the only person who shows up at an open house you're holding to sell your home, is seated next to you and your family on a long flight, or is becoming director of the community playhouse where you like to act in amateur productions? Under what circumstances, if any, would you conduct a clinical or forensic assessment of or provide therapy to your landlord, your internist, your babysitter, or your stockbroker? How about your attorney, one of your best friends, your secretary, your relatives, your tennis partner, the loan officer at your bank, your child's teacher, or someone in your peer-supervision group?

Diverse factors such as our theoretical orientation, the size and nature of the communities we live in, and our personal values influence our responses to these questions. Professional ethics codes, practice guidelines, legislation, and case law can offer guidance, but, as we've written elsewhere, these documents

> cannot do our questioning, thinking, feeling, and responding for us. Such codes can never be a substitute for the active process by which the individual therapist or counselor struggles with the sometimes bewildering, always unique constellation of questions, responsibilities, contexts, and competing demands of helping another person. . . . Ethics must be practical. Clinicians confront an almost unimaginable diversity of situations, each with its own shifting questions, demands, and responsibilities. Every clinician is unique in important ways. Every client is unique in important ways. Ethics that are out of touch with the practical realities of clinical work, with the diversity and constantly changing nature of the therapeutic venture, are useless. (Pope & Vasquez, *Ethics in Psychotherapy and Counseling*, 2nd ed.)

For those looking for resources in this area, the set of Web pages at http://kspope.com/dual/dual.php ("Dual Relationships & Boundary Dilemmas: Trends, Stats, Guides, and Resources") includes several of the most widely used decision-making guides. These include Mike Gottlieb's "Avoiding Exploitive Dual Relationships: A Decision-Making Model;" Jeff Younggren's eight-step model, "Ethical Decision-Making and Dual Relationships;" research articles (e.g., a national survey of 4,800 psychologists, psychiatrists, and social workers); sets of scenarios and questions; and examples of boundary-crossings from one of this book's author's work as a therapist.

What steps, if any, do you take when a client does not show up for a scheduled appointment and does not call? Imagine, for example, that the client has been severely depressed and acutely suicidal.

If a client arrives late, are there any circumstances under which you will extend his or her session time?

What steps do you take if a client does not terminate but simply stops coming to therapy and does not communicate with you in any way? Some therapists prepare a letter to the client, describing the situation and any attempts the therapist has made to reach the client by phone or other means. The letter states that the client has withdrawn from therapy without notice, invites the client to contact the therapist if he or she wishes to explore the possibilities of resuming therapy, addresses any issues of unpaid fees, and wishes the client well. The letter is sent registered mail, return receipt requested, to help ensure that the client—and only the client—receives it. It is important to document clearly in the chart any steps that the therapist takes in regard to a patient who has suddenly stopped therapy without notifying the therapist.

What are your policies and procedures regarding mandatory or discretionary reporting (e.g., child or elder abuse)? Each state and province has a different set of legislation and case law governing reports in regard to issues like child or elder abuse. Each community has its own organizations for receiving these reports. Similarly, the legislation and case law imposing a *duty to protect* third parties differ from state to state. Policies and procedures should provide clear guidance for recognizing and fulfilling these responsibilities.[2]

What are your policies if a client arrives for a session drunk or high on drugs? Some therapists refuse to work with clients under those conditions; other therapists believe that at least a limited session with the client under these conditions can serve an important purpose. What are your policies if a client becomes verbally abusive toward you during a session or seems potentially violent?

What are your policies regarding vacations and other time off? In the relatively early days of psychoanalysis, many therapists seemed to take the month of August off for vacation. How much time you take off, particularly at one time, may be influenced not only by your own needs and wants but also by the nature of your practice. Some therapists working with more fragile clients avoid taking off more than 10 days or 2 weeks at a time. The amount of time you take off each year may also, of course, be influenced by how well you can do without the income you would have earned during the

---

[2]Some state or provincial agencies have put the relevant regulations in regard to such issues as abuse reporting on their Web sites. Links to these online resources are available from the "Psychology Laws & Licensing Boards in Canada & the United States" section of the *Articles, Research, & Resources in Psychology* Web site at http://kspope.com/licensing/index.php. Two other online sources of information about child abuse-reporting regulations are the U.S. National Clearinghouse on Child Abuse and Neglect at http://nccanch.acf.hhs.gov/general/statespecific/index.cfm and "Mandatory Reporting of Child Abuse and Neglect" ("A summary of the important features of statutes mandating persons to report child abuse and neglect. References to statutes, articles and resources in all 50 states"), compiled by attorney Susan K. Smith, at http://www.smith-lawfirm.com/mandatory_reporting.htm. In some situations, it may be helpful to consult Appendix E, "APA Guidelines for Child Custody Evaluations in Divorce Proceedings," and Appendix F, "APA Guidelines for Psychological Evaluations in Child Protection Matters."

time off. Therapists differ in their policies about when they notify their clients about an upcoming break and how much they disclose.

We recommend telling clients about an upcoming break (a vacation, leaving town for a conference, going into the hospital for a medical procedure) as soon as you learn about it. This helps clients plan and adjust their own schedules and prompts them to bring up any concerns they have about the break. It is also consistent with the Golden Rule: The sooner we learn from clients that they will be going on vacation or otherwise missing therapy sessions, the better we're able to reallocate our own schedule (and plan for any lost income due to not receiving that client's fees). Although some therapists say something along the lines of "I'll be away from the office . . . " or "I won't be working on . . . " and leave it at that, declining to answer the client's questions about the reason for the absence, other therapists use self-disclosure in a clinically sound manner, answering virtually any of the client's questions.

8

PREPARING A PROFESSIONAL WILL

Unless a therapist is invulnerable and immortal, it is a good idea to prepare a professional will. Unpleasant as it is to think about, all of us are vulnerable to the unexpected and at any time our lives may be suddenly ended by a drunk driver, a stroke, a mugging, a heart attack, a fire, a plane crash, or countless other misfortunes.

A professional will is a plan for what happens if a therapist dies suddenly or is incapacitated (e.g., falls into a coma) without warning. It helps those whom you designate to respond promptly and effectively to the needs of your clients and to the "unfinished business" of your business. It also gives others the basic information and guidance that can be so hard to come by at a time of shock and mourning.

Preparing a professional will is another of the important steps we recommend you take *before* you open your practice. We can't schedule our personal misfortunes or postpone accidents so that they happen later in our careers. Our professional responsibilities include preparing for the possibility that something may happen to us, taking away our ability to function adequately, at any time without warning. No single professional will with a "one size fits all" approach will work well for every psychologist, every kind of practice, or every situation, but this chapter looks at the items and issues that are useful to address in a professional will.

THE PERSON YOU DESIGNATE TO ASSUME
PRIMARY RESPONSIBILITY

Who would respond effectively in the event that you suddenly die or are incapacitated? Who can make necessary arrangements in a time of great stress; take care of matters sensitively, efficiently, and effectively; and make sure nothing important is overlooked? Who is the best person to talk to many, if not all, of your clients? A good professional will clearly designates a qualified person to serve as the executor of the will and explicitly authorizes that individual to carry out the tasks that the will specifies.

It's useful to provide adequate information about how the designee can be contacted in the event of your sudden death or incapacitation. What is the person's phone, fax, and pager numbers? What are the person's office and e-mail addresses? Are there others likely to know where the person is if he or she proves hard to reach?

THE PEOPLE SERVING AS BACKUPS

Life tends to be full of surprises and sometimes hesitates to cooperate with our plans. At the time he or she needs to step in and take charge, the person you designated to assume primary responsibility may be overseas at a conference or on vacation, attending to a family emergency, seriously ill, or otherwise unavailable. It's important to have a second and third designee, each ready to step in if necessary.

COORDINATED PLANNING

Coordinated planning can make for a much more useful professional will and make it easier for the executor to carry it out. You can meet with your primary designee and both backups to outline what you want done, what needs to be done, and what information the designee will need. One person may think of something that the others have overlooked, and what the psychologist may think "goes without saying" ("You all know that bookshelf where I keep my appointment book, don't you?") may need clarification for the will's executor.

If the designees have trouble relying on a verbal description of where something essential is, they can be shown. They can be introduced to the people they'll need to work with (e.g., your secretary, the executor of your personal will, your accountant, your attorney, your office landlord) and exchange contact information with them. If the time comes that the designee must take charge, he or she will have detailed instructions and information in your professional will, but the designee will also know the rationale for each step (having been involved in the planning process), will know the key people to work with, and will know where the records and other materials are.

YOUR OFFICE, ITS KEYS, AND ITS SECURITY

In addition to providing your office address, it's helpful to be as specific as possible about where each key to your office can be found. For example, "There are four copies of the key to my office. One is on the key ring I always carry with me. It is the key with the blue plastic on it. My partner, whose contact information is _____, also has a key to the office. My secretary, whose contact information is _____, has a key. The building manager, who can be contacted in an emergency at _____, has a key."

There may be separate keys for each of the consulting rooms, the storage room, the filing cabinets, the desks, the computer, and the door to the building itself. It's easy to overlook a key that someone will need to fulfill the responsibilities outlined in your professional will.

Some offices have a security system that requires a code. Be sure to specify the necessary codes, instructions, and where the system is located.

YOUR SCHEDULE

Where is your schedule kept? In a daily planner you keep with you, in an appointment book at the office, on your computer, or in a personal digital assistant (PDA)? Once the record of your scheduled appointments has been located, is additional information needed to access it? For example, if you keep your schedule on your computer, what passwords are used to log on and access the schedule? Where on the drive is the schedule kept? What are the names of the relevant files? Is there a backup somewhere if the copy on your computer has become corrupted of if the computer itself is unavailable (e.g., destroyed in an office fire or earthquake or stolen)?

AVENUES OF COMMUNICATION FROM CLIENTS AND COLLEAGUES

Do clients and colleagues contact you through an answering machine, e-mail, or other method? Clearly describe each one and how the person implementing your professional will can access the messages. What is the code used to retrieve messages from your answering machine? What are the names of any relevant e-mail accounts, along with the user name, password, server address for receiving and sending mail (POP or SMTP), and so on?

CLIENT RECORDS AND CONTACT INFORMATION

Depending on the method of notification you choose, the person implementing your professional will may need to initiate contact with your clients. He or she may also need to return calls from clients whose message lacks a return number. A professional will needs to include clear instructions about how to locate and access client records and contact information. The ability to locate treatment records promptly may become exceptionally important because the sudden death of a therapist may trigger a crisis for some clients. The professional will should also designate whether the person implementing the will or someone else will maintain the therapist's client records. This information can be announced in the local newspapers or filed with the state psychology licensing board and state psychological association.

CLIENT NOTIFICATION

Therapists may choose one or more methods to notify clients of their death. They can choose to have their executor call each client, place a notice in the local newspaper, change the outgoing message on the answering machine to include the announcement or ask clients to call the clinician implementing the deceased therapist's professional will, or by letter. It is worth spending some time considering the potential impact of each method in terms of the Golden Rule and how each of the current and former clients might respond. Would any of us want to learn of our own therapist's or clinical supervisor's death by reading about it in the newspaper or hearing a recorded announcement on an answering machine? Are there resources that our clients might find helpful in these circumstances (e.g., designated colleagues who will make appointments available to your clients to help them deal with the immediate consequences and, if the clients choose, to locate subsequent therapists)? You'll have a good sense of which approaches will work best for your individual practice based on the relationship you have with your clients.

It's important that the notification be made in a way that respects each client's right to privacy. Letters and phone messages can, if not carefully handled, lead unintentionally to the disclosure to a third party that the client is seeing a therapist. Family members and others may not always respect the privacy of someone's mail and may, perhaps "accidentally," open and read something not addressed to them. Someone could also hear a phone message on an answering machine not meant for him or her. In some cases, such unintentional disclosures can place a client at great risk. The abusive partner, for example, of a client who sought therapy because she is a battered woman may become enraged at finding out, through an intercepted letter or phone message, that the client has sought help and may react violently, perhaps lethally.

COLLEAGUE NOTIFICATION

Which colleagues should be notified immediately? Are you a member of a group practice or do you share a suite of offices with someone? Are there clinicians who provide consultation or supervision to you on a regular basis, or are there clinicians who receive those services from you? Do you co-lead a therapy group or family sessions with anyone? Are there conferences or workshops that you present on a regular basis? It can be helpful to look over the listings in your scheduling book for a few months to ensure you don't overlook any colleagues who should be listed (along with contact information) in your professional will for immediate notification.

PROFESSIONAL LIABILITY COVERAGE

It's useful to include the name of the company providing professional liability coverage, their contact information, the policy number, and instructions for the company to be notified immediately after the therapist's death or incapacity.

ATTORNEY FOR PROFESSIONAL ISSUES

Many psychologists have consulted attorneys for professional issues. The attorney might have reviewed the psychologist's office forms (informed consent, release of information, etc.) to ensure they conform to state legislation and case law requirements. The attorney might have discussed the psychologist's policies and procedures, format for keeping records, or particularly troublesome cases that raised puzzling legal questions. The psychologist might have sought legal consultation about how to respond to a subpoena or legal representation in a malpractice suit. It's useful to provide contact information for an attorney whom the psychologist has consulted for practice issues.

BILLING RECORDS, PROCEDURES, AND INSTRUCTIONS

The person whom the professional will designates to take charge will need to know where the billing records are, how to access them (e.g., if they are maintained by computer software), who prepares and processes the bills (e.g., a billing service, accountant, or office clerical worker), and how pending charges are to be handled.

Some therapists may be both financially able (e.g., they have no large outstanding debts and there are adequate funds for their financial dependents) and desirous to forgive part or all of any remaining unpaid bills that were to be paid out of their clients' own pockets (i.e., excluding due or over-due payments from insurance companies). Some may want to provide a ses-sion—at the deceased therapist's expense—for each client, during which the clinician serving as executor of the professional will would work with the client to discuss the situation, assess current needs, and explore options for future therapy. The professional will should include explicit instructions about any such wishes.

EXPENSES

How have the psychologist preparing the professional will and the per-son designated to serve as professional executor decided that the executor will be compensated? Perhaps the easiest arrangement is at the executor's cus-tomary hourly rate, but other approaches can be used (e.g., a flat fee, a token payment, the executor declining any compensation for rendering this service to a friend, or a contribution to a charity chosen by the executor). A profes-sional will needs to include clear instructions about how all business-related expenses are to be paid.

YOUR PERSONAL WILL

To avoid unintended problems and conflicts, it's helpful to review both your professional will and your personal will side by side to ensure they are consistent. If a personal will, for example, directs all its assets to be disbursed in a certain way but makes no mention of the funds to be used to pay the executor of your professional will, problems can arise. It is useful if each will makes explicit reference to the other.

LEGAL REVIEW

A review of the professional will by an attorney skilled and experienced in mental health law can prevent numerous problems. The executor of the professional will can consult with the attorney should any legal quandaries arise in the days, weeks, and months after the psychologist's death. The attor-ney can also advise on whether, in light of state legislation and case law, the professional will is best authenticated simply by the signatures of disinterested witnesses, the seal of a notary, or other means.

COPIES OF THE PROFESSIONAL WILL

Copies of your professional will can be given to those designated as potential executors and to your attorney. Some psychologists may consider making special arrangements to ensure the executors' access to such information as their passwords for retrieving e-mail and answering machine messages is granted *only after their death*. This avoids having this confidential information distributed to others in multiple copies of the will.

REVIEW AND UPDATE

People, practices, times, and situations change. A professional will that is perfectly suited to us when we draw it up may have out-of-date contact information and aspects that don't fit us well at all just a year or two later. It's helpful to review a professional will on a regular basis—say, once a year—and make an immediate update whenever there is a significant change in our circumstances.

9

FINDING CLIENTS AND REFERRAL SOURCES

This chapter reveals 12 strategies—understood by so few therapists that they qualify as "professional secrets"—that are guaranteed to bring you a steady stream of clients.

Not exactly. Okay, not at all. It would be great if there were some set of "one size fits all" techniques to grow and sustain a clinical practice, but what works for one psychologist with a particular kind of practice in a particular location at a particular time can be a complete waste of time, effort, and money for someone else. No method works for all therapists, all practices, all locations.

The search for a way to find clients resembles in some ways the search for a way to help clients. Early psychotherapy research often focused on the question, "Does this therapy work?" In 1967, Gordon Paul suggested a more difficult but also more meaningful and useful question: "What treatment, by whom, is most effective for this individual with that specific problem, and under which set of circumstances?" Psychologists face a similarly complex question when looking for ways to find clients: "What kind of approaches will help me find what kinds of clients for what kind of services in my particular community?"

When evaluating possible approaches to finding clients and referral sources, it's useful to consider how well they fit you as an individual. Some psychologists are quite shy. They do wonderful clinical work and have fulfilling relationships with their family and friends, but they find it agonizing to go out to meet new people. They break into cold sweats at the thought of making "cold calls" on referral sources but might be quite comfortable writing a column for the local paper. Psychologists who enjoy bounding up on a stage to give a dazzling professional presentation packed with information, humor, and entertainment may find that it takes them hours of tortured work to put together a few sentences for an article or brochure. Then afterward they find they don't even like what they've written. Of course, it's always possible to choose one of these "not me" strategies as an attempt at personal growth, learning new skills, or mastering one's fears. But if you're trying to reach new clients or referral sources using a strategy that is unpleasant and unnatural for you and one that you're not very good at, it may not be very effective or worth it. It can be helpful to remember that psychologists are skilled at building relationships and influencing change, which are often major components of marketing oneself, regardless of specific strategies.

Evaluating possible approaches to finding clients and referral sources also includes a realistic assessment of how likely potential clients and referral sources are to encounter our efforts at informing and advertising. It is extremely tempting for most of us to let the degree to which a strategy is easy, inexpensive, or enjoyable become the invalid measure of whether it will reach and influence potential clients and referral sources. We may be so enamored of a life-long hobby and so enjoy the time we spend writing pitches to draw attention to our services in our monthly mental health column, "What's Wrong With You, Anyway? And How I Can Help!" in a hobby magazine that we may not realize that there are surprisingly few subscribers to *Hand-Cancelled Icelandic Stamp Monthly* in our community.

Context can be crucial. An effective yellow pages ad for a particular practice in a remote geographic area in one part of the country may fall flat in a densely populated city in another state. A groundbreaking ad, one that defines a service and establishes why it is needed and how it can be helpful, may bring in new clients from an area where that particular service hasn't been offered before and attract no attention whatsoever in a community where several therapists specialize in that service.

Most therapists—unless they want to cultivate an aura of exclusivity or are in a witness protection program—have a listing in the yellow pages. It's worth checking with therapists in your area to see if large display ads in the local phone books lead to enough calls to justify the expense. Be sure to check your state's licensing regulations to see if specific information (e.g., the number of your psychology license) must be included in advertisements.

"I'm listed in the phone book!" is a solid step toward finding clients. Some may look to the yellow pages to find a therapist, and those who want to schedule an appointment with you can find your phone number. What else can you do to build your practice? Here are some approaches that may be helpful.

DESCRIBING WHO YOU ARE AND WHAT YOU DO
CLEARLY AND QUICKLY

This is not as easy—at least it doesn't seem to be for most people—as it sounds. Imagine that someone has just asked you what you do for a living. Improvise two to four sentences you'd use to reply. If you don't actually try this experiment, it seems hardly a challenge at all. But if you ad lib the sentences without pausing longer than you would were you responding during an actual conversation, you might discover how easy it is for vague abstractions, stilted phrases, professional jargon, or "not exactly what I meant" phrases to invade the response.

It's worthwhile taking some time to work on a brief, to-the-point statement of who you are and what you do. Imagine listening to this statement from a prospective client's or referral source's point of view. Does it make clear what services you provide and how you might be helpful to someone?

Once you craft a basic statement, think of how you might adapt it to different situations, depending on whether you're responding to a question from someone you've just met at a party, you're introducing yourself as you begin a talk to a local PTA, or you're letting your internist or hairdresser know that you'd appreciate referrals.

Once you believe you've got the best possible statement, are comfortable with it, and can adapt it to the listener and setting, try it out with a trusted family member or colleague. Ask for *honest* feedback. (You may have to be persistent: If your listener seems reluctant to say that something is wrong, ask how it might be improved or if there might be other ways to introduce yourself and your work.) When you say who you are and what you do, does it sound direct, natural, and "like you"? Do you maintain eye contact and come across as confident, as someone who knows and likes what they're doing? If it sounds "canned," artificial, stilted, confusing, or rushed, keep tinkering with it.

PREPARING A BROCHURE

Now that you've been working on a statement of who you are and what you do, try transforming it into a brochure. Brochures come in all shapes and sizes, but we lean toward those that are easy to carry and that will fit into someone's pocket or purse. For example, consider a letter-size (8.5" × 11") sheet of paper folded into thirds as if it were going into an envelope. If you turn this folded sheet on its side so that the flaps open to the left and right, it makes a brochure with six sections (i.e., the front and back of each third).

The front of the brochure might include an attractive graphic along with your name or the name of your business (e.g., Lakeside Psychological Services). The other pages might include the specific services you provide;

the problems or populations you specialize in; a statement of your approach or philosophy of treatment; a description of your background, qualifications, or credentials; a photograph; the location of your practice (if it might be hard to find, some psychologists include a map or directions); contact information; and relevant information about insurance coverage, HMOs, or managed care plans. You might take a look at some of your colleagues' brochures to see what aspects appeal to you. For those looking for more detailed guidance, the APA Practice Organization provides a comprehensive step-by-step guide for developing a brochure at http://www.apapractice.org/apo/insider/practice/marketing/brochure.html.

CREATING BUSINESS CARDS THAT ARE RIGHT FOR YOU AND *USING* THEM

Your business card will serve a number of purposes. It tells people your name (which they may have quickly forgotten when you introduced yourself at a party), where your office is, and how to contact you. It also states your degree and license. Be sure to check with your state's licensing requirements to see if your license number or similar information must be included.

How does your business card describe what you do? Some people put only "Psychologist." Some include an adjective: "Clinical Psychologist," "Counseling Psychologist," or "Forensic Psychologist." Still others include specific services such as "Individual, Couples, and Group Psychotherapy," "Neuropsychological Assessment and Rehabilitation," or "Specializing in Eating Disorders." Some describe a therapeutic approach such as "Hypnosis," "Feminist Therapy," or "Behavior Therapy."

The classic business card has black lettering on a white background, a traditional font (e.g., Times Roman), with a landscape orientation (i.e., the words are parallel with the longer sides of the rectangle). Does this style best fit you and your practice? Some psychologists add a logo or other design and artwork, add color to the lettering and background, try a less traditional font (e.g. script), use a portrait orientation (i.e., the words are parallel with the shorter sides of the rectangle), and use textured paper.

If you're going to go to the trouble and expense of preparing business cards, *use* them! Make them available in your waiting room. Carry them with you. If appropriate, enclose a business card with your professional correspondence.

ASKING THE COMMUNITY

Do a formal or informal wants and needs assessment. Use the research techniques that psychology helped develop—interviews, written or phone surveys, and so on—to find out what psychological services people in the area need and want. Are any of these services absent or underrepresented in the area? Are they something that you could provide?

FINDING OUT WHAT PROBLEMS PLAGUE THE COMMUNITY AND CONSIDERING WHETHER PSYCHOLOGICAL SERVICES MIGHT HELP

It may not be apparent to members of the community that a psychologist could be helpful in addressing a variety of problems, so these concerns may not show up in traditional needs and wants investigations. For example, teenagers may feel overwhelmed by the responsibilities of unexpectedly becoming a parent, widespread bullying might be taking place in the local school system, parents may be loud and abusive at youth sporting events, breadwinners may feel anxious and depressed about the threat or reality of being laid off, and older people in the community may be facing a lack of resources. Can you as a psychologist play a helpful role in addressing such problems? If so, you not only give something of value to the community but become known as a trusted and helpful professional.

PARTICIPATING ACTIVELY IN THE LIFE OF THE COMMUNITY

Members of a community may find it hard to contact you for help or refer friends to you if they have no idea that you even exist. Unless you are so naturally outgoing and good at meeting people on your own that you have no need for a plan to bring you into contact with others, consider discovering or creating activities that make you a part of the community, and that are fun, meaningful, and fulfilling to you. What service organizations or social clubs are looking for members? Is there an active Chamber of Commerce or are there other business or civil organizations in your area? Are there networks, classes, get-togethers, leagues, or other structured occasions for people with shared interests?

JOINING OR CREATING A PEER-SUPERVISION, PEER-CONSULTATION, OR PEER-DISCUSSION GROUP

Professionals often tend to refer to colleagues they have met and gotten to know. Joining or creating a small group of colleagues who meet on a regular basis to discuss professional issues is a good way to become known to your colleagues and get to know them (so that you'll have a good basis for referring to them). It can also, as discussed in an earlier chapter, play an important role in self-care.

Some groups focus on current cases, with each member getting collegial feedback, information, support, second opinions, and suggestions about work with a current client. This is an excellent way to learn from colleagues, to contribute to their learning, and to improve the quality of services you provide by having a backup team who can identify possible mistakes and blind spots.

Other groups focus on specific topics. The group may read a specific article or book for discussion during the meeting. In others, each member reads a different work and then summarizes that work's major points. In still others, each member is responsible for discussing recent developments in a different area (e.g., research relevant to assessment and treatment; ethics, malpractice, and professional standards; or medications).

INTRODUCING YOURSELF TO PHYSICIANS AND OTHER REFERRAL SOURCES

One approach for introducing yourself is to send a *brief* letter of introduction to the physicians who practice closest to your office and who might refer patients to you. Address each latter individually and personally (i.e., "Dear Dr. _____" rather than "Dear Colleague").

In a paragraph or two, tell the physician who you are, where your office is, what services you can provide to the physician or the physician's patients, and that you'd appreciate referrals (best to be honest and open about the reason you're writing). Mention that you'll be calling in the next couple of days to answer any questions, see what sorts of referrals from you would be appropriate, and ask whether it might be possible to meet briefly at the physician's office or for a lunch. Enclose your brochure and business card with the letter. Some psychologists also enclose a rolodex card with contact information.

SIGNING UP WITH EAP PROGRAMS

If large companies are located in your area, contact their human resources department and ask to be added to the list of clinicians they use for their Employee Assistance Program (EAP). Often the human resources department will send employees for only a few sessions (perhaps four to six). Some of the employees who come to you for psychological services through this program will want to continue with you, paying out of their own pocket, after their allotted EAP sessions are over.

TALKING TO GROUPS

Develop interesting and informative talks that you can give to local groups and organizations. Among those often looking for speakers or short workshops are local libraries, civics groups, social groups, YMCAs and YWCAs, churches, mosques, synagogues, temples, trade associations, and alumni groups. Offer classes or workshop presentations through local continuing education programs.

Unless you have great talent for improvising in front of an audience, carefully prepare, polish, and practice your talk in front of a supportive friend or family member who will provide you with honest, helpful feedback. Can you maintain eye contact with the audience, avoiding excessive reliance on notes? Does your delivery sound natural, confident, and lively? Are the points you're making clear and well organized?

Find out who your audience will be and make sure your talk is well suited to them. What do you have to say that will be relevant to this audience, that they will care about? What can you assume—and not assume—they already know? Decide in advance whether you will welcome questions during your talk or if you'd rather the audience hold their questions until you're finished. Make that clear to them as you begin to speak.

Be ready to greet all manner of misfortune, interference, and catastrophe with good nature and creativity. Unless you lead a charmed life, you'll probably experience some speaking engagements where the microphone—vital to being heard throughout the hall—doesn't work; one or more babies in the audience decide they aren't charmed by your voice and practice prolonged yowls of protest; the band for the wedding party in the next room drowns out your talk; the refreshments arrive during the midst of your talk, prompting many in the audience to rush toward the back of the room; audience members' beepers going off now and then, prompting someone to look at the display and then leave the room in search of a pay phone; cell phones playing interesting tunes, leading to someone answering and then carrying on a brief conversation that competes with your presentation ("Hey, great to hear from you . . . Yes . . . Yes . . . Look, I can't talk with you now, I'll call you back later. I SAID: I CAN'T TALK WITH YOU NOW, I'LL CALL YOU BACK LATER. What? Really? OK, well, we'll have to talk about it later. No, I gotta meeting after this talk. How about I call you back this evening, say around 7? Well, how about tomorrow then—no, wait, we got auditors coming in all day tomorrow. Hey, you going through a tunnel or something? The signal's breaking up. I SAID I CAN HARDLY HEAR YOU. HELLO!? HELLO!? OK, CALL ME BACK WHEN YOU MAKE IT TO SOUTH STREET, THAT'S WHERE THE SIGNAL GETS STRONGER."); and so many other surprises.

Always have a Plan B ready to go. You may have thought you were on safe ground when invited by a local seniors group to talk about any psychology topic you like. You decide to go with your favorite topic, "Five Fascinating Facts About Memory," in which you summarize recent trends in memory research and how we can put them to use in our everyday lives. You arrive just in time to be introduced: "We're so fortunate to have Dr. Ames with us today to give a talk on whatever topic she's chosen from the field of psychology. I know we're all especially excited to learn more about psychology after last week's presentation by another psychologist, Dr. Brown, on those fascinating findings from recent memory research."

Each time you give a talk don't forget to take along plenty of business cards and brochures, and mention the nature of your practice in your talk. If people in the audience end up liking and respecting you on the basis of your talk, somewhere down the line they may decide to schedule an appointment with you or refer a friend, family member, or coworker to you.

WRITING FOR NEWSPAPERS, MAGAZINES, AND LOCAL PUBLICATIONS

If writing comes naturally to you or you consider it a strength, consider approaching a local newspaper or magazine to see if they might be interested in a regular feature on psychology. This approach to "giving psychology away" provides a service to the community and makes you more visible.

If a regular column doesn't seem right for you, consider writing an occasional op-ed piece or letter to the editor, using the science and discipline of psychology to illuminate a current event or controversy. APA Division 42 (http://www.apa.org/about/division/div42.html) provides a series of brief articles on psychology-related themes that members can adapt for use in their local newspapers.

DISTRIBUTING YOUR OWN NEWSLETTER

Consider writing a newsletter on a regular basis, presenting interesting and useful information about psychology, helpful resources, or news about your practice (e.g., announcing the formation of new therapy groups or specialty services). Some psychologists choose to have the newsletters prepared by a professional printer. Others find it less expensive to use a user-friendly software program and run them off using their own computer. Unless you have no trouble covering the postage expenses for a newsletter, we recommend starting out by simply making them available in your waiting room and other convenient locales. Often local libraries and some businesses will agree to allow you to leave a small stack of newsletters on a regular basis.

HIRING A PROFESSIONAL TO CREATE A WEB SITE FOR YOU

Web sites can create an additional way for clients and referral sources to learn about a psychologist and his or her work. Sometimes the site is an electronic version of the psychologist's brochure. Sometimes it is much more elaborate, containing a variety of sections, information, and resources.

We recommend in most cases that psychologists hire a professional Web designer to create the site and then to work with him or her to maintain, update, and troubleshoot it. Some psychologists may have sufficient knowledge, skill, and experience in the areas of visual design, HTML coding, site organization, and accessibility issues (i.e., ensuring that the site is accessible to people with disabilities; see "Seven Steps Toward Web Accessibility" at http://kpope.com/seven/index.php and "Web Accessibility Verifiers" at http://kpope.com/verify/index.php) to develop a site. However, most will find that they get better results by working with a professional Web designer.

One way to go about finding a good Web designer is to browse the Internet for sites you find attractive, well organized, consumer-friendly, and accessible. Usually, contact information for the designer will be available somewhere on the site. You can also contact the person whose site it is to ask whether they recommend the designer and if they experienced any problems in the working relationship.

In planning your site, it is important to decide whether this is a professional site, a personal site, or some mixture of the two. One of us has four Web sites that range from the personal to the professional, each serving a different purpose: Articles, Research, & Resources in Psychology at http://kspope.com; Accessibility & Disability Information & Resources in Psychology Training & Practice at http://kpope.com; Resources for Companion Animals, Assistance Animals, & Special-Needs Animals at http://catanddoghelp.com; A Family of Special-Needs Dogs & Cats at http://kenpope.com.

VOLUNTEERING AT A LOCAL CHARITY

Donate a few hours a week to a good cause—one that helps people—and you'll get to know and become known by other people in the community who give of themselves. This kind of work often results in surprising referrals.

CONTACTING COLLEAGUES ABOUT SEEING CLIENTS FOR A REDUCED FEE

If you have openings for clients whom you would see on a sliding scale or some other form of reduced fee, contact your colleagues and let them know. Some of those colleagues will likely have full practices and will be looking for good referrals.

DEVELOPING A SPECIALTY

Some psychologists find that developing a well-defined specialty helps them build their practice. They become the go-to professional in their community for that issue.

Is there a special topic you're interested in on which you have or could develop expertise? For those who find the prospect of selecting one specific topic from the vast span of psychology a little overwhelming, or are unsure of how to begin developing a niche practice, fortunately the American Psychological Association's Division of Independent Practice (http://www .apa.org/about/division/div42.html) has developed over 40 guides to provide information and serve as examples. Here is a list of the Division of Independent Practice guides:

- Treatment of Chronic Shyness and Social Anxiety Disorder, Lynne E. Henderson, PhD, and Philip G. Zimbardo, PhD
- Assisting Clients With End-of-Life Decision-Making, James L. Werth Jr., PhD
- Working With Gays, Lesbians and Bisexuals, Hilda F. Besner, PhD, and Charlotte I. Spungin, EdS
- Working With Schools in Preventing School Violence, Adele Besner, PsyD, Hilda F. Besner, PhD, and Charlotte I. Spungin, EdS
- The Supervision of Psychological Services, Jeffrey Barnett, PsyD, and Dorothy Cantor, PsyD
- Clinical Neuropsychology, Rosemarie Scolaro Moser, PhD
- Health Psychology: Primary Care, Behavioral Medicine, and Generalist Care, Esther Freeman, PhD, and Carol Goodheart, EdD
- Infertility, Laurie Kolt, PhD
- Psychologist–Dentist Collaboration, Jeffrey Barnett and Elaine Rodino
- Psychological Management of Migraine and Tension-Type Headache, Gay Lipchik and Kenneth Holroyd
- Psycho-Oncology, Sandra Haber, PhD
- Family Law, Michael Gottlieb, PhD
- Forensic Psychology—Assessment of Clinical Responsibility,[1] David L. Shapiro, PhD
- Forensic Parent Counseling, Elizabeth Thayer, PhD, and Jeffrey Zimmerman, PhD
- Consumer Satisfaction Surveys, James Shulman, PhD

---

[1]See also Appendix N.

- Executive Coaching and Development, Alan Graham, PhD
- Consulting With Business on Workplace Behavior, Marion Gindes, PhD
- Sport Psychology, Kate Hays, PhD
- Treatment of Marital Infidelity, Don–David Lusterman, PhD
- Marital Therapy, Patricia Pitta, PhD
- Domestic Violence and Custody, Leslie Drozd, PhD
- Working With Step Families, James H. Bray, PhD
- Smoking Cessation, Gary DeNelsky, PhD
- Assessment of Substance Abuse, Linda Sobell, PhD, and Mark Sobell, PhD
- Secondary Interventions for Substance Abuse, Mark Sobell, PhD, and Linda Sobell, PhD
- Adolescent Substance Abuse, Robert Margolis, PhD
- ADHD Throughout the Life Span, Robert J. Resnick, PhD
- ADHD Children and Adolescents, Steven Sussman, PhD
- Selecting Empirically Supported Interventions and Treatment Planning, Larry Beutler, PhD
- Treatment of Personality Disorders, Jeffrey Magnavita, PhD
- Eating Disorders: Anorexia Nervosa and Bulimia Nervosa, Ora Gourarie, PhD
- Men's Issues, Gary Brooks, PhD
- Working With Older Adults, Norman Abeles, PhD
- Evaluation and Treatment of the Juvenile Sex Offender, Joseph Poirer, PhD
- Psychotherapy and the Culturally Diverse, Rafael Art Javier, PhD
- Working With the College Aged, Leighton Whitaker, PhD
- Working With Children in the Schools, Laura Barbanel, EdD
- Working With Victims of Violence, Lenore Walker, EdD
- Becoming a Book Author, Lawrence G. Ritt, PhD
- Ethical Considerations in Developing a Niche Practice, Donald Bersoff, PhD
- Burnout Prevention and Treatment: Helping the Helpers, Thomas M. Skovholt, PhD, and Len Jennings, PhD
- Direct Contracting With Employers, Chris Stout, PhD

DOING GOOD WORK

Efforts to expand a practice can depend on the quality of the practice. Even if your practice becomes a household word in your community, it may not do you much good if the people who come to you for help don't receive good services. Word of mouth from those who have benefited from your practice can be the most effective form of advertising, with each person refer-ring you client after client over the years. The meaning, satisfaction, and sometimes joy you receive from fulfilling the deep trust placed in you and from playing a significant role in your clients' healing, growth, and change may be one of the richest rewards you earn from your practice.

10

USING COMPUTERS AND THE INTERNET

The magic that computers weave through the lives of psychologists—imagine calculating a meta-analysis of over 200 studies using only paper and pencil—comes with risks. Ask the client whose clinical records turned up on the hard drive of a newly purchased second-hand computer or the psychologist whose computer crashed and destroyed a year's worth of clinical and financial records. Here are a few suggestions for using computers effectively while minimizing their risks.

POWER AND PRICE

Few of us need a Rolls Royce Silver Shadow, Ferrari 360 Spider, or Lamborghini Diablo to get to and from the office, and few of us need the newest, most powerful computer on the market each year for our practice. A common pitfall is the tendency to waste money on a computer system that isn't well matched to the needs of a practice. Often the extra money spent on a faster, more powerful processor provides no benefit whatsoever. The processor—whose impressive stats the salesperson will tout—may not work well with the computer's other components (which can't keep up with the processor and cause a bottleneck) or the tasks the computer carries out may not make use of the processor's speed and power. For psychologists who use a computer mainly for word processing, e-mail, and financial ledgers or spreadsheets, a midrange or even inexpensive computer is often the best choice.

LOCATION, LOCATION, LOCATION

Carefully consider where you will put any computer that contains sensitive information. Who else will have access to it? Will anyone else be able to see the monitor while you're setting up the next appointment or doing other work? Who, if anyone, will ever be in the same room with the computer when you are not there? What sorts of barriers (e.g., locked doors) are between the computer and anyone who might like to get their hands on it? How difficult would it be for someone to get past those barriers? If someone were able to get into your office (e.g., because the night cleaning crew left your office doors unlocked), would stealing your computer involve anything more than picking it up and carrying it out? For example, is it locked within a desk or secured to the desk in some way?

PASSWORDS

Whenever possible, passwords should be used to make it more difficult for sensitive information to fall into the wrong hands. A password can be required when turning on the computer before the operating system loads. Individual files within the computer can also be password protected. If you sometimes leave your computer on unattended, you can use a screensaver that appears after a short time of inactivity or that can be turned on whenever you step away from the computer. A password can then be a requirement for removing the screensaver.

Avoid choosing a word or phrase as a password. Hackers often use dictionary programs to break into password-protected computers. A strong password that has a good chance of surviving sophisticated password-breaking software must have at least 10 to 12 characters, some of which are lowercase letters, some uppercase, and some numerals and symbols.

If at all possible, avoid writing down your password; try to memorize it. If you don't trust your memory and need to write it down, however, never leave it in the same room as the computer. It is dismaying that so many hackers simply look in the drawers or under the desk pad that the computer sits on to find the relevant passwords. However convenient, it defeats the purpose of a password to leave it on a sticky note affixed to the computer's monitor. Consider carrying the password with your credit cards, and only take it out if no one else can see it.

ENCRYPTION

Encrypting files that contain sensitive data, such as client records, adds an extra layer of protection and helps provide the safeguards for electronically stored and transmitted "electronic protected health information" (EPHI) outlined by the Health Insurance Portability Accountability Act (HIPAA). Both the manufacturers of major operating systems (Apple, Microsoft, etc.) and third-party companies (e.g., PGP at www.pgp.com) offer software for encrypting sensitive files.

FIREWALLS

Firewalls in the form of software or hardware help prevent electronic break-ins. Hackers use an impressive array of strategies to gain entrance to and control over a computer. Sometimes this is done just for fun or for the challenge. Sometimes hackers read and steal the computer's files, use the computer (e.g., to send out spam or viruses), or sometimes just vandalize it (e.g., erase everything on the hard drive). Our view is that when patient records are an issue, the more layers of protection, the better. If some levels fail, others may still work.

The additional levels of protection may also discourage hackers and other data thieves from spending time trying to gain access to your computer. Just as burglars casing a neighborhood may pass by houses with heavy-duty locks on the doors and other security measures in favor of a more inviting residence, many data thieves may turn away from computers secured by multiple protections toward more vulnerable machines.

For these reasons, we recommend that psychologists consider installing both software and hardware firewalls to protect sensitive information. Some of the major software firewalls are ZoneAlarm (http://www.zonelabs.com), NetBarrier (http://www.intego.com), BlackICE (http://www.blackice.com), Personal FirewallPlus (http://us.mcafee.com), Personal Firewall (http://www.symantec.com), and PerimeterScan Firewall (http://www.pandasecurity.com). Some of the major hardware firewalls (often in the form of routers) are made by Linksys (http://www.linksys.com), Netgear (http://www.netgear.com), D-Link (http://www.dlink.com), and Hawking Technology (http://www.hawkingtech.com).

VIRUSES, TROJANS, WORMS, SPYWARE, AND OTHER MALICIOUS CODE

Malicious code in forms such as viruses, worms, spyware, and Trojans have become so powerful, pervasive, sophisticated, and destructive that any computer hooked up to a network or the Internet, or that accepts data from any source (e.g., floppy disks, CDs, or DVDs) other than its own mouse and keyboard, should have a comprehensive program that protects against such threats. The program should check all files in the computer and all files entering the computer (e.g., each e-mail message, including any attachments).

We recommend that psychologists take a look at the current antivirus programs offered by the major companies such as Intego (http://www.intego.com), McAfee (http://www.mcafee.com), Panda (http://www.pandasoftware.com), Symantec (http://www.symantec.com), or Trend Micro (http://www.trendmicro.com) to see which seems to best suit their needs. It's also worth looking at some of the current antispyware programs made by companies such as Lavasoft (http://www.lavasoftusa.com), Pest Patrol (http://pestpatrol.com), and Spybot (http://safer-networking.org). Computer magazines such as *PC Magazine* (http://www.pcmag.com) and *MacWorld* (http://www.macworld.com) provide reviews of the evolving version of these programs.

Programs to protect against malicious code aren't very effective unless their "definitions" are kept up to date. Each time a new virus or Trojan is identified the company creates a "definition," so that the program will recognize the malicious code and protect your computer against it. The best programs include functions that enable the program to automatically download new definitions via the Internet. Unless the program can be notified every time a new definition is available, set the "automatic update" function to check for new definitions as often as possible. The more frequently it checks for new definitions, the shorter the interval that your computer is unprotected against a new form of malicious code.

SOCIAL ENGINEERING

The inner workings of computers are a mystery to most of us. It is easy to imagine that if your computer's security is breached and sensitive information is stolen, the most likely culprit will be a hacker using either his or her extensive knowledge of how computers function or software that uses brute-force computing power (e.g., trying hundreds of thousands of combinations until it happens to hit the right password). However, computers and their contents tend to be much more vulnerable to what should be the specialty of the psychologist: human engineering.

The human engineer takes advantage of basic human psychology to get from people access, actions, and information that they wouldn't usually make available to a stranger. We may receive an e-mail, visit a Web site, or take a phone call and unknowingly disclose enough information to enable a stranger to enter our computer and its files without our knowledge or consent. Someone may come into our office asking for or offering help or we may chat with someone in a social or business setting, and we never realize we are being conned.

The steps to prevent data theft or data destruction through social engineering are basic. If a stranger is asking for information relevant to your computer's security, don't provide it unless (a) you have independently verified who the person is, (b) it is a person or agency whom you trust and rely on, and (c) the person can provide a convincing reason for needing each bit of information.

As an example, someone may call claiming to be working for your Internet service provider (ISP), the company that provides your Internet service, or the local police. You hear that your Internet account has been used to fraudulently purchase merchandise and may have been taken over by an identity thief. Before answering any questions, independently confirm that the person calling you really does work for your ISP or the local police.

You might also receive a call from an inspector for something called the Interagency Internet Compliance Unit (IICU). You begin by trying to confirm that the person really does work for the unit. You ask for the person's name and the phone number of the unit. Then you look up the Interagency Internet Compliance Unit in the phone directory and see that it matches the phone number the person gave to you. Finally, you call the unit, ask to speak to personnel, confirm that the person actually does work for them, clarify the nature and purpose of the unit, and ask to be connected to the person who originally called you.

But before you give any information to the person, wouldn't it be a good idea to do some research first so that you can find out that the IICU, however official it might sound and however convincing a story the person who answers the phone might weave, is bogus? All they might have done to set up the con was take out a directory listing using the name of the fictitious organization. After a week of contacting as many people as possible to steal identities, they'll abandon their "offices." Finally, even if it is a legitimate representative of a trusted organization who is making the inquiry, don't hesitate to ask why each bit of information is needed.

Remain aware of how skillfully social engineers work. They rely on such basic human psychology as our desire to be helpful, our fear and vulnerability when suddenly informed that we may have been the victim of identity theft, and our tendency to take introductions for granted rather than checking them out. They also play on our respect for authority, our tendency to be intimidated by technical talk about computers and our wish not to appear ignorant, our wish to avoid being rude or "difficult," and our attempts to hurry through interruptions to our normal schedule, rather than take time to ask questions and consider alternative explanations for what is happening. Like magicians, they often rely on distraction, suggestion, and misdirection.

PRACTICE MANAGEMENT AND BILLING SOFTWARE

Many psychologists rely on computer programs for billing, scheduling, charting, and other aspects of practice management. Six of the most widely used programs that have both PC and Mac versions are shown in the following list. We also include the URL for the company's Web site, which describes how each functions, how the program handles electronic claim submissions (e.g., whether or not through a clearinghouse), and so on. Some have free trial versions.

We recommend that anyone considering a new billing or management program consider the issue of electronic claims submission, the degree to which the program handles the kind of electronic claims that *you* want to do, and *how* it handles this aspect of billing. Different programs can take very different approaches to electronic billing, and this issue has become more prominent under HIPAA.

It's also important, of course, to see how well each program's approach and features match up with your specific wants and needs. Differences between practices in terms of size, organization, and procedures can make a huge difference in which program works in a given setting, and a program that's terrific for one practice can be a disaster for another.

Here are the six programs and their Web addresses:

- SumTime Practice Management and Billing Software for Therapists (http://www.sumtime.com)
- ShrinkRapt (http://www.sanersoftware.com/upgrade/index.html)
- ChartEvolve (http://thecimsgroup.com/Software.htm)
- TherapySoft (http://www.getphysicalsoftware.com/software/therapysoft/index.cfm)
- PracticeMagic (http://www.practicemagic.com/index.html)
- MedAssist (http://www.getphysicalsoftware.com/software/MedAssist/index.cfm)

MAKING USE OF THE INTERNET

The Internet is rich with resources for psychologists, although finding specifically what you're looking for can be a challenge. An excellent resource is the Psychologist's Internet Guide by Pauline Wallin, PhD, at http://drwallin.com/internetguide.html. Another set of resources, including the article "Some Suggestions For Doing Online Literature Searches," can be found at the Web site maintained by one of this book's authors, Articles, Research, & Resources in Psychology at http://kspope.com.

But the Internet is more than a research tool. It is also a place where psychologists can join each other in virtual communities to discuss topics of shared interest, exchange information, find support, and relax with "water-cooler" conversations. The American Psychological Association sponsors many of these lists for its divisions and other groups at http://listserve.apa .org/cgi-bin/WA.EXE. One of the oldest lists is PsyUSA at http://mael-strom.stjohns.edu/archives/psyusa.html, created originally by the late John Roraback and currently maintained and moderated by Dennis Elias. PsyUSA has a general list focusing on psychology and practice, a PsyChat list for informal conversations, a PsyTech list focusing on computers and the Internet, and a PsyPOV list focusing on opinions and viewpoints.

BACKING UP

The hardware and software we use to protect our data from viruses and other threats can reduce but never eliminate them completely. In addition to attacks, many other causes of damage to data are possible. A malfunction of the hard drive, a software glitch, or a power surge can destroy some or all of what's on your computer.

A possible solution is to back up all the material on your computer unless you wouldn't mind losing it. One strategy is to make a clone or mirror of your computer's hard disk on an external (or removable) disk and keep that backup disk under lock and key in a secure place other than your office building. If a flood or fire occurs, if the building collapses, or if your office is ransacked and everything is stolen, you'll still have access to your backup. One of the safest locations for the backup is a media safe. A media safe protects against humidity, extreme temperature, magnetic or electrical charges, and other factors that might damage or destroy hard drives and other computer media.

Test each backup as you make it. Make sure that no malfunctions take place in the software, in the external disk, or in the backing-up process.

DELETING FILES AND DISCARDING DISKS

Although we like to think that a file has disappeared forever when we delete it, often it has simply been removed from our computer's directory and remains in a form that a simple data-recovery program can retrieve. If the file contains sensitive information, delete it using a program that overwrites the file completely with meaningless data or use another method to destroy the file. If you plan to discard a computer's internal or external hard drive or some other storage device where sensitive data have been stored, make sure it has been either completely degaussed or physically destroyed.

THE VULNERABLE COMPUTER

Any computer hooked up to the Internet is a vulnerable computer. As previously noted, the most high-level security hardware and software can only reduce—never eliminate—a computer's vulnerability to hacking, to malicious code (sometimes called "malware"), and other forms of intrusion. Those who create malware are finding more effective ways to circumvent both antivirus programs and firewalls, to ensure that attachments need not be opened in order to infect the computer, and to use HTML-formatted e-mails to embed destructive codes. They are also devising ways to find the most damaging information (e.g., files containing words like "confidential," "private," "privileged," "clinical," or "password") and then send it to selected addresses in the computer's memory, addresses already contained in the malicious code, or anonymous Web sites.

One of the problems is that many of the new viruses, worms, or Trojans don't "do their stuff" right away. They can "hide" in an almost infinite number of ways on a hard drive, going undetected for a certain period of time. Many have stealth modes and engage in complex functions to avoid detection by antivirus programs and other security software. (Even standard terms like virus, worm, and Trojan are becoming dated and don't fit some of the quickly evolving ways a computer's security is compromised.)

With the threat of confidential clinical, forensic, or other sensitive data being sent out unwillingly to names in the computer's address book, posted to Internet lists, placed on anonymous Web sites, and so on, it may make sense to keep sensitive data in an encrypted form on a removable medium, rather than on the internal hard drive (e.g., an external hard drive, CD, DVD, floppy, Zip or Jaz disk). The medium would be stored safely in a secure area and would only be hooked up to the computer when the psychologist is using it. Certain steps may also help prevent sensitive data from being compromised. As previously mentioned, these include using antivirus programs with frequently updated virus definitions, installing an appropriate firewall, keeping sensitive data on external media, disconnecting the computer when it is not in use, and using sophisticated password systems and encryption.

We strongly recommend that psychologists consider using a separate computer—one that is never connected to the Internet—for storing sensitive material. Because word-processing and related programs use relatively little memory, a very old or a cheap second-hand computer can be used (with all the material backed up). The main criterion is that this computer never be hooked up to anything else (e.g., not part of a network, no phone line, no cable or DSL modem, no Airport)—just a standalone desktop, laptop, or notebook. If used only for clinical data and deprived of any wired or wireless link outside itself, it will lack the means to distribute the confidential information. A different computer can be used for connecting to the Internet, networking, and so on.

11

RESPONDING TO A LICENSING, MALPRACTICE, OR ETHICS COMPLAINT

It happens. A client, former client, or someone else files a formal complaint against you. What now? Here are some considerations you may find helpful.

DON'T PANIC

Okay, panic for a little while if you can't help it or if it feels like the right thing to do. But then take some deep breaths, pull yourself together, and do whatever you have to do to think clearly. The decisions you make—what you do and avoid doing at this point—are crucial. (And avoid letting panic drive or determine the steps you take.)

CONSULT YOUR ATTORNEY FIRST

It's amazing how many psychologists forget this step or experience irresistible impulses to maneuver around it. After opening an envelope to find out that a formal complaint has been filed with the licensing board, a psychologist may figure that by quickly submitting a clear timeline, the relevant documents, and a clear explanation, this unfortunate misunderstanding can be resolved immediately. Receiving notice that a malpractice suit has been filed, a psychologist may hope that asking the client to come in for a free session so that all this can be worked out "without all these lawyers" is the best way to reach a positive resolution and convince the client that a suit should never have been filed in the first place.

Responding to a formal complaint *before* consulting an attorney can lead to needless disasters. An attorney can help guide you through the minefields of formal complaints. In part, this is because you, as a psychologist, are moving into a different realm. Good attorneys are knowledgeable about the complex legislation, case law, and court customs that govern malpractice actions. Attorneys experienced in licensing and ethics hearings can interpret the numerous rules and procedures that the psychologist is now subject to and are familiar with the particular norms and customs of the state or provincial licensing board and ethics committee. In part, the attorney can serve as a guide because he or she has another perspective than you since the attorney is not the object of the complaint. That perspective can be crucial. As the old aphorism has it: The person who represents him- or herself has a fool for a client.

The attorney can show you the pitfalls of certain actions that can otherwise seem to make sense. A psychologist who has not consulted an attorney may talk to colleagues about the case, talk to the opposing attorney, write letters to various people mentioning the case, and blow off steam about the case within earshot of others. Only later will he or she discover that these oral and written statements are not privileged information and are introduced as evidence through testimony and exhibits.

Your attorney may give you strong advice, perhaps a more authoritative list of dos and don'ts, but a good part of what an attorney does is to lay out options and tell you what is and is not known about each option. This enables you to make informed decisions about what you want to do and what you want the attorney to do. For example, the attorney can make you aware of the circumstances, if any, under which you can discuss the case with a supervisor, consultant, colleague, friend, family member, or anyone else and have the discussion remain confidential and privileged. As another example, the attorney can explain the consequences of you declining a settlement offer from the plaintiff in a malpractice suit.

NOTIFY YOUR PROFESSIONAL LIABILITY CARRIER

Your professional liability policy may include a requirement that you notify the company immediately not only if you are sued but also if you have reason to believe you will or may be sued. Regardless of the fine print of such requirements, however, it makes sense to let the carrier know if you become aware of a possible or actual formal complaint. The carrier may give you specific guidance and, under certain circumstances, provide you with an attorney even if a suit has not yet been filed against you. (Chap. 5 discussed petitioning the company to assign the attorney you customarily work with to handle your case, even if that attorney has not previously worked for the carrier.)

WHO IS YOUR ATTORNEY'S CLIENT?

The answer may seem obvious: *You* are your attorney's client. But if your insurance carrier is paying the attorney, it is worth assessing the degree to which the insurance carrier's interests may diverge from your interests. For example, what if the insurance company approves only a very limited discovery, hoping to hold down expenses? What if the carrier believes it makes sense financially (i.e., it is in their financial interests) to settle a case that you believe is bogus and would be decided in your favor were it vigorously defended? The settlement of such a case—which could become a matter of public record—could be devastating to your career, particularly if a substantial portion of your professional time is spent serving as an expert witness.

In some rare circumstances, if you (or you and the attorney) are unable to persuade the carrier to litigate rather than settle the case or provide you with the kind of extensive discovery and vigorous defense you believe you are entitled to, it may be worth considering hiring a separate attorney with your own funds to press your claims with the carrier.

IS THE COMPLAINT VALID?

When someone files a formal complaint against you, it's natural to feel hurt and attacked. Moreover, malpractice trials are adversarial proceedings that can understandably generate much anger and emotional heat. Before that process gets too far under way, take some time to consider whether you actually did what you've been accused of doing. Setting aside defensiveness, rationalization, counterattacks, and the fact that the charges may be considerably overstated or wrong in some details, is there any truth to the allegation that you did something you should not have done or that you failed to do something you should have done?

Being relentlessly honest with ourselves under these circumstances is anything but easy. Acknowledging to ourselves that we may have done something wrong may seem self-destructive, indulging a tendency to "beat ourselves up" when we need all our survival skills to rescue our reputation and career. But holding as firmly as possible to the reality of what actually happened—not what the flattering and self-justifying revisionism of memory can create in place of the unadorned history—may enable us not only to respond effectively to the complaint but also to survive the process in a way that is the very opposite of self-destruction.

DID YOU MAKE A FORMAL COMPLAINT MORE LIKELY?

It's also worth asking yourself, regardless of whether you did or did not do what you are accused of, did you do (or fail to do) anything that made the complaint more likely? Did you, for example, make a normal, run-of-the-mill, human error—not something illegal or unethical—but just a mistake? When confronted by the client, did you refuse to acknowledge it or say you were sorry? Was there a misunderstanding in which the client misperceived that you did something wrong and you didn't clarify or explain yourself? In other words, as you examine the sequence of events with the benefit of hindsight, did your attitude or behavior increase the chances that this complaint would be filed?

In our experience, many formal complaints (but by no means all) seem to have less to do with the existence or magnitude of the therapist's legal or ethical violation and more to do with the therapist-client relationship, how well the therapist has effectively communicated respect, caring, and a reasonable ability to listen. Therapists who communicate these qualities to clients often seem to make all sorts of mistakes, misjudgments, and violations of standards without triggering a complaint, whereas therapists who fail to communicate these qualities must endure complaints even when they have otherwise seemed to adhere to the highest standards. This, of course, does *not* imply that it is somehow okay to bumble our way into careless mistakes, misjudgments, and violations in these circumstances or that we can use what we characterize as "a good relationship with the client" to justify, discount, trivialize, or rationalize what we've done wrong and the consequences of our behavior, a process described in chapter 14. It also does not imply that all therapists who have complaints filed against them fail to communicate these qualities. Nevertheless, some formal complaints seem to represent a client's final attempt to catch the attention of and reach an otherwise unresponsive therapist.

APOLOGIZE AND ACCEPT RESPONSIBILITY?

One crucial decision facing you if the complaint is valid is, do you want to acknowledge what you've done (or failed to do), accept responsibility, and apologize? It seems to be part of the human condition that it is difficult for many of us to admit mistakes, especially when we have hurt someone, and to apologize. It can be much harder when our admission will go "on the record," when it may be influential in sustaining the validity of the complaint, and when it is offered to someone who is angry—perhaps enraged—at you. Your friends and colleagues may advise you to despise the person who filed the complaint and to fight it no matter what the circumstances.

We urge psychologists facing a valid, formal complaint to seriously consider, in consultation with your attorney, apologizing, accepting responsibility, and—if possible and appropriate—trying to make things right. There can be strong reasons both for favoring and opposing this approach, and it's impossible to foresee all the consequences and implications of taking or not taking this path. Each psychologist must attempt to make the choice that is right for him or her as an individual.

WHAT ARE YOU WILLING TO HAVE DONE?

If you plan to contest the charges, consider *before* the adversarial process heats up what you are and aren't willing to allow in defending your case. To examine an extreme hypothetical, imagine that an extremely fragile single mother sues you for malpractice. You believe her to be a basically good and competent person who has mistakenly but in good faith filed suit against you. Whatever your view of her, the claim she has filed threatens your reputation and career. If the verdict goes against you, referral sources for new patients may dry up, the licensing board may launch an investigation, and your work as an expert witness on the standard of care may be in jeopardy.

With all that at stake, would you be willing for your attorney to depose and cross-examine her in a way that misleadingly raises questions about her honesty? Would you be willing to let the attorney use your chart notes to create, through innuendo, the false impression that she is not an adequate mother and that perhaps she even neglected or abused her child?

Or would you consider "clarifying" your chart notes? Those notes may have been done hurriedly, they may not have mentioned everything that was done, and they may be misleading because of the way they were written. Wouldn't it be better to copy over those notes so that they include the material you neglected to put in the first time around on what are, really if you come to think of it, your draft notes? Wouldn't it actually be a service to the court to remove the unintentional ambiguities along with the parts that are relatively unimportant, that clutter up your account of the treatment? In other words (i.e., stripped of its rationalization), would you be willing to hide your actual notes and submit a bogus chart more favorable to your defense?

The struggle to preserve a reputation and career is understandably intense. A question worth asking before the process builds up too much steam is: Am I willing to win at any cost? If not, where do I draw the line? What, if anything, am I unwilling to do—or to have others do in my defense—to "win"?

RECOGNIZE HOW THE COMPLAINT IS AFFECTING YOU

A formal complaint can be a devastating experience. A malpractice suit or other formal complaint can bring all of the following and more into the life of a psychologist:

- A numbing shock that suddenly reputation and career may be at stake
- A sense of betrayal that someone we tried to help has turned against us
- Fear of uncertainty and the horrors in store for us (will we have a practice, a reputation, or a license when this is finally over?)
- Reflexive self-blame, assuming that we must have done something terrible or else we would not be in this fix
- Embarrassment, imagining that our colleagues now think the worst about us
- Self-doubt: If we did so bad with this patient that we wound up in court, what if our other patients sue us?
- Depression
- Suspicion of our other patients (Are they going to sue us?) and colleagues (Who can we trust to talk this over with?)
- Anxiety about what's going to happen, about all the unknowns, about being deposed and cross-examined, about who will be in the courtroom during the trial (the media?), and on and on
- Obsessive and intrusive thoughts, finding it hard to think about anything else
- Insomnia, tossing and turning, thinking endlessly about what's happened and what may happen
- Catastrophizing, seeing only the most horrible possibilities unfolding
- A loss of appetite or taking in too much food, alcohol, or other substances as a response to the stress

Our view is that for some psychologists, being sued can bring on reactions similar to those of post-traumatic stress disorder (PTSD). If we can be rigorously honest about our reactions to encountering a formal complaint, we are in a better position to address those reactions constructively and realistically.

GET THE HELP AND SUPPORT YOU NEED

As you monitor your reactions to the complaint process, realistically assess what help, if any, you need in dealing with these reactions. Some psychologists return to therapy or seek it for the first time. Some reach out to friends, colleagues, and family. An attorney's guidance can be invaluable in ensuring that what you say to others doesn't unintentionally become part of the case against you. Ethics experts in your state may be able to provide you and your attorney with additional consultation.

WHAT YOU CAN LEARN

As the process unfolds, it's worth asking what, if anything, is to be learned from this. It's probably fair to say—in fact, it's probably an understatement—that *no one* ever wishes for a formal complaint. But this unwelcome process brings with it opportunity.

Psychologists may discover flaws and weaknesses in their policies, procedures, and ways of approaching clinical work. They may learn to recognize and attend more carefully to red flags in their practice. They may learn about their colleagues, about who can be counted on for support and who avoids them. They may learn about how both their own work and the allegations against them are evaluated during adversarial procedures. And in their reactions and decisions, they may learn about themselves.

12

AVOIDING PITFALLS IN PSYCHOLOGICAL ASSESSMENT

The final three chapters focus on avoiding common pitfalls that—especially in the day-to-day complexities and pressures of practice—can easily entrap any of us. Most psychology practices involve assessment in some form. This chapter spotlights seven of the most widespread and troublesome assessment pitfalls (see also Appendix L).

MISMATCHED VALIDITY

Some tests are useful in diverse situations, but no test works well for all tasks with all people in all situations. As mentioned in chapter 9, Gordon Paul helped move psychology away from the oversimplified search for effective therapies in the 1960s toward a more difficult but meaningful question: "What treatment, by whom, is most effective for this individual with that specific problem, and under which set of circumstances?"

Selecting assessment instruments involves similarly complex questions, such as, "Has research established sufficient reliability and validity (as well

---

This chapter is adapted from "Fallacies & Pitfalls in Psychology" © by Ken Pope, available at http://kspope.com

as sensitivity, specificity, and other relevant features) for this test, with an individual from this population, for this task (i.e., the purpose of the assessment), in this set of circumstances?" It is important to note that as the population, task, or circumstances change, the measures of validity, reliability, and sensitivity will also tend to change.

To determine whether tests are well matched with the task, individual, and situation at hand, it is crucial that the psychologist ask a basic question at the outset: Why exactly am I conducting this assessment?

CONFIRMATION BIAS

Often we tend to seek, recognize, and value information that is consistent with our attitudes, beliefs, and expectations. If we form an initial impression, we may favor findings that support that impression, and discount, ignore, or misconstrue data that don't fit. This premature cognitive commitment to an initial impression, which can form a strong cognitive set through which we sift all subsequent findings, is similar to the logical fallacy of hasty generalization.

To help protect ourselves against confirmation bias (in which we give preference to information that confirms our expectations), it is useful to search actively for data that disconfirm our expectations and to try out alternate interpretations of the available data.

CONFUSING RETROSPECTIVE AND PREDICTIVE ACCURACY (SWITCHING CONDITIONAL PROBABILITIES)

Predictive accuracy begins with an individual's test results and asks, what is the likelihood, expressed as a conditional probability, that a person with these results has condition (or ability, aptitude, quality, etc.) X? Retrospective accuracy begins with the condition (or ability, aptitude, or quality) X and asks, what is the likelihood, expressed as a conditional probability, that a person who has X will show these test results? Confusing the "directionality" of the inference causes numerous assessment errors. An example of such an error would be confusing the likelihood that those who score positive on a hypothetical predictor variable will fall into a specific group with the likelihood that those in a specific group will score positive on the predictor variable.

This mistake of confusing retrospective with predictive accuracy often resembles the affirming the consequent logical fallacy:

People with condition X are overwhelmingly likely to have these specific test results.
Person Y has these specific test results.
Therefore, Person Y is overwhelmingly likely to have condition X.

UNSTANDARDIZING STANDARDIZED TESTS

Standardized tests gain their power from their standardization. Norms, validity, reliability, specificity, sensitivity, and similar measures emerge from an actuarial base: a well-selected sample of people providing data (through answering questions, performing tasks, etc.) in response to a uniform procedure in (reasonably) uniform conditions. When we change the instructions, the test items themselves, or the way items are administered or scored, we depart from that standardization, and our attempts to draw on the actuarial base become questionable.

Standardization can be defeated in other ways as well. People may show up for an assessment session without adequate reading glasses or having taken cold medication that affects their alertness. They may have experienced a family emergency or loss that leaves them unable to concentrate, or they stayed up all night with a loved one and now can barely keep their eyes open. The professional conducting the assessment must be alert to these situational factors, how they can threaten the assessment's validity, and how they can best be addressed.

Any of us who conduct assessments can fall prey to these same situational factors and, on a given day, be unable to function adequately. We can also fall short of conducting an adequate assessment through a lack of competence. It is important to administer only those tests for which there has been adequate education, training, and supervised experience. We may function well in one area (e.g., counseling psychology, clinical psychology, sport psychology, organizational psychology, school psychology, or forensic psychology) and falsely assume that our competence transfers easily to the other areas. It is our responsibility to recognize the limits of competence and to ensure that any assessment is based on adequate competence in the relevant areas of practice, the relevant issues, and the relevant instruments.

In the same way that searching for disconfirming data and alternative explanations can help avoid confirmation bias, it can be helpful to search for conditions, incidents, or other factors that may undermine the validity of the assessment, so that these factors can be taken into account and explicitly addressed in the assessment report.

IGNORING THE EFFECTS OF LOW BASE RATES

Ignoring base rates can play a role in many testing problems, but very low base rates seem particularly troublesome. Imagine you've been commissioned to develop an assessment procedure that will identify crooked judges so that candidates for judicial appointment can be screened. It's a difficult challenge, in part because only 1 out of 500 judges is (hypothetically speaking) dishonest.

You pull together all the actuarial data you can find and discover that you are able to develop a screening test for crookedness based on a variety of characteristics, personal history, and test results. Your method is 90% accurate. When your method is used to screen the next 5,000 judicial candidates, there might be 10 candidates who are crooked (because about 1 out of 500 is crooked). A 90% accurate screening method will identify 9 of these 10 crooked candidates as crooked and 1 as honest.

So far, so good. The problem is the 4,990 honest candidates. Because the screening is wrong 10% of the time, and the only way for the screening to be wrong about honest candidates is to identify them as crooked, it will falsely classify 10% of the honest candidates as crooked. Therefore, this screening method will incorrectly classify 499 of these 4,990 honest candidates as crooked.

So out of the 5,000 candidates who were screened, the 90% accurate test has classified 508 of them as crooked (i.e., 9 who actually were crooked and 499 who were honest). Every 508 times the screening method indicates crookedness, it tends to be right only 9 times. And it has falsely branded 499 honest people as crooked.

MISINTERPRETING DUAL HIGH BASE RATES

As part of a disaster response team, you are flown in to work at a community mental health center in a city that has experienced a severe earthquake. Taking a quick look at the records the center has compiled, you note that 200 people have come for services since the earthquake. Within that group, 162 are of a particular religious faith and are diagnosed with post-traumatic stress disorder (PTSD) related to the earthquake, and 18 people of that faith came for services unrelated to it. Of those who are not of that faith, 18 have been diagnosed with PTSD related to the earthquake, and 2 have come for services unrelated to it.

It seems almost self-evident that a strong association exists between that particular religious faith and developing PTSD related to the earthquake: 81% of the people who came for services were of that religious faith and had developed PTSD. Perhaps this faith makes people vulnerable to PTSD, or perhaps it is a more subtle association: This faith might make it easier for people with PTSD to seek mental heath services.

But the inference of an association is a fallacy. The records compiled by the center suggest that faith and the development of PTSD in this community are independent factors. Ninety percent of the people who seek services at this center happen to be of that specific religious faith (i.e., 90% of those who developed PTSD and 90% who had come for other reasons), and 90% of the people who sought services after the earthquake (i.e., 90% of those of that particular religious faith and 90% of those who are not) developed

PTSD. The two factors appear to be associated because both have high base rates, but they are statistically unrelated.

UNCERTAIN GATEKEEPING

Psychologists who conduct assessments are gatekeepers of sensitive information that may have profound and lasting effects on the life of the client. The following scenario illustrates some gatekeeping decisions psychologists may be called on to make. This passage is taken from *Ethics in Psychotherapy and Counseling* (2nd ed.):[1]

> A 17-year-old boy comes to your office and asks for a comprehensive psychological evaluation. He has been experiencing some headaches, anxiety, and depression. A high-school dropout, he has been married for a year and has a 1-year-old baby, but has left his wife and child and returned to live with his parents. He works full time as an auto mechanic and has insurance that covers the testing procedures. You complete the testing.
>
> During the following year you receive requests for information about the testing from
>
> - The boy's physician, an internist
> - The boy's parents, who are concerned about his depression
> - The boy's employer, in connection with a worker's compensation claim filed by the boy
> - The attorney for the insurance company that is contesting the worker's compensation claim
> - The attorney for the boy's wife, who is suing for divorce and for custody of the baby
> - The boy's attorney, who is considering suing you for malpractice because he does not like the results of the tests
>
> Each of the requests asks for the full formal report, the original test data, and copies of each of the tests you administered (for example, instructions and all items for the MMPI-2).
>
> To which of these people are you ethically or legally obligated to supply all the information requested, partial information, a summary of the report, or no information at all? Which requests require having the boy's written, informed consent before information can be released?
>
> It is unfortunately all too easy, in the crush of a busy schedule or a hurried lapse of attention, to release data to those who are not legally or ethically entitled to it, and it sometimes leads to disastrous results. Clarifying these issues while planning an assessment is important because if the psy-

---

[1]Pope, K. S., & Vasquez, M. J. T. (1998). *Ethics in psychotherapy and counseling* (2nd ed.). San Francisco: Jossey–Bass.

chologist does not clearly understand them, it is impossible to communicate the information effectively as part of the process of informed consent and informed refusal. Information about who will or won't have access to an assessment report may be the key to an individual's decision to give or withhold informed consent for an assessment. The psychologist is responsible for remaining aware of the evolving legal, ethical, and practical frameworks that inform gatekeeping decisions.

For each of the requests for information described in the previous passage, it would be wonderful if there were one clear answer to the question, "How should the therapist respond to this request?" But these gatekeeping responsibilities exist within a complex framework of federal (e.g., Health Insurance Portability Accountability Act [HIPAA]), state, and provincial legislation and case law, as well as other relevant regulations, codes, and contexts. The responsibilities to provide or withhold the information requested in each instance differs from province to province and from state to state. And as emphasized throughout this book, such requirements can change over time. A requirement to withhold certain health care data in a specific situation in a given jurisdiction may be transformed the following year by new legislation, case law, or regulations into a requirement to provide the data.

13

AVOIDING LOGICAL FALLACIES IN PSYCHOLOGY

Practicing psychology requires countless decisions. We consider the options, context, and implications in areas that are diverse, complex, and changing. We try to think through the issues—those that fall within and beyond the scope of this short book—as clearly as we can.

In this chapter, we've tried to pull together some of the most basic ways that this process of thinking through can go wrong. Our list of 18 logical fallacies is not, of course, comprehensive. We've tried to choose those fallacies that seem to thrive, that cause much mischief in psychology practices, and that are unlikely to appear on the "endangered species" list in the psychological literature and in psychological discussions.

The fallacies are denying the antecedent; composition fallacy; affirming the consequent; division fallacy; Golden Mean fallacy; appeal to ignorance (ad ignorantium); disjunctive fallacy; false dilemma; mistaking deductive validity for truth; post hoc, ergo propter hoc (after this, therefore because of this); red herring; ad hominem; straw person; you too (tu quoque); naturalistic fallacy; false analogy; begging the question (petitio principii); and argument to logic (argumentum ad logicam). The name of each fallacy is followed

---

This chapter is adapted from "Fallacies & Pitfalls in Psychology" © by Ken Pope, available at http://kspope.com

by a brief description and an example, often in exaggerated form, from the field of psychology.

DENYING THE ANTECEDENT

This fallacy takes the form of

If x, then y.
Not x.
Therefore, not y.

Example: "If clients or colleagues using wheelchairs came to this office, there would be a reason to make my office accessible. But no one using a wheelchair comes into my office, so there's no reason too make it wheelchair-accessible."

COMPOSITION FALLACY

This fallacy takes the form of assuming that a group possesses the characteristics of its individual members.

Example: "Several years ago, a group of 10 psychologists started a group practice. Each of those psychologists is efficient, effective, and highly regarded. Their group practice must be efficient, effective, and highly regarded."

AFFIRMING THE CONSEQUENT

This fallacy takes the form of

If x, then y.
y.
Therefore, x.

Example: "Good mental health attorneys have a lot of clients. My attorney has a lot of clients, so she must be good."

Alternate example: "If this client is competent to stand trial, he will certainly know the answers to at least 80% of the questions on this standardized test. He knows the answers to 87% of the test questions. Therefore, he is competent to stand trial."

DIVISION FALLACY

The division fallacy or decomposition fallacy takes the form of assuming that the members of a group possess the characteristics of the group.

Example: "This clinic sure makes a lot of money. Each of the psychologists who work there must earn a large income."

GOLDEN MEAN FALLACY

The fallacy of the Golden Mean (fallacy of compromise or fallacy of moderation) takes the form of assuming that the most valid conclusion is that which accepts the best compromise between two competing positions.

Example: "The co-owner of my practice believes the best office is on the top floor of this high-rise office building, with its wonderful view. I believe that the best office is on the first floor, which is more convenient to our clients and would be seen by countless people as they walk to the elevators. We'll probably compromise and get an office on one of the floors about halfway to the top."

APPEAL TO IGNORANCE (AD IGNORANTIUM)

The appeal to ignorance fallacy takes the following form:

There is no (or insufficient) evidence establishing that x is false. Therefore, x is true.

Example: "In the 6 years that I have been practicing my new and improved brand of cognitive–humanistic–dynamic–behavioral–deconstructive–metaregressive–deontological psychotherapy (now with biofeedback!), which I developed, not one published study has shown that it fails to work or that it has ever harmed a patient. It is clearly one of the safest and most effective interventions ever devised."

DISJUNCTIVE FALLACY

This fallacy takes the form of

Either x or y.
x.
Therefore, not y.

Example: "This new brochure doesn't seem to be bringing in many new clients and it's either because I didn't distribute as many copies as I'd thought or it's not that great a brochure. Going over my records, I see that I didn't distribute as many copies as I'd thought. It's a great brochure."

FALSE DILEMMA

Also known as the "either/or" fallacy or the fallacy of false choices, this takes the form of only acknowledging two options (one of which is usually extreme) from a continuum or other array of possibilities.

Example: "Either I can make enough to live on within a couple of months of starting my new practice or I'm just no good as a therapist."

MISTAKING DEDUCTIVE VALIDITY FOR TRUTH

This fallacy takes the form of assuming that because an argument is a logical syllogism the conclusion must therefore be true. It ignores the possibility that the premises of the argument may be false.

Example: "I just read a book that proves that the book's author knows the best way to market a psychology practice. He has a chart showing that every other method can fail sometimes, but that his always works. That proves his method is best."

POST HOC, ERGO PROPTER HOC (AFTER THIS, THEREFORE ON ACCOUNT OF THIS)

The post hoc, ergo propter hoc fallacy takes the form of confusing correlation with causation and concluding that because y follows x, y must be a result of x.

Example: "Luckily, I practice in a town where there are not many malpractice suits. One of my colleagues was sued by a client whose diagnosis was borderline personality disorder, and another was sued by a client whose diagnosis was anxiety disorder. That's reason enough for me to avoid clients with those diagnoses."

RED HERRING

This fallacy takes the form of introducing or focusing on irrelevant information to distract from the valid evidence and reasoning. It takes its name from the strategy of dragging a herring or other fish across a path to distract the hounds or other tracking dogs and throw them off the scent of whatever they are searching for.

> Example: "Some of you have objected to the new test batteries that I purchased for our group practice, alleging that they have no demonstrable validity, were not adequately normed for the kind of clients we see from various cultures, and are unusable for clients with physical disabilities. What you have conveniently failed to take into account, however, is that they cost less than a third of the price for the other tests we had been using, are much easier to learn, and can be administered and scored in less than half the time of the tests we used to use."

AD HOMINEM

The argumentum ad hominem or ad feminam attempts to discredit an argument or position by drawing attention to characteristics of the person who is making the argument or who holds the position.

> Example: "I spoke with a senior colleague who has an established practice in my community. She gave me a number of suggestions about how to market my practice to the clientele I'm interested in. However, I didn't think she dressed in a very professional manner so I'm not inclined to pursue her suggestions."

STRAW PERSON

The straw person, straw man, or straw woman fallacy takes the form of mischaracterizing someone else's position in a way that makes it weak, false, or ridiculous.

> Example: "The idea that I should do any retirement planning is the kind of notion that assumes you can control everything in the future."

YOU TOO! (TU QUOQUE)

This fallacy takes the form of distracting attention from one's error or weakness by claiming that an opposing argument, person, or position has the same error or weakness.

> Example: "I have been accused of stealing a colleague's promotional materials just because I printed up copies of her brochure after substituting my name and practice address for hers. But I'm pretty sure that she got that brochure from someone else!"

NATURALISTIC FALLACY

The naturalistic fallacy takes the form of logically deducing values (e.g., what is good, best, right, ethical, or moral) based only on statements of fact.

Example: "There is no intervention for survivors of domestic violence that has more empirical support from controlled studies than this one. It is clear that this is the right way to address this problem, and we should all be providing this therapy whenever survivors of domestic violence come to us for help."

FALSE ANALOGY

The false or faulty analogy fallacy takes the form of argument by an analogy in which the comparison is misleading in at least one important aspect.

Example: "I know at least five very senior practitioners in this building who do no marketing whatsoever and yet have a waiting list. It seems foolish for me to waste my time and money on marketing, especially now while I'm just starting a practice and am on a very tight budget."

BEGGING THE QUESTION (PETITIO PRINCIPII)

This fallacy, one of the fallacies of circularity, takes the form of statements that simply assume or restate their own truth rather than providing relevant evidence and logical arguments.

Examples: Sometimes this fallacy literally takes the form of a question, such as, "Have you stopped using those terrible marketing brochures yet?" (The question assumes—and a "yes" or "no" response to the question affirms—that your brochures are terrible.) Or "Why must you always use such a nonsensical fee scale?" (The question assumes that the practitioner's method of setting fees makes no sense.) Sometimes this fallacy takes the form of a statement such as, "No one can deny that my approach to marketing is the only effective way to market psychological services," or "It must be acknowledged that the forms I use are the only legitimate approach to informed consent." Sometimes it takes the form of a logical argument such as, "My new billing software is the most effective there is because it is the only computer billing program capable of such effectiveness, the only one that has ever approached such a high level of functioning, and the only one that works so well."

ARGUMENT TO LOGIC (ARGUMENTUM AD LOGICAM)

The argument to logic fallacy takes the form of assuming that a proposition must be false because an argument offered in support of that proposition was fallacious.

> Example: "I thought that declaring my new swimming pool, tango lessons, and vacation in Aruba as business expenses was prohibited by the tax laws, but I just found out that all three of the colleagues who told me that are not CPAs, have not read the tax code lately, and didn't really understand my situation, so the deductions must be okay."

14

AVOIDING ETHICAL RATIONALIZATIONS

Faced with the complex demands, human costs, constant risks, and often limited resources of our work as psychologists, we may experience the very human temptation to try to make life easier for ourselves by nullifying some of our fundamental ethical responsibilities. Not wanting to view ourselves (or have others view us) as unethical, however, we use common fallacies and rationalizations to justify our unethical behavior and to quiet a noisy conscience. These attempts to disguise unethical behavior might be termed ethical substandards, although they are in no way ethical, and many are so far beneath the standards of the profession that "substandard" seems an understatement. The justifications can make even the most hurtful and reprehensible behaviors seem ethical or at least insignificant.

These substandards afflict all too many practices, and all of us at one time or another have probably endorsed at least some of them and could probably extend the list. If some excuses seem absurd and humorous to us, it is likely that we have not yet had to resort to using those particular rationalizations. At some

For additional information about ethics, please see Appendixes B and C, and http://kspope.com/ethics/index.php. Adapted from *Ethics in Psychotherapy and Counseling, Second Edition* (pp. 13–15), by K. Pope and M. Vasquez, 1998, New York: John Wiley & Sons, Inc. Adapted with permission.

future moment of great stress or exceptional temptation, those funny absurdities may gain considerable plausibility if not a comforting certitude. These substandards that we commonly rely on to justify the unjustifiable include the following:

- It's not unethical as long as you don't talk about ethics. The principle of general denial is at work here. As long as neither you nor your colleagues mention ethical aspects of practice, no course of action could be identified as unethical.
- It's not unethical as long as you don't know a law, ethical principle, or professional standard that prohibits it. This substandard encompasses two principles: specific ignorance and specific literalization. The principle of specific ignorance states that even if there is, say, a law prohibiting an action, what you do is not illegal as long as you are unaware of the law. The principle of literalization states that if you cannot find specific mention of a particular incident anywhere in legal, ethical, or professional standards, it must he ethical. In desperate times, when the specific incident is unfortunately mentioned in the standards and you are aware of it, it is still perfectly ethical as long as the standard does not mention your theoretical orientation. Thus, if the formal standard prohibits sexual involvement with patients, violations of confidentiality, or diagnosing without actually meeting with the client, a behavioral, humanistic, or psychodynamic therapist may legitimately engage in these activities as long as the standard does not explicitly mention behavioral, humanistic, or psychodynamic therapy.
- It's not unethical as long as you can name at least five other clinicians right off the top of your head who do the same thing. (There are probably countless thousands more who you don't know about or who you could name if you just had the time.)
- It's not unethical as long as none of your clients has ever complained about it.
- It's not unethical as long as your client wanted you to do it.
- It's not unethical as long as your clients' condition (probably borderline) made them so difficult to treat and so troublesome and risky to be around that they elicited whatever it was you did (not, of course, to admit that you actually did anything).
- It's not unethical as long as you weren't really feeling well that day and thus couldn't be expected to perform up to your usual level of quality. No fair-minded person would hold you as a professional accountable for what you did when it is clear that it was the stress you were under—along with all sorts of other powerful factors—that must be held responsible.

- It's not unethical as long as a friend of yours knew someone that said an ethics committee somewhere once issued an opinion that it's okay.

- It's not unethical as long as you're sure that legal, ethical, and professional standards were made up by people who don't understand the hard realities of psychological practice.

- It's not unethical as long as you're sure that the people involved in enforcing standards (e.g., licensing boards or administrative law judges) are dishonest, stupid, and extremist; are unlike you in some significant way; or are conspiring against you.

- It's not unethical as long as it results in a higher income or more prestige.

- It's not unethical as long as it's more convenient than doing things another way.

- It's not unethical as long as no one else finds out—or if whoever might find out probably wouldn't care anyway.

- It's not unethical as long as you're observing most of the other ethical standards. This means that everyone can, by fiat, nullify one or two ethical principles as long as the other, more important standards are observed. In a pinch, it's okay to observe a majority of the standards. In a real emergency, it's acceptable simply to have observed one of the ethical principles in some situation at some time in your life or to have thought about observing it.

- It's not unethical as long as there's no intent to do harm.

- It's not unethical as long as there is no body of universally accepted, scientific studies showing, without any doubt whatsoever, that exactly what you did was the sole cause of harm to the client. This view was vividly and succinctly stated by a member of the Texas pesticide regulatory board charged with protecting Texas citizens against undue risks from pesticides. In discussing Chlordane, a chemical used to kill termites, one member said, "Sure, it's going to kill a lot of people, but they may be dying of something else anyway" ("Perspectives," Newsweek, April 23, 1990, p. 17).

- It's not unethical as long as you don't intend to do it more than once.

- It's not unethical as long as no one can prove you did it.

- It's not unethical as long as you're an important person. The criteria for importance in this context generally include being rich, well known, extensively published, or tenured; having a large practice; having what you think of as a "following" of like-minded people; or having discovered and given clever names to at least five new diagnoses described on television talk shows as reaching epidemic proportions. . . Actually, if you just think you're important, you'll have no problem finding proof.

- It's not unethical as long as you're busy. After all, given your workload and responsibilities, who could reasonably expect you to obtain informed consent from all your clients, keep your chart notes in a secured area, be thorough when conducting assessments, and follow every little law?

SOME FINAL THOUGHTS

For many psychologists, the practicalities of practice are uncharted territory. Graduate schools and internships are part of the supportive, challenging structure teaching us the content and skills of psychology. We learn, grow, and develop within a network of teachers, supervisors, mentors, and others. Over the course of training, our knowledge of the science and discipline of psychology and our clinical skills expand and deepen. We encounter year after year of tests—including the licensing examination—designed to ensure that we understand psychological theory and research, and that we know what we're doing when we conduct an assessment or provide therapy.

Most of us start a practice with relatively little—if any—formal training in business principles, marketing, and the other practicalities that can determine whether this venture succeeds or fails. We do the best we can, learning as we go along, mostly by trial and error. We often work without a net—for many, a psychology practice is the major or sole source of income.

Our hope is that this collection of information, ideas, and resources will help those whose clinical training, knowledge, and skills are not matched by their training, knowledge, and skills in the practicalities of practice. Even when you decide that certain suggestions we make (e.g., in regard to making a business plan, finding a good attorney before trouble finds you, or developing a support network) don't fit you and your practice, we hope that this material is helpful in your thinking through the best course for you.

Our view is that a psychology practice is more than just working with clients and consulting. It is also a business, and a lack of training, knowledge, and skills in business principles and other practical aspects can weigh down or sink even the most skilled clinician's attempts to build, expand, or maintain a practice.

A psychology practice is also—for most of us—much more than a business. It is what we have chosen to do with our time and our lives. We look to it for much more than financial support. For many, our practice is a source of joy, meaning, and fulfillment, but sometimes it can become a drain. It takes more out of the practitioner's life than it gives back. We hope that the information, ideas, and resources in this book can help bring about change, especially for practitioners caught in such circumstances. For *all* practitioners who want to start, expand, strengthen, rethink, redirect, or improve a psychology practice, we hope that this book gives you some helpful tools, guidance, and support.

APPENDIX A

Contact Information for Psychology Licensing Boards in Canada and the United States

CANADA

Alberta
College of Alberta Psychologists
10123-99 Street, 2100 Sunlife Place
Edmonton, AB T5J 3H1
(780) 424-5070

British Columbia
College of Psychologists of British Columbia
1755 West Broadway, Suite 404
Vancouver, BC V6J 4S5
(604) 736-6164

Manitoba
Psychological Association of Manitoba
162-2025 Corydon Avenue, #253
Winnipeg, MB R3P 0N5
(204) 487-0784

New Brunswick
College of Psychologists of New Brunswick
238 St. George Street, Suite 5
Moncton, NB E1C 1V9
(506) 382-1994

Newfoundland
Newfoundland Board of Examiners in Psychology
P.O. Box 5666, Station C
St. John's, NL A1C 5W8
(709) 579-6313

Nova Scotia Board of Examiners in Psychology
Halifax Professional Centre, Suite 455
5991 Spring Garden Road
Halifax, Nova Scotia B3H 1Y6
(902) 423-2238

Ontario
The College of Psychologists of Ontario
L'Ordre des Psychologues de L'Ontario
110 Eglinton Avenue West, Suite 500
Toronto, Ontario M4R 1A3
(416) 961-8817

Prince Edward Island Psychologists Registration Board
Registrar—Dr. Philip Smith,
Department of Psychology
University of Prince Edward Island
Charlottetown, PE C1A 4P3
(902) 566-0549

Quebec
Ordre des Psychologues du Quebec
1100, rue Beaumont #510
Mont-Royal, Quebec H3P 3H5
(514) 738-1881, ext. 225

Saskatchewan
Saskatchewan College of Psychologists
384 Albert Street
Regina, SK S4R 2N2
(306) 352-1699

UNITED STATES

Alabama Board of Examiners in Psychology
660 Adams Avenue, Suite 360
Montgomery, AL 36104
(334) 242-4127

Alaska Board of Psychologist
    and Psychological Associate Examiners
333 Willoughby Avenue, 9th Floor, SOB
P.O. Box 110806
Juneau, AK 99811-0806
(907) 465-3811

Arizona Board of Psychologist Examiners
1400 West Washington, Room 235
Phoenix, AZ 85007
(602) 542-8162

Arkansas Board of Psychology
101 East Capitol, Suite 415
Little Rock, AR 72201
(501) 682-6168

California Board of Psychology
1422 Howe Avenue, Suite 22
Sacramento, CA 95825-3200
(916) 263-2696

Colorado Board of Psychologist Examiners
1560 Broadway, Suite 880
Denver, CO 80202
(303) 894-7768

Connecticut Board of Examiners of Psychologists
Department of Public Health
P.O. Box 340308
410 Capitol Avenue, MS# 12APP
Hartford, CT 06134
(860) 509-7603

Delaware Board of Examiners of Psychology
861 Silver Lake Boulevard, Cannon Building, Suite 203
Dover, DE 19904
(302) 739-4522, ext. 220

District of Columbia Board of Psychology
825 North Capitol Street NE, Suite 2224
Washington, DC 20002
(202) 442-4766

Florida Board of Psychology
4052 Bald Cypress Way, Bin #C05
Tallahassee, FL 32399-3255
(850) 245-4373

Georgia State Board of Examiners of Psychologists
237 Coliseum Drive
Macon, GA 31217-3858
(478) 207-1670

Hawaii Board of Psychology
Department of Commerce and Consumer Affairs
335 Merchant Street
Honolulu, HI 96813
(808) 586-2693

Idaho Board of Psychologist Examiners
Bureau of Occupational Licenses
1109 Main Street, Suite 220
Boise, ID 83702
(208) 334-3233

Illinois Clinical Psychologists Licensing & Disciplinary Committee
Division of Professional Regulation
320 West Washington Street, 3rd Floor
Springfield, IL 62786
(217) 782-0458

Indiana State Psychology Board
Health Profession Bureau
402 W. Washington Street, Suite W066
Indianapolis, IN 46204
(317) 234-2057

Iowa Board of Psychology Examiners
Department of Public Health
321 East 12th Street, Lucas State Office Building, 5th Floor
Des Moines, IA 50319-0075
(515) 281-4401

Kansas Behavioral Sciences Regulatory Board
712 S. Kansas Avenue
Topeka, KS 66603-3817
(785) 296-3240

Kentucky State Board of Examiners of Psychology
P.O. Box 1360
Frankfort, KY 40602-0456
(502) 564-3296, ext. 225

Louisiana State Board of Examiners of Psychologists
8280 YMCA Plaza Drive
One Oak Square, Building 8-B
Baton Rouge, LA 70810
(225) 763-3935

Maine Board of Examiners of Psychologists
35 State House Station
Augusta, ME 04333-0035
(207) 624-8600

Maryland Board of Examiners of Psychologists
4201 Patterson Avenue
Baltimore, MD 21215-2299
(410) 764-4787

Massachusetts Board of Registration of Psychologists
Division of Registration
239 Causeway Street
Boston, MA 02114
(617) 727-0592

Michigan Board of Psychology
P.O. Box 30670
Lansing, MI 48909
(517) 335-0918

Minnesota Board of Psychology
2829 University Avenue SE, Suite 320
St. Paul, MN 55414-3237
(612) 617-2230

Mississippi Board of Psychology
419 E. Broadway
Yazoo City, MS 13769
(662) 716-3934

Missouri State Committee of Psychologists
3605 Missouri Boulevard
Jefferson City, MO 65109
(573) 751-0099

Montana Board of Psychologists
301 South Park Avenue, Room 430
Helena, MT 59620-0513
(406) 841-2394

Nebraska Board of Psychologists
301 Centennial Mall South, 3rd Floor
P.O. Box 94986
Lincoln, NE 68509-4986
(402) 471-2117

State of Nevada Board of Psychological Examiners
P.O. Box 2286
Reno, NV 89505-2286
(775) 688-1268

New Hampshire Board of Mental Health Practice
49 Donovan Street
Concord, NH 03301
(603) 271-6762

New Jersey State Board of Psychological Examiners
P.O. Box 45017
Newark, NJ 07101
(973) 504-6470

New Mexico Board of Psychologist Examiners
2550 Cerrillos Road
Santa Fe, NM 87505
(505) 476-4607

New York State Board for Psychology
New York State Education Department
Office of the Professions
89 Washington Avenue, 2nd Floor, East Wing
Albany, NY 12234-1000
(518) 474-3817, ext. 150

North Carolina Psychology Board
895 State Farm Road, Suite 101
Boone, NC 28607
(828) 262-2258

North Dakota State Board of Psychologist Examiners
P.O. Box 7458
Bismark, ND 58507-7458
(701) 250-8691

Ohio State Board of Psychology
77 S. High Street, Suite 1830
Columbus, OH 43215-6108
(614) 466-8808

Oklahoma State Board of Examiners of Psychologists
201 NE 38th Terrace, Suite 3
Oklahoma City, OK 73105
(405) 524-9094

Oregon State Board of Psychologist Examiners
3218 Pringle Road SE, Suite 130
Salem, OR 97302-6309
(503) 378-4154

Pennsylvania State Board of Psychology
2601 N. 3rd Street
Harrisburg, PA 17110
(717) 783-7155, ext. 3

Rhode Island Board of Psychology
Office of Health Professionals Regulations
Cannon Building
3 Capitol Hill, Room 104
Providence, RI 02908-5097
(401) 222-2827

South Carolina Board of Examiners in Psychology
P.O. Box 11329
Columbia, SC 29211-1329
(803) 896-4664

South Dakota Board of Examiners of Psychologists
135 East Illinois, Suite 214
Spearfish, SD 57783
(605) 642-1600

Tennessee Board of Examiners in Psychology
425 5th Avenue North
First Floor, Cordell Hull Building
Nashville, TN 37243
(615) 532-5127

Texas State Board of Examiners of Psychologists
333 Guadalupe, Tower 2, Room 450
Austin, TX 78701
(512) 305-7700

Utah Psychologist Licensing Board
Division of Occupational & Professional Licensing
160 E. 300 S, Box 146741
Salt Lake City, UT 84114-6741
(801) 530-6628

Vermont Board of Psychological Examiners
Office of Professional Regulation
26 Terrace Street
Montpelier, VT 05609-1106
(802) 828-2373

Virgin Islands
Executive Secretary to Medical Boards
Office of the Commissioner
Roy L. Schneider Hospital
St. Thomas, VI 00801
(340) 776-8311 ext. 5078

Virginia Board of Psychology
6603 West Broad Street, 5th Floor
Richmond, VA 23230-1717
(804) 662-9913

Washington State Examining Board of Psychology
Department of Health
P.O. Box 47869
Olympia, WA 98504-7869
(360) 236-4912

West Virginia Board of Examiners of Psychologists
P.O. Box 3955
Charleston, WV 25339-3955
(304) 558-3040

Wisconsin Psychology Examining Board
Department of Regulation & Licensing
Bureau of Health Service Professions
P.O. Box 8935
Madison, WI 53708-8935
(608) 266-2112

Wyoming State Board of Psychology
2020 Carey Avenue, Suite 201
Cheyenne, WV 82002
(307) 777-6529

APPENDIX B

APA Ethical Principles of Psychologists and Code of Conduct

CONTENTS

Introduction and Applicability

Preamble

General Principles

ETHICAL STANDARDS

From "Ethical Principles of Psychologists and Code of Conduct," by the American Psychological Association, 2002, *American Psychologist, 57*, pp. 1597–1611. Copyright 2002 by the American Psychological Association. Retrieved September 23, 2004, from PsychNET® Web site: http://www.apa.org/ethics/code2002.html

Introduction and Applicability

The American Psychological Association's (APA's) Ethical Principles of Psychologists and Code of Conduct (hereinafter referred to as the Ethics Code) consists of an introduction, a Preamble, five General Principles (A–E), and specific Ethical Standards. The Introduction discusses the intent, organization, procedural considerations, and scope of application of the Ethics Code. The Preamble and General Principles are aspirational goals to guide psychologists toward the highest ideals of psychology. Although the Preamble and General Principles are not themselves enforceable rules, they should be considered by psychologists in arriving at an ethical course of action. The Ethical Standards set forth enforceable rules for conduct as psychologists. Most of the Ethical Standards are written broadly, in order to apply to psychologists in varied roles, although the application of an Ethical Standard may vary depending on the context. The Ethical Standards are not exhaustive. The fact that

[This version of the APA Ethics Code was adopted by the American Psychological Association's Council of Representatives during its meeting, August 21, 2002, and is effective beginning June 1, 2003. Inquiries concerning the substance or interpretation of the APA Ethics Code should be addressed to the Director, Office of Ethics, American Psychological Association, 750 First Street, NE, Washington, DC 20002-4242. The Ethics Code and information regarding the Code can be found on the APA Web site, http://www.apa.org/ethics. The standards in this Ethics Code will be used to adjudicate complaints brought concerning alleged conduct occurring on or after the effective date. Complaints regarding conduct occurring prior to the effective date will be adjudicated on the basis of the version of the Ethics Code that was in effect at the time the conduct occurred.]

a given conduct is not specifically addressed by an Ethical Standard does not mean that it is necessarily either ethical or unethical.

This Ethics Code applies only to psychologists' activities that are part of their scientific, educational, or professional roles as psychologists. Areas covered include but are not limited to the clinical, counseling, and school practice of psychology; research; teaching; supervision of trainees; public service; policy development; social intervention; development of assessment instruments; conducting assessments; educational counseling; organizational consulting; forensic activities; program design and evaluation; and administration. This Ethics Code applies to these activities across a variety of contexts, such as in person, postal, telephone, Internet, and other electronic transmissions. These activities shall be distinguished from the purely private conduct of psychologists, which is not within the purview of the Ethics Code.

Membership in the APA commits members and student affiliates to comply with the standards of the APA Ethics Code and to the rules and procedures used to enforce them. Lack of awareness or misunderstanding of an Ethical Standard is not itself a defense to a charge of unethical conduct.

The procedures for filing, investigating, and resolving complaints of unethical conduct are described in the current Rules and Procedures of the APA Ethics Committee. APA may impose sanctions on its members for violations of the standards of the Ethics Code, including termination of APA membership, and may notify other bodies and individuals of its actions. Actions that violate the standards of the Ethics Code may also lead to the imposition of sanctions on psychologists or students whether or not they are APA members by bodies other than APA, including state psychological associations, other professional groups, psychology boards, other state or federal agencies, and payors for health services. In addition, APA may take action against a member after his or her conviction of a felony, expulsion or suspension from an affiliated state psychological association, or suspension or loss of licensure. When the sanction to be imposed by APA is less than expulsion, the 2001 Rules and Procedures do not guarantee an opportunity for an in-person hearing, but generally provide that complaints will be resolved only on the basis of a submitted record.

The Ethics Code is intended to provide guidance for psychologists and standards of professional conduct that can be applied by the APA and by other bodies that choose to adopt them. The Ethics Code is not intended to be a basis of civil liability. Whether a psychologist has violated the Ethics Code standards does not by itself determine whether the psychologist is legally liable in a court action, whether a contract is enforceable, or whether other legal consequences occur.

The modifiers used in some of the standards of this Ethics Code (e.g., *reasonably, appropriate, potentially*) are included in the standards when they would (1) allow professional judgment on the part of psychologists, (2) eliminate injustice or inequality that would occur without the modifier,

(3) ensure applicability across the broad range of activities conducted by psychologists, or (4) guard against a set of rigid rules that might be quickly outdated. As used in this Ethics Code, the term *reasonable* means the prevailing professional judgment of psychologists engaged in similar activities in similar circumstances, given the knowledge the psychologist had or should have had at the time.

In the process of making decisions regarding their professional behavior, psychologists must consider this Ethics Code in addition to applicable laws and psychology board regulations. In applying the Ethics Code to their professional work, psychologists may consider other materials and guidelines that have been adopted or endorsed by scientific and professional psychological organizations and the dictates of their own conscience, as well as consult with others within the field. If this Ethics Code establishes a higher standard of conduct than is required by law, psychologists must meet the higher ethical standard. If psychologists' ethical responsibilities conflict with law, regulations, or other governing legal authority, psychologists make known their commitment to this Ethics Code and take steps to resolve the conflict in a responsible manner. If the conflict is unresolvable via such means, psychologists may adhere to the requirements of the law, regulations, or other governing authority in keeping with basic principles of human rights.

Preamble

Psychologists are committed to increasing scientific and professional knowledge of behavior and people's understanding of themselves and others and to the use of such knowledge to improve the condition of individuals, organizations, and society. Psychologists respect and protect civil and human rights and the central importance of freedom of inquiry and expression in research, teaching, and publication. They strive to help the public in developing informed judgments and choices concerning human behavior. In doing so, they perform many roles, such as researcher, educator, diagnostician, therapist, supervisor, consultant, administrator, social interventionist, and expert witness. This Ethics Code provides a common set of principles and standards upon which psychologists build their professional and scientific work.

This Ethics Code is intended to provide specific standards to cover most situations encountered by psychologists. It has as its goals the welfare and protection of the individuals and groups with whom psychologists work and the education of members, students, and the public regarding ethical standards of the discipline.

The development of a dynamic set of ethical standards for psychologists' work-related conduct requires a personal commitment and lifelong effort to act ethically; to encourage ethical behavior by students, supervisees, employees, and colleagues; and to consult with others concerning ethical problems.

General Principles

This section consists of General Principles. General Principles, as opposed to Ethical Standards, are aspirational in nature. Their intent is to guide and inspire psychologists toward the very highest ethical ideals of the profession. General Principles, in contrast to Ethical Standards, do not represent obligations and should not form the basis for imposing sanctions. Relying upon General Principles for either of these reasons distorts both their meaning and purpose.

Principle A: Beneficence and Nonmaleficence. Psychologists strive to benefit those with whom they work and take care to do no harm. In their professional actions, psychologists seek to safeguard the welfare and rights of those with whom they interact professionally and other affected persons, and the welfare of animal subjects of research. When conflicts occur among psychologists' obligations or concerns, they attempt to resolve these conflicts in a responsible fashion that avoids or minimizes harm. Because psychologists' scientific and professional judgments and actions may affect the lives of others, they are alert to and guard against personal, financial, social, organizational, or political factors that might lead to misuse of their influence. Psychologists strive to be aware of the possible effect of their own physical and mental health on their ability to help those with whom they work.

Principle B: Fidelity and Responsibility. Psychologists establish relationships of trust with those with whom they work. They are aware of their professional and scientific responsibilities to society and to the specific communities in which they work. Psychologists uphold professional standards of conduct, clarify their professional roles and obligations, accept appropriate responsibility for their behavior, and seek to manage conflicts of interest that could lead to exploitation or harm. Psychologists consult with, refer to, or cooperate with other professionals and institutions to the extent needed to serve the best interests of those with whom they work. They are concerned about the ethical compliance of their colleagues' scientific and professional conduct. Psychologists strive to contribute a portion of their professional time for little or no compensation or personal advantage.

Principle C: Integrity. Psychologists seek to promote accuracy, honesty, and truthfulness in the science, teaching, and practice of psychology. In these activities psychologists do not steal, cheat, or engage in fraud, subterfuge, or intentional misrepresentation of fact. Psychologists strive to keep their promises and to avoid unwise or unclear commitments. In situations in which deception may be ethically justifiable to maximize benefits and minimize harm, psychologists have a serious obligation to consider the need for, the possible consequences of, and their responsibility to correct any resulting mistrust or other harmful effects that arise from the use of such techniques.

Principle D: Justice. Psychologists recognize that fairness and justice entitle all persons to access to and benefit from the contributions of psychology and to equal quality in the processes, procedures, and services being conducted by psychologists. Psychologists exercise reasonable judgment and take precautions to ensure that their potential biases, the boundaries of their competence, and the limitations of their expertise do not lead to or condone unjust practices.

Principle E: Respect for People's Rights and Dignity. Psychologists respect the dignity and worth of all people, and the rights of individuals to privacy, confidentiality, and self-determination. Psychologists are aware that special safeguards may be necessary to protect the rights and welfare of persons or communities whose vulnerabilities impair autonomous decision making. Psychologists are aware of and respect cultural, individual, and role differences, including those based on age, gender, gender identity, race, ethnicity, culture, national origin, religion, sexual orientation, disability, language, and socioeconomic status and consider these factors when working with members of such groups. Psychologists try to eliminate the effect on their work of biases based on those factors, and they do not knowingly participate in or condone activities of others based upon such prejudices.

Ethical Standards

1. Resolving Ethical Issues

1.01 Misuse of Psychologists' Work. If psychologists learn of misuse or misrepresentation of their work, they take reasonable steps to correct or minimize the misuse or misrepresentation.

1.02 Conflicts Between Ethics and Law, Regulations, or Other Governing Legal Authority. If psychologists' ethical responsibilities conflict with law, regulations, or other governing legal authority, psychologists make known their commitment to the Ethics Code and take steps to resolve the conflict. If the conflict is unresolvable via such means, psychologists may adhere to the requirements of the law, regulations, or other governing legal authority.

1.03 Conflicts Between Ethics and Organizational Demands. If the demands of an organization with which psychologists are affiliated or for whom they are working conflict with this Ethics Code, psychologists clarify the nature of the conflict, make known their commitment to the Ethics Code, and to the extent feasible, resolve the conflict in a way that permits adherence to the Ethics Code.

1.04 Informal Resolution of Ethical Violations. When psychologists believe that there may have been an ethical violation by another psychologist, they attempt to resolve the issue by bringing it to the attention of that individual, if an informal resolution appears appropriate and the intervention does not violate any confidentiality rights that may be involved. (See also

Standards 1.02, Conflicts Between Ethics and Law, Regulations, or Other Governing Legal Authority, and 1.03, Conflicts Between Ethics and Organizational Demands.)

1.05 Reporting Ethical Violations. If an apparent ethical violation has substantially harmed or is likely to substantially harm a person or organization and is not appropriate for informal resolution under Standard 1.04, Informal Resolution of Ethical Violations, or is not resolved properly in that fashion, psychologists take further action appropriate to the situation. Such action might include referral to state or national committees on professional ethics, to state licensing boards, or to the appropriate institutional authorities. This standard does not apply when an intervention would violate confidentiality rights or when psychologists have been retained to review the work of another psychologist whose professional conduct is in question. (See also Standard 1.02, Conflicts Between Ethics and Law, Regulations, or Other Governing Legal Authority.)

1.06 Cooperating With Ethics Committees. Psychologists cooperate in ethics investigations, proceedings, and resulting requirements of the APA or any affiliated state psychological association to which they belong. In doing so, they address any confidentiality issues. Failure to cooperate is itself an ethics violation. However, making a request for deferment of adjudication of an ethics complaint pending the outcome of litigation does not alone constitute noncooperation.

1.07 Improper Complaints. Psychologists do not file or encourage the filing of ethics complaints that are made with reckless disregard for or willful ignorance of facts that would disprove the allegation.

1.08 Unfair Discrimination Against Complainants and Respondents. Psychologists do not deny persons employment, advancement, admissions to academic or other programs, tenure, or promotion, based solely upon their having made or their being the subject of an ethics complaint. This does not preclude taking action based upon the outcome of such proceedings or considering other appropriate information.

2. Competence

2.01 Boundaries of Competence (a) Psychologists provide services, teach, and conduct research with populations and in areas only within the boundaries of their competence, based on their education, training, supervised experience, consultation, study, or professional experience.

(b) Where scientific or professional knowledge in the discipline of psychology establishes that an understanding of factors associated with age, gender, gender identity, race, ethnicity, culture, national origin, religion, sexual orientation, disability, language, or socioeconomic status is essential for effective implementation of their services or research, psychologists have or obtain the training, experience, consultation, or supervision necessary to ensure the competence of their services, or they make appropriate referrals, except as provided in Standard 2.02, Providing Services in Emergencies.

(c) Psychologists planning to provide services, teach, or conduct research involving populations, areas, techniques, or technologies new to them undertake relevant education, training, supervised experience, consultation, or study.

(d) When psychologists are asked to provide services to individuals for whom appropriate mental health services are not available and for which psychologists have not obtained the competence necessary, psychologists with closely related prior training or experience may provide such services in order to ensure that services are not denied if they make a reasonable effort to obtain the competence required by using relevant research, training, consultation, or study.

(e) In those emerging areas in which generally recognized standards for preparatory training do not yet exist, psychologists nevertheless take reasonable steps to ensure the competence of their work and to protect clients/patients, students, supervisees, research participants, organizational clients, and others from harm.

(f) When assuming forensic roles, psychologists are or become reasonably familiar with the judicial or administrative rules governing their roles.

2.02 *Providing Services in Emergencies.* In emergencies, when psychologists provide services to individuals for whom other mental health services are not available and for which psychologists have not obtained the necessary training, psychologists may provide such services in order to ensure that services are not denied. The services are discontinued as soon as the emergency has ended or appropriate services are available.

2.03 *Maintaining Competence.* Psychologists undertake ongoing efforts to develop and maintain their competence.

2.04 *Bases for Scientific and Professional Judgments.* Psychologists' work is based upon established scientific and professional knowledge of the discipline. (See also Standards 2.01e, Boundaries of Competence, and 10.01b, Informed Consent to Therapy.)

2.05 *Delegation of Work to Others.* Psychologists who delegate work to employees, supervisees, or research or teaching assistants or who use the services of others, such as interpreters, take reasonable steps to (1) avoid delegating such work to persons who have a multiple relationship with those being served that would likely lead to exploitation or loss of objectivity; (2) authorize only those responsibilities that such persons can be expected to perform competently on the basis of their education, training, or experience, either independently or with the level of supervision being provided; and (3) see that such persons perform these services competently. (See also Standards 2.02, Providing Services in Emergencies; 3.05, Multiple Relationships; 4.01,

Maintaining Confidentiality; 9.01, Bases for Assessments; 9.02, Use of Assessments; 9.03, Informed Consent in Assessments; and 9.07, Assessment by Unqualified Persons.)

2.06 *Personal Problems and Conflicts*. (a) Psychologists refrain from initiating an activity when they know or should know that there is a substantial likelihood that their personal problems will prevent them from performing their work-related activities in a competent manner.

(b) When psychologists become aware of personal problems that may interfere with their performing work-related duties adequately, they take appropriate measures, such as obtaining professional consultation or assistance, and determine whether they should limit, suspend, or terminate their work-related duties. (See also Standard 10.10, Terminating Therapy.)

3. Human Relations

3.01 *Unfair Discrimination*. In their work-related activities, psychologists do not engage in unfair discrimination based on age, gender, gender identity, race, ethnicity, culture, national origin, religion, sexual orientation, disability, socioeconomic status, or any basis proscribed by law.

3.02 *Sexual Harassment*. Psychologists do not engage in sexual harassment. Sexual harassment is sexual solicitation, physical advances, or verbal or nonverbal conduct that is sexual in nature, that occurs in connection with the psychologist's activities or roles as a psychologist, and that either (1) is unwelcome, is offensive, or creates a hostile workplace or educational environment, and the psychologist knows or is told this or (2) is sufficiently severe or intense to be abusive to a reasonable person in the context. Sexual harassment can consist of a single intense or severe act or of multiple persistent or pervasive acts. (See also Standard 1.08, Unfair Discrimination Against Complainants and Respondents.)

3.03 *Other Harassment*. Psychologists do not knowingly engage in behavior that is harassing or demeaning to persons with whom they interact in their work based on factors such as those persons' age, gender, gender identity, race, ethnicity, culture, national origin, religion, sexual orientation, disability, language, or socioeconomic status.

3.04 *Avoiding Harm*. Psychologists take reasonable steps to avoid harming their clients/patients, students, supervisees, research participants, organizational clients, and others with whom they work, and to minimize harm where it is foreseeable and unavoidable.

3.05 *Multiple Relationship*. (a) A multiple relationship occurs when a psychologist is in a professional role with a person and (1) at the same time is in another role with the same person, (2) at the same time is in a relationship with a person closely associated with or related to the person with whom the psychologist has the professional relationship, or (3) promises to enter into another relationship in the future with the person or a person closely associated with or related to the person.

A psychologist refrains from entering into a multiple relationship if the multiple relationship could reasonably be expected to impair the psychologist's objectivity, competence, or effectiveness in performing his or her functions as a psychologist, or otherwise risks exploitation or harm to the person with whom the professional relationship exists.

Multiple relationships that would not reasonably be expected to cause impairment or risk exploitation or harm are not unethical.

(b) If a psychologist finds that, due to unforeseen factors, a potentially harmful multiple relationship has arisen, the psychologist takes reasonable steps to resolve it with due regard for the best interests of the affected person and maximal compliance with the Ethics Code.

(c) When psychologists are required by law, institutional policy, or extraordinary circumstances to serve in more than one role in judicial or administrative proceedings, at the outset they clarify role expectations and the extent of confidentiality and thereafter as changes occur. (See also Standards 3.04, Avoiding Harm, and 3.07, Third-Party Requests for Services.)

3.06 Conflict of Interest. Psychologists refrain from taking on a professional role when personal, scientific, professional, legal, financial, or other interests or relationships could reasonably be expected to (1) impair their objectivity, competence, or effectiveness in performing their functions as psychologists or (2) expose the person or organization with whom the professional relationship exists to harm or exploitation.

3.07 Third-Party Requests for Services. When psychologists agree to provide services to a person or entity at the request of a third party, psychologists attempt to clarify at the outset of the service the nature of the relationship with all individuals or organizations involved. This clarification includes the role of the psychologist (e.g., therapist, consultant, diagnostician, or expert witness), an identification of who is the client, the probable uses of the services provided or the information obtained, and the fact that there may be limits to confidentiality. (See also Standards 3.05, Multiple Relationships, and 4.02, Discussing the Limits of Confidentiality.)

3.08 Exploitative Relationships. Psychologists do not exploit persons over whom they have supervisory, evaluative, or other authority such as clients/patients, students, supervisees, research participants, and employees. (See also Standards 3.05, Multiple Relationships; 6.04, Fees and Financial Arrangements; 6.05, Barter with Clients/Patients; 7.07, Sexual Relationships with Students and Supervisees; 10.05, Sexual Intimacies With Current Therapy Clients/Patients; 10.06, Sexual Intimacies With Relatives or Significant Others of Current Therapy Clients/Patients; 10.07, Therapy With Former Sexual Partners; and 10.08, Sexual Intimacies With Former Therapy Clients/Patients.)

3.09 Cooperation With Other Professionals. When indicated and professionally appropriate, psychologists cooperate with other professionals in order to serve their clients/patients effectively and appropriately. (See also Standard 4.05, Disclosures.)

3.10 Informed Consent. (a) When psychologists conduct research or provide assessment, therapy, counseling, or consulting services in person or via electronic transmission or other forms of communication, they obtain the informed consent of the individual or individuals using language that is reasonably understandable to that person or persons except when conducting such activities without consent is mandated by law or governmental regulation or as otherwise provided in this Ethics Code. (See also Standards 8.02, Informed Consent to Research; 9.03, Informed Consent in Assessments; and 10.01, Informed Consent to Therapy.)

(b) For persons who are legally incapable of giving informed consent, psychologists nevertheless (1) provide an appropriate explanation, (2) seek the individual's assent, (3) consider such persons' preferences and best interests, and (4) obtain appropriate permission from a legally authorized person, if such substitute consent is permitted or required by law. When consent by a legally authorized person is not permitted or required by law, psychologists take reasonable steps to protect the individual's rights and welfare.

(c) When psychological services are court ordered or otherwise mandated, psychologists inform the individual of the nature of the anticipated services, including whether the services are court ordered or mandated and any limits of confidentiality, before proceeding.

(d) Psychologists appropriately document written or oral consent, permission, and assent. (See also Standards 8.02, Informed Consent to Research; 9.03, Informed Consent in Assessments; and 10.01, Informed Consent to Therapy.)

3.11 Psychological Services Delivered to or Through Organizations. (a) Psychologists delivering services to or through organizations provide information beforehand to clients and when appropriate those directly affected by the services about (1) the nature and objectives of the services, (2) the intended recipients, (3) which of the individuals are clients, (4) the relationship the psychologist will have with each person and the organization, (5) the probable uses of services provided and information obtained, (6) who will have access to the information, and (7) limits of confidentiality. As soon as feasible, they provide information about the results and conclusions of such services to appropriate persons.

(b) If psychologists will be precluded by law or by organizational roles from providing such information to particular individuals or groups, they so inform those individuals or groups at the outset of the service.

3.12 Interruption of Psychological Services Unless otherwise covered by contract, psychologists make reasonable efforts to plan for facilitating services in the event that psychological services are interrupted by factors such as the psychologist's illness, death, unavailability, relocation, or retirement or by the client's/patient's relocation or financial limitations. (See also Standard 6.02c, Maintenance, Dissemination, and Disposal of Confidential Records of Professional and Scientific Work.)

4. Privacy and Confidentiality

4.01 Maintaining Confidentiality. Psychologists have a primary obligation and take reasonable precautions to protect confidential information obtained through or stored in any medium, recognizing that the extent and limits of confidentiality may be regulated by law or established by institutional rules or professional or scientific relationship. (See also Standard 2.05, Delegation of Work to Others.)

4.02 Discussing the Limits of Confidentiality. (a) Psychologists discuss with persons (including, to the extent feasible, persons who are legally incapable of giving informed consent and their legal representatives) and organizations with whom they establish a scientific or professional relationship (1) the relevant limits of confidentiality and (2) the foreseeable uses of the information generated through their psychological activities. (See also Standard 3.10, Informed Consent.)

(b) Unless it is not feasible or is contraindicated, the discussion of confidentiality occurs at the outset of the relationship and thereafter as new circumstances may warrant.

(c) Psychologists who offer services, products, or information via electronic transmission inform clients/patients of the risks to privacy and limits of confidentiality.

4.03 Recording. Before recording the voices or images of individuals to whom they provide services, psychologists obtain permission from all such persons or their legal representatives. (See also Standards 8.03, Informed Consent for Recording Voices and Images in Research; 8.05, Dispensing with Informed Consent for Research; and 8.07, Deception in Research.)

4.04 Minimizing Intrusions on Privacy. (a) Psychologists include in written and oral reports and consultations, only information germane to the purpose for which the communication is made.

(b) Psychologists discuss confidential information obtained in their work only for appropriate scientific or professional purposes and only with persons clearly concerned with such matters.

4.05 Disclosures. (a) Psychologists may disclose confidential information with the appropriate consent of the organizational client, the individual client/patient, or another legally authorized person on behalf of the client/patient unless prohibited by law.

(b) Psychologists disclose confidential information without the consent of the individual only as mandated by law, or where permitted by law for a valid purpose such as to (1) provide needed professional services; (2) obtain appropriate professional consultations; (3) protect the client/patient, psychologist, or others from harm; or (4) obtain payment for services from a client/patient, in which instance disclosure is limited to the minimum that is necessary to achieve the purpose. (See also Standard 6.04e, Fees and Financial Arrangements.)

4.06 *Consultations.* When consulting with colleagues, (1) psychologists do not disclose confidential information that reasonably could lead to the identification of a client/patient, research participant, or other person or organization with whom they have a confidential relationship unless they have obtained the prior consent of the person or organization or the disclosure cannot be avoided, and (2) they disclose information only to the extent necessary to achieve the purposes of the consultation. (See also Standard 4.01, Maintaining Confidentiality.)

4.07 *Use of Confidential Information for Didactic or Other Purposes.* Psychologists do not disclose in their writings, lectures, or other public media, confidential, personally identifiable information concerning their clients/patients, students, research participants, organizational clients, or other recipients of their services that they obtained during the course of their work, unless (1) they take reasonable steps to disguise the person or organization, (2) the person or organization has consented in writing, or (3) there is legal authorization for doing so.

5. Advertising and Other Public Statements

5.01 *Avoidance of False or Deceptive Statements* (a) Public statements include but are not limited to paid or unpaid advertising, product endorsements, grant applications, licensing applications, other credentialing applications, brochures, printed matter, directory listings, personal resumes or curricula vitae, or comments for use in media such as print or electronic transmission, statements in legal proceedings, lectures and public oral presentations, and published materials. Psychologists do not knowingly make public statements that are false, deceptive, or fraudulent concerning their research, practice, or other work activities or those of persons or organizations with which they are affiliated.

(b) Psychologists do not make false, deceptive, or fraudulent statements concerning (1) their training, experience, or competence; (2) their academic degrees; (3) their credentials; (4) their institutional or association affiliations; (5) their services; (6) the scientific or clinical basis for, or results or degree of success of, their services; (7) their fees; or (8) their publications or research findings.

(c) Psychologists claim degrees as credentials for their health services only if those degrees (1) were earned from a regionally accredited educational institution or (2) were the basis for psychology licensure by the state in which they practice.

5.02 Statements by Others. (a) Psychologists who engage others to create or place public statements that promote their professional practice, products, or activities retain professional responsibility for such statements.

(b) Psychologists do not compensate employees of press, radio, television, or other communication media in return for publicity in a news item. (See also Standard 1.01, Misuse of Psychologists' Work.)

(c) A paid advertisement relating to psychologists' activities must be identified or clearly recognizable as such.

5.03 Descriptions of Workshops and Non-Degree-Granting Educational Programs. To the degree to which they exercise control, psychologists responsible for announcements, catalogs, brochures, or advertisements describing workshops, seminars, or other non-degree-granting educational programs ensure that they accurately describe the audience for which the program is intended, the educational objectives, the presenters, and the fees involved.

5.04 Media Presentations. When psychologists provide public advice or comment via print, Internet, or other electronic transmission, they take precautions to ensure that statements (1) are based on their professional knowledge, training, or experience in accord with appropriate psychological literature and practice; (2) are otherwise consistent with this Ethics Code; and (3) do not indicate that a professional relationship has been established with the recipient. (See also Standard 2.04, Bases for Scientific and Professional Judgments.)

5.05 Testimonials. Psychologists do not solicit testimonials from current therapy clients/patients or other persons who because of their particular circumstances are vulnerable to undue influence.

5.06 In-Person Solicitation. Psychologists do not engage, directly or through agents, in uninvited in-person solicitation of business from actual or potential therapy clients/patients or other persons who because of their particular circumstances are vulnerable to undue influence. However, this prohibition does not preclude (1) attempting to implement appropriate collateral contacts for the purpose of benefiting an already engaged therapy client/patient or (2) providing disaster or community outreach services.

6. Record Keeping and Fees

6.01 Documentation of Professional and Scientific Work and Maintenance of Records. Psychologists create, and to the extent the records are under their control, maintain, disseminate, store, retain, and dispose of records and data relating to their professional and scientific work in order to (1) facilitate provision of services later by them or by other professionals, (2) allow for replication of research design and analyses, (3) meet institutional requirements, (4) ensure accuracy of billing and payments, and (5) ensure compliance with law. (See also Standard 4.01, Maintaining Confidentiality.)

6.02 Maintenance, Dissemination, and Disposal of Confidential Records of Professional and Scientific Work. (a) Psychologists maintain confidentiality in creating, storing, accessing, transferring, and disposing of records under their control, whether these are written, automated, or in any other medium. (See also Standards 4.01, Maintaining Confidentiality, and 6.01, Documentation of Professional and Scientific Work and Maintenance of Records.)

(b) If confidential information concerning recipients of psychological services is entered into databases or systems of records available to persons whose access has not been consented to by the recipient, psychologists use coding or other techniques to avoid the inclusion of personal identifiers.

(c) Psychologists make plans in advance to facilitate the appropriate transfer and to protect the confidentiality of records and data in the event of psychologists' withdrawal from positions or practice. (See also Standards 3.12, Interruption of Psychological Services, and 10.09, Interruption of Therapy.)

6.03 Withholding Records for Nonpayment. Psychologists may not withhold records under their control that are requested and needed for a client's/patient's emergency treatment solely because payment has not been received.

6.04 Fees and Financial Arrangements. (a) As early as is feasible in a professional or scientific relationship, psychologists and recipients of psychological services reach an agreement specifying compensation and billing arrangements.

(b) Psychologists' fee practices are consistent with law.

(c) Psychologists do not misrepresent their fees.

(d) If limitations to services can be anticipated because of limitations in financing, this is discussed with the recipient of services as early as is feasible. (See also Standards 10.09, Interruption of Therapy, and 10.10, Terminating Therapy.)

(e) If the recipient of services does not pay for services as agreed, and if psychologists intend to use collection agencies or legal measures to collect the fees, psychologists first inform the person that such measures will be taken and provide that person an opportunity to make prompt payment. (See also Standards 4.05, Disclosures; 6.03, Withholding Records for Nonpayment; and 10.01, Informed Consent to Therapy.)

6.05 Barter With Clients/Patients. Barter is the acceptance of goods, services, or other nonmonetary remuneration from clients/patients in return for psychological services. Psychologists may barter only if (1) it is not clinically contraindicated, and (2) the resulting arrangement is not exploitative. (See also Standards 3.05, Multiple Relationships, and 6.04, Fees and Financial Arrangements.)

6.06 Accuracy in Reports to Payors and Funding Sources. In their reports to payors for services or sources of research funding, psychologists take reasonable steps to ensure the accurate reporting of the nature of the service provided or research conducted, the fees, charges, or payments, and where applicable, the identity of the provider, the findings, and the diagnosis. (See also Standards 4.01, Maintaining Confidentiality; 4.04, Minimizing Intrusions on Privacy; and 4.05, Disclosures.)

6.07 Referrals and Fees When psychologists pay, receive payment from, or divide fees with another professional, other than in an employer–employee relationship, the payment to each is based on the services provided (clinical, consultative, administrative, or other) and is not based on the referral itself. (See also Standard 3.09, Cooperation With Other Professionals.)

7. Education and Training

7.01 Design of Education and Training Programs. Psychologists responsible for education and training programs take reasonable steps to ensure that the programs are designed to provide the appropriate knowledge and proper experiences, and to meet the requirements for licensure, certification, or other goals for which claims are made by the program. (See also Standard 5.03, Descriptions of Workshops and Non-Degree-Granting Educational Programs.)

7.02 Descriptions of Education and Training Programs. Psychologists responsible for education and training programs take reasonable steps to ensure that there is a current and accurate description of the program content (including participation in required course- or program-related counseling, psychotherapy, experiential groups, consulting projects, or community service), training goals and objectives, stipends and benefits, and requirements that must be met for satisfactory completion of the program. This information must be made readily available to all interested parties.

7.03 Accuracy in Teaching. (a) Psychologists take reasonable steps to ensure that course syllabi are accurate regarding the subject matter to be covered, bases for evaluating progress, and the nature of course experiences. This standard does not preclude an instructor from modifying course content or requirements when the instructor considers it pedagogically necessary or desirable, so long as students are made aware of these modifications in a manner that enables them to fulfill course requirements. (See also Standard 5.01, Avoidance of False or Deceptive Statements.)

(b) When engaged in teaching or training, psychologists present psychological information accurately. (See also Standard 2.03, Maintaining Competence.)

7.04 Student Disclosure of Personal Information. Psychologists do not require students or supervisees to disclose personal information in course- or program-related activities, either orally or in writing, regarding sexual history, history of abuse and neglect, psychological treatment, and relationships with parents, peers, and spouses or significant others except if (1) the program or training facility has clearly identified this requirement in its admissions and program materials or (2) the information is necessary to evaluate or obtain assistance for students whose personal problems could reasonably be judged to be preventing them from performing their training or professionally related activities in a competent manner or posing a threat to the students or others.

7.05 *Mandatory Individual or Group Therapy.* (a) When individual or group therapy is a program or course requirement, psychologists responsible for that program allow students in undergraduate and graduate programs the option of selecting such therapy from practitioners unaffiliated with the program. (See also Standard 7.02, Descriptions of Education and Training Programs.)

(b) Faculty who are or are likely to be responsible for evaluating students' academic performance do not themselves provide that therapy. (See also Standard 3.05, Multiple Relationships.)

7.06 *Assessing Student and Supervisee Performance.* (a) In academic and supervisory relationships, psychologists establish a timely and specific process for providing feedback to students and supervisees. Information regarding the process is provided to the student at the beginning of supervision.

(b) Psychologists evaluate students and supervisees on the basis of their actual performance on relevant and established program requirements.

7.07 *Sexual Relationships With Students and Supervisees* Psychologists do not engage in sexual relationships with students or supervisees who are in their department, agency, or training center or over whom psychologists have or are likely to have evaluative authority. (See also Standard 3.05, Multiple Relationships.)

8. *Research and Publication*

8.01 *Institutional Approval.* When institutional approval is required, psychologists provide accurate information about their research proposals and obtain approval prior to conducting the research. They conduct the research in accordance with the approved research protocol.

8.02 *Informed Consent to Research.* (a) When obtaining informed consent as required in Standard 3.10, Informed Consent, psychologists inform participants about (1) the purpose of the research, expected duration, and procedures; (2) their right to decline to participate and to withdraw from the research once participation has begun; (3) the foreseeable consequences of declining or withdrawing; (4) reasonably foreseeable factors that may be expected to influence their willingness to participate such as potential risks, discomfort, or adverse effects; (5) any prospective research benefits; (6) limits of confidentiality; (7) incentives for participation; and (8) whom to contact for questions about the research and research participants' rights. They provide opportunity for the prospective participants to ask questions and receive answers. (See also Standards 8.03, Informed Consent for Recording Voices and Images in Research; 8.05, Dispensing with Informed Consent for Research; and 8.07, Deception in Research.)

(b) Psychologists conducting intervention research involving the use of experimental treatments clarify to participants at the outset of the research (1) the experimental nature of the treatment; (2) the services that will or will not be available to the control group(s) if appropriate; (3) the means by which assignment to treatment and control groups will be made; (4) available treatment alternatives if an individual does not wish to participate in the research or wishes to withdraw once a study has begun; and (5) compensation for or monetary costs of participating including, if appropriate, whether reimbursement from the participant or a third-party payor will be sought. (See also Standard 8.02a, Informed Consent to Research.)

8.03 *Informed Consent for Recording Voices and Images in Research.* Psychologists obtain informed consent from research participants prior to recording their voices or images for data collection unless (1) the research consists solely of naturalistic observations in public places, and it is not anticipated that the recording will be used in a manner that could cause personal identification or harm, or (2) the research design includes deception, and consent for the use of the recording is obtained during debriefing. (See also Standard 8.07, Deception in Research.)

8.04 *Client/Patient, Student, and Subordinate Research Participants.* (a) When psychologists conduct research with clients/patients, students, or subordinates as participants, psychologists take steps to protect the prospective participants from adverse consequences of declining or withdrawing from participation.

(b) When research participation is a course requirement or an opportunity for extra credit, the prospective participant is given the choice of equitable alternative activities.

8.05 *Dispensing With Informed Consent for Research.* Psychologists may dispense with informed consent only (1) where research would not reasonably be assumed to create distress or harm and involves (a) the study of normal educational practices, curricula, or classroom management methods conducted in educational settings; (b) only anonymous questionnaires, naturalistic observations, or archival research for which disclosure of responses would not place participants at risk of criminal or civil liability or damage their financial standing, employability, or reputation, and confidentiality is protected; or (c) the study of factors related to job or organization effectiveness conducted in organizational settings for which there is no risk to participants' employability, and confidentiality is protected or (2) where otherwise permitted by law or federal or institutional regulations.

8.06 *Offering Inducements for Research Participation.* (a) Psychologists make reasonable efforts to avoid offering excessive or inappropriate financial or other inducements for research participation when such inducements are likely to coerce participation.

(b) When offering professional services as an inducement for research participation, psychologists clarify the nature of the services, as well as the risks, obligations, and limitations. (See also Standard 6.05, Barter With Clients/Patients.)

8.07 *Deception in Research.* (a) Psychologists do not conduct a study involving deception unless they have determined that the use of deceptive techniques is justified by the study's significant prospective scientific, educational, or applied value and that effective nondeceptive alternative procedures are not feasible.

(b) Psychologists do not deceive prospective participants about research that is reasonably expected to cause physical pain or severe emotional distress.

(c) Psychologists explain any deception that is an integral feature of the design and conduct of an experiment to participants as early as is feasible, preferably at the conclusion of their participation, but no later than at the conclusion of the data collection, and permit participants to withdraw their data. (See also Standard 8.08, Debriefing.)

8.08 *Debriefing.* (a) Psychologists provide a prompt opportunity for participants to obtain appropriate information about the nature, results, and conclusions of the research, and they take reasonable steps to correct any misconceptions that participants may have of which the psychologists are aware.

(b) If scientific or humane values justify delaying or withholding this information, psychologists take reasonable measures to reduce the risk of harm.

(c) When psychologists become aware that research procedures have harmed a participant, they take reasonable steps to minimize the harm.

8.09 *Humane Care and Use of Animals in Research.* (a) Psychologists acquire, care for, use, and dispose of animals in compliance with current federal, state, and local laws and regulations, and with professional standards.

(b) Psychologists trained in research methods and experienced in the care of laboratory animals supervise all procedures involving animals and are responsible for ensuring appropriate consideration of their comfort, health, and humane treatment.

(c) Psychologists ensure that all individuals under their supervision who are using animals have received instruction in research methods and in the care, maintenance, and handling of the species being used, to the extent appropriate to their role. (See also Standard 2.05, Delegation of Work to Others.)

(d) Psychologists make reasonable efforts to minimize the discomfort, infection, illness, and pain of animal subjects.

(e) Psychologists use a procedure subjecting animals to pain, stress, or privation only when an alternative procedure is unavailable and the goal is justified by its prospective scientific, educational, or applied value.

(f) Psychologists perform surgical procedures under appropriate anesthesia and follow techniques to avoid infection and minimize pain during and after surgery.

(g) When it is appropriate that an animal's life be terminated, psychologists proceed rapidly, with an effort to minimize pain and in accordance with accepted procedures.

8.10 *Reporting Research Results.* (a) Psychologists do not fabricate data. (See also Standard 5.01a, Avoidance of False or Deceptive Statements.)

(b) If psychologists discover significant errors in their published data, they take reasonable steps to correct such errors in a correction, retraction, erratum, or other appropriate publication means.

8.11 *Plagiarism.* Psychologists do not present portions of another's work or data as their own, even if the other work or data source is cited occasionally.

8.12 *Publication Credit* (a) Psychologists take responsibility and credit, including authorship credit, only for work they have actually performed or to which they have substantially contributed. (See also Standard 8.12b, Publication Credit.)

(b) Principal authorship and other publication credits accurately reflect the relative scientific or professional contributions of the individuals involved, regardless of their relative status. Mere possession of an institutional position, such as department chair, does not justify authorship credit. Minor contributions to the research or to the writing for publications are acknowledged appropriately, such as in footnotes or in an introductory statement.

(c) Except under exceptional circumstances, a student is listed as principal author on any multiple-authored article that is substantially based on the student's doctoral dissertation. Faculty advisors discuss publication credit with students as early as feasible and throughout the research and publication process as appropriate. (See also Standard 8.12b, Publication Credit.)

8.13 *Duplicate Publication of Data.* Psychologists do not publish, as original data, data that have been previously published. This does not preclude republishing data when they are accompanied by proper acknowledgment.

8.14 *Sharing Research Data for Verification.* (a) After research results are published, psychologists do not withhold the data on which their conclusions are based from other competent professionals who seek to verify the substantive claims through reanalysis and who intend to use such data only for that purpose, provided that the confidentiality of the participants can be protected and unless legal rights concerning proprietary data preclude their release. This does not preclude psychologists from requiring that such individuals or groups be responsible for costs associated with the provision of such information.

(b) Psychologists who request data from other psychologists to verify the substantive claims through reanalysis may use shared data only for the declared purpose. Requesting psychologists obtain prior written agreement for all other uses of the data.

8.15 Reviewers. Psychologists who review material submitted for presentation, publication, grant, or research proposal review respect the confidentiality of and the proprietary rights in such information of those who submitted it.

9. *Assessment*

9.01 Bases for Assessments. (a) Psychologists base the opinions contained in their recommendations, reports, and diagnostic or evaluative statements, including forensic testimony, on information and techniques sufficient to substantiate their findings. (See also Standard 2.04, Bases for Scientific and Professional Judgments.)

(b) Except as noted in 9.01c, psychologists provide opinions of the psychological characteristics of individuals only after they have conducted an examination of the individuals adequate to support their statements or conclusions. When, despite reasonable efforts, such an examination is not practical, psychologists document the efforts they made and the result of those efforts, clarify the probable impact of their limited information on the reliability and validity of their opinions, and appropriately limit the nature and extent of their conclusions or recommendations. (See also Standards 2.01, Boundaries of Competence, and 9.06, Interpreting Assessment Results.)

(c) When psychologists conduct a record review or provide consultation or supervision and an individual examination is not warranted or necessary for the opinion, psychologists explain this and the sources of information on which they based their conclusions and recommendations.

9.02 Use of Assessments (a) Psychologists administer, adapt, score, interpret, or use assessment techniques, interviews, tests, or instruments in a manner and for purposes that are appropriate in light of the research on or evidence of the usefulness and proper application of the techniques.

(b) Psychologists use assessment instruments whose validity and reliability have been established for use with members of the population tested. When such validity or reliability has not been established, psychologists describe the strengths and limitations of test results and interpretation.

(c) Psychologists use assessment methods that are appropriate to an individual's language preference and competence, unless the use of an alternative language is relevant to the assessment issues.

9.03 Informed Consent in Assessments. (a) Psychologists obtain informed consent for assessments, evaluations, or diagnostic services, as described in Standard 3.10, Informed Consent, except when (1) testing is mandated by law or governmental regulations; (2) informed consent is implied because testing is conducted as a routine educational, institutional, or organizational activity (e.g., when participants voluntarily agree to assessment when applying for a job); or (3) one purpose of the testing is to evaluate decisional capacity. Informed consent includes an explanation of the nature and purpose of the assessment, fees, involvement of third parties, and limits of confidentiality and sufficient opportunity for the client/patient to ask questions and receive answers.

(b) Psychologists inform persons with questionable capacity to consent or for whom testing is mandated by law or governmental regulations about the nature and purpose of the proposed assessment services, using language that is reasonably understandable to the person being assessed.

(c) Psychologists using the services of an interpreter obtain informed consent from the client/patient to use that interpreter, ensure that confidentiality of test results and test security are maintained, and include in their recommendations, reports, and diagnostic or evaluative statements, including forensic testimony, discussion of any limitations on the data obtained. (See also Standards 2.05, Delegation of Work to Others; 4.01, Maintaining Confidentiality; 9.01, Bases for Assessments; 9.06, Interpreting Assessment Results; and 9.07, Assessment by Unqualified Persons.)

9.04 *Release of Test Data.* (a) The term *test data* refers to raw and scaled scores, client/patient responses to test questions or stimuli, and psychologists' notes and recordings concerning client/patient statements and behavior during an examination. Those portions of test materials that include client/patient responses are included in the definition of *test data*. Pursuant to a client/patient release, psychologists provide test data to the client/patient or other persons identified in the release. Psychologists may refrain from releasing test data to protect a client/patient or others from substantial harm or misuse or misrepresentation of the data or the test, recognizing that in many instances release of confidential information under these circumstances is regulated by law. (See also Standard 9.11, Maintaining Test Security.)

(b) In the absence of a client/patient release, psychologists provide test data only as required by law or court order.

9.05 *Test Construction.* Psychologists who develop tests and other assessment techniques use appropriate psychometric procedures and current scientific or professional knowledge for test design, standardization, validation, reduction or elimination of bias, and recommendations for use.

9.06 *Interpreting Assessment Results.* When interpreting assessment results, including automated interpretations, psychologists take into account the purpose of the assessment as well as the various test factors, test-taking abilities, and other characteristics of the person being assessed, such as situational, personal, linguistic, and cultural differences, that might affect psychologists' judgments or reduce the accuracy of their interpretations. They indicate any significant limitations of their interpretations. (See also Standards 2.01b and c, Boundaries of Competence, and 3.01, Unfair Discrimination.)

9.07 *Assessment by Unqualified Persons.* Psychologists do not promote the use of psychological assessment techniques by unqualified persons, except when such use is conducted for training purposes with appropriate supervision. (See also Standard 2.05, Delegation of Work to Others.)

9.08 *Obsolete Tests and Outdated Test Results.* (a) Psychologists do not base their assessment or intervention decisions or recommendations on data or test results that are outdated for the current purpose.

(b) Psychologists do not base such decisions or recommendations on tests and measures that are obsolete and not useful for the current purpose.

9.09 *Test Scoring and Interpretation Services.* (a) Psychologists who offer assessment or scoring services to other professionals accurately describe the purpose, norms, validity, reliability, and applications of the procedures and any special qualifications applicable to their use.

(b) Psychologists select scoring and interpretation services (including automated services) on the basis of evidence of the validity of the program and procedures as well as on other appropriate considerations. (See also Standard 2.01b and c, Boundaries of Competence.)

(c) Psychologists retain responsibility for the appropriate application, interpretation, and use of assessment instruments, whether they score and interpret such tests themselves or use automated or other services.

9.10 *Explaining Assessment Results.* Regardless of whether the scoring and interpretation are done by psychologists, by employees or assistants, or by automated or other outside services, psychologists take reasonable steps to ensure that explanations of results are given to the individual or designated representative unless the nature of the relationship precludes provision of an explanation of results (such as in some organizational consulting, preemployment or security screenings, and forensic evaluations), and this fact has been clearly explained to the person being assessed in advance.

9.11. *Maintaining Test Security.* The term *test materials* refers to manuals, instruments, protocols, and test questions or stimuli and does not include *test data* as defined in Standard 9.04, Release of Test Data. Psychologists make reasonable efforts to maintain the integrity and security of test materials and other assessment techniques consistent with law and contractual obligations, and in a manner that permits adherence to this Ethics Code.

10. Therapy

10.01 *Informed Consent to Therapy.* (a) When obtaining informed consent to therapy as required in Standard 3.10, Informed Consent, psychologists inform clients/patients as early as is feasible in the therapeutic relationship about the nature and anticipated course of therapy, fees, involvement of third parties, and limits of confidentiality and provide sufficient opportunity for the client/patient to ask questions and receive answers. (See also Standards 4.02, Discussing the Limits of Confidentiality, and 6.04, Fees and Financial Arrangements.)

(b) When obtaining informed consent for treatment for which generally recognized techniques and procedures have not been established, psychologists inform their clients/patients of the developing nature of the treatment, the potential risks involved, alternative treatments that may be available, and the voluntary nature of their participation. (See also Standards 2.01d, Boundaries of Competence, and 3.10, Informed Consent.)

(c) When the therapist is a trainee and the legal responsibility for the treatment provided resides with the supervisor, the client/patient, as part of the informed consent procedure, is informed that the therapist is in training and is being supervised and is given the name of the supervisor.

10.02 *Therapy Involving Couples or Families*. (a) When psychologists agree to provide services to several persons who have a relationship (such as spouses, significant others, or parents and children), they take reasonable steps to clarify at the outset (1) which of the individuals are clients/patients and (2) the relationship the psychologist will have with each person. This clarification includes the psychologist's role and the probable uses of the services provided or the information obtained. (See also Standard 4.02, Discussing the Limits of Confidentiality.)

(b) If it becomes apparent that psychologists may be called on to perform potentially conflicting roles (such as family therapist and then witness for one party in divorce proceedings), psychologists take reasonable steps to clarify and modify, or withdraw from, roles appropriately. (See also Standard 3.05c, Multiple Relationships.)

10.03 *Group Therapy*. When psychologists provide services to several persons in a group setting, they describe at the outset the roles and responsibilities of all parties and the limits of confidentiality.

10.04 *Providing Therapy to Those Served by Others*. In deciding whether to offer or provide services to those already receiving mental health services elsewhere, psychologists carefully consider the treatment issues and the potential client's/patient's welfare. Psychologists discuss these issues with the client/patient or another legally authorized person on behalf of the client/patient in order to minimize the risk of confusion and conflict, consult with the other service providers when appropriate, and proceed with caution and sensitivity to the therapeutic issues.

10.05 *Sexual Intimacies With Current Therapy Clients/Patients*. Psychologists do not engage in sexual intimacies with current therapy clients/patients.

10.06 *Sexual Intimacies With Relatives or Significant Others of Current Therapy Clients/Patients*. Psychologists do not engage in sexual intimacies with individuals they know to be close relatives, guardians, or significant others of current clients/patients. Psychologists do not terminate therapy to circumvent this standard.

10.07 Therapy With Former Sexual Partners. Psychologists do not accept as therapy clients/patients persons with whom they have engaged in sexual intimacies.

10.08 Sexual Intimacies With Former Therapy Clients/Patients. (a) Psychologists do not engage in sexual intimacies with former clients/patients for at least two years after cessation or termination of therapy.

(b) Psychologists do not engage in sexual intimacies with former clients/patients even after a two-year interval except in the most unusual circumstances. Psychologists who engage in such activity after the two years following cessation or termination of therapy and of having no sexual contact with the former client/patient bear the burden of demonstrating that there has been no exploitation, in light of all relevant factors, including (1) the amount of time that has passed since therapy terminated; (2) the nature, duration, and intensity of the therapy; (3) the circumstances of termination; (4) the client's/patient's personal history; (5) the client's/patient's current mental status; (6) the likelihood of adverse impact on the client/patient; and (7) any statements or actions made by the therapist during the course of therapy suggesting or inviting the possibility of a posttermination sexual or romantic relationship with the client/patient. (See also Standard 3.05, Multiple Relationships.)

10.09 Interruption of Therapy. When entering into employment or contractual relationships, psychologists make reasonable efforts to provide for orderly and appropriate resolution of responsibility for client/patient care in the event that the employment or contractual relationship ends, with paramount consideration given to the welfare of the client/patient. (See also Standard 3.12, Interruption of Psychological Services.)

10.10 Terminating Therapy. (a) Psychologists terminate therapy when it becomes reasonably clear that the client/patient no longer needs the service, is not likely to benefit, or is being harmed by continued service.

(b) Psychologists may terminate therapy when threatened or otherwise endangered by the client/patient or another person with whom the client/patient has a relationship.

(c) Except where precluded by the actions of clients/patients or third-party payors, prior to termination psychologists provide pretermination counseling and suggest alternative service providers as appropriate.

The APA has previously published its Ethics Code as follows:

American Psychological Association. (1953). *Ethical standards of psychologists.* Washington, DC: Author.

American Psychological Association. (1959). Ethical standards of psychologists. *American Psychologist, 14,* 279–282.

American Psychological Association. (1963). Ethical standards of psychologists. *American Psychologist, 18,* 56–60.

American Psychological Association. (1968). Ethical standards of psychologists. *American Psychologist, 23*, 357–361.

American Psychological Association. (1977, March). Ethical standards of psychologists. *APA Monitor*, 22–23.

American Psychological Association. (1979). *Ethical standards of psychologists.* Washington, DC: Author.

American Psychological Association. (1981). Ethical principles of psychologists. *American Psychologist, 36*, 633–638.

American Psychological Association. (1990). Ethical principles of psychologists (Amended June 2, 1989). *American Psychologist, 45*, 390–395.

American Psychological Association. (1992). Ethical principles of psychologists and code of conduct. *American Psychologist, 47*, 1597–1611.

Request copies of the APA's Ethical Principles of Psychologists and Code of Conduct from the APA Order Department, 750 First Street, NE, Washington, DC 20002-4242, or phone (202) 336-5510.

APPENDIX C
Canadian Code of Ethics for Psychologists, Third Edition

TABLE OF CONTENTS

Principle II: Responsible Caring

- Values Statement
- Ethical Standards
- General caring
- Competence and self-knowledge
- Risk/benefit analysis
- Maximize benefit
- Minimize harm
- Offset/correct harm
- Care of animals
- Extended responsibility

Principle III: Integrity in Relationships

- Values Statement
- Ethical Standards
- Accuracy/honesty
- Objectivity/lack of bias
- Straightforwardness/openness
- Avoidance of incomplete disclosure
- Avoidance of conflict of interest
- Reliance on the discipline
- Extended responsibility

Principle IV: Responsibility to Society

- Values Statement
- Ethical Standards
- Development of knowledge
- Beneficial activities
- Respect for society
- Development of society
- Extended responsibility
- CPA Publications/CPA Homepage

CANADIAN CODE OF ETHICS FOR PSYCHOLOGISTS

Introduction

Every discipline that has relatively autonomous control over its entry requirements, training, development of knowledge, standards, methods, and practices does so only within the context of a contract with the society in which it functions. This social contract is based on attitudes of mutual respect and trust, with society granting support for the autonomy of a discipline in exchange for a commitment by the discipline to do everything it can to assure that its members act ethically in conducting the affairs of the discipline within society; in particular, a commitment to try to assure that each member will place the welfare of the society and individual members of that society above the welfare of the discipline and its own members. By virtue of this social contract, psychologists have a higher duty of care to members of society than the general duty of care that all members of society have to each other.

The Canadian Psychological Association recognizes its responsibility to help assure ethical behaviour and attitudes on the part of psychologists. Attempts to assure ethical behaviour and attitudes include articulating ethical principles, values, and standards; promoting those principles, values, and standards through education, peer modelling, and consultation; developing and implementing methods to help psychologists monitor the ethics of their behaviour and attitudes; adjudicating complaints of unethical behaviour; and, taking corrective action when warranted.

This *Code* articulates ethical principles, values, and standards to guide all members of the Canadian Psychological Association, whether scientists, practitioners, or scientist practitioners, or whether acting in a research, direct service, teaching, student, trainee, administrative, management, employer, employee, supervisory, consultative, peer review, editorial, expert witness, social policy, or any other role related to the discipline of psychology.

Structure and Derivation of Code

Structure. Four ethical principles, to be considered and balanced in ethical decision making, are presented. Each principle is followed by a statement of those values that are included in and give definition to the principle. Each values statement is followed by a list of ethical standards that illustrate the application of the specific principle and values to the activities of psychologists. The standards range from minimal behavioural expectations (e.g., Standards I.28, II.28, III.33, IV.27) to more idealized, but achievable, attitudinal and behavioural expectations (e.g., Standards I.12, II.12, III.10, IV.6). In the margin, to the left of the standards, key words are placed to guide the reader through the standards and to illustrate the relationship of the specific standards to the values statement.

Derivation. The four principles represent those ethical principles used most consistently by Canadian psychologists to resolve hypothetical ethical dilemmas sent to them by the CPA Committee on Ethics during the initial development of the *Code*. In addition to the responses provided by Canadian psychologists, the values statements and ethical standards have been derived from interdisciplinary and international ethics codes, provincial and specialty codes of conduct, and ethics literature.

When Principles Conflict

- **Principle I: Respect for the Dignity of Persons.** This principle, with its emphasis on moral rights, generally should be given the highest weight, except in circumstances in which there is a clear and imminent danger to the physical safety of any person.
- **Principle II: Responsible Caring.** This principle generally should be given the second highest weight. Responsible caring requires competence and should be carried out only in ways that respect the dignity of persons.
- **Principle III: Integrity in Relationships.** This principle generally should be given the third highest weight. Psychologists are expected to demonstrate the highest integrity in all of their relationships. However, in rare circumstances, values such as openness and straightforwardness might need to be subordinated to the values contained in the Principles of Respect for the Dignity of Persons and Responsible Caring.
- **Principle IV: Responsibility to Society.** This principle generally should be given the lowest weight of the four principles when it conflicts with one or more of them. Although it is necessary and important to consider responsibility to society in every ethical decision, adherence to this principle must be subject to and guided by Respect for the Dignity of Persons, Responsible Caring, and Integrity in Relationships. When a person's welfare appears to conflict with benefits to society, it is often possible to find ways of working for the benefit of society that do not violate respect and responsible caring for the person. However, if this is not possible, the dignity and well-being of a person should not be sacrificed to a vision of the greater good of society, and greater weight must be given to respect and responsible caring for the person.

Even with the above ordering of the principles, psychologists will be faced with ethical dilemmas that are difficult to resolve. In these circumstances, psychologists are expected to engage in an ethical decision-making process that is explicit enough to bear public scrutiny. In some cases, resolution might be a matter of personal conscience. However, decisions of personal conscience are also expected to be the result of a decision-making process that is based on a reasonably coherent set of ethical principles and that can bear public scrutiny. If the psychologist can demonstrate that every reasonable effort was made to apply the ethical principles of this *Code* and resolution of the conflict has had to depend on the personal conscience of the psychologist, such a psychologist would be deemed to have followed this *Code*.

The Ethical Decision-Making Process

The ethical decision-making process might occur very rapidly, leading to an easy resolution of an ethical issue. This is particularly true of issues for which clear-cut guidelines or standards exist and for which there is no conflict between principles. On the other hand, some ethical issues (particularly those in which ethical principles conflict) are not easily resolved, might be emotionally distressful, and might require time-consuming deliberation.

The following basic steps typify approaches to ethical decision making:

1. Identification of the individuals and groups potentially affected by the decision.
2. Identification of ethically relevant issues and practices, including the interests, rights, and any relevant characteristics of the individuals and groups involved and of the system or circumstances in which the ethical problem arose.
3. Consideration of how personal biases, stresses, or self-interest might influence the development of or choice between courses of action.
4. Development of alternative courses of action.
5. Analysis of likely short-term, ongoing, and long-term risks and benefits of each course of action on the individual(s)/group(s) involved or likely to be affected (e.g., client, client's family or employees, employing institution, students, research participants, colleagues, the discipline, society, self).
6. Choice of course of action after conscientious application of existing principles, values, and standards.
7. Action, with a commitment to assume responsibility for the consequences of the action.
8. Evaluation of the results of the course of action.
9. Assumption of responsibility for consequences of action, including correction of negative consequences, if any, or re-engaging in the decision-making process if the ethical issue is not resolved.
10. Appropriate action, as warranted and feasible, to prevent future occurrences of the dilemma (e.g., communication and problem solving with colleagues; changes in procedures and practices).

Psychologists engaged in time-consuming deliberation are encouraged and expected to consult with parties affected by the ethical problem, when appropriate, and with colleagues and/or advisory bodies when such persons can add knowledge or objectivity to the decision-making process. Although the decision for action remains with the individual psychologist, the seeking and consideration of such assistance reflects an ethical approach to ethical decision making.

Uses of the Code

This *Code* is intended to guide psychologists in their everyday conduct, thinking, and planning, and in the resolution of ethical dilemmas; that is, it advocates the practice of both proactive and reactive ethics.

The *Code* also is intended to serve as an umbrella document for the development of codes of conduct or other more specific codes. For example, the *Code* could be used as an ethical framework for the identification of behaviours that would be considered enforceable in a jurisdiction, the violation of which would constitute misconduct; or, jurisdictions could identify those standards in the *Code* that would be considered of a more serious nature and, therefore, reportable and subject to possible discipline. In addition, the principles and values could be used to help specialty areas develop standards that are specific to those areas. Some work in this direction has already occurred within CPA (e.g., *Guidelines for the Use of Animals in Research and Instruction in Psychology, Guidelines for Non-Discriminatory Practice, Guidelines for Psychologists in Addressing Recovered Memories*). The principles and values incorporated into this *Code*, insofar as they come to be reflected in other documents guiding the behaviour of psychologists, will reduce inconsistency and conflict between documents.

A third use of the *Code* is to assist in the adjudication of complaints against psychologists. A body charged with this responsibility is required to investigate allegations, judge whether unacceptable behaviour has occurred, and determine what corrective action should be taken. In judging whether unacceptable conduct has occurred, many jurisdictions refer to a code of conduct. Some complaints, however, are about conduct that is not addressed directly in a code of conduct. The *Code* provides an ethical framework for determining whether the complaint is of enough concern, either at the level of the individual psychologist or at the level of the profession as a whole, to warrant corrective action (e.g., discipline of the individual psychologist, general educational activities for members, or incorporation into the code of conduct). In determining corrective action for an individual psychologist, one of the judgments the adjudicating body needs to make is whether an individual conscientiously engaged in an ethical decision-making process and acted in good faith, or whether there was a negligent or willful disregard of ethical principles. The articulation of the ethical decision-making process contained in this *Code* provides guidance for making such judgements.

Responsibility of the Individual Psychologist

The discipline's contract with society commits the discipline and its members to act as a moral community that develops its ethical awareness and sensitivity, educates new members in the ethics of the discipline, manages its affairs and its members in an ethical manner, is as self-correcting as possible, and is accountable both internally and externally.

However, responsibility for ethical action depends foremost on the integrity of each individual psychologist; that is, on each psychologist's commitment to behave as ethically as possible in every situation. Acceptance to membership in the Canadian Psychological Association, a scientific and professional association of psychologists, commits members:

1. To adhere to the Association's *Code* in all current activities as a psychologist.
2. To apply conscientiously the ethical principles and values of the *Code* to new and emerging areas of activity.
3. To assess and discuss ethical issues and practices with colleagues on a regular basis.
4. To bring to the attention of the Association ethical issues that require clarification or the development of new guidelines or standards.
5. To bring concerns about possible unethical actions by a psychologist directly to the psychologist when the action appears to be primarily a lack of sensitivity, knowledge, or experience, and attempt to reach an agreement on the issue and, if needed, on the appropriate action to be taken.
6. To bring concerns about possible unethical actions of a more serious nature (e.g., actions that have caused or could cause serious harm, or actions that are considered misconduct in the jurisdiction) to the person(s) or body(ies) best suited to investigating the situation and to stopping or offsetting the harm.
7. To consider seriously others' concerns about one's own possibly unethical actions and attempt to reach an agreement on the issue and, if needed, take appropriate action.
8. In bringing or in responding to concerns about possible unethical actions, not to be vexatious or malicious.
9. To cooperate with duly constituted committees of the Association that are concerned with ethics and ethical conduct.

Relationship of Code to Personal Behaviour

This *Code* is intended to guide and regulate only those activities a psychologist engages in by virtue of being a psychologist. There is no intention to guide or regulate a psychologist's activities outside of this context. Personal behaviour becomes a concern of the discipline only if it is of such a nature that it undermines public trust in the discipline as a whole or if it raises questions about the psychologist's ability to carry out appropriately his/her responsibilities as a psychologist.

Relationship of Code to Provincial Regulatory Bodies

In exercising its responsibility to articulate ethical principles, values, and standards for those who wish to become and remain members in good standing, the Canadian Psychological Association recognizes the multiple memberships that some psychologists have (both regulatory and voluntary). The *Code* has attempted to encompass and incorporate those ethical principles most prevalent in the discipline as a whole, thereby minimizing the possibility of variance with provincial/territorial regulations and guidelines. Psychologists are expected to respect the requirements of their provincial/territorial regulatory bodies. Such requirements might define particular behaviours that constitute misconduct, are reportable to the regulatory body, and/or are subject to discipline.

Definition of Terms

For the purposes of this Code:

a. **"Psychologist"** means any person who is a Fellow, Member, Student Affiliate or Foreign Affiliate of the Canadian Psychological Association, or a member of any psychology voluntary association or regulatory body adopting this *Code*. (Readers are reminded that provincial/territorial jurisdictions might restrict the legal use of the term psychologist in their jurisdiction and that such restrictions are to be honoured.)

b. **"Client"** means an individual, family, or group (including an organization or community) receiving service from a psychologist.

c. Clients, research participants, students, and any other persons with whom psychologists come in contact in the course of their work, are **"independent"** if they can independently contract or give informed consent. Such persons are **"partially dependent"** if the decision to contract or give informed consent is shared between two or more parties (e.g., parents and school boards, workers and Workers' Compensation Boards, adult members of a family). Such persons are considered to be **"fully dependent"** if they have little or no choice about whether or not to receive service or participate in an activity (e.g., patients who have been involuntarily committed to a psychiatric facility, or very young children involved in a research project).

d. **"Others"** means any persons with whom psychologists come in contact in the course of their work. This may include, but is not limited to: clients seeking help with individual, family, organizational, industrial, or community issues; research participants;

employees; students; trainees; supervisees; colleagues; employers; third party payers; and, members of the general public.

e. **"Legal or civil rights"** means those rights protected under laws and statutes recognized by the province or territory in which the psychologist is working.

f. **"Moral rights"** means fundamental and inalienable human rights that might or might not be fully protected by existing laws and statutes. Of particular significance to psychologists, for example, are rights to: distributive justice; fairness and due process; and, developmentally appropriate privacy, self-determination, and personal liberty. Protection of some aspects of these rights might involve practices that are not contained or controlled within current laws and statutes. Moral rights are not limited to those mentioned in this definition.

g. **"Unjust discrimination"** or **"unjustly discriminatory"** means activities that are prejudicial or promote prejudice to persons because of their culture, nationality, ethnicity, colour, race, religion, sex, gender, marital status, sexual orientation, physical or mental abilities, age, socio-economic status, or any other preference or personal characteristic, condition, or status.

h. **"Sexual harassment"** includes either or both of the following: (i) The use of power or authority in an attempt to coerce another person to engage in or tolerate sexual activity. Such uses include explicit or implicit threats of reprisal for noncompliance, or promises of reward for compliance. (ii) Engaging in deliberate and/or repeated unsolicited sexually oriented comments, anecdotes, gestures, or touching, if such behaviours: are offensive and unwelcome; create an offensive, hostile, or intimidating working, learning, or service environment; or, can be expected to be harmful to the recipient.[1]

i. The **"discipline of psychology"** refers to the scientific and applied methods and knowledge of psychology, and to the structures and procedures used by its members for conducting their work in relationship to society, to members of the public, to students or trainees, and to each other.

Review Schedule

To maintain the relevance and responsiveness of this *Code*, it will be reviewed regularly by the CPA Board of Directors, and revised as needed. You are invited to forward comments and suggestions, at any time, to the CPA

---

1. Adapted from: Canadian Psychological Association. (1985). *Guidelines for the elimination of sexual harassment.* Ottawa, Author.

office. In addition to psychologists, this invitation is extended to all readers, including members of the public and other disciplines.

PRINCIPLE I: RESPECT FOR THE DIGNITY OF PERSONS

Values Statement

In the course of their work as scientists, practitioners, or scientist-practitioners, psychologists come into contact with many different individuals and groups, including: research participants; clients seeking help with individual, family, organizational, industrial, or community issues; students; trainees; supervisees; employees; business partners; business competitors; colleagues; employers; third party payers; and, the general public.

In these contacts, psychologists accept as fundamental the principle of respect for the dignity of persons; that is, the belief that each person should be treated primarily as a person or an end in him/herself, not as an object or a means to an end. In so doing, psychologists acknowledge that all persons have a right to have their innate worth as human beings appreciated and that this worth is not dependent upon their culture, nationality, ethnicity, colour, race, religion, sex, gender, marital status, sexual orientation, physical or mental abilities, age, socio-economic status, or any other preference or personal characteristic, condition, or status.

Although psychologists have a responsibility to respect the dignity of all persons with whom they come in contact in their role as psychologists, the nature of their contract with society demands that their greatest responsibility be to those persons in the most vulnerable position. Normally, persons directly receiving or involved in the psychologist's activities are in such a position (e.g., research participants, clients, students). This responsibility is almost always greater than their responsibility to those indirectly involved (e.g., employers, third party payers, the general public).

Adherence to the concept of moral rights is an essential component of respect for the dignity of persons. Rights to privacy, self-determination, personal liberty, and natural justice are of particular importance to psychologists, and they have a responsibility to protect and promote these rights in all of their activities. As such, psychologists have a responsibility to develop and follow procedures for informed consent, confidentiality, fair treatment, and due process that are consistent with those rights.

As individual rights exist within the context of the rights of others and of responsible caring (see Principle II), there might be circumstances in which the possibility of serious detrimental consequences to themselves or others, a diminished capacity to be autonomous, or a court order, would disallow some aspects of the rights to privacy, self-determination, and personal liberty. Indeed, such circumstances might be serious enough to create a duty to warn or protect others (see Standards I.45 and II.39). However, psychologists still have a responsibility to respect the rights of the person(s) involved to the greatest extent possible under the circumstances, and to do what is necessary and reasonable to reduce the need for future disallowances.

Psychologists recognize that, although all persons possess moral rights, the manner in which such rights are promoted, protected, and exercised varies across communities and cultures. For instance, definitions of what is considered private vary, as does the role of families and other community members in personal decision making. In their work, psychologists acknowledge and respect such differences, while guarding against clear violations of moral rights.

In addition, psychologists recognize that as individual, family, group, or community vulnerabilities increase, or as the power of persons to control their environment or their lives decreases, psychologists have an increasing responsibility to seek ethical advice and to establish safeguards to protect the rights of the persons involved. For this reason, psychologists consider it their responsibility to increase safeguards to protect and promote the rights of persons involved in their activities proportionate to the degree of dependency and the lack of voluntary initiation. For example, this would mean that there would be more safeguards to protect and promote the rights of fully dependent persons than partially dependent persons, and more safeguards for partially dependent than independent persons.

Respect for the dignity of persons also includes the concept of distributive justice. With respect to psychologists, this concept implies that all persons are entitled to benefit equally from the contributions of psychology and to equal quality in the processes, procedures, and services being conducted by psychologists, regardless of the person's characteristics, condition, or status. Although individual psychologists might specialize and direct their activities to particular populations, or might decline to engage in activities based on the limits of their competence or acknowledgment of problems in some relationships, psychologists must not exclude persons on a capricious or unjustly discriminatory basis.

By virtue of the social contract that the discipline has with society, psychologists have a higher duty of care to members of society than the general duty of care all members of society have to each other. However, psychologists are entitled to protect themselves from serious violations of their own moral rights (e.g., privacy, personal liberty) in carrying out their work as psychologists.

Ethical Standards

In adhering to the Principle of Respect for the Dignity of Persons, psychologists would:

General respect

I.1 Demonstrate appropriate respect for the knowledge, insight, experience, and areas of expertise of others.

I.2 Not engage publicly (e.g., in public statements, presentations, research reports, or with clients) in degrading comments about others, including demeaning jokes based on such characteristics as culture, nationality, ethnicity, colour, race, religion, sex, gender, or sexual orientation.

I.3 Strive to use language that conveys respect for the dignity of persons as much as possible in all written or oral communication.

I.4 Abstain from all forms of harassment, including sexual harassment.

General rights

I.5 Avoid or refuse to participate in practices disrespectful of the legal, civil, or moral rights of others.

I.6 Refuse to advise, train, or supply information to anyone who, in the psychologist's judgement, will use the knowledge or skills to infringe on human rights.

I.7 Make every reasonable effort to ensure that psychological knowledge is not misused, intentionally or unintentionally, to infringe on human rights.

I.8 Respect the right of research participants, clients, employees, supervisees, students, trainees, and others to safeguard their own dignity.

Non-discrimination

I.9 Not practice, condone, facilitate, or collaborate with any form of unjust discrimination.

I.10 Act to correct practices that are unjustly discriminatory.

I.11 Seek to design research, teaching, practice, and business activities in such a way that they contribute to the fair distribution of benefits to individuals and groups, and that they do not unfairly exclude those who are vulnerable or might be disadvantaged.

Fair treatment/due process

I.12 Work and act in a spirit of fair treatment to others.

I.13 Help to establish and abide by due process or other natural justice procedures for employment, evaluation, adjudication, editorial, and peer review activities.

I.14 Compensate others fairly for the use of their time, energy, and knowledge, unless such compensation is refused in advance.

I.15 Establish fees that are fair in light of the time, energy, and knowledge of the psychologist and any associates or employees, and in light of the market value of the product or service. (Also see Standard IV.12.)

Informed consent

I.16 Seek as full and active participation as possible from others in decisions that affect them, respecting and integrating as much as possible their opinions and wishes.

I.17 Recognize that informed consent is the result of a process of reaching an agreement to work collaboratively, rather than of simply having a consent form signed.

I.18 Respect the expressed wishes of persons to involve others (e.g., family members, community members) in their decision making regarding informed consent. This would include respect for written and clearly expressed unwritten advance directives.

I.19 Obtain informed consent from all independent and partially dependent persons for any psychological services provided to them except in circumstances of urgent need (e.g., disaster or other crisis). In urgent circumstances, psychologists would proceed with the assent of such persons, but fully informed consent would be obtained as soon as possible. (Also see Standard I.29.)

I.20 Obtain informed consent for all research activities that involve obtrusive measures, invasion of privacy, more than minimal risk of harm, or any attempt to change the behaviour of research participants.

I.21 Establish and use signed consent forms that specify the dimensions of informed consent or that acknowledge that such dimensions have been explained and are understood, if such forms are required by law or if such forms are desired by the psychologist, the person(s) giving consent, or the organization for whom the psychologist works.

I.22 Accept and document oral consent, in situations in which signed consent forms are not acceptable culturally or in which there are other good reasons for not using them.

I.23 Provide, in obtaining informed consent, as much information as reasonable or prudent persons would want to know before making a decision or consenting to the activity. The psychologist would relay this information in language that the persons understand (including providing translation into another language, if necessary) and would take whatever reasonable steps are needed to ensure that the information was, in fact, understood.

I.24 Ensure, in the process of obtaining informed consent, that at least the following points are understood: purpose and nature of the activity; mutual responsibilities; confidentiality protections and limitations; likely benefits and risks; alternatives; the likely consequences of non-action; the option to refuse or withdraw at any time, without prejudice; over what period of time the consent applies; and, how to rescind consent if desired. (Also see Standards III.23–30.)

I.25 Provide new information in a timely manner, whenever such information becomes available and is significant enough that it reasonably could be seen as relevant to the original or ongoing informed consent.

I.26 Clarify the nature of multiple relationships to all concerned parties before obtaining consent, if providing services to or conducting research at the request or for the use of third parties. This would include, but not be limited to: the purpose of the service or research; the reasonably anticipated use that will be made of information collected; and, the limits on confidentiality. Third parties may include schools, courts, government agencies, insurance companies, police, and special funding bodies.

Freedom of consent

I.27 Take all reasonable steps to ensure that consent is not given under conditions of coercion, undue pressure, or undue reward. (Also see Standard III.32.)

I.28 Not proceed with any research activity, if consent is given under any condition of coercion, undue pressure, or undue reward. (Also see Standard III.32.)

I.29 Take all reasonable steps to confirm or re-establish freedom of consent, if consent for service is given under conditions of duress or conditions of extreme need.

I.30 Respect the right of persons to discontinue participation or service at any time, and be responsive to non-verbal indications of a desire to discontinue if a person has difficulty with verbally communicating such a desire (e.g., young children, verbally disabled persons) or, due to culture, is unlikely to communicate such a desire orally.

Protections for vulnerable persons

I.31 Seek an independent and adequate ethical review of human rights issues and protections for any research involving members of vulnerable groups, including persons of diminished capacity to give informed consent, before making a decision to proceed.

I.32 Not use persons of diminished capacity to give informed consent in research studies, if the research involved may be carried out equally well with persons who have a fuller capacity to give informed consent.

I.33 Seek to use methods that maximize the understanding and ability to consent of persons of diminished capacity to give informed consent, and that reduce the need for a substitute decision maker.

I.34 Carry out informed consent processes with those persons who are legally responsible or appointed to give informed consent on behalf of persons not competent to consent on their own behalf, seeking to ensure respect for any previously expressed preferences of persons not competent to consent.

I.35 Seek willing and adequately informed participation from any person of diminished capacity to give informed consent, and proceed without this assent only if the service or research activity is considered to be of direct benefit to that person.

I.36 Be particularly cautious in establishing the freedom of consent of any person who is in a dependent relationship to the psychologist (e.g., student, employee). This may include, but is not limited to, offering that person an alternative activity to fulfill their educational or employment goals, or offering a range of research studies or experience opportunities from which the person can select, none of which is so onerous as to be coercive.

Privacy

I.37 Seek and collect only information that is germane to the purpose(s) for which consent has been obtained.

I.38 Take care not to infringe, in research, teaching, or service activities, on the personally, developmentally, or culturally defined private space of individuals or groups, unless clear permission is granted to do so.

I.39 Record only that private information necessary for the provision of continuous, coordinated service, or for the goals of the particular research study being conducted, or that is required or justified by law. (Also see Standards IV.17 and IV.18.)

I.40 Respect the right of research participants, employees, supervisees, students, and trainees to reasonable personal privacy.

I.41 Collect, store, handle, and transfer all private information, whether written or unwritten (e.g., communication during service provision, written records, e-mail or fax communication, computer files, video-tapes), in a way that attends to the needs for privacy and security. This would include having adequate plans for records in circumstances of one's own serious illness, termination of employment, or death.

I.42 Take all reasonable steps to ensure that records over which they have control remain personally identifiable only as long as necessary in the interests of those to whom they refer and/or to the research project for which they were collected, or as required or justified by law (e.g., the possible need to defend oneself against future allegations), and render anonymous or destroy any records under their control that no longer need to be personally identifiable. (Also see Standards IV.17 and IV.18.)

Confidentiality

I.43 Be careful not to relay information about colleagues, colleagues' clients, research participants, employees, supervisees, students, trainees, and members of organizations, gained in the process of their activities as psychologists, that the psychologist has reason to believe is considered confidential by those persons, except as required or justified by law. (Also see Standards IV.17 and IV.18.)

I.44 Clarify what measures will be taken to protect confidentiality, and what responsibilities family, group, and community members have for the protection of each other's confidentiality, when engaged in services to or research with individuals, families, groups, or communities.

I.45 Share confidential information with others only with the informed consent of those involved, or in a manner that the persons involved cannot be identified, except as required or justified by law, or in circumstances of actual or possible serious physical harm or death. (Also see Standards II.39, IV.17, and IV.18.)

Extended responsibility

I.46 Encourage others, in a manner consistent with this *Code*, to respect the dignity of persons and to expect respect for their own dignity.

I.47 Assume overall responsibility for the scientific and professional activities of their assistants, employees, students, supervisees, and trainees with regard to Respect for the Dignity of Persons, all of whom, however, incur similar obligations.

PRINCIPLE II: RESPONSIBLE CARING

Values Statement

A basic ethical expectation of any discipline is that its activities will benefit members of society or, at least, do no harm. Therefore, psychologists demonstrate an active concern for the welfare of any individual, family, group, or community with whom they relate in their role as psychologists. This concern includes both those directly involved and those indirectly involved in their activities. However, as with Principle I, psychologists' greatest responsibility is to protect the welfare of those in the most vulnerable position. Normally, persons directly involved in their activities (e.g., research participants, clients, students) are in such a position. Psychologists' responsibility to those indirectly involved (e.g., employers, third party payers, the general public) normally is secondary.

As persons usually consider their own welfare in their personal decision making, obtaining informed consent (see Principle I) is one of the best methods for ensuring that their welfare will be protected. However, it is only when such consent is combined with the responsible caring of the psychologist that there is considerable ethical protection of the welfare of the person(s) involved.

Responsible caring leads psychologists to take care to discern the potential harm and benefits involved, to predict the likelihood of their occurrence, to proceed only if the potential benefits outweigh the potential harms, to develop and use methods that will minimize harms and maximize benefits, and to take responsibility for correcting clearly harmful effects that have occurred as a direct result of their research, teaching, practice, or business activities.

In order to carry out these steps, psychologists recognize the need for competence and self-knowledge. They consider incompetent action to be unethical per se, as it is unlikely to be of benefit and likely to be harmful. They engage only in those activities in which they have competence or for which they are receiving supervision, and they perform their activities as competently as possible. They acquire, contribute to, and use the existing knowledge most relevant to the best interests of those concerned. They also engage in self-reflection regarding how their own values, attitudes, experiences, and social context (e.g., culture, ethnicity, colour, religion, sex, gender, sexual orientation, physical and mental abilities, age, and socio-economic status) influence their actions, interpretations, choices, and recommendations. This is done with the intent of increasing the probability that their activities will benefit and not harm the individuals, families, groups, and communities to whom they relate in their role as psychologists. Psychologists define harm and benefit in terms of both physical and psychological dimensions. They are concerned about such factors as: social, family, and community relationships; personal and cultural identity; feelings of self-worth, fear, humiliation, interpersonal trust, and cynicism; self-knowledge and general knowledge; and, such factors as physical safety, comfort, pain, and injury. They are concerned about immediate, short-term, and long-term effects.

Responsible caring recognizes and respects (e.g., through obtaining informed consent) the ability of individuals, families, groups, and communities to make decisions for themselves and to care for themselves and each other. It does not replace or undermine such ability, nor does it substitute one person's opinion about what is in the best interests of another person for that other person's competent decision making. However, psychologists recognize that, as vulnerabilities increase or as power to control one's own life decreases, psychologists have an increasing responsibility to protect the well-being of the individual, family, group, or community involved. For this reason, as in Principle I, psychologists consider it their responsibility to increase safeguards proportionate to the degree of dependency and the lack of voluntary initiation on the part of the persons involved. However, for Principle II, the safeguards are for the well-being of persons rather than for the rights of persons.

Psychologists' treatment and use of animals in their research and teaching activities are also a component of responsible caring. Although animals do not have the same moral rights as persons (e.g., privacy), they do have the right to be treated humanely and not to be exposed to unnecessary discomfort, pain, or disruption.

By virtue of the social contract that the discipline has with society, psychologists have a higher duty of care to members of society than the general duty of care all members of society have to each other. However, psychologists are entitled to protect their own basic well-being (e.g., physical safety, family relationships) in their work as psychologists.

Ethical Standards

In adhering to the Principle of Responsible Caring, psychologists would:

General caring

II.1 Protect and promote the welfare of clients, research participants, employees, supervisees, students, trainees, colleagues, and others.

II.2 Avoid doing harm to clients, research participants, employees, supervisees, students, trainees, colleagues, and others.

II.3 Accept responsibility for the consequences of their actions.

II.4 Refuse to advise, train, or supply information to anyone who, in the psychologist's judgment, will use the knowledge or skills to harm others.

II.5 Make every reasonable effort to ensure that psychological knowledge is not misused, intentionally or unintentionally, to harm others.

Competence and self-knowledge

II.6 Offer or carry out (without supervision) only those activities for which they have established their competence to carry them out to the benefit of others.

II.7 Not delegate activities to persons not competent to carry them out to the benefit of others.

II.8 Take immediate steps to obtain consultation or to refer a client to a colleague or other appropriate professional, whichever is more likely to result in providing the client with competent service, if it becomes apparent that a client's problems are beyond their competence.

II.9 Keep themselves up to date with a broad range of relevant knowledge, research methods, and techniques, and their impact on persons and society, through the reading of relevant literature, peer consultation, and continuing education activities, in order that their service or research activities and conclusions will benefit and not harm others.

II.10 Evaluate how their own experiences, attitudes, culture, beliefs, values, social context, individual differences, specific training, and stresses influence their interactions with others, and integrate this awareness into all efforts to benefit and not harm others.

II.11 Seek appropriate help and/or discontinue scientific or professional activity for an appropriate period of time, if a physical or psychological condition reduces their ability to benefit and not harm others.

II.12 Engage in self-care activities that help to avoid conditions (e.g., burnout, addictions) that could result in impaired judgment and interfere with their ability to benefit and not harm others.

Risk/benefit analysis

II.13 Assess the individuals, families, groups, and communities involved in their activities adequately enough to ensure that they will be able to discern what will benefit and not harm the persons involved.

II.14 Be sufficiently sensitive to and knowledgeable about individual, group, community, and cultural differences and vulnerabilities to discern what will benefit and not harm persons involved in their activities.

II.15 Carry out pilot studies to determine the effects of all new procedures and techniques that might carry more than minimal risk, before considering their use on a broader scale.

II.16 Seek an independent and adequate ethical review of the balance of risks and potential benefits of all research and new interventions that involve procedures of unknown consequence, or where pain, discomfort, or harm are possible, before making a decision to proceed.

II.17 Not carry out any scientific or professional activity unless the probable benefit is proportionately greater than the risk involved.

Maximize benefit

II.18 Provide services that are coordinated over time and with other service providers, in order to avoid duplication or working at cross purposes.

II.19 Create and maintain records relating to their activities that are sufficient to support continuity and appropriate coordination of their activities with the activities of others.

II.20 Make themselves aware of the knowledge and skills of other disciplines (e.g., law, medicine, business administration) and advise the use of such knowledge and skills, where relevant to the benefit of others.

II.21 Strive to provide and/or obtain the best possible service for those needing and seeking psychological service. This may include, but is not limited to: selecting interventions that are relevant to the needs and characteristics of the client and that have reasonable theoretical or empirically-supported efficacy in light of those needs and characteristics; consulting with, or including in service delivery, persons relevant to the culture or belief systems of those served; advocating on behalf of the client; and, recommending professionals other than psychologists when appropriate.

II.22 Monitor and evaluate the effect of their activities, record their findings, and communicate new knowledge to relevant others.

II.23 Debrief research participants in such a way that the participants' knowledge is enhanced and the participants have a sense of contribution to knowledge. (Also see Standards III.26 and III.27.)

II.24 Perform their teaching duties on the basis of careful preparation, so that their instruction is current and scholarly.

II.25 Facilitate the professional and scientific development of their employees, supervisees, students, and trainees by ensuring that these persons understand the values and ethical prescriptions of the discipline, and by providing or arranging for adequate working conditions, timely evaluations, and constructive consultation and experience opportunities.

II.26 Encourage and assist students in publication of worthy student papers.

Minimize harm

II.27 Be acutely aware of the power relationship in therapy and, therefore, not encourage or engage in sexual intimacy with therapy clients, neither during therapy, nor for that period of time following therapy during which the power relationship reasonably could be expected to influence the client's personal decision making. (Also see Standard III.31.)

II.28 Not encourage or engage in sexual intimacy with students or trainees with whom the psychologist has an evaluative or other relationship of direct authority. (Also see Standard III.31.)

II.29 Be careful not to engage in activities in a way that could place incidentally involved persons at risk.

II.30 Be acutely aware of the need for discretion in the recording and communication of information, in order that the information not be misinterpreted or misused to the detriment of others. This includes, but is not limited to: not recording information that could lead to misinterpretation and misuse; avoiding conjecture; clearly labelling opinion; and, communicating information in language that can be understood clearly by the recipient of the information.

II.31 Give reasonable assistance to secure needed psychological services or activities, if personally unable to meet requests for needed psychological services or activities.

II.32 Provide a client, if appropriate and if desired by the client, with reasonable assistance to find a way to receive needed services in the event that third party payments are exhausted and the client cannot afford the fees involved.

II.33 Maintain appropriate contact, support, and responsibility for caring until a colleague or other professional begins service, if referring a client to a colleague or other professional.

II.34 Give reasonable notice and be reasonably assured that discontinuation will cause no harm to the client, before discontinuing services.

II.35 Screen appropriate research participants and select those least likely to be harmed, if more than minimal risk of harm to some research participants is possible.

II.36 Act to minimize the impact of their research activities on research participants' personalities, or on their physical or mental integrity.

Offset/correct harm

II.37 Terminate an activity when it is clear that the activity carries more than minimal risk of harm and is found to be more harmful than beneficial, or when the activity is no longer needed.

II.38 Refuse to help individuals, families, groups, or communities to carry out or submit to activities that, according to current knowledge, or legal or professional guidelines, would cause serious physical or psychological harm to themselves or others.

II.39 Do everything reasonably possible to stop or offset the consequences of actions by others when these actions are likely to cause serious physical harm or death. This may include reporting to appropriate authorities (e.g., the police), an intended victim, or a family member or other support person who can intervene, and would be done even when a confidential relationship is involved. (Also see Standard I.45.)

II.40 Act to stop or offset the consequences of seriously harmful activities being carried out by another psychologist or member of another discipline, when there is objective information about the activities and the harm, and when these activities have come to their attention outside of a confidential client relationship between themselves and the psychologist or member of another discipline. This may include reporting to the appropriate regulatory body, authority, or committee for action, depending on the psychologist's judgment about the person(s) or body(ies) best suited to stop or offset the harm, and depending upon regulatory requirements and definitions of misconduct.

II.41 Act also to stop or offset the consequences of harmful activities carried out by another psychologist or member of another discipline, when the harm is not serious or the activities appear to be primarily a lack of sensitivity, knowledge, or experience, and when the activities have come to their attention outside of a confidential client relationship between themselves and the psychologist or member of another discipline. This may include talking informally with the psychologist or member of the other discipline, obtaining objective information and, if possible and relevant, the assurance that the harm will discontinue and be corrected. If in a vulnerable position (e.g., employee, trainee) with respect to the other psychologist or member of the other discipline, it may include asking persons in less vulnerable positions to participate in the meeting(s).

II.42 Be open to the concerns of others about perceptions of harm that they as a psychologist might be causing, stop activities that are causing harm, and not punish or seek punishment for those who raise such concerns in good faith.

II.43 Not place an individual, group, family, or community needing service at a serious disadvantage by offering them no service in order to fulfill the conditions of a research design, when a standard service is available.

II.44 Debrief research participants in such a way that any harm caused can be discerned, and act to correct any resultant harm. (Also see Standards III.26 and III.27.)

Care of animals

II.45 Not use animals in their research unless there is a reasonable expectation that the research will increase understanding of the structures and processes underlying behaviour, or increase understanding of the particular animal species used in the study, or result eventually in benefits to the health and welfare of humans or other animals.

II.46 Use a procedure subjecting animals to pain, stress, or privation only if an alternative procedure is unavailable and the goal is justified by its prospective scientific, educational, or applied value.

II.47 Make every effort to minimize the discomfort, illness, and pain of animals. This would include performing surgical procedures only under appropriate anaesthesia, using techniques to avoid infection and minimize pain during and after surgery and, if disposing of experimental animals is carried out at the termination of the study, doing so in a humane way.

II.48 Use animals in classroom demonstrations only if the instructional objectives cannot be achieved through the use of videotapes, films, or other methods, and if the type of demonstration is warranted by the anticipated instructional gain.

Extended responsibility

II.49 Encourage others, in a manner consistent with this *Code*, to care responsibly.

II.50 Assume overall responsibility for the scientific and professional activities of their assistants, employees, supervisees, students, and trainees with regard to the Principle of Responsible Caring, all of whom, however, incur similar obligations.

PRINCIPLE III: INTEGRITY IN RELATIONSHIPS

Values Statement

The relationships formed by psychologists in the course of their work embody explicit and implicit mutual expectations of integrity that are vital to the advancement of scientific knowledge and to the maintenance of public confidence in the discipline of psychology. These expectations include: accuracy and honesty; straightforwardness and openness; the maximization of objectivity and minimization of bias; and, avoidance of conflicts of interest. Psychologists have a responsibility to meet these expectations and to encourage reciprocity.

In addition to accuracy, honesty, and the obvious prohibitions of fraud or misrepresentation, meeting expectations of integrity is enhanced by self-knowledge and the use of critical analysis. Although it can be argued that science is value-free and impartial, scientists are not. Personal values and self-interest can affect the questions psychologists ask, how they ask those questions, what assumptions they make, their selection of methods, what they observe and what they fail to observe, and how they interpret their data.

Psychologists are not expected to be value-free or totally without self-interest in conducting their activities. However, they are expected to understand how their backgrounds, personal needs, and values interact with their activities, to be open and honest about the influence of such factors, and to be as objective and unbiased as possible under the circumstances.

The values of openness and straightforwardness exist within the context of Respect for the Dignity of Persons (Principle I) and Responsible Caring (Principle II). As such, there will be circumstances in which openness and straightforwardness will need to be tempered. Fully open and straightforward disclosure might not be needed or desired by others and, in some circumstances, might be a risk to their dignity or well-being, or considered culturally inappropriate. In such circumstances, however, psychologists have a responsibility to ensure that their decision not to be fully open or straightforward is justified by higher-order values and does not invalidate any informed consent procedures.

Of special concern to psychologists is the provision of incomplete disclosure when obtaining informed consent for research participation, or temporarily leading research participants to believe that a research project has a purpose other than its actual purpose. These actions sometimes occur in research where full disclosure would be likely to influence the responses of the research participants and thus invalidate the results. Although research that uses such techniques can lead to knowledge that is beneficial, such benefits must be weighed against the research participant's right to self-determination and the importance of public and individual trust in psychology. Psychologists have a serious obligation to avoid as much as possible the use of such research procedures. They also have a serious obligation to consider the need for, the possible consequences of, and their responsibility to correct any resulting mistrust or other harmful effects from their use.

As public trust in the discipline of psychology includes trusting that psychologists will act in the best interests of members of the public, situations that present real or potential conflicts of interest are of concern to psychologists. Conflict-of-interest situations are those that can lead to distorted judgment and can motivate psychologists to act in ways that meet their own personal, political, financial, or business interests at the expense of the best interests of members of the public. Although avoidance of all conflicts of interest and potential exploitation of others is not possible, some are of such a high risk to protecting the interests of members of the public and to maintaining the trust of the public, that they are considered never acceptable (see Standard III.31). The risk level of other conflicts of interest (e.g., dual or multiple relationships) might be partially dependent on cultural factors and the specific type of professional relationship (e.g., long-term psychotherapy vs. community development activities). It is the responsibility of psychologists to avoid dual or multiple relationships and other conflicts of interest when appropriate and possible. When such situations cannot be avoided or are inappropriate to avoid, psychologists have a responsibility to declare that they have a conflict of interest, to seek advice, and to establish safeguards to ensure that the best interests of members of the public are protected.

Integrity in relationships implies that psychologists, as a matter of honesty, have a responsibility to maintain competence in any specialty area for which they declare competence, whether or not they are currently practising in that area. It also requires that psychologists, in as much as they present themselves as members and representatives of a specific discipline, have a responsibility to actively rely on and be guided by that discipline and its guidelines and requirements.

Ethical Standards

In adhering to the Principle of Integrity in Relationships, psychologists would:

Accuracy/honesty

III.1 Not knowingly participate in, condone, or be associated with dishonesty, fraud, or misrepresentation.

III.2 Accurately represent their own and their colleagues' credentials, qualifications, education, experience, competence, and affiliations, in all spoken, written, or printed communications, being careful not to use descriptions or information that could be misinterpreted (e.g., citing membership in a voluntary association of psychologists as a testament of competence).

III.3 Carefully protect their own and their colleagues' credentials from being misrepresented by others, and act quickly to correct any such misrepresentation.

III.4 Maintain competence in their declared area(s) of psychological competence, as well as in their current area(s) of activity. (Also see Standard II.9.)

III.5 Accurately represent their own and their colleagues' activities, functions, contributions, and likely or actual outcomes of their activities (including research results) in all spoken, written, or printed communication. This includes, but is not limited to: advertisements of services or products; course and workshop descriptions; academic grading requirements; and, research reports.

III.6 Ensure that their own and their colleagues' activities, functions, contributions, and likely or actual outcomes of their activities (including research results) are not misrepresented by others, and act quickly to correct any such misrepresentation.

III.7 Take credit only for the work and ideas that they have actually done or generated, and give credit for work done or ideas contributed by others (including students), in proportion to their contribution.

III.8 Acknowledge the limitations of their own and their colleagues' knowledge, methods, findings, interventions, and views.

III 9. Not suppress disconfirming evidence of their own and their colleagues' findings and views, acknowledging alternative hypotheses and explanations.

Objectivity/lack of bias

III.10 Evaluate how their personal experiences, attitudes, values, social context, individual differences, stresses, and specific training influence their activities and thinking, integrating this awareness into all attempts to be objective and unbiased in their research, service, and other activities.

III.11 Take care to communicate as completely and objectively as possible, and to clearly differentiate facts, opinions, theories, hypotheses, and ideas, when communicating knowledge, findings, and views.

III.12 Present instructional information accurately, avoiding bias in the selection and presentation of information, and publicly acknowledge any personal values or bias that influence the selection and presentation of information.

III.13 Act quickly to clarify any distortion by a sponsor, client, agency (e.g., news media), or other persons, of the findings of their research.

Straightforwardness/openness

III.14 Be clear and straightforward about all information needed to establish informed consent or any other valid written or unwritten agreement (for example: fees, including any limitations imposed by third-party payers; relevant business policies and practices; mutual concerns; mutual responsibilities; ethical responsibilities of psychologists; purpose and nature of the relationship, including research participation; alternatives; likely experiences; possible conflicts; possible outcomes; and, expectations for processing, using, and sharing any information generated).

III.15 Provide suitable information about the results of assessments, evaluations, or research findings to the persons involved, if appropriate and if asked. This information would be communicated in understandable language.

III.16 Fully explain reasons for their actions to persons who have been affected by their actions, if appropriate and if asked.

III.17 Honour all promises and commitments included in any written or verbal agreement, unless serious and unexpected circumstances (e.g., illness) intervene. If such circumstances occur, then the psychologist would make a full and honest explanation to other parties involved.

III.18 Make clear whether they are acting as private citizens, as members of specific organizations or groups, or as representatives of the discipline of psychology, when making statements or when involved in public activities.

III.19 Carry out, present, and discuss research in a way that is consistent with a commitment to honest, open inquiry, and to clear communication of any research aims, sponsorship, social context, personal values, or financial interests that might affect or appear to affect the research.

III.20 Submit their research, in some accurate form and within the limits of confidentiality, to persons with expertise in the research area, for their comments and evaluations, prior to publication or the preparation of any final report.

III.21 Encourage and not interfere with the free and open exchange of psychological knowledge and theory between themselves, their students, colleagues, and the public.

III.22 Make no attempt to conceal the status of a trainee and, if a trainee is providing direct client service, ensure that the client is informed of that fact.

Avoidance of incomplete disclosure

III.23 Not engage in incomplete disclosure, or in temporarily leading research participants to believe that a research project or some aspect of it has a different purpose, if there are alternative procedures available or if the negative effects cannot be predicted or offset.

III.24 Not engage in incomplete disclosure, or in temporarily leading research participants to believe that a research project or some aspect of it has a different purpose, if it would interfere with the person's understanding of facts that clearly might influence a decision to give adequately informed consent (e.g., withholding information about the level of risk, discomfort, or inconvenience).

III.25 Use the minimum necessary incomplete disclosure or temporary leading of research participants to believe that a research project or some aspect of it has a different purpose, when such research procedures are used.

III.26 Debrief research participants as soon as possible after the participants' involvement, if there has been incomplete disclosure or temporary leading of research participants to believe that a research project or some aspect of it has a different purpose.

III.27 Provide research participants, during such debriefing, with a clarification of the nature of the study, seek to remove any misconceptions that might have arisen, and seek to re-establish any trust that might have been lost, assuring the participants that the research procedures were neither arbitrary nor capricious, but necessary for scientifically valid findings. (Also see Standards II.23 and II.44.)

III.28 Act to re-establish with research participants any trust that might have been lost due to the use of incomplete disclosure or temporarily leading research participants to believe that the research project or some aspect of it had a different purpose.

III.29 Give a research participant the option of removing his or her data, if the research participant expresses concern during the debriefing about the incomplete disclosure or the temporary leading of the research participant to believe that the research project or some aspect of it had a different purpose, and if removal of the data will not compromise the validity of the research design and hence diminish the ethical value of the participation of the other research participants.

III.30 Seek an independent and adequate ethical review of the risks to public or individual trust and of safeguards to protect such trust for any research that plans to provide incomplete disclosure or temporarily lead research participants to believe that the research project or some aspect of it has a different purpose, before making a decision to proceed.

Avoidance of conflict of interest

III.31 Not exploit any relationship established as a psychologist to further personal, political, or business interests at the expense of the best interests of their clients, research participants, students, employers, or others. This includes, but is not limited to: soliciting clients of one's employing agency for private practice; taking advantage of trust or dependency to encourage or engage in sexual intimacies (e.g., with clients not included in Standard II.27, with clients' partners or relatives, with students or trainees not included in Standard II.28, or with research participants); taking advantage of trust or dependency to frighten clients into receiving services; misappropriating students' ideas, research or work; using the resources of one's employing institution for purposes not agreed to; giving or receiving kickbacks or bonuses for referrals; seeking or accepting loans or investments from clients; and, prejudicing others against a colleague for reasons of personal gain.

III.32 Not offer rewards sufficient to motivate an individual or group to participate in an activity that has possible or known risks to themselves or others. (Also see Standards I.27, I.28, II.2, and II.49.)

III.33 Avoid dual or multiple relationships (e.g. with clients, research participants, employees, supervisees, students, or trainees) and other situations that might present a conflict of interest or that might reduce their ability to be objective and unbiased in their determinations of what might be in the best interests of others.

III.34 Manage dual or multiple relationships that are unavoidable due to cultural norms or other circumstances in such a manner that bias, lack of objectivity, and risk of exploitation are minimized. This might include obtaining ongoing supervision or consultation for the duration of the dual or multiple relationship, or involving a third party in obtaining consent (e.g., approaching a client or employee about becoming a research participant).

III.35 Inform all parties, if a real or potential conflict of interest arises, of the need to resolve the situation in a manner that is consistent with Respect for the Dignity of Persons (Principle I) and Responsible Caring (Principle II), and take all reasonable steps to resolve the issue in such a manner.

Reliance on the discipline

III.36 Familiarize themselves with their discipline's rules and regulations, and abide by them, unless abiding by them would be seriously detrimental to the rights or welfare of others as demonstrated in the Principles of Respect for the Dignity of Persons or Responsible Caring. (See Standards IV.17 and IV.18 for guidelines regarding the resolution of such conflicts.)

III.37 Familiarize themselves with and demonstrate a commitment to maintaining the standards of their discipline.

III.38 Seek consultation from colleagues and/or appropriate groups and committees, and give due regard to their advice in arriving at a responsible decision, if faced with difficult situations.

Extended responsibility

III.39 Encourage others, in a manner consistent with this *Code*, to relate with integrity.

III.40 Assume overall responsibility for the scientific and professional activities of their assistants, employees, supervisees, students, and trainees with regard to the Principle of Integrity in Relationships, all of whom, however, incur similar obligations.

PRINCIPLE IV: RESPONSIBILITY TO SOCIETY

Values Statement

Psychology functions as a discipline within the context of human society[2]. Psychologists, both in their work and as private citizens, have responsibilities to the societies in which they live and work, such as the neighbourhood or city, and to the welfare of all human beings in those societies.

---

2. Society is used here in the broad sense of a group of persons living as members of one or more human communities, rather than in the limited sense of state or government.

Two of the legitimate expectations of psychology as a science and a profession are that it will increase knowledge and that it will conduct its affairs in such ways that it will promote the welfare of all human beings.

Freedom of enquiry and debate (including scientific and academic freedom) is a foundation of psychological education, science, and practice. In the context of society, the above expectations imply that psychologists will exercise this freedom through the use of activities and methods that are consistent with ethical requirements.

The above expectations also imply that psychologists will do whatever they can to ensure that psychological knowledge, when used in the development of social structures and policies, will be used for beneficial purposes, and that the discipline's own structures and policies will support those beneficial purposes. Within the context of this document, social structures and policies that have beneficial purposes are defined as those that more readily support and reflect respect for the dignity of persons, responsible caring, integrity in relationships, and responsibility to society. If psychological knowledge or structures are used against these purposes, psychologists have an ethical responsibility to try to draw attention to and correct the misuse. Although this is a collective responsibility, those psychologists having direct involvement in the structures of the discipline, in social development, or in the theoretical or research data base that is being used (e.g., through research, expert testimony, or policy advice) have the greatest responsibility to act. Other psychologists must decide for themselves the most appropriate and beneficial use of their time and talents to help meet this collective responsibility.

In carrying out their work, psychologists acknowledge that many social structures have evolved slowly over time in response to human need and are valued by the societies that have developed them. In such circumstances, psychologists convey respect for such social structures and avoid unwarranted or unnecessary disruption. Suggestions for and action toward changes or enhancement of such structures are carried out through processes that seek to achieve a consensus within those societies and/or through democratic means.

On the other hand, if structures or policies seriously ignore or oppose the principles of respect for the dignity of persons, responsible caring, integrity in relationships, or responsibility to society, psychologists involved have a responsibility to speak out in a manner consistent with the principles of this *Code*, and advocate for appropriate change to occur as quickly as possible.

In order to be responsible and accountable to society, and to contribute constructively to its ongoing development, psychologists need to be willing to work in partnership with others, be self-reflective, and be open to external suggestions and criticisms about the place of the discipline of psychology in society. They need to engage in even-tempered observation and interpretation of the effects of societal structures and policies, and their process of change, developing the ability of psychologists to increase the beneficial use of psychological knowledge and structures, and avoid their misuse. The discipline needs to be willing to set high standards for its members, to do what it can to assure that such standards are met, and to support its members in their attempts to maintain the standards. Once again, individual psychologists must decide for themselves the most appropriate and beneficial use of their time and talents in helping to meet these collective responsibilities.

Ethical Standards

In adhering to the Principle of Responsibility to Society, psychologists would:

Development of knowledge

IV.1 Contribute to the discipline of psychology and of society's understanding of itself and human beings generally, through free enquiry and the acquisition, transmission, and expression of knowledge and ideas, unless such activities conflict with other basic ethical requirements.

IV.2 Not interfere with, or condone interference with, free enquiry and the acquisition, transmission, and expression of knowledge and ideas that do not conflict with other basic ethical requirements.

IV.3 Keep informed of progress in their area(s) of psychological activity, take this progress into account in their work, and try to make their own contributions to this progress.

Beneficial activities

IV.4 Participate in and contribute to continuing education and the professional and scientific growth of self and colleagues.

IV.5 Assist in the development of those who enter the discipline of psychology by helping them to acquire a full understanding of their ethical responsibilities, and the needed competencies of their chosen area(s), including an understanding of critical analysis and of the variations, uses, and possible misuses of the scientific paradigm.

IV.6 Participate in the process of critical self-evaluation of the discipline's place in society, and in the development and implementation of structures and procedures that help the discipline to contribute to beneficial societal functioning and changes.

IV.7 Provide and/or contribute to a work environment that supports the respectful expression of ethical concern or dissent, and the constructive resolution of such concern or dissent.

IV.8   Engage in regular monitoring, assessment, and reporting (e.g., through peer review, and in programme reviews, case management reviews, and reports of one's own research) of their ethical practices and safeguards.

IV.9   Help develop, promote, and participate in accountability processes and procedures related to their work.

IV.10 Uphold the discipline's responsibility to society by promoting and maintaining the highest standards of the discipline.

IV.11 Protect the skills, knowledge, and interpretations of psychology from being misused, used incompetently, or made useless (e.g., loss of security of assessment techniques) by others.

IV.12 Contribute to the general welfare of society (e.g., improving accessibility of services, regardless of ability to pay) and/or to the general welfare of their discipline, by offering a portion of their time to work for which they receive little or no financial return.

IV.13 Uphold the discipline's responsibility to society by bringing incompetent or unethical behaviour, including misuses of psychological knowledge and techniques, to the attention of appropriate authorities, committees, or regulatory bodies, in a manner consistent with the ethical principles of this *Code*, if informal resolution or correction of the situation is not appropriate or possible.

IV.14 Enter only into agreements or contracts that allow them to act in accordance with the ethical principles and standards of this *Code*.

Respect for society

IV.15 Acquire an adequate knowledge of the culture, social structure, and customs of a community before beginning any major work there.

IV.16 Convey respect for and abide by prevailing community mores, social customs, and cultural expectations in their scientific and professional activities, provided that this does not contravene any of the ethical principles of this *Code*.

IV.17 Familiarize themselves with the laws and regulations of the societies in which they work, especially those that are related to their activities as psychologists, and abide by them. If those laws or regulations seriously conflict with the ethical principles contained herein, psychologists would do whatever they could to uphold the ethical principles. If upholding the ethical principles could result in serious personal consequences (e.g., jail or physical harm), decision for final action would be considered a matter of personal conscience.

IV.18 Consult with colleagues, if faced with an apparent conflict between abiding by a law or regulation and following an ethical principle, unless in an emergency, and seek consensus as to the most ethical course of action and the most responsible, knowledgeable, effective, and respectful way to carry it out.

Development of society

IV.19 Act to change those aspects of the discipline of psychology that detract from beneficial societal changes, where appropriate and possible.

IV.20 Be sensitive to the needs, current issues, and problems of society, when determining research questions to be asked, services to be developed, content to be taught, information to be collected, or appropriate interpretation of results or findings.

IV.21 Be especially careful to keep well informed of social issues through relevant reading, peer consultation, and continuing education, if their work is related to societal issues.

IV.22 Speak out, in a manner consistent with the four principles of this *Code*, if they possess expert knowledge that bears on important societal issues being studied or discussed.

IV.23 Provide thorough discussion of the limits of their data with respect to social policy, if their work touches on social policy and structure.

IV.24 Consult, if feasible and appropriate, with groups, organizations, or communities being studied, in order to increase the accuracy of interpretation of results and to minimize risk of misinterpretation or misuse.

IV.25 Make themselves aware of the current social and political climate and of previous and possible future societal misuses of psychological knowledge, and exercise due discretion in communicating psychological information (e.g., research results, theoretical knowledge), in order to discourage any further misuse.

IV.26 Exercise particular care when reporting the results of any work regarding vulnerable groups, ensuring that results are not likely to be misinterpreted or misused in the development of social policy, attitudes, and practices (e.g., encouraging manipulation of vulnerable persons or reinforcing discrimination against any specific population).

IV.27 Not contribute to nor engage in research or any other activity that contravenes international humanitarian law, such as the development of methods intended for use in the torture of persons, the development of prohibited weapons, or destruction of the environment.

IV.28 Provide the public with any psychological knowledge relevant to the public's informed participation in the shaping of social policies and structures, if they possess expert knowledge that bears on the social policies and structures.

IV.29 Speak out and/or act, in a manner consistent with the four principles of this *Code*, if the policies, practices, laws, or regulations of the social structure within which they work seriously ignore or contradict any of the principles of this *Code*.

Extended responsibility

IV.30 Encourage others, in a manner consistent with this *Code*, to exercise responsibility to society.

IV.3 Assume overall responsibility for the scientific and professional activities of their assistants, employees, supervisees, students, and trainees with regard to the Principle of Responsibility to Society, all of whom, however, incur similar obligations.

APPENDIX D
APA Record Keeping Guidelines

INTRODUCTION[1]

The guidelines that follow are based on the General Guidelines, adopted by the American Psychological Association (APA) in July 1987 (APA, 1987). The guidelines receive their inspirational guidance from specific APA *Ethical Principles of Psychologists and Code of Conduct* (APA, 1992).

These guidelines are aspirational and professional judgment must be used in specific applications. They are intended for use by providers of health care services.[2, 3] The language of these guidelines must be interpreted in light of their aspirational intent, advancements in psychology and the technology of record keeping, and the professional judgment of the individual psychologist.

From "APA Record Keeping Guidelines," by the American Psychological Association, 1993, *American Psychologist, 48*, pp. 984–986. Copyright 1993 by the American Psychological Association. Retrieved from PsychNET® Web site: http://www.apa.org/practice/recordkeeping.html

1. In 1988 the Board of Professional Affairs (BPA) directed the Committee on Professional Practice and Standards (COPPS) to determine whether record keeping guidelines would be appropriate. COPPS was informed that these guidelines would supplement the provisions contained in the *General Guidelines for Providers of Psychological Services*, which had been amended two years earlier. The Council of Representatives approved the General Guidelines records provisions after extended debate on the minimum recordation concerning the nature and contents of psychological services. The General Guidelines reflect a compromise position that psychologists hold widely varying views on the wisdom of recording the content of the psychotherapeutic relationship. In light of the Council debate on the content of psychological records and the absence of an integrated document, BPA instructed COPPS to assess the need for such guidelines, and, if necessary, the likely content.

COPPS undertook a series of interviews with psychologists experienced in this area. The consensus of the respondents indicated that practicing psychologists could benefit from guidance in this area. In addition, an APA legal intern undertook a 50-state review of laws governing psychologists with respect to record keeping provisions. The survey demonstrated that while some states have relatively clear provisions governing certain types of records, many questions are often left unclear. In addition, there is a great deal of variability among the states, so that consistent treatment of records as people move from state to state, or as records are sought from other states, may not be easy to achieve.

Based on COPPS' survey and legal research, BPA in 1989 directed COPPS to prepare an initial set of record keeping guidelines. This document resulted.

2. These guidelines apply to Industrial/Organizational psychologists providing health care services but generally not to those providing non-health care I/O services. For instance, in I/O psychology, written records may constitute the primary work product, such as a test instrument or a job analysis, while psychologists providing health care services may principally use records to document non-written services and to maintain continuity.

3. Rather than keeping their own record system, psychologists practicing in institutional settings comply with the institution's policies on record keeping, so long as they are consistent with legal and ethical standards.

It is important to highlight that professional judgment is not preempted by these guidelines; rather, the intent is to enhance it.

UNDERLYING PRINCIPLES AND PURPOSE

Psychologists maintain records for a variety of reasons, the most important of which is the benefit of the client. Records allow a psychologist to document and review the delivery of psychological services. The nature and extent of the record will vary depending upon the type and purpose of psychological services. Records can provide a history and current status in the event that a user seeks psychological services from another psychologist or mental health professional.

Conscientious record keeping may also benefit psychologists themselves, by guiding them to plan and implement an appropriate course of psychological services, to review work as a whole, and to self-monitor more precisely.

Maintenance of appropriate records may also be relevant for a variety of other institutional, financial, and legal purposes. State and federal laws in many cases require maintenance of appropriate records of certain kinds of psychological services. Adequate records may be a requirement for receipt or third party payment for psychological services.

In addition, well documented records may help protect psychologists from professional liability, if they become the subject of legal or ethical proceedings. In these circumstances, the principal issue will be the professional action of the psychologist, as reflected in part by the records.

At times, there may be conflicts between the federal, state or local laws governing record keeping, the requirements of institutional rules, and these guidelines. In these circumstances, psychologists bear in mind their obligations to conform to applicable law. When laws or institutional rules appear to conflict with the principles of these guidelines, psychologists use their education, skills and training to identify the relevant issues, and to attempt to resolve it in a way that, to the maximum extent feasible, conforms both to law and to professional practice, as required by ethical principles.

Psychologists are justifiably concerned that, at times, record keeping information will be required to be disclosed against the wishes of the psychologist or client, and may be released to persons unqualified to interpret such records. These guidelines assume that no record is free from disclosure all of the time, regardless of the wishes of the client or the psychologist.

1. Content of Records

Records include any information (including information stored in a computer) that may be used to document the nature, delivery, progress, or results of psychological services. Records can be reviewed and duplicated.

Records of psychological services minimally include (a) identifying data, (b) dates of services, (c) types of services, (d) fees, (e) any assessment, plan for intervention, consultation, summary reports, and/or testing reports and supporting data as may be appropriate, and (f) any release of information obtained.

As may be required by their jurisdiction and circumstances, psychologists maintain to a reasonable degree accurate, current, and pertinent records of psychological services. The detail is sufficient to permit planning for continuity in the event that another psychologist takes over delivery of services, including, in the event of death, disability, and retirement. In addition, psychologists maintain records in sufficient detail for regulatory and administrative review of psychological service delivery.

Records kept beyond the minimum requirements are a matter of professional judgment for the psychologist. The psychologist takes into account the nature of the psychological services, the source of the information recorded, the intended use of the records, and his or her professional obligation.

Psychologists make reasonable efforts to protect against the misuse of records. They take into account the anticipated use by the intended or anticipated recipients when preparing records. Psychologists adequately identify impressions and tentative conclusions as such.

2. Construction and Control of Records

Psychologists maintain a system that protects the confidentiality of records. They must take reasonable steps to establish and maintain the confidentiality of information arising from their own delivery of psychological services, or the services provided by others working under their supervision.

Psychologists have ultimate responsibility for the content of their records and the records of those under their supervision. Where appropriate, this requires that the psychologist oversee the design and implementation of record keeping procedures, and monitor their observance.

Psychologists maintain control over their clients' records, taking into account the policies of the institutions in which they practice. In situations where psychologists have control over their clients' records and where circumstances change such that it is no longer feasible to maintain control over such records, psychologists seek to make appropriate arrangements for transfer.

Records are organized in a manner that facilitates their use by the psychologist and other authorized persons. Psychologists strive to assure that record entries are legible. Records are to be completed in a timely manner.

Records may be maintained in a variety of media, so long as their utility, confidentiality and durability are assured.

3. Retention of Records

The psychologist is aware of relevant federal, state and local laws and regulations governing records retention. Such laws and regulations supersede the requirements of these guidelines. In the absence of such laws and regulations, complete records are maintained for a minimum of 3 years after the last contact with the client. Records, or a summary, are then maintained for an additional 12 years before disposal.[4] If the client is a minor, the record period is extended until 3 years after the age of majority.

All records, active and inactive, are maintained safely, with properly limited access, and from which timely retrieval is possible.

4. Outdated Records

Psychologists are attentive to situations in which record information has become outdated, and may therefore be invalid, particularly in circumstances where disclosure might cause adverse effects. Psychologists ensure that when disclosing such information that its outdated nature and limited utility are noted using professional judgment and complying with applicable law.

When records are to be disposed of, this is done in an appropriate manner that ensures nondisclosure (or preserves confidentiality) (see Section 3a).

5. Disclosure of Record Keeping Procedures

When appropriate, psychologists may inform their clients of the nature and extent of their record keeping procedures. This information includes a statement on the limitations of the confidentiality of the records.

---

4. These time limits follow the APA's specialty guidelines. If the specialty guidelines should be revised, a simple 7-year requirement for the retention of the complete record is preferred, which would be a more stringent requirement than any existing state statute.

Psychologists may charge a reasonable fee for review and reproduction of records. Psychologists do not withhold records that are needed for valid healthcare purposes solely because the client has not paid for prior services.

REFERENCES

American Psychological Association. (1987). *General guidelines for providers of psychological services.* Washington, DC: Author

American Psychological Association. (1992). *Ethical principles of psychologists and code of conduct.* Washington, DC: Author.

APPENDIX E

APA Guidelines for Child Custody Evaluations in Divorce Proceedings

INTRODUCTION

Decisions regarding child custody and other parenting arrangements occur within several different legal contexts, including parental divorce, guardianship, neglect or abuse proceedings, and termination of parental rights. The following guidelines were developed for psychologists conducting child custody evaluation, specifically within the context of parental divorce. These guidelines build upon the American Psychological Association's *Ethical Principles of Psychologists and Code of Conduct* (APA, 1992) and are aspirational in intent. *As guidelines, they are not intended to be either mandatory or exhaustive. The goal of the guidelines is to promote proficiency in using psychological expertise in conducting child custody evaluations.*

Parental divorce requires a restructuring of parental rights and responsibilities in relation to children. If the parents can agree to a restructuring arrangement, which they do in the overwhelming proportion (90%) of divorce custody cases (Melton, Petrila, Poythress, & Slobogin, 1987), there is no dispute for the court to decide. However, if the parents are unable to reach such an agreement, the court must help to determine the relative allocation of decision making authority and physical contact each parent will have with the child. The courts typically apply a "best interest of the child" standard in determining this restructuring of rights and responsibilities.

Psychologists provide an important service to children and the courts by providing competent, objective, impartial information in assessing the best interests of the child; by demonstrating a clear sense of direction and purpose in conducting a child custody evaluation; by performing their roles ethically; and by clarifying to all involved the nature and scope of the evaluation. The Ethics Committee of the American Psychological Association has noted that psychologists' involvement in custody disputes has at times raised questions in regard to the misuse of psychologists' influence, sometimes resulting in complaints against psychologists being brought to the attention of the APA Ethics Committee (APA Ethics Committee, 1985; Hall & Hare-Mustin, 1983; Keith-Spiegel & Koocher, 1985; Mills, 1984) and raising questions in the legal and forensic literature (Grisso, 1986; Melton et al., 1987; Mnookin, 1975; Ochroch, 1982; Okpaku, 1976; Weithorn, 1987).

Particular competencies and knowledge are required for child custody evaluations to provide adequate and appropriate psychological services to the court. Child custody evaluation in the context of parental divorce can be an extremely demanding task. For competing parents the stakes are high as they participate in a process fraught with tension and anxiety. The stress on the psychologist/evaluator can become great. Tension surrounding child custody evaluation can become further heightened when there are accusations of child abuse, neglect, and/or family violence.

Psychology is in a position to make significant contributions to child custody decisions. Psychological data and expertise, gained through a child custody evaluation, can provide an additional source of information and an additional perspective not otherwise readily available to the court on what appears to be in a child's best interest, and thus can increase the fairness of the determination the court must make.

GUIDELINES FOR CHILD CUSTODY EVALUATIONS IN DIVORCE PROCEEDINGS

I. Orienting Guidelines: Purpose of a Child Custody Evaluation

1. **The primary purpose of the evaluation is to assess the best psychological interests of the child.**
   The primary consideration in a child custody evaluation is to assess the individual and family factors that affect the best psychological interests of the child. More specific questions may be raised by the court.
2. **The child's interests and well-being are paramount.**
   In a child custody evaluation, the child's interests and well-being are paramount. Parents competing for custody, as well as others, may have legitimate concerns, but the child's best interests must prevail.
3. **The focus of the evaluation is on parenting capacity, the psychological and developmental needs of the child, and the resulting fit.**
   In considering psychological factors affecting the best interests of the child, the psychologist focuses on the parenting capacity of the prospective custodians in conjunction with the psychological and developmental needs of each involved child.

This involves (a) an assessment of the adults' capacities for parenting, including whatever knowledge, attributes, skills, and abilities, or lack thereof, are present; (b) an assessment of the psychological functioning and developmental needs of each child and of the wishes of each child where appropriate; and (c) an assessment of the functional ability of each parent to meet these needs, including an evaluation of the interaction between each adult and child.

The values of the parents relevant to parenting, ability to plan for the child's future needs, capacity to provide a stable and loving home, and any potential for inappropriate behavior or misconduct that might negatively influence the child also are considered. Psychopathology may be relevant to such an assessment, insofar as it has impact on the child or the ability to parent, but it is not the primary focus.

II. General Guidelines: Preparing for a Child Custody Evaluation

4. **The role of the psychologist is that of a professional expert who strives to maintain an objective, impartial stance.**
   The role of the psychologist is as a professional expert. The psychologist does not act as a judge, who makes the ultimate decision applying the law to all relevant evidence. Neither does the psychologist act as an advocating attorney, who strives to present his or her client's best possible case. The psychologist, in a balanced, impartial manner, informs and advises the court and the prospective custodians of the child of the relevant psychological factors pertaining to the custody issue. The psychologist should be impartial regardless of whether he or she is retained by the court or by a party to the proceedings. If either the psychologist or the client cannot accept this neutral role, the psychologist should consider withdrawing from the case. If not permitted to withdraw, in such circumstances, the psychologist acknowledges past roles and other factors that could affect impartiality.

5. **The psychologist gains specialized competence.**
   A. A psychologist contemplating performing child custody evaluations is aware that special competencies and knowledge are required for the undertaking of such evaluations. Competence in performing psychological assessments of children, adults, and families is necessary but not sufficient. Education, training, experience, and/or supervision in the areas of child and family development, child and family psychopathology, and the impact of divorce on children

help to prepare the psychologist to participate competently in child custody evaluations. The psychologist also strives to become familiar with applicable legal standards and procedures, including laws governing divorce and custody adjudications in his or her state or jurisdiction.

B.   The psychologist uses current knowledge of scientific and professional developments, consistent with accepted clinical and scientific standards, in selecting data collection methods and procedures. The *Standards for Educational and Psychological Testing* (APA, 1985) are adhered to in the use of psychological tests and other assessment tools.

C.   In the course of conducting child custody evaluations, allegations of child abuse, neglect, family violence, or other issues may occur that are not necessarily within the scope of a particular evaluator's expertise. If this is so, the psychologist seeks additional consultation, supervision, and/or specialized knowledge, training, or experience in child abuse, neglect, and family violence to address these complex issues. The psychologist is familiar with the laws of his or her state addressing child abuse, neglect, and family violence and acts accordingly.

6. **The psychologist is aware of personal and societal biases and engages in nondiscriminatory practice.**

The psychologist engaging in child custody evaluations is aware of how biases regarding age, gender, race, ethnicity, national origin, religion, sexual orientation, disability, language, culture, and socioeconomic status may interfere with an objective evaluation and recommendations. The psychologist recognizes and strives to overcome any such biases or withdraws from the evaluation.

7. **The psychologist avoids multiple relationships.**

Psychologists generally avoid conducting a child custody evaluation in a case in which the psychologist served in a therapeutic role for the child or his or her immediate family or has had other involvement that may compromise the psychologist's objectivity. This should not, however, preclude the psychologist from testifying in the case as a fact witness concerning treatment of the child. In addition, during the course of a child custody evaluation, a psychologist does not accept any of the involved participants in the evaluation as a therapy client. Therapeutic contact with the child or involved participants following a child custody evaluation is undertaken with caution.

A psychologist asked to testify regarding a therapy client who is involved in a child custody case is aware of the limitations and possible biases inherent in such a role and the possible impact on the ongoing therapeutic relationship. Although the court may require the psychologist to testify as a fact witness regarding factual information he or she became aware of in a professional relationship with a client, that psychologist should generally decline the role of an expert witness who gives a professinal opinion regarding custody and visitation issues (see Ethical Standard 7.03) unless so ordered by the court.

III. Procedural Guidelines: Conducting a Child Custody Evaluation

8. **The scope of the evaluation is determined by the evaluator, based on the nature of the referral question.**

   The scope of the custody-related evaluation is determined by the nature of the question or issue raised by the referring person or the court, or is inherent in the situation. Although comprehensive child custody evaluations generally require an evaluation of all parents or guardians and children, as well as observations of interactions between them, the scope of the assessment in a particular case may be limited to evaluating the parental capacity of one parent without attempting to compare the parents or to make recommendations. Likewise, the scope may be limited to evaluating the child. Or a psychologist may be asked to critique the assumptions and methodology of the assessment of another mental health professional. A psychologist also might serve as an expert witness in the area of child development, providing expertise to the court without relating it specifically to the parties involved in a case.

9. **The psychologist obtains informed consent from all adult participants and, as appropriate, informs child participants.**

   In undertaking child custody evaluations, the psychologist ensures that each adult participant is aware of (a) the purpose, nature, and method of the evaluation; (b) who has requested the psychologist's services; and (c) who will be paying the fees. The psychologist informs adult participants about the nature of the assessment instruments and techniques and informs those participants about the possible disposition of the data collected. The psychologist provides this information, as appropriate, to children, to the extent that they are able to understand.

10. **The psychologist informs participants about the limits of confidentiality and the disclosure of information.**

A psychologist conducting a child custody evaluation ensures that the participants, including children to the extent feasible, are aware of the limits of confidentiality characterizing the professional relationship with the psychologist. The psychologist informs participants that in consenting to the evaluation, they are consenting to disclosure of the evaluation's findings in the context of the forthcoming litigation and in any other proceedings deemed necessary by the courts. A psychologist obtains a waiver of confidentiality from all adult participants or from their authorized legal representatives.

11. **The psychologist uses multiple methods of data gathering.**

The psychologist strives to use the most appropriate methods available for addressing the questions raised in a specific child custody evaluation and generally uses multiple methods of data gathering, including, but not limited to, clinical interviews, observation, and/or psychological assessments. Important facts and opinions are documented from at least two sources whenever their reliability is questionable. The psychologist, for example, may review potentially relevant reports (e.g., from schools, health care providers, child care providers, agencies, and institutions). Psychologists may also interview extended family, friends, and other individuals on occasions when the information is likely to be useful. If information is gathered from third parties that is significant and may be used as a basis for conclusions, psychologists corroborate it by at least one other source wherever possible and appropriate and document this in the report.

12. **The psychologist neither overinterprets nor inappropriately interprets clinical or assessment data.**

The psychologist refrains from drawing conclusions not adequately supported by the data. The psychologist interprets any data from interviews or tests, as well as any questions of data reliability and validity, cautiously and conservatively, seeking convergent validity. The psychologist strives to acknowledge to the court any limitations in methods or data used.

13. **The psychologist does not give any opinion regarding the psychological functioning of any individual who has not been personally evaluated.**

This guideline, however, does not preclude the psychologist from reporting what an evaluated individual (such as the parent or child) has stated or from addressing theoretical issues or hypothetical questions, so long as the limited basis of the information is noted.

14. **Recommendations, if any, are based on what is in the best psychological interests of the child.**

   Although the profession has not reached consensus about whether psychologists ought to make recommendations about the final custody determination to the courts, psychologists are obligated to be aware of the arguments on both sides of this issue and to be able to explain the logic of their position concerning their own practice.

   If the psychologist does choose to make custody recommendations, these recommendations should be derived from sound psychological data and must be based on the best interests of the child in the particular case. Recommendations are based on articulated assumptions, data, interpretations, and inferences based upon established professional and scientific standards. Psychologists guard against relying on their own biases or unsupported beliefs in rendering opinions in particular cases.

15. **The psychologist clarifies financial arrangements.**

   Financial arrangements are clarified and agreed upon prior to commencing a child custody evaluation. When billing for a child custody evaluation, the psychologist does not misrepresent his or her services for reimbursement purposes.

16. **The psychologist maintains written records.**

   All records obtained in the process of conducting a child custody evaluation are properly maintained and filed in accord with the APA *Record Keeping Guidelines* (APA, 1993) and relevant statutory guidelines.

   All raw data and interview information are recorded with an eye toward their possible review by other psychologists or the court, where legally permitted. Upon request, appropriate reports are made available to the court.

REFERENCES

American Psychological Association. (1985). *Standards for educational and psychological testing.* Washington, DC: Author.

American Psychological Association. (1992). Ethical principles of psychologists and code of conduct. *American Psychologist, 47,* 1597–1611.

American Psychological Association. (1993). *Record keeping guidelines.* Washington, DC: Author.

American Psychological Association, Ethics Committee. (1985). *Annual report of the American Psychological Association Ethics Committee.* Washington, DC: Author.

Grisso, T. (1986). *Evaluating competencies: Forensic assessments and instruments.* New York: Plenum.

Hall, J. E., & Hare-Mustin, R. T. (1983). Sanctions and the diversity of ethical complaints against psychologists. *American Psychologist, 38,* 714–729.

Keith-Spiegel, P., & Koocher, G. P. (1985). *Ethics in psychology.* New York: Random House.

Melton, G. B., Petrila, J., Poythress, N. G., & Slobogin, C. (1987). *Psychological evaluations for the courts: A handbook for mental health professionals and lawyers.* New York: Guilford Press.

Mills, D. H. (1984). Ethics education and adjudication within psychology. *American Psychologist, 39,* 669–675.

Mnookin, R. H. (1975). Child-custody adjudication: Judicial functions in the face of indeterminacy. *Law and Contemporary Problems, 39,* 226–293.

Ochroch, R. (1982, August). *Ethical pitfalls in child custody evaluations.* Paper presented at the 90th Annual Convention of the American Psychological Association, Washington, DC.

Okpaku, S. (1976). Psychology: Impediment or aid in child custody cases? *Rugers Law Review, 29,* 1117–1153.

Weithorn, L. A. (1987). *Psychology and child custody determinations: Knowledge, roles, and expertise.* Lincoln: University of Nebraska Press.

OTHER RESOURCES

State Guidelines

Georgia Psychological Association. 1990
   Recommendations for psychologists' involvement in child custody cases. Atlanta, GA: Author.

Metropolitan Denver Interdisciplinary Committee on Child Custody. 1989
   Guidelines for child custody evaluations. Denver, CO: Author.

Nebraska Psychological Association. 1986
   Guidelines for child custody evaluations. Lincoln, NE: Author.

New Jersey State Board of Psychological Examiners. 1993
   Specialty guidelines for psychologists in custody/visitation evaluations. Newark, NJ: Author.

North Carolina Psychological Association. 1993
   Child custody guidelines. Unpublished manuscript.

Oklahoma Psychological Association. 1988
   Ethical guidelines for child custody evaluations. Oklahoma City, OK: Author.

Forensic Guidelines

Committee on Ethical Guidelines for Forensic Psychologists. 1991
Specialty guidelines for forensic psychologists. *Law and Human Behavior, 6,* 655–665.

Pertinent Literature

Ackerman, M. J., Kane, A. W. 1993
Psychological experts in divorce, personal injury and other civil actions. New York: Wiley.

American Psychological Association, Board of Ethnic Minority Affairs. 1991
Guidelines for providers of psychological services to ethnic, linguistic, and culturally diverse populations. Washington, DC: American Psychological Association.

American Psychological Association, Committee on Women in Psychology and Committee on Lesbian and Gay Concerns. 1988
Lesbian parents and their children: A resource paper for psychologists. Washington, DC: American Psychological Association.

Beaber, R. J. 1982, Fall
Custody quagmire: Some psycholegal dilemmas. *Journal of Psychiatry & Law,* 309–326.

Bennett, B. E., Bryant, B. K., VandenBos, G. R., Greenwood, A. 1990
Professional liability and risk management. Washington, DC: American Psychological Association.

Bolocofsky, D. N. 1989
Use and abuse of mental health experts in child custody determinations. *Behavioral Sciences and the Law, 7* (2), 197–213.

Bozett, F. 1987
Gay and lesbian parents. New York: Praeger.

Bray, J. H. 1993
What's the best interest of the child?: Children's adjustment issues in divorce. *The Independent Practitioner. 13,* 42–45.

Bricklin, B. 1992
Data-based tests in custody evaluations. American Journal of Family Therapy, 20, 254–265.

Cantor, D. W., Drake, E. A. 1982
Divorced parents and their children: A guide for mental health professionals. New York: Springer.

Chesler, P. 1991
Mothers on trial: The battle for children and custody. New York: Harcourt Brace Jovanovich.

Deed, M. L. 1991
Court-ordered child custody evaluations: Helping or victimizing vulnerable families. *Psychotherapy, 28,* 76–84.

Falk, P. J. 1989
   Lesbian mothers: Psychosocial assumptions in family law. *American Psychologist*, *44*, 941–947.

Gardner, R. A. 1989
   Family evaluation in child custody mediation, arbitration, and litigation. Cresskill, NJ: Creative Therapeutics.

Gardner, R. A. 1992
   The parental alienation syndrome: A guide for mental health and legal professionals. Cresskill, NJ: Creative Therapeutics.

Gardner, R. A. 1992
   True and false accusations of child abuse. Cresskill, NJ: Creative Therapeutics.

Goldstein, J., Freud, A., Solnit, A. J. 1980
   Before the best interests of the child. New York: Free Press.

Goldstein, J., Freud, A., Solnit, A. J., Goldstein, S. 1986
   In the best interests of the child. New York: Free Press.

Grisso, T. 1990
   Evolving guidelines for divorce/custody evaluations. *Family and Conciliation Courts Review*, *28*(1), 35–41.

Halon, R. L. 1990
   The comprehensive child custody evaluation. *American Journal of Forensic Psychology*, *8*(3), 19–46.

Hetherington, E. M. 1990
   Coping with family transitions: Winners, losers, and survivors. *Child Development*, *60*, 1–14.

Hetherington, E. M., Stanley-Hagen, M., Anderson, E. R. 1988
   Marital transitions: A child's perspective. *American Psychologist*, *44*, 303–312.

Johnston, J., Kline, M., Tschann, J. 1989
   Ongoing postdivorce conflict: Effects on children of joint custody and frequent access. *Journal of Orthopsychiatry*, *59*, 576–592.

Koocher, G. P., Keith-Spiegel, P. C. 1990
   Children, ethics, and the law: Professional issues and cases. Lincoln: University of Nebraska Press.

Kreindler, S. 1986
   The role of mental health professions in custody and access disputes. In R. S. Parry, E. A. Broder, E. A. G. Schmitt, E. B. Saunders, & E. Hood (Eds.), *Custody disputes: Evaluation and intervention.* New York: Free Press.

Martindale, D. A., Martindale, J. L., Broderick, J. E. 1991
   Providing expert testimony in child custody litigation. In P. A. Keller & S. R. Heyman (Eds.), *Innovations in clinical practice: A source book* (Vol. 10, pp. 481–497). Sarasota, FL: Professional Resource Exchange.

Patterson, C. J. in press
   Children of lesbian and gay parents. *Child Development.*

Pennsylvania Psychological Association, Clinical Division Task Force on Child Custody Evaluation. 1991
Roles for psychologists in child custody disputes. Unpublished manuscript.

Saunders, T. R. 1991
An overview of some psycholegal issues in child physical and sexual abuse. *Psychotherapy in Private Practice, 9*(2), 61–78.

Schutz, B. M., Dixon, E. B., Lindenberger, J. C., Ruther, N. J. 1989
Solomon's sword: A practical guide to conducting child custody evaluations. San Francisco: Jossey-Bass.

Stahly, G. B., 1989, August 9
Testimony on child abuse policy to APA Board. Paper presented at the meeting of the American Psychological Association Board of Directors, New Orleans, LA.

Thoennes, N., Tjaden, P. G. 1991
The extent, nature, and validity of sexual abuse allegations in custody/visitation disputes. *Child Abuse & Neglect, 14,* 151–163.

Wallerstein, J. S., Blakeslee, S. 1989
Second chances: Men, women, and children a decade after divorce. New York: Ticknor & Fields.

Wallerstein, J. S., Kelly, J. B. 1980
Surviving the breakup. New York: Basic Books.

Weissman, H. N. 1991
Child custody evaluations: Fair and unfair professional practices. *Behavioral Sciences and the Law, 9,* 469–476.

Weithorn, L. A., Grisso, T. 1987
Psychological evaluations in divorce custody: Problems, principles, and procedures. In L. A. Weithorn (Ed.), *Psychology and child custody determinations* (pp. 157–158). Lincoln: University of Nebraska Press.

White, S. 1990
The contamination of children's interviews. *Child Youth and Family Services Quarterly, 13*(3), 6, 17–18.

Wyer, M. M., Gaylord, S. J., Grove, E. T.
The legal context of child custody evaluations. In L. A. Weithorn (Ed.), *Psychology and child custody determinations* (pp. 3–23). Lincoln: University of Nebraska Press.

APPENDIX F

APA Guidelines for Psychological Evaluations in Child Protection Matters

COMMITTEE ON PROFESSIONAL PRACTICE AND STANDARDS[1]
BOARD OF PROFESSIONAL AFFAIRS
APPROVED BY THE COUNCIL OF REPRESENTATIVES
AMERICAN PSYCHOLOGICAL ASSOCIATION
FEBRUARY 1998

GUIDELINES FOR PSYCHOLOGICAL EVALUATIONS IN CHILD PROTECTION MATTERS

The problems of abused and neglected children are epidemic in our society (U.S. Advisory Board on Child Abuse and Neglect (ABCAN, 1995) and create issues that psychologists may be called upon to address. According to the U.S. Advisory Board on Child Abuse and Neglect (ABCAN), conservative estimates indicate that almost two thousand infants and young children die from abuse and neglect by parents or caretakers each year, or five children every day. McClain's research at the Center for Disease Control and Prevention (CDC) suggests that abuse and neglect kills 5.4 out of every 100,000 children age four and under (McClain et al., 1993; McClain, 1995).

From *Guidelines for Psychological Evaluations in Child Practice and Standards*, by the American Psychological Association Committee on Professional Practice and Standards, 1998, Washington, DC: American Psychological Association. Copyright 1998 by the American Psychological Association. Retrieved September 23, 2004, from PsychNET® Web site: http://www.apa.org/practice/childprotection.html

Suggested citation: American Psychological Association Committee on Professional Practice and Standards (1998). *Guidelines for psychological evaluations in child protection matters*. Washington, DC: American Psychological Association.

1. These guidelines were drafted by the Committee on Professional Practice and Standards (COPPS), a committee of the Board of Professional Affairs (BPA). COPPS is responsible for developing and recommending to BPA standards and guidelines for providers of psychological services and for monitoring, evaluating, and developing information regarding the scientific and professional aspects of psychological services. This paper was developed under the auspices of COPPS, reviewed by numerous APA divisions, committees, and state psychological associations, and is endorsed by the BPA. The document reflects the contributions of many psychologists. The manuscript was drafted by COPPS members Catherine Acuff, PhD; Steven Bisbing, PhD; Michael Gottlieb, PhD; Lisa Grossman, PhD; Jody Porter, PhD; Richard Reichbart, PhD; Steven Sparta, PhD; and C. Eugene Walker, PhD. COPPS also acknowledges and appreciates the support of APA staff members Billie Hinnefeld and Cherie Jones. Correspondence concerning this paper should be addressed to the Practice Directorate, American Psychological Association, 750 First Street, NE, Washington, DC 20002-4242.

According to ABCAN, fatalities are not the entire story. There are tens of thousands of victims overwhelmed by lifelong psychological trauma, thousands of traumatized siblings and family members and thousands of near-death survivors who, as adults, continue to bear physical and psychological scars. Each year, 18,000 children are left permanently disabled (Baladerian, 1991). Some may turn to crime or domestic violence or become abusers themselves (ABCAN, 1995).

When a child is at risk for harm, psychologists may become involved. Psychologists are in a position to make significant contributions to child welfare decisions. Psychological data and expertise may provide additional sources of information and a perspective not otherwise readily available to the court regarding the functioning of parties, and thus may increase the fairness of the determination by the court, state agency or other party.

As the complexity of psychological practice increases and the reciprocal involvement between psychologists and the public broadens, the need for guidelines to educate the profession, the public and the other interested parties regarding desirable professional practice in child protection matters has expanded and will probably continue to expand in the foreseeable future. Although psychologists may assume various roles and responsibilities in such proceedings, the following guidelines were developed primarily for psychologists conducting psychological evaluations in child protection matters.[2] These guidelines build upon the American Psychological Association's *Ethical Principals of Psychologists and Code of Conduct* (APA, 1992)[3] and are aspirational in intent. The term "guidelines" refers to pronouncements, statements, or declarations that suggest or recommend specific professional behavior, endeavor, or conduct for psychologists (APA, 1992a). Guidelines differ from standards in that standards are mandatory and may be accompanied by an enforcement mechanism (APA, 1993).

Thus, as guidelines, they are not intended to be either mandatory or exhaustive and may not always be applicable to legal matters. Their aspirational intent is to facilitate the continued systematic development of the profession and help to assure a high level of professional practice by psychologists. These guidelines should not be construed as definitive or intended to take precedence over the judgement of psychologists. The specific goal of the guidelines is to promote proficiency in using

---

2. For example, the role of psychologists acting as psychotherapists, conducting individual or family psychotherapy, is very different from the role of psychologists conducting formal child protection evaluations (Greenberg & Schumann, 1997).

3. At times, these guidelines refer to other APA documents such as the ethics code, test standards, and record keeping guidelines. These documents undergo periodic review and revision. Therefore, the reader is advised to refer to the most recent edition.

psychological expertise in conducting psychological evaluations in child protection matters.

Parents[4] enjoy important civil and constitutional rights regarding the care for their children. A child has a fundamental interest in being protected from abuse and neglect. Child protection laws attempt to strike a balance between these interests. Under the concept of *parens patriae*, all states have the right to intervene in cases where a child is at risk for harm. State interventions most commonly occur in three stages. In the first stage, following a report of suspected child abuse and neglect[5], an investigation occurs. In the second stage, if the findings of the investigation stage indicate the child is at sufficient risk for harm, the state may assume care and/or custody of the child and may make recommendations for rehabilitation of the parents. The third stage may occur if such rehabilitative conditions have failed to create a safe environment for the child's return to the parent(s), or if the child has been returned unsuccessfully. At this point the state may request a hearing for a final disposition. The final dispositional stage may result in involuntary termination of parental rights. Such a disposition typically requires not only a finding of abuse and/or neglect by the parent(s), but also a finding that various rehabilitative efforts with the parent(s) have failed. Psychologists are aware that the most extreme disposition—termination of parental rights—has a finality requiring both due process protection and a higher standard of proof[6] than may be used in other child protection matters.

Jurisdictions have statutory or case law requirements that diligent efforts must be made to rehabilitate the parent(s) and reunite the child with his/her parent(s). Typically, these requirements must be met prior to a disposition of parental termination. Different states may have different statutory or case law requirements. In conducting an evaluation, psychologists should be familiar with applicable law.[7]

---

4. For the purposes of this document, the term parent may also refer to a person other than a biological parent, such as, but not limited to, a grandparent, foster parent, or legal guardian. However, it should be noted that at this time, only biological and adoptive parents have a *Constitutional* right to care for their child.

5. While these guidelines usually refer to parents, it is recognized that children are potentially abused by a wide variety of individuals, including but not limited to, siblings, companions of parents, care givers or strangers.

6. The U.S. Supreme Court overturned a preponderance of evidence standard and instituted one of a clear and convincing burden of proof in order to involuntarily terminate parental rights (*Santosky v. Kramer*, 455 U.S. 745 1982).

7. There are circumstances where Federal rather than state law may apply, e.g. on military installations, Native American territories.

During any of the above-mentioned stages, psychologists may be asked to evaluate different parties for different purposes. Psychologists may act as agents of the court, the child protection agency, or may be directly retained by the parent(s). Psychologists may also be retained by a guardian *ad litem* if one has been appointed to represent the child.

As evaluators in child protection cases, psychologists are frequently asked to address such questions as:

1. How seriously has the child's psychological well-being been affected?
2. What therapeutic interventions would be recommended to assist the child?
3. Can the parent(s) be successfully treated to prevent harm to the child in the future? If so, how? If not, why not?
4. What would be the psychological effect upon the child if returned to the parent(s)?
5. What would be the psychological effect upon the child if separated from the parents or if parental rights are terminated?

In the course of their evaluations, and depending upon the specific needs of a given case, psychologists may wish to evaluate the parent(s) and/or the child individually or together. Psychologists may wish to gather information on family history, assess relevant personality functioning, assess developmental needs of the child, explore the nature and quality of the parent-child relationship and assess evidence of trauma. Psychologists are encouraged to consider specific risk factors such as substance abuse or chemical dependency, domestic violence, financial circumstance, health status of family members and the entire family context. Psychologists may wish to review information from other sources including an assessment of cultural, educational, religious and community factors.

Particular competencies and knowledge are necessary when performing psychological evaluations in child protection matters so that adequate and appropriate psychological services can be provided to the court, state agencies or other parties. For example, in cases involving physical disability, such as hearing impairments, orthopedic handicaps, etc., psychologists strive to seek consultation from experts in these areas. Particular attention should also be given to other aspects of human diversity such as, but not limited to, ethnic minority status, sexual orientation and socioeconomic status.

Conducting psychological evaluations in child protection matters can be a demanding and stressful task. The demand of such evaluations can become heightened because the issues involved may include child abuse, neglect and/or family violence. Psychologists are alert to these personal stressors, and when appropriate, undertake relevant study, training, supervision and/or consultation.

GUIDELINES FOR PSYCHOLOGICAL EVALUATIONS
IN CHILD PROTECTION MATTERS

I. Orienting Guidelines

1. *The primary purpose of the evaluation is to provide relevant, professionally sound results or opinions, in matters where a child's health and welfare may have been and/or may in the future be harmed.* The specific purposes of the evaluation will be determined by the nature of the child protection matter. In investigative proceedings, a primary purpose of the evaluation is to assist in determining whether the child's health and welfare may have been harmed. When the child is already identified as being at risk for harm, the evaluation often focuses on rehabilitation recommendations, designed to protect the child and help the family. An additional purpose of such an evaluation may be to make recommendations for interventions that promote the psychological and physical well-being of the child, and if appropriate, facilitate the reunification of the family. Psychologists appreciate the value of expediting family reunification when safe and appropriate.

In proceedings involving termination of parental rights, the primary purpose of the evaluation is to assess not only abuse or neglect by the parent(s), but also whether rehabilitation efforts for and by the parent(s) have succeeded in creating a safe environment for the child's return.

2. *In child protection cases, the child's interest and well-being are paramount.* In these cases, the state is intervening in the family based on the concern that the child's needs at that time are not being served by the family, resulting in the child's psychological or physical harm. Thus, the child's interest and well-being are paramount. In proceedings where involuntary termination of parental rights is being considered, there is an additional focus: whether the parents have been or can be successfully rehabilitated.

3. *The evaluation addresses the particular psychological and developmental needs of the child and/or parent(s) that are relevant to child protection issues such as physical abuse, sexual abuse, neglect, and/or serious emotional harm.* In considering psychological factors affecting the health and welfare of the child, psychologists may focus on parental capacities in conjunction with the psychological and developmental needs of the child. This may involve an assessment of:

(a) the adult's capacities for parenting, including those attributes, skills and abilities most relevant to abuse and/or neglect concerns;

(b) the psychological functioning and developmental needs of the child, particularly with regard to vulnerabilities and special needs of the child as well as the strength of the child's attachment to the parent(s) and the possible detrimental effects of separation from the parent(s);

(c) the current and potential functional abilities of the parent(s) to meet the needs of the child, including an evaluation of the relationship between the child and the parent(s);

(d) the need for and likelihood of success of clinical interventions for observed problems, which may include recommendations regarding treatment focus, frequency of sessions, specialized kinds of intervention, parent education and placement.

II. General Guidelines: Preparing for a Child Protection Evaluation

4. *The role of psychologists conducting evaluations is that of professional expert who strives to maintain an unbiased, objective stance.* In performing protection evaluations, psychologists do not act as judges, who make the ultimate decision by applying the law to all relevant evidence, or as advocating attorneys for any particular party. Whether retained by the court, the child protection agency, the parent(s) or the guardian ad litem for the child, psychologists should strive to be objective. Psychologists rely on scientifically and professionally derived knowledge when making judgements and describe fairly the bases for their testimonies and conclusions. If psychologists cannot accept this unbiased objective stance, they should consider withdrawing from the case. If not permitted to withdraw, psychologists disclose factors that may bias their findings and/or compromise their objectivity.

5. *The serious consequences of psychological assessment in child protection matters place a heavy burden on psychologists.* Because psychologists' professional judgements have great potential to affect the lives of others, psychologists are alert to guard against factors that might lead to misuse of their findings. For example, in an initial dispositional hearing, psychologists' findings may be used to separate the child from her/his parent(s). In a final dispositional hearing, the psychologists' findings may be a factor in the decision to terminate parental rights. The gravity and potential permanence of this consequence underscore the importance for psychologists to reasonably insure the objectivity of the assessment procedure and findings.

6. *Psychologists gain specialized competence.*

A. Psychologists who conduct evaluations in child protection matters are aware that special competencies and knowledge may be necessary for the undertaking of such evaluations. Competence in performing psychological assessments of children, adults and families is necessary but not sufficient. Education, training, experience and/or supervision in the areas of forensic practice, child and family development, child and family psychopathology, the impact of separation on the child, the nature of various types of child abuse and the role of human differences[8] may help to prepare psychologists to participate competently in psychological evaluations in child protection matters.

B. Psychologists make reasonable effort to use current knowledge of scholarly and professional developments, consistent with generally accepted clinical and scientific practice, in selecting evaluation methods and procedures. The current *Standards for Educational and Psychological Testing* (APA, 1985) are adhered to in the use of psychological tests and other assessment tools.

C. Psychologists also strive to become familiar with applicable legal and regulatory standards and procedures, including state and Federal laws governing child protection issues. These may include laws and regulations addressing child abuse, neglect and termination of parental rights.

7. *Psychologists are aware of personal and societal biases and engage in nondiscriminatory practice.* Psychologists engaging in psychological evaluations in child protection matters are aware of how biases regarding age, gender, race, ethnicity, national origin, religion, sexual orientation, disability, language, culture and socioeconomic status may interfere with an objective evaluation and recommendations. Psychologists recognize and strive to overcome any such biases or withdraw from the evaluation. When interpreting evaluation results, psychologists strive to be aware that there are diverse cultural and community methods of child rearing, and consider these in the context of the existing state and Federal[9] laws. Also, psychologists should use, whenever available, tests and norms based on populations similar to those evaluated.

8. *Psychologists avoid multiple relationships.* In conducting psychological evaluations in child protective matters, psychologists are aware that there may be a need to avoid confusion about role boundaries. Psychologists generally do not conduct psychological evaluations in child protection matters in which they serve in a therapeutic role for the child or the immediate family or have had other involvement that may compromise their objectivity. This does not, however, preclude psychologists from testifying in cases as fact or expert witnesses concerning therapeutic treatment of the children, parents or families. In addition, during the course of a psychological evaluation in child protection matters, psychologists do not accept any of the participants involved in the evaluation as therapy clients. Therapeutic contact with the child or involved participants following a child protection evaluation is discouraged and when done, is undertaken with caution.

---

8. "Human differences" refers to differences of age, gender, race, ethnicity, national origin, religion, sexual orientation, disability, language and/or socio-economic status.

9. For example, see Indian Child Welfare Act of 1978.

Psychologists asked to testify regarding a therapy client who is involved in a child protection case are aware of the limitations and possible biases inherent in such a role and the possible impact on ongoing therapeutic relationships. Although the court may order psychologists to testify as fact or expert witnesses regarding information they became aware of in a professional relationship with a client, psychologists must appreciate the difference in roles and methods between being psychotherapists and being child protection evaluators.

III. Procedural Guidelines: Conducting a Psychological Evaluation in Child Protection Matters

In child protection matters, there are many different situations representing a wide variety of legal and/or ethical considerations. The appropriate procedure in one case may not be appropriate in another. Psychologists should be alert to applicable laws which govern the evaluation, as well as applicable sections of the *Ethical Principles and Code of Conduct for Psychologists*, particularly those sections dealing with confidentiality. In addition, psychologists appreciate the need for timeliness in child protection matters (e.g., response to evaluation referral, scheduling appointments, completion of report).

9. Based on the nature of the referral questions, the scope of the evaluation is determined by the evaluator. The scope of the protection-related evaluation is determined by the nature of the questions or issues raised by the referring agency, person or court, or is inherent in the situation. In child protection matters, psychologists are frequently asked to address parenting deficits. Consequently, psychologists are often asked to propose a rehabilitation plan for the parent(s) or to discuss why prior rehabilitation attempts have failed. The scope and methods of the assessment should be based upon consideration of the referral questions and the appropriate methods by which to evaluate them. Sometimes the evaluation is limited to one parent without attempting to compare the parents. Likewise, the scope may be limited to evaluating the child. At other times, psychologists may be asked to critique the assumptions and methodology of another mental health professional's assessment. Psychologists may also identify relevant issues not anticipated in the referral questions that could enlarge the scope of the evaluation. Also, psychologists might serve as pure expert witnesses in such areas as child development or social psychology, providing expertise to the court without relating it specifically to the parties involved in a particular case.

10. Psychologists performing psychological evaluations in child protection matters obtain appropriate informed consent from all adult participants, and as appropriate, inform the child participant. Psychologists need to be particularly sensitive to informed consent issues. Psychological evaluations in child protection matters are often performed at the request of an agency, by order of a court or at the request of another individual, such as an attorney. Due to the nature of child protection matters, the complexity of the legal issues involved and the potential serious consequences of the evaluation, psychologists need to be particularly sensitive to informed consent issues. Efforts toward obtaining informed consent should make clear to the participant the nature of the evaluation, its purpose, to whom the results will be provided and the role of the psychologist in relation to the referring party (see APA Ethical Principles of Psychologists and Code of Conduct, Standards 1.21 and 1.216 re: third party request for services). This information should be provided in language understandable to the recipient.

Because participants in this type of evaluation may feel compelled to cooperate, psychologists should attempt to obtain confirmation of the participants' understanding of and agreement to the evaluation, including its purposes and its implications, prior to the initiation of the evaluation. The *Ethical Principles of Psychologists and Code of Conduct* requires appropriate informed consent and many state laws require written consent. Should there be refusal to give consent, it may be advisable to refer the individual back to his/her own attorney or seek the guidance of the court or referring agency before proceeding. The purpose of the evaluation, the results and where and to whom the results are distributed are all determined by the individual characteristics of the case as well as by legal requirements and agency regulations.

The *Ethical Principles of Psychologists and Code of Conduct* suggests that psychologists provide information to the child as appropriate, to the extent that the child is able to understand. Psychologists explain to the child the nature of the evaluation procedures. Psychologists attempt to make it clear to the child that his/her safety is the primary interest and because of that interest, the information will be shared with others. Psychologists allow time for questions by the child and answer them in a developmentally and culturally appropriate fashion.

11. Psychologists inform participants about the disclosure of information and the limits of confidentiality. Psychologists conducting a psychological evaluation in child protection matters ensure that the participants, including the child (to the extent feasible), are aware of the limits of confidentiality for the evaluation results. Psychologists recognize that evaluation results could be sought by a child protection investigation agency, the court, a guardian *ad litem* for the child or an attorney for either parent. When an evaluation is court-ordered, there may be special considerations regarding the limits of confidentiality and the disclosure of information. In such cases, psychologists will seek to reconcile the APA ethical standards with fulfilling the demands of the court. A clear explanation of the nature of the evaluation and to whom it will be released takes place.

12. Psychologists use multiple methods of data gathering. Psychologists strive to use the most appropriate methods available for addressing the questions raised in a specific child protection evaluation. Psychologists generally use multiple methods of data gathering, including but not limited to, clinical interviews, observation and/or psychological testing that are sufficient to provide appropriate substantiation for their findings. Psychologists may review relevant reports (e.g. from child protection agencies, social service providers, law enforcement agencies, health care providers, child care providers, schools and institutions). In evaluating parental capacity to care for a particular child or the child-parent interaction, psychologists make efforts to observe the child together with the parent and recognize the value of these observations occurring in natural settings. This may not always be possible, for example, in cases where the safety of the child is in jeopardy or parental contact with the child has been prohibited by the court. Psychologists may also attempt to interview extended family members and other individuals when appropriate (e.g., caretakers, grandparents and teachers). If information gathered from a third party is used as a basis for conclusions, psychologists attempt to corroborate it from at least one other source wherever possible. The corroboration should be documented in the report.

13. *Psychologists neither over-interpret nor inappropriately interpret clinical or assessment data.* Psychologists refrain from drawing conclusions not adequately supported by the data. Psychologists interpret any data from interviews or tests cautiously and conservatively, strive to be knowledgeable about cultural norms and present findings in a form understandable to the recipient. Psychologists strive to acknowledge to the court any limitations in methods or data used. In addition, psychologists are aware that in compelled evaluations the situation may lend itself to defensiveness by the participant, given the potentially serious consequences of an adverse finding. Consequently, the situational determinants should be borne in mind when interpreting test findings.

14. *Psychologists conducting a psychological evaluation in child protection matters provide an opinion regarding the psychological functioning of an individual only after conducting an evaluation of the individual adequate to support their statements or conclusions.* This guideline does not preclude psychologists from reporting what an individual has stated or from addressing theoretical issues or hypothetical questions, so long as any limitations of the basis of such information are noted. When, despite reasonable effort, a personal evaluation of an individual is not feasible, psychologists report this and appropriately limit the nature and extent of their conclusions or recommendations.

15. *Recommendations, if offered, are based on whether the child's health and welfare have been and/or may be seriously harmed.* When conducting a psychological evaluation in child protection matters, psychologists may choose to make a variety of recommendations, including but not limited to, psychological treatment for the child, psychological treatment for the parent(s), and/or suggestions for parental rehabilitation that would help create a safe environment for the child.

If recommendations are made, the primary focus must be the child's health and welfare. Recommendations are based on sound psychological data, such as clinical data, interpretations and inferences founded on generally accepted psychological theory and practice. Particular attention may be given to outcomes research on interventions with abusive families. Psychologists strive to disclose relevant information and clinical data pertaining to the issues being evaluated while maintaining an awareness of the limitations in predicting future violent behavior. They also explain the reasoning behind their conclusions.

The profession has not reached consensus about whether making dispositional recommendations in child protection evaluations is within the purview of psychological practice. However, if psychologists choose to make dispositional recommendations, the recommendations should be derived from sound psychological data and must be based on considerations of the child's health and welfare in the particular case.

16. *Psychologists clarify financial arrangements.* Financial arrangements are clarified and agreed upon prior to conducting a child protection evaluation. When billing for an evaluation, psychologists accurately describe the services provided for reimbursement purposes.

17. *Psychologists maintain appropriate records.* All data obtained in the process of conducting a child protection evaluation are properly maintained and stored in accordance with the APA *Record Keeping Guidelines* (APA, 1993). All records, including raw data and interview information, are recorded with the understanding that they may be reviewed by other psychologists, the court or the client.

GLOSSARY OF TERMS

The following definitions are written generally and are intended solely to familiarize readers to some common terms used in child protection matters. These are not to be construed as uniformly accepted legal definitions or applied in specific legal matters. Readers wishing to use these terms as part of their evaluations are encouraged to confer with a licensed attorney in the state in which they are providing the evaluation.[10]

Abuse, emotional: also referred to as 'psychological maltreatment' generally defined as a repeated pattern of behavior that conveys to children that they are worthless, unwanted or only of value in meeting another's needs; may include serious threats of physical or psychological violence.

---

[10]Many definitions contained in the glossary have been taken from: The National Center on Child Abuse and Neglect (1995). *Working with Courts in Child Protection.* U.S. Dept. of Health and Human Services.

Abuse, physical: generally defined as the suffering by a child, or sub-stantial risk that a child will imminently suffer, a physical harm, inflicted non-accidentally upon him/her by his/her parents or caretaker.

Abuse, sexual (child): generally defined as contacts between a child and an adult or other person significantly older or in a position of power or control over the child, where the child is being used for sexual stimulation of the adult or other person.

Abuse, neglect: (see Neglect)

Burden of proof: an obligation by a party (e.g., plaintiff in civil cases, the state in a termination of parental rights matter) to demonstrate to the court that the weight of the evidence in a legal action favors his/her side, position or argument.

Beyond a reasonable doubt: highest standard of proof used in cases where the loss of liberty interests are at stake (e.g., incarceration or loss of life). Generally defined as the highest degree of support or level of certainty (90–95% chance).

Child Protective Services (CPS): The social service agency (in most states) designated to receive reports, investigate and provide rehabilitation services to children and families with problems of child maltreatment. Fre-quently, this agency is located within a large public entity, such as a depart-ment of social services or human services.

Clear and convincing: intermediate standard of proof used in cases when significant liberty interests are at stake (e.g., loss of parental rights, civil commitment). Generally defined as a high degree of support or level of cer-tainty (75% chance).

Disposition hearing: held by the Juvenile/Family Court to determine the disposition of children after cases have been adjudicated, includes deter-minations regarding placement of the child in out-of-home care when nec-essary and services needed by the children and family to reduce the risks and address the effects of maltreatment.

Evidence: any form of proof presented by a party for the purpose of sup-porting its factual allegation or arguments before the court.

Expert witness: an individual who by reason of education or specialized experience possesses superior knowledge respecting a subject about which per-sons having no particular training are incapable of forming an accurate opin-ion or deducing correct conclusions. A witness who has been qualified as an expert will be allowed (through his/her answers to questions posted) to assist the jury in understanding complicated and technical subjects not within the understanding of the average lay person. Experts are also allowed to provide testimony based on "hypothetical" scenarios or information/opinions which are not specifically related to the parties in particular legal action.

Fact witness: generally defined as an individual who by being present, personally sees or perceives a thing; a beholder, spectator or eyewitness. One who testifies to what he/she has seen, heard, or otherwise observed regarding a circumstance, event or occurrence as it actually took place; a physical object or appearance, as it usually exists or existed. Fact witnesses are generally not allowed to offer opinion, address issues that they do not have personal knowledge of or respond to hypothetical situations.

Family/Juvenile court: courts specifically established to hear cases concerning minors and related domestic matters such as child abuse, neglect, child support, determination of paternity, termination of parental rights, juvenile delinquency, and family domestic offenses.

Family preservation/reunification: the philosophical belief of social service agencies, established in law and policy, that children and families should be maintained together if the safety of the children can be ensured.

Guardian *ad litem*: generally defined as an adult appointed by the court to represent and make decisions for someone (such as a minor) legally incapable of doing so on his/her own in a civil legal proceeding. The guardian *ad litem* can be any adult with a demonstrated interest.

Guardianship: legal right given to a person to be responsible for the necessities (e.g., food, shelter, health care) of another person legally deemed incapable of providing these necessities for him/herself.

Maltreatment: generally defined as actions that are abusive, neglectful, or otherwise threatening to a child's welfare. Commonly used as a general term for child abuse and neglect.

Neglect: generally defined as an act of omission, specifically the failure of a parent or other person legally responsible for a child's welfare to provide for the child's basic needs and proper level of care with respect to food, shelter, hygiene, medical attention or supervision.

a. emotional: generally defined as the passive or passive-aggressive inattention to a child's emotional needs, nurturing or emotional well-being. Also referred to as psychological unavailability to a child.

b. physical: generally defined as a child suffering, or in substantial risk of imminently suffering, physical harm causing disfigurement, impairment of bodily functioning, or other serious physical injury as a result of conditions created by a parent or other person legally responsible for the child's welfare, or by the failure of a parent or person legally responsible for the child's welfare to adequately supervise or protect him/her.

Out-of-home care: child care, foster care, or residential care provided by persons, organizations, and institutions to children who are placed outside of their families, usually under the jurisdiction of Juvenile/Family Court.

***Parens patriae*:** refers traditionally to the role of state as sovereign and guardian of persons under legal disability. It is a concept of standing utilized to protect those quasi-sovereign interests such as health, comfort and welfare of the people, interstate water rights, general economy of the state, etc. Literally means "parent of the country."

Petition: a formal written application to the court requesting judicial action on a particular matter.

Preponderance of evidence: lowest of the three standards of proof, and applied in most civil actions; generally defined as "probable" degree of certainty (e.g., "more likely than not" or 51% chance).

Protection order: may be ordered by the judge to restrain or control the conduct of the alleged maltreating adult or any other person who might harm the child or interfere with the disposition.

Review hearing: held by the Juvenile/Family Court to review dispositions (usually every 6 months) and to determine the need to maintain placement in out-of-home care and/or court jurisdiction of a child. Every state requires state courts, agency panels, or citizen review boards to hold periodic reviews to reevaluate the child's circumstances if s/he has been placed in out-of-home care. Federal law requires, as a condition of Federal funding eligibility, that a review hearing be held within at least 18 months from disposition, and continue to be held at regular intervals to determine the ultimate resolution of the case (i.e., whether the child will be returned home, continued in out-of-home care for a specified period, placed for adoption, or continued in long-term foster care).

Termination of parental rights hearing: formal judicial proceeding where the legal rights and responsibility for a child are permanently or indefinitely severed and no longer legally recognized and where the state assumes legal responsibility for the care and welfare of the child.

REFERENCES

American Psychological Association. (1985). *Standards for educational and psychological testing.* Washington, DC: Author.

American Psychological Association. (1992). Ethical principles of psychologists and code of conduct. *American Psychologist, 47,* 1597–1611.

American Psychological Association. (1993). Record keeping guidelines. *American Psychologist, 48,* 984–986.

Baladerian, N. J. (1991). Abuse causes disabilities. *Disability and the Family.* Culver City, CA: SPECTRUM Institute.

Greenberg, S., & Shuman, D. W. (1997). Irreconcilable conflict between therapeutic and forensic roles. *Professional Psychology: Research and Practice, 28,* 50–57.

McClain, P. (1995). [Centers for Disease Control and Prevention] (Anne Marie Finn). Atlanta, GA.

McClain, P., Sacks, J., & Frohlke, R. (1993). Estimates of fatal child abuse and neglect, United States, 1979–1988. *Pediatrics, 91,* 338–343.

Santosky v. Kramer, 455 U.S. 745 (1982).

U.S. Advisory Board on Child Abuse and Neglect. (1995). *A national shame: Fatal child abuse and neglect in the U.S.* (5th Report). Washington, DC: U.S. Government Printing Office.

BIBLIOGRAPHY

American Psychological Association. (1985). *Standards for educational and psychological testing.* Washington, DC: Author.

American Psychological Association. (1992). Ethical principles of psychologists and code of conduct. *American Psychologist, 47,* 1597–1611.

American Psychological Association. (1993). Record keeping guidelines. *American Psychologist, 48,* 984–986.

Butcher, J. N., & Pope, K. S. (1993). Seven issues in conducting forensic assessments: Ethical responsibilities in light of new standards and new tests. *Ethics and Behavior, 3,* 267–288.

Briere, J. (Ed.). (1991). Treating victims of child sexual abuse. *New Directions for Mental Health Services series, 51.*

Ceci, S. (1995). *Jeopardy in the courtroom.* Washington, DC: American Psychological Association.

Committee on Ethical Guidelines for Forensic Psychologists. (1991). Specialty guidelines for forensic psychologists. *Law and Human Behavior, 6,* 655–665.

Conte, J. R. (1986). *A look at child sexual abuse.* Chicago: National Committee for Prevention of Child Abuse.

Coulborn-Faller, K. (1988). *Child sexual abuse: An Interdisciplinary manual for diagnosis case management and treatment.* New York: Columbia University Press.

Daro, D. H., & McCurdy, K. (1993). *Current trends in child abuse reporting and fatalities: The results of the 1993 annual fifty state survey.* Chicago: National Committee to Prevent Child Abuse.

Doris, J. (Ed.). (1991). *The suggestibility of children's recollection: Implications for eye witness testimony.* Washington, DC: American Psychological Association.

English, D. J. (1989). *Risk assessment: Issues and concerns.* Denver, CO: American Humane Society.

Faller, K. C., Everson, M. D. (Eds.). (1996). Child interviewing, Part I. *Child Maltreatment 1,* 83–175.

Faller, K. C., Everson, M. D. (Eds.). (1996). Child interviewing, Part II. *Child Maltreatment 1,* 187–212.

Friedreich, W. N. (1990). *Psychotherapy of sexually abused children and their families.* New York: Norton.

Goldstein, J., Frend A., Solnit A. J., & Goldstein, S. (1986). *In the best interests of the child.* New York: Free Press.

Grisso, T. (1986). *Evaluating competencies: Forensic assessments and instruments.* New York: Plenum.

Hagans, K. B., & Case, J. (1988). *When your child has been molested: A parent's guide to healing and recovery.* New York: Lexington Books.

Hass, L. J. (1993). Competence and quality in the performance of forensic psychologists. *Ethics and Behavior, 3,* 251–266.

Helfar, R. E., & Kempe, R. S. (Eds.). (1987). *The battered child* (4th ed.). Chicago: University of Chicago Press.

Kalichman, S. C. (1993). *Mandated reporting of suspected child abuse: Ethics, law and policy.* Washington, DC: American Psychological Association.

Kalichman, S. C., Craig, M. E., & Follingstad, D. R. (1988). Factors influencing the reporting of father-child sexual abuse; study of licensed practicing psychologists. *Professional Psychology, 20,* 84–89.

Koocher, G. P., & Keith-Spiegel, P. C. (1990). *Children ethics, and the law: Professional issues and cases.* Lincoln: University of Nebraska Press.

Kuehnle, K. (1996). *Assessing allegations of child sexual abuse.* Sarasota, FL: Professional Resource Press.

Melton, G. B., Petrila, J., Poythress, N. G., & Slobogin, C. (1997). *Psychological evaluations for the courts: A handbook for mental health professionals and lawyers.* New York: Guilford Press.

Myers, J. E. B. (1997). *Evidence in child abuse and neglect cases* (Vols. 1–2). New York: John Wiley & Sons.

Reiser, M. (1991). Recantation of child sexual abuse cases. *Child Welfare, 70,* 611–623.

Roane, T. (1992). Male victims of sexual abuse: A case review within a child protective team. *Child Welfare, 71,* 231–241.

Sales, B., & Simon, L. (1993). Institutional constraints on the ethics of expert testimony. *Ethics and Behavior, 3,* 231–249.

Santosky v. Kramer, 102 S. Ct. 1388 (1982).

Saunders, T. R. (1991). An overview of some psychological issues in child physical and sexual abuse. *Psychotherapy in Private Practice, 9(2),* 61–78.

U.S. Advisory Board on Child Abuse and Neglect. (1995). *A National Shame: Fatal Child Abuse and Neglect in the U.S.* (5th Report). Washington, DC: U.S. Government Printing Office.

Walker, C. E., Bonner, B. L., & Kaufman, K. L. (1988). *The physically and sexually abused child: Evaluation and treatment.* Elmsford, NY: Pergamon Press.

Watson, H., & Levine, M. (1989). Psychotherapy and mandated reporting of child abuse. *American Journal of Orthopsychiatry, 59,* 246–255.

Weissman, H. (1991). Forensic psychological examination of the child witness in cases of alleged sexual abuse. *American Journal of Orthopsychiatry, G1, 1,* 48–58.

White, S. (1990). The contamination of children's interviews. *Child Youth and Family Service Quarterly 13(3)* 6, 17–18.

Willis, D. J., Bagwell, W., Broyhill, G. C., & Campbell, M. M. (1991). *Child abuse: Abstracts of the psychological and behavioral literature: Vol. 2, 1986–1990.* Washington, DC: American Psychological Association.

Willis, D. J., Bagwell, W. & Campbell, M. M. (1991). *Child abuse: Abstracts of the psychological and behavioral literature: Vol. 1, 1967–1985.* Washington, DC: American Psychological Association.

RELATED JOURNALS

Child Abuse and Neglect: The International Journal
Child Welfare
Journal of Child Sexual Abuse
Journal of Family Violence
Journal of Interpersonal Violence
Child Maltreatment: Journal of the American
Professional Society of the Abuse of Children

ADDITIONAL RESOURCES

American Academy of Pediatrics
141 Northwest Point Boulevard
P.O. Box 927
Elk Grove, IL 60009-0927
(800) 433-9016

American Bar Association Center on Children and the Law
1800 M Street, NW, Suite 200
Washington, DC 20036
(202) 331-2250

American Professional Society on the Abuse of Children
407 South Dearborn, Suite 1300
Chicago, IL 60605
(312) 554-0166

Child Welfare League of America
440 First Street, NE, Suite 310
Washington, DC 20001-2085
(202) 638-2952

Clearinghouse on Child Abuse and Neglect Information
P.O. Box 1182
Washington, DC 20013
(703) 385-7565

Family Violence and Sexual Assault Institute
1310 Clinic Drive
Tyler, TX 75701
(903) 534-5100

National Association of Counsel for Children
1205 Oneida Street
Denver, CO 80220
(303) 321-3963

National Clearinghouse on Child Abuse and Neglect Information
U.S. Department of Health and Human Services
P.O. Box 1182
Washington, DC 20013
(800) FYI-3366

National Committee to Prevent Child Abuse
332 S. Michigan Avenue, Suite 1600
Chicago, IL 60604-4357
(312) 663-3520

National Resource Center on Child Sexual Abuse
Information Service
2204 Whitesburg Drive, Suite 200
Huntsville, AL 35801
(800) 543-7006

APPENDIX G

APA Guidelines for Psychological Practice With Older Adults

AMERICAN PSYCHOLOGICAL ASSOCIATION

TABLE OF CONTENTS

Guideline 1. Psychologists are encouraged to work with older adults within their scope of competence, and to seek consultation or make appropriate referrals when indicated.

Guideline 2. Psychologists are encouraged to recognize how their attitudes and beliefs about aging and about older individuals may be relevant to their assessment and treatment of older adults, and to seek consultation or further education about these issues when indicated.

Author's Note. This document was approved as policy of the American Psychological Association (APA) by the APA Council of Representatives in August, 2003. From *APA Guidelines for Psychological Practice With Older Adults,* by the American Psychological Association, 2003, Washington, DC: American Psychological Association. Copyright 2003 by the American Psychological Association. Retrieved September 23, 2004, from PsychNET® Web site: http://www.apa.org/practice/Guidelines_for_Psychological_Practice_with_Older_Adults.pdf

These guidelines were developed by the Division 12-Section II (Section on Clinical Geropschology) and Division 20 (Division of Adult Development and Aging) Interdivisional Task Force on Practice in Clinical Geropsychology (TF). The TF cochairs were George Niederehe, PhD (National Institute of Mental Health), and Linda Teri, PhD (University of Washington). The TF members included Michael Duffy, PhD (Texas A&M University); Barry Edelstein, PhD (West Virginia University); Dolores Gallagher-Thompson, PhD (Stanford University School of Medicine); Margaret Gatz, PhD (University of Southern California); Paula Hartman-Stein, PhD (independent practice, Kent, OH); Gregory Hinrichsen, PhD (The Zucker Hillside Hospital, North Shore-Long Island Jewish Health System, Glen Oaks, NY); Asenath LaRue, PhD (independent practice, Richland Center, WI); Peter Lichtenberg, PhD (Wayne State University); and George Taylor, PhD (independent practice, Atlanta, GA). Additional input on the guidelines was provided by members of the APA Committee on Aging during 2002 and 2003, including John Cavanaugh, PhD, Bob Knight, PhD, Martita Lopez, PhD, Leonard Poon, PhD, Forrest Scogin, PhD, Beth Hudnall Stamm, PhD, and Antonette Zeiss, PhD.

223

General Knowledge About Adult Development, Aging, and Older Adults

Guideline 3. Psychologists strive to gain knowledge about theory and research in aging.

Guideline 4. Psychologists strive to be aware of the social/psychological dynamics of the aging process.

Guideline 5. Psychologists strive to understand diversity in the aging process, particularly how sociocultural factors such as gender, ethnicity, socioeconomic status, sexual orientation, disability status, and urban/rural residence may influence the experience and expression of health and of psychological problems in later life.

Guideline 6. Psychologists strive to be familiar with current information about biological and health-related aspects of aging.

Clinical Issues

Guideline 7. Psychologists strive to be familiar with current knowledge about cognitive changes in older adults.

Guideline 8. Psychologists strive to understand problems in daily living among older adults.

Guideline 9. Psychologists strive to be knowledgeable about psychopathology within the aging population and cognizant of the prevalence and nature of that psychopathology when providing services to older adults.

Assessment

Guideline 10. Psychologists strive to be familiar with the theory, research, and practice of various methods of assessment with older

The TF wishes to extend thanks to the working group established by the Council of Representatives to offer recommendations about an earlier version of these guidelines for their thorough and thoughtful review and editorial suggestions. In addition to TF members Taylor (working group convener) and Niederehe, the working group included Lisa Grossman, PhD, JD; Satoru Izutsu, PhD; Arthur Kovacs, PhD; Neil Massoth, PhD; Janet Matthews, PhD; Katherine Nordal, PhD (Board of Directors); and Ronald Rozensky, PhD. APA staff liaisons for the working group included Geoffrey Reed, PhD (APA Assistant Executive Director for Professional Development), and Jayne Lux. The TF also wishes to acknowledge and thank the many other APA colleagues who have offered consultation and comments on earlier drafts of these guidelines, Sarah Jordan (APA Office of Divisional Services) for staff liaison assistance, the Board of Directors of Division 12-Section II and the Executive Committee of Division 20 for support throughout the process of guideline development, and these Boards and those of Division 12 (Society of Clinical Psychology) and Division 17 (Society of Counseling Psychology) for endorsing prior versions of the guidelines document.

Correspondence regarding this document should be directed to the Practice Directorate, American Psychological Association, 750 First Street, NE, Washington, DC 20002-4242.

This document is scheduled to expire as APA policy by August 31, 2010. After this date, users are encouraged to contact the APA Practice Directorate to confirm that this document remains in effect.

adults, and knowledgeable of assessment instruments that are psychometrically suitable for use with them.

Guideline 11. Psychologists strive to understand the problems of using assessment instruments created for younger individuals when assessing older adults, and to develop skill in tailoring assessments to accommodate older adults' specific characteristics and contexts.

Guideline 12. Psychologists strive to develop skill at recognizing cognitive changes in older adults, and in conducting and interpreting cognitive screening and functional ability evaluations.

Intervention, Consultation and Other Service Provision

Guideline 13. Psychologists strive to be familiar with the theory, research, and practice of various methods of intervention with older adults, particularly with current research evidence about their efficacy with this age group.

Guideline 14. Psychologists strive to be familiar with and develop skill in applying specific psychotherapeutic interventions and environmental modifications with older adults and their families, including adapting interventions for use with this age group.

Guideline 15. Psychologists strive to understand the issues pertaining to the provision of services in the specific settings in which older adults are typically located or encountered.

Guideline 16. Psychologists strive to recognize issues related to the provision of prevention and health promotion services with older adults.

Guideline 17. Psychologists strive to understand issues pertaining to the provision of consultation services in assisting older adults.

Guideline 18. In working with older adults, psychologists are encouraged to understand the importance of interfacing with other disciplines, and to make referrals to other disciplines and/or to work with them in collaborative teams and across a range of sites, as appropriate.

Guideline 19. Psychologists strive to understand the special ethical and/or legal issues entailed in providing services to older adults.

Education

Guideline 20. Psychologists are encouraged to increase their knowledge, understanding and skills with respect to working with older adults through continuing education, training, supervision and consultation.

References

GUIDELINES FOR PSYCHOLOGICAL PRACTICE
WITH OLDER ADULTS

In recent years, professional psychology practice with older adults has been increasing, due both to the changing demography of our population and changes in service settings and market forces. For instance, federal legislation contained in the 1987 Omnibus Budget and Reconciliation Act (OBRA, 1987) has led to increased accountability for some mental health issues. Psychologists' inclusion in Medicare has expanded reimbursement opportunities. For example, whereas in 1986 psychological practice in nursing homes was rare, by 1996 as many as a dozen large companies and numerous smaller organizations were providing psychological services in nursing homes. As well, clinicians and researchers have made impressive strides toward identifying the unique aspects of knowledge that facilitate the accurate psychological assessment and effective treatment of older adults, and the psychological literature in this area has been burgeoning. Unquestionably, the demand for psychologists with a substantial understanding of the clinical issues pertaining to older adults will expand in future years as the older population grows and service demands increase, and as cohorts of middle-aged and younger individuals who are attuned to psychological services move into old age (Gatz & Finkel, 1995; Koenig, George, & Schneider, 1994).

General practice psychologists as well as those specifically identified as geropsychologists are interested in this area of practice. Relatively few psychologists, however, have received formal training in the psychology of aging as part of their generic training in psychology. A recent survey of APA-member practicing psychologists indicated that the vast majority (69%) conduct some clinical work with older adults, at least occasionally, but that fewer than 30% report having had any graduate coursework in geropsychology, and fewer than 20% any supervised practicum or internship experience with older adults (Qualls, Segal, Norman, Niederehe, & Gallagher-Thompson, 2002). Many psychologists may be reluctant to work with older adults, feeling ill prepared in knowledge and skills. In the above practitioner survey (Qualls et al., 2002), a high proportion of the respondents (58%) reported that they needed further training as a basis for their work with older adults, and 70% said that they were interested in attending specialized education programs in clinical geropsychology. In other research, over half of the psychology externs and interns studied desired further education and training in this area, and 90% expressed interest in providing clinical services to older adults (Hinrichsen, 2000). As another indication of the perceived need for psychologists to acquire increased preparation for this area of practice, recent legislation in California has made graduate or continuing education coursework in aging and long-term care a prerequisite for psychology licensure (California State Senate Bill 953, 2002). In addition, the 2003 Congressional appropriation for the Graduate Psychology Education (GPE) program in the Health

Resources and Services Administration's Bureau of Health Professions included funding specifically designated as support for training in Geropsychology as a public health shortage area ("Congress Triples Funding," 2003).

The present document is intended to assist psychologists in evaluating their own readiness for working clinically with older adults, and in seeking and using appropriate education and training to increase their knowledge, skills and experience relevant to this area of practice, when desired and appropriate. The specific goals of these guidelines are to provide practitioners with (a) a frame of reference for engaging in clinical work with older adults and (b) basic information and further references in the areas of attitudes, general aspects of aging, clinical issues, assessment, intervention, consultation, and continuing education and training relative to work with older adults. These guidelines build on, and are intended to be entirely consistent with, the APA's (2002) "Ethical Principles of Psychologists and Code of Conduct" and other APA policies.

The term *guidelines* refers to statements that suggest or recommend specific professional behavior, endeavors, or conduct for psychologists. Guidelines differ from "standards" in that standards are mandatory and may be accompanied by an enforcement mechanism. Thus, these guidelines are aspirational in intent. They are intended to facilitate the continued systematic development of the profession and to help assure a high level of professional practice by psychologists in their work with older adults and their families. These guidelines are not intended to be mandatory or exhaustive and may not be applicable to every professional and clinical situation. They are not definitive and are not intended to take precedence over the judgment of psychologists. Federal and state statutes, when applicable, also supersede these guidelines. These guidelines are intended for use by psychologists who work clinically with older adults. Because of increasing service needs, it is hoped that psychologists in general practice will work clinically with older adults and continue to seek education in support of their practice skills.

The guidelines are intended to assist psychologists and facilitate their work with older adults, rather than to restrict or exclude any psychologist from practicing in this area or to require specialized certification for this work. The guidelines also recognize that some psychologists will specialize in working clinically with older adults, and will therefore seek more extensive training consistent with practicing within the formally recognized proficiency/ practice emphasis of Clinical Geropsychology[1], identifying themselves as geropsychologists.

---

[1]In 1998, at the recommendation of the Commission for the Recognition of Specialties and Proficiencies in Professional Psychology (CRSPPP), the APA Council of Representatives formally recognized Clinical Geropsychology as "a proficiency in professional psychology concerned with helping older persons and their families maintain well-being, overcome problems, and achieve maximum potential during later life" (archival description available at http://www.apa.org/crsppp/gero.html).

The guidelines further recognize and appreciate that there are numerous methods and pathways whereby psychologists may gain expertise and/or seek training in working with older adults. This document is designed to offer recommendations on those areas of knowledge and clinical skills considered as applicable to this work, rather than prescribing specific training methods to be followed.

Guidelines Development Process

In 1992, APA organized a "National Conference on Clinical Training in Psychology: Improving Services for Older Adults," which recommended that APA not only "aid professionals seeking to specialize in clinical geropsychology," but also "develop criteria to define the expertise necessary for working with older adults and their families and for evaluating competencies at both the generalist and specialist levels" (Knight, Teri, Wohlford, & Santos, 1995; Teri, Storandt, Gatz, Smyer, & Stricker, 1992). Section II (Clinical Geropsychology) of APA Division 12 (Society of Clinical Psychology) and Division 20 (Adult Development and Aging) jointly followed up on this Training Conference recommendation by forming an Interdivisional Task Force on Practice in Clinical Geropsychology, charged to address the perceived need for guidance on appropriate preparation for clinical work with older adults. The Task Force included members with expertise and professional involvements in adult development and aging as applied to diverse areas within professional psychology; they represented not only the specialty formally designated as clinical psychology, but also clinical neuropsychology, health psychology, and counseling psychology, related areas of interest such as rehabilitation psychology and community psychology, and licensed psychologists who engage in independent psychological practice with older adults and/or their families.

Consistent with its composition, the Task Force adopted an inclusive understanding and use of the term "clinical." Thus, these guidelines use "clinical work" and its variants (e.g., working clinically) as generic terms meant to encompass the practice of professional psychology by licensed practitioners from a variety of psychological subdisciplines—including all those represented within the Task Force and, potentially, others. This usage is similar to that of the federal Centers for Medicare and Medicaid Services (formerly Health Care Financing Administration) which, under the Medicare program, recognizes as a clinical psychologist "an individual who (1) holds a doctoral degree in psychology; and (2) is licensed or certified, on the basis of the doctoral degree in psychology, by the State in which he or she practices, at the independent practice level of psychology to furnish diagnostic, assessment, preventive and therapeutic services directly to individuals."

Task Force members considered the relevant background literature within their individual areas of expertise, as they saw fit. They participated in formulating and/or reviewing all portions of the guidelines document and made suggestions about the inclusion of specific content and literature citations. The initial document went through multiple drafts, until a group consensus was reached, and suggested literature references were retained if they met with general consensus. The draft document was subsequently circulated broadly within APA several times in accordance with Association Rule 100–1.5 (governing review of divisionally generated guidelines documents). Comments were invited and received from APA boards, committees, divisions, state associations, directorates, offices, and individual psychologists with interests pertinent to this area of practice. At the time of their consideration of the document, both the Board of Directors and the Council of Representatives arranged for special reviews by guidelines consultants who made recommendations about content, formatting and wording. The Task Force carefully considered each round of comments, and incorporated revisions intended to be responsive to the suggestions.

Minor financial support for mailing expenses and the costs of other Task Force operations (e.g., conference calls) was provided by Division 12-Section II and Division 20. Prior drafts of the document were reviewed and formally endorsed by the executive boards of these organizations, as well as those of Division 12 and Division 17 (Society of Counseling Psychology). No other financial support was received from any group or individual, and no financial benefit to the Task Force members or their sponsoring organizations is anticipated from approval or implementation of these guidelines.

These guidelines are organized into six sections: (a) attitudes; (b) general knowledge about adult development, aging, and older adults; (c) clinical issues; (d) assessment; (e) intervention, consultation and other service provision; and (f) education.

ATTITUDES

Guideline 1. Psychologists are encouraged to work with older adults within their scope of competence, and to seek consultation or make appropriate referrals when indicated. A balancing of considerations is useful in pursuing work with older adults, recognizing both that training in professional psychology provides general skills that can be applied to the potential benefit of older adults, and that special skills and knowledge may be essential for assessing and treating some older adults' problems. Psychologists have many skills that can be of benefit to and significantly increase the well-being of older adults. They are often called upon to evaluate and/or assist older adults with regard to serious illness, disability, stress or crisis. They also work with elders who seek psychological assistance to cope with adaptational issues; psychologists can help older adults in maintaining healthy function and adaptation, accomplishing new life-cycle developmental tasks, and/or achieving positive psychological growth in their later years. Some problems of older adults are essentially the same as those of other ages, and generally will respond to the same repertoire of skills and techniques in which all professional psychologists have generic training. Given such commonalities across age groups, considerably more psychologists may want to work with older adults, since many of their already existing skills can be effective with these clients.

On the other hand, because of the aging process and circumstances specific to later life, older adults may manifest their developmental struggles and health-related problems in distinctive ways, challenging psychologists to recognize and characterize these issues accurately and sensitively. In addition, other special clinical problems arise uniquely in old age, and may require additional diagnostic skills or intervention methods that can be applied, with appropriate adaptations, to the particular circumstances of older adults. Clinical work with older adults may involve a complex interplay of factors, including developmental issues specific to late life, cohort (generational) perspectives and preferences, comorbid physical illness, the effects of taking multiple medications, cognitive or sensory impairments, and history of medical or mental disorders. This complex interplay makes the field highly challenging, and calls for clinicians to apply psychological knowledge and methods skillfully. Education and training in the aging process and associated difficulties can help ascertain the nature of the older adult's clinical issues. Thus, those psychologists who work with the aged can benefit from specific preparation for this work.

While it would be ideal for all practice-oriented psychologists to have had some courses relating to the aging process and older adulthood as part of their clinical training (Teri et al., 1992), this is not the case for most practicing psychologists (Qualls et al., 2002). In the spirit of continuing education and self-study, psychologists already in practice can review the guidelines below and determine how these might apply to their own knowledge base or need for continuing education. Having evaluated their own scope of competence for working with older adults, psychologists can match the extent and types of their work with their competence, and can seek consultation or make appropriate referrals when the problems encountered lie outside their expertise. As well, they can use this information to shape their own learning program.

Guideline 2. Psychologists are encouraged to recognize how their attitudes and beliefs about aging and about older individuals may be relevant to their assessment and treatment of older adults, and to seek consultation or further education about these issues when indicated. Principle E of the APA Ethics Code (APA, 2002a) urges psychologists to eliminate the effect of age-related biases on their work. In addition, the APA Council of Representatives in 2002 passed a resolution opposing ageism and committing the Association to its elimination as a matter of APA policy (APA, 2002b).

Ageism refers to prejudice toward, stereotyping of, and/or discrimination against people simply because they are perceived or defined as "old" (Butler, 1969; Nelson, 2002; Schaie, 1993). Ageist biases can foster a higher recall of negative traits regarding older persons than of positive ones and encourage discriminatory practices (Perdue & Gurtman, 1990).

There are many inaccurate stereotypes of older adults that can contribute to negative biases and affect the delivery of psychological services (Abeles et al., 1998; Rodeheaver, 1990). These include, for example, that: (1) with age inevitably comes senility; (2) older adults have increased rates of mental illness, particularly depression; (3) older adults are inefficient in the workplace; (4) most older adults are frail and ill; (5) older adults are socially isolated; (6) older adults have no interest in sex or intimacy; and (7) older adults are inflexible and stubborn (Edelstein & Kalish, 1999). Such views can become self-fulfilling prophecies, leading to misdiagnosis of disorders and inappropriately decreased expectations for improvement, so-called "therapeutic nihilism" (Goodstein, 1985; Perlick & Atkins, 1984; Settin, 1982), and to the lack of preventive actions and treatment (Dupree & Paterson, 1985). For example, complaints such as anxiety, tremors, fatigue, confusion, and irritability may be attributed to "old age" or "senility" (Goodstein, 1985). Likewise, older adults with treatable depression who report lethargy, decreased appetite, and lack of interest in activities may have these symptoms attributed to old age. Inaccurately informed therapists may assume that older adults are too old to change (Zarit, 1980) or less likely than younger adults to profit from psychosocial therapies (Gatz & Pearson, 1988), though discriminatory behavior by health providers toward older adults may be linked more to provider biases about physical health conditions associated with age than to ageism as such (Gatz & Pearson, 1988; James & Haley, 1995). Older people themselves can harbor ageist attitudes.

Some health professionals may avoid serving older adults because such work evokes discomfort related to their own aging or own relationships with parents or other older family members, a phenomenon sometimes termed "gerophobia" (Verwoerdt, 1976). As well, it is not uncommon for therapists to take a paternalistic role with older adult patients who manifest significant functional limitations, even if the limitations are unrelated to their abilities to benefit from interventions (Sprenkel, 1999). Paternalistic attitudes and behavior can potentially compromise the therapeutic relationship (Horvath & Bedi, 2002; Knight, 1996; Newton & Jacobowitz, 1999) and reinforce dependency (Baltes, 1996).

Positive stereotypes (e.g., the viewpoint that older adults are "cute," "childlike," or "grandparentlike"), which are often overlooked in discussions of age-related biases (Edelstein & Kalish, 1999), can also adversely affect the assessment and therapeutic process and outcomes (Kimerling, Zeiss, & Zeiss, 2000; Zarit, 1980). Such biases due to sympathy or the desire to make allowances for shortcomings can result in inflated estimates of older adults' skills or mental health and consequent failure to intervene appropriately (Braithwaite, 1986). Psychologists are encouraged to develop more realistic perceptions of the capabilities and vulnerabilities of this segment of the population and to eliminate biases that can impede their work with older adults by examining their attitudes towards aging and older adults and (since some biases may constitute "blind spots") by seeking consultation from colleagues or others, preferably from others who are experienced in working with older adults.

GENERAL KNOWLEDGE ABOUT ADULT DEVELOPMENT, AGING, AND OLDER ADULTS

Guideline 3. Psychologists strive to gain knowledge about theory and research in aging. APA training conferences have recommended that, as part of their knowledge base for working clinically with older adults, psychologists acquire familiarity with the biological, psychological, and social content and contexts associated with normal aging (Knight et al., 1995; Santos & VandenBos, 1982). Moreover, given the likelihood that most practicing psychologists will deal with patients, family members, and caregivers of diverse ages, a rounded preparatory education encompasses training with a lifespan-developmental perspective that provides knowledge of a range of age groups, including older adults (Abeles et al., 1998). Over the past 30 years, a substantial scientific knowledge base has developed in the psychology of aging, as reflected in numerous scholarly publications. *The Psychology of Adult Development and Aging* (Eisdorfer & Lawton, 1973), printed by APA, was a landmark publication that laid out the current status of substantive knowledge, theory, and methods in psychology and aging. It was followed by *Aging in the 1980s: Psychological Issues* (Poon, 1980), and more recently by *Psychology and the Aging Revolution* (Qualls & Abeles, 2000). The successive editions of the *Handbook of the Psychology of Aging* (Birren & Schaie, 1977, 1985, 1990, 1996, 2001) and various other compilations (e.g., Lawton & Salthouse, 1998) have provided an overview of advances in knowledge about normal aging as well as psychological assessment and intervention with older adults. On its home page, APA Division 20 presents extensive information on resource materials now available for instructional coursework or self-study in geropsychology, including course syllabi, textbooks, films and videotapes, and literature references (see http://aging.ufl.edu/apadiv20/apadiv20.htm).

Training within a lifespan-developmental perspective usually includes such topics as concepts of age and aging, stages of the life cycle, longitudinal change and cross-sectional differences, cohort differences, and research designs for adult development and aging (e.g., Bengtson & Schaie, 1999; Cavanaugh & Whitbourne, 1999). Longitudinal studies, where individuals are followed over many years, permit observation of how individual trajectories of change unfold. Cross-sectional studies, where individuals of different ages are compared, allow age groups to be characterized. However, individuals are inextricably bound to their own time in history. People are born, mature, and grow old within a given generation (or "cohort" of persons born within a given period of historical time). Therefore, it is useful to combine longitudinal and cross-sectional methods in order to identify which age-related characteristics reflect change over the lifespan and which reflect differences in cohort or generation (Schaie, 1977). For example, older adults may be less familiar with using scantron answer sheets to respond to questionnaires or personality inventories, compared to college students of today. Rather than varying by stage of life, differing political attitudes may reflect various age cohorts' different experiences with World War II, the Korean War, the war in Viet Nam, or the Gulf War. Appreciating an older adult's cohort can be an integral aspect of understanding the individual within his or her cultural context (Knight, 1996).

There are a variety of conceptions of successful aging (Rowe & Kahn, 1998) and of positive mental health in older adults (e.g., Erikson, Erikson, & Kivnick, 1986). Inevitably, aging includes the need to accommodate to physical changes, functional limitations, and other losses. Baltes and Baltes (1990; Baltes, 1997) describe the behavioral strategies involved in such adaptation in terms of "selective optimization with compensation," in which older adults set priorities, selecting goals which they feel are most crucial or domains where they feel most competent, refine the means to achieve those goals, and use compensatory strategies to make up for aging-related losses. Another key aspect of a lifespan-developmental viewpoint is to emphasize that aging be seen not only according to a biologically based decrement model, but also as including positive aspects of psychological growth and maturation (Gutmann, 1994; Schaie, 1993). Such theories of the normal aging process have applicability for clinicians who strive to build a lifespan-developmental perspective into their interventions (Gatz, 1998; Staudinger, Marsiske, & Baltes, 1995).

Guideline 4. Psychologists strive to be aware of the social/psychological dynamics of the aging process. As part of the broader developmental continuum of the life cycle, aging is a dynamic process that challenges the aging individual to make continuing behavioral adaptations (Diehl, Coyle, & Labouvie-Vief, 1996). Many psychological issues in late life are similar in nature to difficulties at earlier life stages—coping with life transitions such as retirement (Sterns & Gray, 1999) or changes in residence, bereavement and widowhood (Kastenbaum, 1999), couples' problems or sexual difficulties (Levenson, Carstensen, & Gottman, 1993), social discrimination, traumatic events (Hyer & Sohnle, 2001), social isolation and loneliness, or issues of modifying one's self-concept and goals in light of altered life circumstances or continuing progression through the life cycle (Tobin, 1999). Other issues, however, may be more specific to late life, such as grandparenting problems (Robertson, 1995; Szinovacz, 1998), adapting to typical age-related physical changes, including health problems (Schulz & Heckhausen, 1996), or needs for integrating or coming to terms with one's personal lifetime of aspirations, achievements and failures (Butler, 1963). Older adults also routinely experience the effects of social attitudes toward the older population, including societal stereotypes about the aged (Kite & Wagner, 2002), and often are coping with particular economic and legal issues (Smyer, Schaie, & Kapp, 1996).

Among the special stresses of old age are a variety of significant losses. Loss—whether of significant persons, objects, animals, roles, belongings, independence, health, or financial well-being—may trigger problematic reactions, particularly in individuals predisposed to depression, anxiety or other mental disorders. Among the elderly, losses are often multiple, and their effects cumulative. Nevertheless, confronting loss in the context of one's long life often offers unique possibilities for achieving reconciliation, healing, or deeper wisdom (Baltes & Staudinger, 2000; Sternberg & Lubart, 2001). Moreover, the vast majority of older people maintain positive outlooks and morale, and express enjoyment and high life satisfaction for the perspectives and experiences (including decreased social expectations) that accompany later life (Magai, 2001; Mroczek & Kolarz, 1998). Despite the multiple stresses and infirmities of old age, it is noteworthy that, other than for the dementias, older adults have a lower prevalence of psychological disorders than do younger adults. In working with older adults, psychologists have found it useful to remain cognizant of the strengths that many older people possess, the many commonalities they retain with younger adults and with themselves at earlier ages, and the opportunities for using skills developed over the lifespan for continued psychological growth in late life.

In older adults, there is both a great deal of continuity of personality traits (Costa, Yang, & McCrae, 1998; McCrae & Costa, 1990) and considerable subjective change across the second half of life (Ryff, Kwan, & Singer, 2001). Of particular interest is how sense of well-being is maintained. For example, although people of all ages reminisce about the past, older adults are more likely to use reminiscence in psychologically intense ways to integrate experiences, to maintain intimacy and to prepare for death (Webster, 1995). Dimensions of well-being that are useful for psychologists to consider include self-acceptance, autonomy, and sense of purpose in life (Ryff et al., 2001). Later-life family, intimate, friendship and other social relations (Blieszner & Bedford, 1995) and intergenerational issues (Bengtson, 2001) figure prominently in the aging process. One influential theoretical perspective suggests that aging typically brings a heightened awareness that one's remaining time and opportunities are limited, leading to increased selectivity in one's goals and social relationships and goals, and a growing concentration on those which are most emotionally satisfying (Carstensen, Isaacowitz, & Charles, 1999). For these and other reasons, older adults' voluntary social networks often shrink with age, showing a progressive focusing on interactions with family and close associates. Families and other support systems are critical aspects of the context for most older adults (Antonucci, 2001; Antocucci & Akiyama, 1995). Working with older adults often involves dealing with their families and other support or, not infrequently, their absence. Psychologists often appraise the social support context in detail (Abeles et al., 1998), and typically seek to find interventions and solutions to problems that strike a balance between respecting the dignity and autonomy of the older person and recognizing others' perspectives on the older individual's needs for care (see Guideline 19).

Though the individuals who care for older adults are usually family members related by blood ties or marriage, increasingly, psychologists may encounter complex, varied and nontraditional relationships as part of older adults' patterns of intimacy, residence and support. This document uses the term "family" broadly to include all such relationships, and recognizes that continuing changes in this context are likely in future generations. Awareness of and training in these issues will be useful to psychologists in dealing with older adults manifesting diverse family relationships and forms of support.

Guideline 5. Psychologists strive to understand diversity in the aging process, particularly how sociocultural factors such as gender, ethnicity, socioeconomic status, sexual orientation, disability status, and urban/rural residence may influence the experience and expression of health and of psychological problems in later life. The older adult population is highly diverse, including considerable sociocultural, socioeconomic, and demographic variation (U.S. Bureau of the Census, 2001). According to some research, the heterogeneity among older adults surpasses that seen in other age groups (Crowther & Zeiss, 2003; Nelson & Dannefer, 1992). The psychological problems experienced by older adults may differ according to such factors as age cohort, gender, ethnicity and cultural background, sexual orientation, rural/frontier living status, differences in education and socioeconomic status, religion, as well as transitions in social status and living situations. Clinical presentations of symptoms and syndromes in older individuals often reflect interactions among these factors and specifics of the clinical setting (such as the nursing home or the homebound living context). In addition, adults in the relatively earlier stages of their old age often differ considerably from the very old in physical health, functional abilities, living situations, or other characteristics.

An important factor to take into account when providing psychological services to older adults is the influence of cohort or generational issues. Each generation has unique historical circumstances that shape that generation's collective social and psychological perspectives throughout the lifespan. For the current group of American older adults, the economic depression of the 1930's and World War II were formative early life experiences that built a strong ethic of self-reliance (Elder, 1999; Elder & Hareven, 1994). Likewise, these individuals may have been socialized in communities in which negative attitudes toward mental health issues and professionals were prevalent. As a result, older adults may be more reluctant than younger adults to access mental health services and to accept a psychological frame for problems.

A striking demographic fact of late life is the preponderance of females surviving to older ages (Federal Interagency Forum on Aging-Related Statistics, 2000), which infuses aging with many gender-related issues (Huyck, 1990). Notably, because of the greater longevity of women, on average the older patient is more likely to be a woman than a man. This greater longevity has many repercussions. For example, it means that, as they age, most women will provide care to infirm husbands, experience widowhood, and be at increasing risk themselves for dementia and other health conditions associated with advanced age. Moreover, the current generation of older women was less likely to engage in competitive employment than the younger generation and therefore has fewer economic resources in later life than their male counterparts. Financial instability may be particularly salient for the growing numbers of women grandparents raising grandchildren (Fuller-Thompson & Minkler, 2003). Women's issues frequently arise as concerns to be dealt with throughout the processes of assessing and treating older adults (Banks, Ackerman, & Clark, 1986; Trotman & Brody, 2002). Consideration of special issues affecting older men is similarly germane, though many of these have not been sufficiently researched (Bengtson, Rosenthal, & Burton, 1996).

It is critical also to consider the pervasive influence of crosscultural and minority factors on the experience of aging (Jackson, 1985; Miles, 1999). The population of older adults today is predominantly white but by the year 2050, non-white minorities will represent one-third of all older adults in the United States (Gerontological Society of America Task Force on Minority Issues in Gerontology, 1994; U.S. Bureau of the Census, 1993). Earlier life experiences of older adults were often conditioned by racial or ethnic identity. Many older minority persons faced discrimination and were denied access to jobs, housing, healthcare, and other services. As a result, older minority persons have fewer economic resources than majority persons. For example, 47% of black women aged 65 to 74 years live in poverty. As a consequence of these and other factors, minority older adults have more physical health problems than the majority of older persons and they often delay or refrain from accessing needed health and mental health services (Abramson, Trejo, & Lai, 2002; Vasquez & Clavigo, 1995; Yeo & Hikoyeda, 1993).

In addition to ethnic and minority older adults, there are sexual minorities including gay, lesbian, bisexual, and transgendered persons (Kimmel, 1995; Reid, 1995). They have also suffered discrimination from the larger society, including the mental health professions, which previously labeled sexual variation as psychopathology and utilized psychological and biological treatments to try to alter sexual orientation. Guideline 12 of APA's Guidelines for Psychotherapy With Lesbian, Gay, & Bisexual Clients (2000) discusses particular challenges faced by older adults in this minority status.

Aging presents special issues for individuals with developmental and other longstanding disabilities (e.g., mental retardation, autism, cerebral palsy, seizure disorders, traumatic brain injury), as well as physical impairments such as blindness, deafness, and musculoskeletal impairments (Janicki & Dalton, 1999). Nowadays, given available supports, life expectancy for persons with serious disability may approach or equal that of the general population (Janicki, Dalton, Henderson, & Davidson, 1999). Many chronic impairments may affect risk for age-associated changes (e.g., Zigman, Silverman, & Wisniewski, 1996), and/or may have implications for psychological assessment, diagnosis, and treatment of persons who are aging with these conditions.

Aging is also conditioned by a multiplicity of environmental and ecological factors (Scheidt & Windley, 1998; Wahl, 2001), including rural/frontier issues and relocation. Place of residence affects access to health services, and places obstacles to providers in delivering services. Older adults residing in rural areas often have problems accessing aging resources (e.g., transportation, community centers, meals programs) and as a consequence experience low levels of social support and high levels of isolation (Guralnick, Kemel, Stamm, & Greving, 2003; Russell, Cutrona, de la Mora, & Wallace, 1997). Rural elders also have less access to community mental health services and to mental health specialists in nursing homes compared to non-rural older adults (Burns, Wagner, Taube, Magaziner, Permutt, & Landerman, 1993; Coburn & Bolda, 1999). Homebound older adults also find it particularly difficult to obtain psychological services since there are few programs that bring such services to older adults' residences.

Guideline 6. Psychologists strive to be familiar with current information about biological and health-related aspects of aging. In working with older adults, psychologists often find it useful to be informed about the normal biological changes that accompany aging. Though there are individual differences in rates of change, with advancing age the older individual inevitably experiences such changes as decreases in sensory acuity, alterations in physical appearance and body composition, hormonal changes, reductions in the peak performance capacity of most body organ systems, and weakened immunological responses and greater susceptibility to illness. Such biological aging processes may have significant hereditary or genetically related components (McClearn & Vogler, 2001), about which older adults and their families may often have keen interests or concerns. Adjusting to such physical changes with age is a core task of the normal psychological aging process (Whitbourne, 1996, 1998). When older clients discuss their physical health, most often their focus may be on changes with significant experiential components, such as changes in vision, hearing, sleep, continence, energy levels or fatiguability, and the like. In such contexts, it is useful for the psychologist to be able to distinguish normative patterns of change from symptoms of serious illness, to recognize when psychological symptoms might represent a side effect of medication or the consequence of a physical illness, and to provide informed help to older adults with respect to coping with physical changes and managing chronic disease (Frazer, 1995).

Over 80% of older adults have at least one chronic health condition, and most have multiple conditions, each requiring medication and/or management. The most commonly experienced chronic health conditions of late life include arthritis, hypertension, hearing impairments, heart disease, and cataracts (National Academy on an Aging Society, 1999). Other common medical problems include diabetes, osteoporosis, vascular diseases, neurological diseases, including stroke, and respiratory diseases (Segal, 1996). Many of these physical conditions have associated mental health conditions, either mediated physiologically (e.g., poststroke depression) or in reaction to disability, pain, or prognosis (Frazer, Leicht, & Baker, 1996).

Because older adults so commonly take medications for these conditions, it often is useful to have knowledge about various aspects of pharmacology. For example, pharmacokinetic and pharmacodynamic changes tied to aging affect older adults' metabolism of and sensitivity to medications, leading to consequent considerations about dosing. It is helpful to be familiar with medications typically used by older adults, including psychotropic medications, and potential interactions among them (Levy & Uncapher, 2000; Smyer & Downs, 1995). Numerous problems seen among older adults can stem from the multiplicity of medications they often are taking (so-called polypharmacy issues; Schneider, 1996).

Psychologists working with older adults may find behavioral medicine information useful in helping older adults with lifestyle and behavioral issues in maintaining or improving their health, such as nutrition, diet, and exercise (Bortz & Bortz, 1996). They can help older adults achieve pain control and manage their chronic illnesses and associated medications with greater compliance (Watkins, Shifrin, Park, & Morrell, 1999). Other health-related issues that are often encountered include preventive measures for dealing with the risk of falls and associated injury, management of incontinence (Burgio & Locher, 1996), and dealing with terminal illness (Kastenbaum, 1999). Behavioral medicine approaches have great potential for contributing to effective and humane geriatric health care, and improving older adults' functional status and health-related quality of life (Siegler, Bastian, Steffens, Bosworth, & Costa, 2002).

For example, while many older adults experience some changes in sleep, it is often difficult to determine whether these are inherent in the aging process or may stem from changes in physical health or other causes. Sleep complaints in older adults are sometimes dismissed as part of normal age-related change, but can also signal depression or other mental health problems (Bootzin, Epstein, Engle-Friedman, & Salvio, 1996). Sleep can often be improved by implementing simple sleep hygiene procedures and by behavioral treatment, including relaxation, cognitive restructuring, and stimulus control instructions (Ancoli-Israel, Pat-Horenczyk, & Martin, 2001; *Older Adults and Insomnia Resource Guide*, 2001).

CLINICAL ISSUES

Guideline 7. Psychologists strive to be familiar with current knowledge about cognitive changes in older adults. Numerous reference volumes offer comprehensive coverage of research on cognitive aging (e.g., Blanchard-Fields & Hess, 1996; Craik & Salthouse, 2000; Park & Schwartz, 2000). For most older adults, the changes in cognition that occur with aging are mild in degree and do not significantly interfere with daily functioning (Abeles et al., 1998). While some decline in capacity and/or efficiency may be demonstrated in most cognitive domains, the vast majority of older adults continue to engage in their longstanding pursuits, interact intellectually with others, actively solve real-life problems, and achieve new learning.

Various cognitive abilities show differential rates and trajectories of change in normal aging (Schaie, 1994). Among the changes most commonly associated with normal aging are slowing in reaction times and the overall speed of information processing (Salthouse, 1996; Sliwinski & Buschke, 1999), and reduction in visuospatial and motor control abilities. Memory changes with age are also common, in particular those involving retrieval processes and so-called working memory (retaining information while using it in performance of another mental task) (Bäckman, Small, & Wahlin, 2001; Smith, 1996; Zacks, Hasher, & Li, 2000). Attention is also affected, particularly the ability to divide one's attention, to shift focus rapidly, and to deal with complex situations (Rogers & Fisk, 2001). Cognitive functions that are better preserved with age include learning, language and vocabulary skills, reasoning, and other skills that rely primarily on stored information and knowledge. Older adults remain capable of new learning, though typically at a somewhat slower pace than younger individuals. Changes in executive abilities, when they occur, tend to be quite predictive of functional disability (Royall, Chiodo, & Polk, 2000).

A large variety of factors influence both lifetime levels of cognitive achievement and patterns of maintenance or decline in intellectual performance in old age, including genetic, constitutional, health, sensory, affective and other variables. Sensory deficits, particularly when present in vision and hearing, often significantly impede and limit older adults' intellectual functioning and ability to interact with their environments, and may be linked in more fundamental ways with higher-order cognitive changes (Baltes & Lindenberger, 1997). Many of the illnesses and chronic physical conditions that are common in old age tend to have significant impacts on particular aspects of cognition, as do many of the medications used to treat them (Waldstein, 2000). Cumulatively, such factors may account for much of the decline that older adults experience in intellectual functioning, as opposed to simply the normal aging process in itself. In addition to sensory integrity and physical health, psychological factors such as affective state, sense of control and self-efficacy (Eizenman et al., 1997), as well as active use of information processing strategies and continued practice of existing mental skills (Schooler, Mulatu, & Oates, 1999) may influence older adults' level of cognitive performance.

At the same time, there is a relatively high prevalence of more serious cognitive disorders within the older adult population, and an appreciable minority of older adults suffers significantly impaired function and quality of life as a result. Advanced age is tied to increased risk of cognitive impairment, in varying forms and degrees. Population-based research has found that the prevalence of dementia increases dramatically with age, with various estimates indicating that as many as 25% to 50% of all those over age 85 suffer from this condition (Bachman et al., 1992; Evans et al., 1989). The most common types of dementia are Alzheimer's disease and vascular dementia; however, quite commonly, cognitive impairment in old age exists in milder forms that are not inevitably progressive and for which the etiology may not be clearly definable. Depression or anxiety sometimes triggers reversible cognitive impairments in older, vulnerable adults who had previously appeared normal in cognitive function (Butters et al., 2000). Reversible cognitive impairment or mental confusion can also result from medical conditions or side effects of medications. Acute confusional states (delirium) often signal underlying physical conditions or illness processes, which generally deserve prompt medical attention and sometimes may even be life-threatening (Dolan et al., 2000; Miller & Lipowski, 1991).

Largely as a consequence of the affected older adults' increased needs for assistance and supervision, cognitively impairing disorders typically place great time demands and stress on caregiving family members as well as the affected individuals, and represent a very costly burden for society as a whole.

Guideline 8. Psychologists strive to understand problems in daily living among older adults. Older adults confront many of the problems in daily life that younger persons do. For example, increasingly, many older adults may remain in the work force, facing job pressures and decisions about retirement versus continued employment (Sterns & Gray, 1999). However, the increasing presence of acute or chronic health problems as persons age may exacerbate existing problems or create new difficulties. Intimate relationships may become strained by the presence of health problems in one or both partners. Discord among adult children may be precipitated or exacerbated because of differing expectations about how much care each child should provide to the impaired parent (Qualls, 1999). Increasing use of health care can be frustrating for older adults because of demands on time, finances, transportation, and lack of communication among care providers.

It is important to understand how issues of daily living for many older adults center around the degree to which the individual retains "everyday competence" or the ability for independent function, or is disabled to such extent as having to depend on others for basic elements of self-care (Baltes, 1996; Diehl, 1998; Femia, Zarit, & Johansson, 2001). For example, for some older adults, health problems have an adverse effect on ability to complete activities of daily living, requiring the use of paid home health care assistants. Some older adults find the presence of health care assistants in their homes to be stressful because of the financial demands of such care, differences in expectations about how care should be provided, racial and cultural differences between care provider and recipient, or beliefs that family members are the only acceptable caregivers. Theoretical perspectives of person-environment fit or congruence (e.g., Kahana, Kahana, & Riley, 1989; Smyer & Allen-Burge, 1999; Wahl, 2001) have considerable applicability in such situations, and often are helpful in elucidating their remediable aspects. A useful general principle is the so-called "environmental docility" thesis, namely, that while behavior is a function of both person and environment, as older adults' personal competence declines, environmental variables often play a correspondingly greater role in determining their level of functioning (Lawton, 1989).

Loss of mental abilities such as those found in Alzheimer's disease and other dementias and associated emotional and behavioral problems often have a significant impact on both older adults and family members (Schulz, O'Brien, Bookwala, & Fleissner, 1995). Older adults and family members confront difficult decisions about whether the older person with waning cognitive ability can manage finances, drive, live independently, or manage medications and make decisions about medical care. Older persons with dementia and their families must also deal with the financial and legal implications of the condition. Family members who experience caregiving stress are at increased risk for experiencing depression, anxiety, anger and frustration (Gallagher-Thompson & DeVries, 1994), and compromised immune system function (Cacioppo et al., 1998; Kiecolt-Glaser, Dura, Speicher, Trask, & Glaser, 1991). In addition, older adults who are responsible for others, such as the aging parents of adult offspring with longstanding disabilities or severe psychiatric disorders, may experience considerable duress in arranging for the future care or oversight of their dependents (Greenberg, Seltzer, & Greenley, 1993; Seltzer, Greenberg, Krauss, & Hong, 1997). Older grandparents who assume primary responsibilities for raising their grandchildren may face many similar problems and strains (Fuller-Thomson, Minkler, & Driver, 1997; Robertson, 1995; Szinovacz, DeViney, & Atkinson, 1999). Partly as a result of such tensions, mentally or physically frail older adults are at increased risk for abuse and neglect (Curry & Stone, 1995; *Elder Abuse and Neglect*, 1999; Wilber & McNeilly, 2001; Wolf, 1998).

Even older adults who remain in relatively good cognitive and physical health are witness to a changing social world as older family members and friends experience health declines (Myers, 1999). Relationships change, access to friends and family becomes more difficult, and demands to provide care to others increase. Of note, many individuals subject to caregiving responsibilities and stresses are themselves older adults, who may be contending with physical health problems and psychological adjustment to aging. Death of friends and older family members is something most older people experience (Kastenbaum, 1999). The oldest old (those 85 years and older) sometimes find they are the only surviving members of the age peers they have known. These older people must not only deal with the emotional ramifications of these losses but also the practical challenges of how to reconstitute a meaningful social world.

Guideline 9. Psychologists strive to be knowledgeable about psychopathology within the aging population and cognizant of the prevalence and nature of that psychopathology when providing services to older adults. Prevalence estimates suggest that approximately 20% to 22% of older adults may meet criteria for some form of mental disorder, including dementias (Administration on Aging, 2001; Gatz & Smyer, 2001; Jeste et al., 1999; Surgeon General, 1999). Older adults may present a broad array of psychological issues for clinical attention. These issues include almost all of the problems that affect younger adults. In addition, older adults may seek or benefit from psychological services when they experience challenges specific to late life, including developmental issues and social changes. Some problems that rarely affect younger adults, notably dementias due to degenerative brain diseases and stroke, are much more common in old age (see Guideline 7).

Older adults may suffer recurrences of psychological disorders they experienced when younger (e.g., Bonwick & Morris, 1996; Hyer & Sohnle, 2001) or develop new problems because of the unique stresses of old age or neuropathology. Other older persons have histories of chronic mental illness or personality disorder, the presentation of which may change or become further complicated because of cognitive impairment, medical comorbidity, polypharmacy, and end-of-life issues (Light & Lebowitz, 1991; Meeks & Murrell, 1997; Rosowsky, Abrams, & Zweig, 1999). Among older adults seeking health services, depression and anxiety disorders are common, as are adjustment disorders and problems stemming from inadvertent misuse of prescription medications (Fisher & Noll, 1996; Gallo & Lebowitz, 1999; Reynolds & Charney, 2002). Suicide is a particular concern in conjunction with depression in late life, as suicide rates are higher among older adults than in other age groups (see Guideline 16). Dementing disorders including Alzheimer's disease are also commonly seen among older adults who come to clinical attention. The vast majority of older adults with mental health problems seek help from primary medical care settings, rather than in specialty mental health facilities (Phillips & Murrell, 1994).

Older adults often have multiple problems. Both mental and behavioral disorders may be evident in older adults (for example, those with Axis I disorders who also manifest concurrent substance abuse or Axis II personality disorders). Likewise, older adults suffering from progressive dementias typically evidence coexistent psychological symptoms, which may include depression, anxiety, paranoia, and behavioral disturbances. Because medical disorders are more prevalent in old age than in younger years, mental and behavioral problems are often comorbid with medical illness (Lebowitz & Niederehe, 1992). Being alert to comorbid physical and mental health problems is a key concept in evaluating older adults. Further complicating the clinical picture, older adults often receive multiple medications and have sensory or motor impairments. All of these factors may interact in ways that are difficult to disentangle diagnostically. For example, sometimes depressive symptoms in older adults are caused by medical conditions (Frazer, Leicht, & Baker, 1996; Weintraub, Furlan, & Katz, 2002). At other times, depression is a response to the experience of physical illness. Depression may increase the risk that physical illness will recur and reduce treatment compliance, or otherwise dampen the outcomes of medical care. Growing evidence links depression in older adults to increased mortality, not attributable to suicide (Schulz, Martire, Beach, & Scherer, 2000).

Some mental disorders may have unique presentations in older adults. For example, late-life depression may coexist with cognitive impairment and other symptoms of dementia, or may be expressed in forms that lack overt manifestations of sadness (Gallo & Rabins, 1999). It may thus be difficult to determine whether symptoms such as apathy and withdrawal are caused by a depressive syndrome and/or impaired brain functioning (Lamberty & Bieliauskas, 1993). Furthermore, depressive symptoms may at times reflect older adults' confrontation with developmentally challenging aspects of aging, coming to terms with the existential reality of physical decline and death, or spiritual crises. Familiarity with the mental disorders of late life usually evident in clinical settings, their presentations in older adults, and relationship with physical health problems will facilitate accurate recognition of and appropriate therapeutic response to these syndromes.

Other issues that often come to clinical attention in older adults include substance abuse (Blow, Oslin, & Barry, 2002), complicated grief (Frank, Prigerson, Shear, & Reynolds, 1997), sexual dysfunction, psychotic disorders, including schizophrenia and delusional disorders (Palmer, Folsom, Bartels, & Jeste, 2002), and behavioral disturbances (e.g, wandering, aggressive behavior) in those suffering from dementia or other cognitive impairment (Cohen-Mansfield, Werner, Culpepper, Wolfson, & Bickel, 1996). Many comprehensive reference volumes are available as resources for clinicians with respect to late-life mental disorders (e.g., Butler, Lewis, & Sunderland, 1998; Edelstein, 2001; Kennedy, 2000; Smyer & Qualls, 1999; Whitbourne, 2000; Woods, 1999; Zarit & Zarit, 1998), and the literature in this area is rapidly expanding.

ASSESSMENT

Guideline 10. Psychologists strive to be familiar with the theory, research, and practice of various methods of assessment with older adults, and knowledgeable of assessment instruments that are psychometrically suitable for use with them. Relevant methods may include clinical interviewing; use of self-report measures; cognitive performance testing; direct behavioral observation; psychophysiological techniques; and use of informant data.

A thorough geriatric assessment is preferably an interdisciplinary one, determining how problems interrelate and taking account of contributing factors. In evaluating older adults it is, for example, almost always useful to ascertain the possible influence of medications on the presenting mental health or psychological picture, and the nature and extent of the individual's familial or other social support. In many contexts, particularly hospital and outpatient care settings, psychologists are frequently asked to evaluate older adults for the presence of depression or other affective disorder, suicidal potential, psychotic symptoms, and like issues. As part of this process, in addition to employing clinical interview and behavioral observation techniques (Edelstein & Kalish, 1999; Edelstein & Semenchuk, 1996), psychologists may conduct various forms of standardized assessment.

Developing knowledge and skill with respect to standardized measures involves understanding the importance of using assessments that have been shown to be reliable and valid with older adults (e.g., Ivnik et al., 1992). For example, when assessing late-life issues in personality and characteristic patterns of behavior in relationship to older adults' clinical symptoms, psychologists frequently administer and interpret both symptom scales (such as those for depression or anxiety) and trait/personality measures (e.g., Costa & McCrae, 1988). Likewise, gaining an understanding of the clinical problem may require assessments of other persistent behavior patterns (e.g., assertiveness, dependency) and/or of contextual factors (such as family interaction patterns, degree of social support). Such assessments are likely to be most accurate and useful when based on measures designed for use with, or that have known psychometric properties relative to, older adults. The *Geropsychology Assessment Resource Guide* (1996) produced by the Veterans Administration and other resources (e.g., Lawton & Teresi, 1994; Poon et al., 1986) offer commentary on assessment instruments for use with geriatric patients.

As well, behavioral assessment has many applications in working with older adults, particularly for psychologists working in hospital, rehabilitation, or other institutionalized settings (Fisher & Carstensen, 1990; Hersen & Van Hasselt, 1992; Lundervold & Lewin, 1992). Behavioral analysis (and associated intervention techniques) may often be useful with patients who show potentially harmful behavior such as wandering (Algaze, 2001) or assaultiveness (Fisher, Swingen, & Harsin, 2001), sexual disinhibition, or excess disability (i.e., impairment of function greater than that directly attributable to disease; Roberts, 1986). These techniques can also be valuable in determining elderly individuals' skills and weaknesses and targeting areas in which to strengthen adaptive behavior.

In assessing older adults, particularly those with cognitive impairments, psychologists may rely considerably on data provided by other informants. It is useful to be aware of empirical findings about effective ways of gathering such information, and general considerations about how to interpret it in relation to other data (e.g., Teri & Wagner, 1991). Likewise, evaluations of older adults may often be clarified by conducting repeated-measures assessments at more than a single time point. Such longitudinal assessment is useful particularly with respect to such matters as the older adult's affective state or functional capacities, and can help in examining the degree to which these are stable or vary according to situational factors, time of day, or the like.

Psychologists may do assessments for more than diagnostic purposes. They may also use them to help generate appropriate intervention strategies with the older patient, the family, other support providers, or professional caregivers, and to evaluate the outcomes of these interventions. For example, assessments may be used to appraise patient satisfaction with psychological interventions in nursing homes, to determine the key efficacious components of day care programs, or to evaluate the cost-benefit of respite care programs designed to help family caregivers maintain their demented relatives at home. Assessments may thus play an important role in determining the therapeutic and programmatic efficacy and efficiency of interventions, whether made at individual, group, program, or systems levels. Such program evaluations can lead to improved services for older adults.

Guideline 11. Psychologists strive to understand the problems of using assessment instruments created for younger individuals when assessing older adults, and to develop skill in tailoring assessments to accommodate older adults' specific characteristics and contexts. When assessment tools appropriately validated and normed for use with this age group are not available, psychologists may find themselves in the position of using instruments imperfectly suited for the situation and exercising professional judgment to evaluate the probable impact of aging on test performance. At other times, the challenge may be to adapt the assessment procedures to accommodate the special frailties, impairments or living contexts of older adults (e.g., Hunt & Lindley, 1989). For example, with older adults who have sensory or communication problems, elements of the evaluation process may include assessing the extent of these impediments, modifying other assessments to work around such problems, and taking these modifications into account when interpreting the test findings.

It may be useful to modify the assessment environment in various ways in order to reduce the influence of sensory problems or other preexisting (e.g., motor or longstanding intellectual) impairments on test results. In particular, clinicians would not want to confuse cognitive impairment with sensory deficits. Hearing difficulties in older adults tend to be worse at higher frequencies, and background noise can be especially distracting (Vernon, 1989). Thus, it can be helpful for the clinician to minimize surrounding noise and for female psychologists, in particular, to lower the pitch of their voice. To be useful, self-administered assessment forms may have to be reprinted in larger type, and high-gloss paper is best avoided.

Aging individuals with developmental disabilities or other preexisting physical or cognitive impairments may present unique challenges for psychological assessment, as well as for intervention (Janicki, Heller, & Hogg, 1996). Often it is not useful to apply the same techniques as employed with nondisabled individuals. Sensitivity to these special circumstances may demand exercising special care in selecting assessment procedures appropriate for the individual, and/or making adjustments in methods and diagnostic decisionmaking (Burt & Aylward, 1999; Working Group for the Establishment of Criteria for the Diagnosis of Dementia, 2000).

Another common challenge in conducting assessments is taking account of the potential influence of both psychopharmacological and other medications, and other substance use (Blow, 2000; Blow et al., 2002). Substance abuse assessment, particularly with respect to alcohol use but spanning the full range of abused substances, is frequently very valuable in clinical work with older adults. Whereas work demands and legal problems make alcohol abuse more apparent in younger adults, in older adults it is often more difficult to detect or may present itself via atypical symptoms. Also, because of the multiple medications that many older adults take, psychologists may frequently find it useful to evaluate prescription and over-the-counter medication misuse (whether inadvertent or not).

Other special challenges in assessing older adults include interpreting the significance of somatic complaints; appraising the nature and extent of familial and other social support; evaluating potential elder abuse or neglect; and identification of strengths and potential compensatory skills.

Guideline 12. Psychologists strive to develop skill at recognizing cognitive changes in older adults, and in conducting and interpreting cognitive screening and functional ability evaluations. Quite commonly, when evaluating geriatric patients, psychologists may use specialized procedures and tests to help determine the nature of and bases for an older adult's cognitive difficulties, functional impairment, or behavioral disturbances (*Geropsychology Assessment Resource Guide*, 1996; LaRue, 1992; Lichtenberg, 1999; Poon et al., 1986; Storandt & VandenBos, 1994). For example, the referral question may be whether the individual's impairments exceed the extent of change expected from age alone, or whether the observed problems stem from a dementing process, depression, and/or other causes (Kaszniak & Christenson, 1994; Lamberty & Bieliauskas, 1993). Differentiating cognitive deficits that reflect early dementia from those associated with normal aging, and mild dementia from depression can be diagnostically challenging (Butters, Salmon, & Butters, 1994; Kaszniak & Christenson, 1994; Spencer, Tompkins, & Schulz, 1997). Clarification is often provided by comprehensive neuropsychological studies and longitudinal, repeated-measures evaluation. While impairment in delayed recall is a hallmark of Alzheimer's disease, the illness can present quite variably, and other dementing disorders may also present with poor retention. Disproportionate deficits in visuospatial or executive functions may indicate other etiologies. Prompt evaluation of memory complaints may be useful in identifying potentially reversible causes of cognitive impairment (APA Presidential Task Force on the Assessment of Age-Consistent Memory Decline and Dementia, 1998), though such complaints are also influenced by mood and many other factors and in themselves are generally not reliable indices of objectively measured cognitive decline (Niederehe, 1998; Smith, Petersen, Ivnik, Malec, & Tangalos, 1996).

The ability to make accurate assessments and appropriate referrals in this area depends upon knowledge of normal and abnormal aging, including age-related changes in intellectual abilities. In conducting such assessments, psychologists rely upon their familiarity with age-related brain changes, diseases that affect the brain, tests of cognition, and age-appropriate normative data on cognitive functioning (Albert & Moss, 1988; Green, 2000; Ivnik et al., 1992; Nussbaum, 1997; Park, Zec, & Wilson, 1993), as well as upon knowledge of how performance can be influenced by preexisting impairments and individual differences in cognitive abilities. Brief cognitive screening tests do not substitute for more thorough evaluation in challenging cases. Psychologists make referrals to clinical neuropsychologists (for comprehensive neuropsychological assessments[2]), neurologists, or other specialists as appropriate.

Psychologists sometimes do functional capacity assessments and consult on questions regarding an older person's functional abilities (Diehl, 1998; Willis et al., 1998). For example, they may be asked to assess the individual's abilities to make medical or legal decisions (Marson, Chatterjee, Ingram, & Harrell, 1996; Moye, 1999; Smyer, 1993; Smyer & Allen-Burge, 1999) or to exercise specific behavioral competencies, such as medication management (Park, Morrell, & Shifrin, 1999) or driving (Ball, 1997; Odenheimer et al., 1994). Other questions, including those of a forensic nature, may involve the elder's capacity for continued independent living, capacity for making advanced directives or a valid will, or need for legal guardianship (*Assessment*

---

[2]In 1996, at the recommendation of the Commission for Recognition of Specialties and Proficiencies in Professional Psychology (CRSPPP), the APA Council of Representatives formally recognized Clinical Neuropsychology as a "specialty that applies principles of assessment and intervention based upon the scientific study of human behavior as it relates to normal and abnormal functioning of the central nervous system" and that "is dedicated to enhancing the understanding of brain-behavior relationships and the application of such knowledge to human problems" (archival description available at http://www.apa.org/crsppp/neuro.html).

of *Competency and Capacity of the Older Adult*, 1997; Marson, 2002; Smyer, Schaie, & Kapp, 1996). In addressing questions in these areas, the psychologist typically evaluates cognitive skills, higher-order executive functioning (such as ability to plan, organize and implement complex behaviors), and other aspects of psychological function, using assessment procedures within their expertise and competence that have demonstrated validity concerning the referral questions. Furthermore, to make ecologically valid recommendations in these areas, he or she often integrates the assessment results with clinical interview information gathered from both the older adult and collateral sources, with direct observations of the older adult's functional performance, and with other pertinent considerations (such as the immediate physical environment, available social supports, or local legal standards).

INTERVENTION, CONSULTATION AND OTHER SERVICE PROVISION

Guideline 13. Psychologists strive to be familiar with the theory, research, and practice of various methods of intervention with older adults, particularly with current research evidence about their efficacy with this age group. Psychologists have been adapting their treatments and doing psychological interventions with older adults over the entire history of psychotherapy (Knight, Kelly, & Gatz, 1992). As different theoretical approaches have emerged, each has been applied to older adults, e.g., psychoanalysis, behavior modification, cognitive therapy, and community mental health consultation. In addition, efforts have been made to use the knowledge base from research on developmental processes in later life in order to inform intervention efforts (e.g., Knight, 1996).

Increasing evidence documents that older adults respond well to a variety of forms of psychotherapy and can benefit from psychological interventions to a degree comparable with younger adults (Pinquart & Soerensen, 2001; Zarit & Knight, 1996), though often responding somewhat more slowly. Cognitive-behavioral, psychodynamic, interpersonal and other approaches have shown utility in the treatment of specific problems among the aged (Gatz et al., 1998; Teri & McCurry, 1994). The problems for which efficacious psychological interventions have been demonstrated in older adults include depression (Areán & Cook, 2002; Niederehe & Schneider, 1998; Scogin & McElreath, 1994), anxiety (Stanley, Beck, & Glassco, 1996; Mohlman et al., 2003; Wetherell, 1998; 2002), sleep disturbance (Morin, Colecchi, Stone, Sood, & Brink, 1999; Morin, Kowatch, Barry, & Walton, 1993), and alcohol abuse (Blow, 2000). Cognitive training techniques, behavior modification strategies, and socio-environmental modifications may have particular relevance both for treating depression and improving functional abilities in cognitively impaired older adults (Burgio, 1996; Camp

& McKitrick, 1992; Floyd & Scogin, 1997; Neely & Bäckman, 1995; Teri, Logsdon, Uomoto, & McCurry, 1997). Reminiscence or life review therapy has shown utility as a technique in various applications, including the treatment of depression (Areán et al., 1993) and post-traumatic stress disorder (Maercker, 2002). The research knowledge base in treatment of late-life mental disorders is less adequate, however, with respect to establishing the efficacy of psychological interventions with ethnic minority older adults (Areán, 2003).

Psychological interventions are also effective in the behavioral medicine arena as adjunctive approaches for managing a variety of issues in care for those with primary medical conditions, such as managing pain (Watkins et al., 1999) and behavioral aspects of urinary incontinence (Burgio, 1998). They also can provide valuable assistance to older adults in dealing with the developmental issues of later life (Gutmann, 1994; Tobin, 1999), adapting to changing life circumstances, improving interpersonal relationships, and the like (e.g., see *Aging and Human Sexuality Resource Guide*, 2000).

Guideline 14. Psychologists strive to be familiar with and develop skill in applying specific psychotherapeutic interventions and environmental modifications with older adults and their families, including adapting interventions for use with this age group. Such interventions may include individual, group, couples and family techniques, and may employ both methods used for direct patient care and others designed for working with older adults' families and caregivers. Examples of interventions that may be unique to older adults or that are very commonly used with this population include reminiscence and life review; grief therapy; psychotherapy focusing on developmental issues and behavioral adaptations in late life; expressive therapies for those with communication difficulties; methods for enhancing cognitive function in later years; and psychoeducational programs for older adults, family members and other caregivers (Zarit & Knight, 1996; Duffy, 1999a).

No single modality of psychological intervention is preferable for all older adults. The selection of the most appropriate treatments and modes of delivery depends on the nature of the problem(s) involved, the clinical goals, the immediate situation, and the individual patient's characteristics, preferences and place on the continuum of care (for case examples, see Karel, Ogland-Hand, & Gatz, 2002; Knight, 1992). For example, community dwelling elders who are quite functional both physically and mentally may respond very well to outpatient forms of psychotherapy (individual, group, family, etc.). On the other hand, many disorders of late life are chronic or recurrent rather than acute, and the clinical objectives typically involve symptom management and rehabilitative maximization of function rather than cure (Knight & Satre, 1999). Accordingly, frail elders who are cognitively impaired, bed-bound, and depressed may respond most positively to behavioral techniques or modified psychotherapeutic approaches, emphasizing interpersonal support and environmental modifications designed to maximize functional abilities (Lichtenberg & Hartman-Stein, 1997; Wisocki, 1991).

The research literature provides evidence of the importance of specialized skills in working with the older adult population (Pinquart & Soerensen, 2001). A variety of special issues characterize work with older adults that may require that psychologists show particular sensitivities or utilize specialized techniques of intervention (*Psychotherapy and Older Adults Resource Guide*, 2003). For example, because many older adults lack familiarity with psychological services or harbor negative attitudes toward mental health issues, therapists often take special steps to educate older patients about ways in which psychological intervention may be helpful. In some clinical situations, intervention techniques developed particularly for use with older adults, such as reminiscence therapy, may be appropriate. Reminiscence is frequently used as a supportive therapeutic intervention to assist older adults in integrating their experiences, both as an element of other therapies (e.g., Birren & Deutchman, 1991; Peake, 1998) and as a separate, special technique (Haight, 1991; Haight & Webster, 1995; Sherman, 1991).

Because the issues are so commonly present, psychological intervention with older adults frequently also incorporates ways of addressing medical and other forms of comorbidity (for example, pain management, or enhancing compliance with medical treatment; Park, Morrell, & Shriffin, 1999). When facing physical illness, older adults may require assistance with adjusting to disabilities, bringing awareness and autonomy to the dying process (Kastenbaum, 2000), or altering patterns of relationship to family members, friends or significant others.

Though the procedures and techniques of clinical psychology in general are useful in working with older adults, and helpful in facilitating continued psychological growth at this stage of the life cycle, the appropriate and effective application of these methods to older adults involves expertise in adapting and tailoring them to fit the specific needs and situations of this age group (Jongsma & Frazer, 1998). Various adaptations of therapies have been advocated. For example, the processes of problem-solving, new learning, and behavior change often unfold more slowly when working with older adults (Gallagher-Thompson & Thompson, 1996); and sometimes modifications may be helpful to make the therapy more "user friendly" for older adults (Duffy, 1999a). These modifications may range from using larger print on forms for self-monitoring behavior or mood, to incorporating expressive techniques into the therapeutic interaction, to therapists' conducting home visits when mobility is impaired (Buschmann, Hollinger-Smith, & Peterson-Kokkas, 1999; Duffy, 1999b; Zeiss & Steffen, 1996).

Such changes may be prompted more by specific issues that older adults face (e.g., chronic illness and disability, grieving for loved ones, caregiving), the specific environments in which some older adults live or spend time (e.g., age-segregated social programs, skilled nursing facilities), or generational or cohort differences, than by clients' age per se (Knight, 1996). Many of the unique aspects of intervening with older adults thus may come from the content, rather than from the processes, of the therapy, where there is more attention to physical illness, grief, cognitive decline, and stressful practical problems associated with being old (Knight & Satre, 1999). It is also important to adapt interventions to fit the environmental context of the work, whether that be a private office, home, hospital or long-term care facility setting (see Guideline 15).

Furthermore, in addition to providing individual forms of treatment, many times psychologists deal with older adults as active participants in family or other social systems and work extensively with other interacting persons. Psychologists often assist family members or other care providers by providing education and/or emotional support, facilitating conceptualization of problems and potential solutions, and improving communication and the coordination of care (Qualls, 1995). While treating emotional and behavioral symptoms in older adults with progressive dementias generally involves attending to the affected older person as an individual (Kasl-Godley & Gatz, 2000), often families may also need help in understanding and coping with the behavioral problems that accompany dementia (Thompson & Gallagher-Thompson, 1996). Psychological interventions with family members who are providing care to older adults is a distinctive area of practice, with organized programs of intervention, training for providers, and evaluation of effectiveness (Coon, Gallagher-Thompson, & Thompson, 2003; Gallagher-Thompson & Steffen, 1994; Knight, Lutsky, & Macofsky-Urban, 1993; Mittelman et al., 1995; Teri et al., 1997).

Guideline 15. Psychologists strive to understand the issues pertaining to the provision of services in the specific settings in which older adults are typically located or encountered. Psychologists often work with older adults in a variety of settings, reflecting the "continuum of care" along which most services are delivered (Gelfand, 1999; Scheidt & Windley, 1998). These service delivery sites encompass various community settings where older people are to be found, including community-based and in-home care settings (e.g., senior centers, their own homes or apartments); outpatient settings (e.g., mental health or primary care clinics, private practitioner offices, HMO settings, or outpatient group programs); "day" programs (such as day hospitals or health care centers, day care centers, psychiatric partial hospitalization programs) serving elders with multiple or more complex problems; inpatient medical or psychiatric hospital settings; and long term care settings (such as nursing homes, residential care, assisted living, hospice and other congregate care sites; see Smyer & Allen-Burge, 1999). Some institutions include a variety of care settings. For example, consultation in Continuing Care Retirement Communities may run the gamut from older adults living in independent apartments to assisted living settings to the skilled nursing facility (SNFs). Because residence patterns are often concentrated by virtue of service needs, older adults seen in these various contexts usually differ in degree of impairment and functional ability. In the outpatient setting, for instance, a psychologist will most likely see functionally capable older adults, whereas in long term care facilities the clinician will usually treat physically frail and/or cognitively impaired elders (Lichtenberg & Hartman-Stein, 1997).

Understanding the financing and reimbursement systems, such as Medicare and Medicaid, that govern the organization and operation of various facilities is an important aspect of professional function in these settings (Norris, 2000; Norris, Molinari, & Rosowsky, 1998).

A set of practice guidelines is available for psychologists who provide services in long term care settings (Lichtenberg et al., 1998), as well as useful volumes discussing various facets of such professional practice (Lichtenberg, 1994; Molinari, 2000; Norris, Molinari, & Ogland-Hand, 2002; see also *Psychological Services for Long Term Care Resource Guide*, 2000).

Guideline 16. Psychologists strive to recognize issues related to the provision of prevention and health promotion services with older adults. Psychologists may contribute to the health and well-being of older adults by helping to provide psychoeducational programs (e.g., Gallagher-Thompson & DeVries, 1994) and by involvement in broader prevention efforts and other community-oriented interventions, as well as by advocacy within health care and political-legal systems (Gatz & Smyer, 2001; Hartman-Stein, 1998; Norris, 2000). In such activities, psychologists integrate their knowledge of clinical problems and techniques with consultation skills, strategic interventions, and preventive community or organizational programming to benefit substantial numbers of older adults. Such work may entail becoming familiar with outreach, case finding, referral and early intervention, as these relate to particular groups of at risk older adults. An important aspect of this emphasis is for psychologists to understand the strengths and limitations of local community resources relative to their domains of practice, or the risk factors affecting the older adult group of concern. For example, if attempting to reduce isolation as a risk factor for depression (Fees, Martin, & Poon, 1999), it might be pertinent to consider the availability of organized opportunities for older adult socialization and whether to increase these. Similarly, relative to fostering older adults' general sense of well-being, it might be useful to advocate for more health promotion activities designed to facilitate their participation in exercise, good nutrition and healthy lifestyles (Bortz & Bortz, 1996; Rowe & Kahn, 1998).

An area of particular concern for preventive efforts in the older adult population is that of suicide prevention (*Depression and Suicide in Older Adults Resource Guide*, 2002; Pearson, 2002). Older adults, and especially older white males, are the age group at highest risk for suicide (Conwell & Duberstein, 2001). A large study conducted in Finland indicated that depression was a particularly common precursor among older women who attempted or committed suicide, whereas older men in this category were more likely to have financial or physical health difficulties or substance abuse problems (Suominen et al., 1996). According to such data, assessment for suicide risk and prevention interventions might be directed towards older adults with depression and/or substance abuse. An influential observation has been that 70% to 75% of older adults who commit suicide have seen a physician quite recently (Carney, Rich, Burke, & Fowler, 1994). Based on this logic, it is important to enlist primary care physicians in efforts to prevent late-life suicide, through improved recognition of depressive symptoms and other risk factors, and referral to appropriate treatment (Pearson & Brown, 2000).

Guideline 17. Psychologists strive to understand issues pertaining to the provision of consultation services in assisting older adults. Psychologists who work with older adults are frequently asked to provide consultation to families and other caregivers of older adults, as well as to other professionals, self-help and support groups, institutions, agencies, and community organizations. In particular, they may often play key roles in providing training to staff who work directly with older adults in a variety of settings (Kramer & Smith, 2000), and in leading or contributing to program development, evaluation and quality assurance (Hartman-Stein, 1998; Knight & Kaskie, 1995). In the changing health care system, psychologists are increasingly likely to fill such consultative, supervisory, and educational roles in the organization and delivery of services to impaired older persons (e.g., particularly in nursing home settings; see Smyer, Cohn, & Brannon, 1988). If current trends continue, they may spend even more time than is already the case training and clinically supervising other health care providers for work with the aged.

Guideline 18. In working with older adults, psychologists are encouraged to understand the importance of interfacing with other disciplines, and to make referrals to other disciplines and/or to work with them in collaborative teams and across a range of sites, as appropriate. In their work with older adults, psychologists frequently may be cognizant of the importance of a coordinated care approach and may collaborate with other health, mental health, or social service professionals who are responsible for and/or provide particular forms of care to the same older individuals. Other disciplines typically involved in coordinated care, either as part of a team or to which referrals may be appropriate, include physicians, nurses and other associated health professionals, social workers, clergy, and lawyers. Psychologists can help a group of professionals become a team that is interdisciplinary in function, rather than merely multidisciplinary in structure, by generating effective strategies for integrating and coordinating the services provided by the various team members (Zeiss & Steffen, 1998).

For effective collaboration with other professionals, whether through actual teamwork or referrals, it is useful for psychologists to be knowledgeable about the services available from other disciplines and their potential contributions to a coordinated effort (e.g., see *Resource Directory for Older*

People, 2001). To make their particular contribution to such an effort, psychologists may often find it important to educate others as to the skills and role of the psychologist, and to present both clinical and didactic material in language understandable to other specific disciplines. The ability to communicate, educate, and coordinate with other concerned individuals may often be a key element in providing effective psychological services to older adults.

To provide psychological services in particular settings, it is important to learn how to collaborate in an interdisciplinary fashion with other disciplines operating in those environments. For this, it is useful to be familiar with the issues affecting particular service settings, such as age-related residential settings and services programs, and existing and emerging health care delivery systems, and to understand how various locales (e.g., in-home, outpatient, partial or day care, inpatient, extended care) fit into the broader continuum of care (see Guideline 15). It is also useful to understand entitlement programs for older adults (e.g., Social Security), provider reimbursement programs such as Medicare (see Administration on Aging, 2001; *Medicare Handbook: A Guide for Psychologists*, 2003; *Medicare Local Medical Review Policies Tool Kit*, 2003; Norris, 2000; Norris, Molinari, & Rosowsky, 1998), and how entitlement and reimbursement issues affect each of the disciplines on the team.

Sometimes psychologists are not able to operate within a team approach because they work in a private practice setting or other clinical context that lacks close linkages with other professions. In such settings psychologists may often see older adults with treatable problems for which they are not receiving adequate or timely professional attention. In such cases, another important role for the psychologist is to be proactively involved in outreach and appropriate referral to other professionals. Once having assured that such older adults receive more comprehensive care (whether that be in terms of social services, medications or other forms of care), psychologists can take steps to improve overall coordination and management of the care. They can attempt to tailor their psychological services to fit into an integral care plan suitable for the older individual and work towards helping the other care providers understand how each professional service being offered may affect the patient's response to other aspects of ongoing care. Such coordination of services is often key in the care of older adults, even in the private practice setting.

Guideline 19. Psychologists strive to understand the special ethical and/or legal issues entailed in providing services to older adults. It is important for psychologists to insure the safety of the older adults with whom they work but also to allow them to direct their own lives. Conflicts arise particularly with physically frail or cognitively impaired older adults because their ability to exercise autonomy is presumed to be impaired. Psychologists working with older adults are encouraged to be prepared to work through difficult ethical dilemmas in ways that balance considerations of the ethical principles of beneficence and autonomy, guarding the older adult's safety and well-being as well as recognizing the individual's right to make his or her own decisions to the extent possible, and to avoid adding their own value preferences to an already complex mix (Gilhooly, 1986; Yarhouse & DeVries, 1998).

Similar considerations regarding informed consent for treatment apply in work with older adults as in work with younger people. Special considerations tend to enter the picture to the degree that cognitive impairment (whether due to longstanding disabilities or age-associated changes) is present, or that the older individual may lack familiarity with the treatments that are being discussed as options. For example, while refusals of treatment always deserve to be respected, extra efforts may also be essential to assure that an older adult is making a treatment decision on an adequately informed basis. Older adults who may initially display an unwillingness to consent to participate in psychotherapy sometimes change this stance when informed that the therapy is short term, that it does not involve inpatient commitment, and that they will have the opportunity to decide their own treatment goals. As older adults are often brought in for therapy by family members, it is also important to assure that the older individual can make his or her own treatment decision independently of the desires of the family. Insistence on obtaining the individual's personal consent often may be an important part of building rapport with the older adult (Knight, 1996).

A diagnosis of dementia is not equivalent to incapacity. Even older adults with dementia often maintain the capacity to give or withhold consent until the illness has progressed to a point at which incapacity can be clearly established (Moye, 2000; Smyer & Allen-Burge, 1999). The particular point at which this occurs depends on the specific decision to be made. Even after incapacity becomes clear-cut, the individual often remains able to indicate assent to decisions.

Psychologists working with older adults may often encounter confidentiality issues in situations that involve families, multidisciplinary teams, long-term care settings, or other support systems. A common values conflict with regard to confidentiality involves older persons who are moderately to severely cognitively impaired and may be in some danger of causing harm to themselves or others as a result. Though it constitutes an exception to the general rules concerning confidentiality and deserves to be thought through with care, in such cases, it may be allowable to contact and share information with others. At the same time, for some individuals, preserving the individual's continued freedom and autonomy may be worth tolerating some risk of self-injury or allowing them to remain in a substandard living environment (Norris, Molinari, & Ogland-Hand, 2002).

In some settings (e.g., nursing homes, board and care facilities), mental health services may be provided in the residence in which the older adult lives. In these settings psychologists may be particularly challenged to protect client confidentiality. For example, it may be difficult to find a place to meet that is private. In addition, in such settings it is important to establish clear boundaries about what will and will not be shared with residence staff, both verbally and in written records (Lichtenberg et al., 1998).

Psychologists working with older adults may at times experience pressure from family members or other helping professionals who are also involved to share information about the older person. Such information sharing is often justified in terms of the need to help the older adult, and the collaboration with others may be very advantageous. Nonetheless, older adults in treatment relationships have as much right to full confidentiality as younger adults, and deserve to be asked to consent (in writing, if possible) to the sharing of information as long as able to provide consent (Knight, 1996).

Another set of ethical issues involves handling potential conflicts of interest between older adults and family members, particularly in situations of substitute decision making (Smyer & Allen-Burge, 1999). Even when cognitive incapacity does interfere with a demented person's ability to exercise autonomy in the present, it may remain possible to ascertain what the individual's wishes have been in the past and act according to those wishes. The question arises as to who decides what is in the demented person's best interests: one or another family member, a professional person, the residential facility in which the demented person resides, the director of a research program and so on. In each instance, there may be some risk that the substitute decision maker will act for his or her own good rather than in the best interests of the demented older adult (Allen-Burge & Haley, 1997). This potential for conflict of interests arises both with formally and legally appointed guardians as well as with informal substitute decision making by family members.

Psychologists may experience role conflicts when working in nursing homes. For example, instances arise in which the best interests of the older adult may be at odds with those of the staff or facility management. Such ethical dilemmas are best resolved by reserving uppermost priority for serving the best interests of the older adult, even when the psychologist has been hired by the facility (Abeles et al., 1998).

At times, psychologists may encounter situations in which it is suspected that older adults may be victims of abuse or neglect, and will be legally obligated to report these to appropriate authorities. Serving older adults well under these circumstances entails being knowledgeable about applicable statutory requirements as well as local community resources, and collaborating in arranging for the involvement of adult protective services (*Elder Abuse and Neglect*, 1999; Pollack & Weiner, 1995; Wolf, 1998). Likewise, because death and dying are age-related, psychologists who work with the older adult population may often find it useful to be well informed regarding legal concerns and professional ethics surrounding these matters (APA Working Group on Assisted Suicide and End-of-Life Decisions, 2000).

EDUCATION

Guideline 20. Psychologists are encouraged to increase their knowledge, understanding and skills with respect to working with older adults through continuing education, training, supervision and consultation. Psychologists can obtain training in working clinically with older adults through various pathways, including respecialization programs, postdoctoral fellowships, continuing education activities (workshops, in-service training/seminars, distance learning), self-study and/or supervised self-study, or combinations of such alternatives. Newly trained psychologists fortunate enough to be given supervised experience in clinical work with older adults as part of their graduate training most commonly receive it within clinical internships or postdoctoral fellowships, although some graduate programs may provide such training opportunities as part of clinical practicum course work. Those already in practice but unable to participate in concentrated, formal training programs may be able to accumulate continuing education credits. Many practicing psychologists perceive a need for and express interest in continuing education in clinical geropsychology (Qualls et al., 2002), and opportunities for obtaining continuing education in this area are expanding. Individuals in practice may also enroll over time for course work relating to the provision of services to the older adult, and gain consultation or supervised experience working with older adults by arrangements with local clinical service organizations and/or individual psychologists who are already skilled in this area.

The research and practice literature relevant to working with older adults is available through various major professional journals, including a growing number of applied clinical journals. Research and practice developments are also disseminated to practitioners through various professional organizations. Within APA, both Division 20 (Adult Development and Aging), and Division 12-Section II (Clinical Geropsychology) have newsletters, e-mail networks, and web sites offering information useful to practicing psychologists. For example, among its "Resources for Educators," the Division 20 Web site features extensive listings of relevant reference materials, including books, films and videotapes, sample syllabi for various undergraduate and graduate courses in the psychology of aging, and a guide to doctoral programs in adult development and aging, including clinical geropsychology (APA Division 20 Education Committee, 2002). The Division 12-Section II Web site features a directory of pre- and postdoctoral training opportunities in clinical work with older adults (Hinrichsen & Arnold, 2001). Likewise, the Office on Aging page on the main APA Web site provides access to a number of aging-related APA publications, some of them downloadable (see http://www.apa.org/pi/aging).

Psychologists in Long Term Care (PLTC) is an independent organization that convenes regularly in conjunction with APA Conventions and annual meetings of the Gerontological Society of America (GSA). PTLC frequently provides workshop training for psychologists interested in developing assessment, therapeutic and consultation skills in serving older adults in long term care settings. The GSA has a multidisciplinary membership and, as part of its annual meeting, promotes information sharing and networking among the health professions which serve older adults in sessions held by standing interest groups on numerous topics (e.g., mental health practice, end-of-life issues). Other special interest groups on aging have operated for varying periods of time and with variable intensity within the Association for Advancement of Behavior Therapy (AABT), and in additional practice-oriented APA Divisions, such as Division 17 (Counseling Psychology), Division 29 (Psychotherapy), Division 38 (Health Psychology), and Division 42 (Independent Practice).

REFERENCES

Abeles, N., Cooley, S., Deitch, I. M., Harper, M. S., Hinrichsen, G., Lopez, M. A., & Molinari, V. A. (1998). What practitioners should know about working with older adults. *Professional Psychology: Research and Practice, 29,* 413–427. [electronic version] Retrieved August 19, 2002, from http://www.apa.org/pi/aging/practitioners.pdf

Abramson, T. A., Trejo, L., & Lai, D. W. L. (2002). Culture and mental health: Providing appropriate services for a diverse older population. *Generations: Journal of the American Society on Aging, 26,* 21–27.

Administration on Aging. (2001). *Older adults and mental health: Issues and opportunities* [electronic version]. Retrieved February 6, 2003, from the AOA Web site: http://www.aoa.gov/mh/report2001/default.htm

Aging and Human Sexuality Resource Guide. (2000). Washington, DC: American Psychological Association. Retrieved February 6, 2003, from the APA Office on Aging Web site: http://www.apa.org/pi/aging/sexuality.html

Albert, M. S., & Moss, M. B. (Eds.). (1988). *Geriatric neuropsychology.* New York: Guilford.

Algase, D. L. (2001). Wandering. In B. Edelstein (Ed.), *Clinical geropsychology.* New York: Pergamon.

Allen-Burge, R., & Haley, W. E. (1997). Individual differences and surrogate medical decisions: Differing preferences for life-sustaining treatments. *Aging & Mental Health, 1*(2), 121–131.

American Psychological Association. (2002a). Ethical principles of psychologists and code of conduct. *American Psychologist, 57*(12), 1060–1073. [electronic version] Retrieved December 18, 2002, from http://www2.apa.org/ethics/code2002.doc

American Psychological Association. (2002b). *Resolution on ageism* [electronic version]. Retrieved February 6, 2003, from the APA Office on Aging Web site: http://www.apa.org/pi/aging/ageism.html

APA Division 20 Education Committee. (2002). *Guide to graduate study in the psychology of adult development and aging (Data from 1998–1999; updates 11/2002)* [electronic version]. Washington, DC: Author. Retrieved August 19, 2002, from APA Division of Adult Development and Aging Web site: http://aging.ufl.edu/apadiv20/guide01.htm

APA Presidential Task Force on the Assessment of Age-Consistent Memory Decline and 40 Dementia. (1998). *Guidelines for the evaluation of dementia and age-related cognitive decline* [electronic version]. Washington, DC: American Psychological Association. Retrieved July 8, 2000, from the APA Practice Directorate Web site: http://www.apa.org/practice/dementia.html

APA Working Group on Assisted Suicide and End-of-Life Decisions. (2000). *Report to the Board of Directors of APA from the Working Group on Assisted Suicide and End-of-Life Decisions.* Washington, DC: American Psychological Association. Retrieved February 6, 2003, from http://www.apa.org/pi/aseolf.html

Ancoli-Israel, S., Pat-Horenczyk, R., & Martin, J. (2001). Sleep disorders. In B. Edelstein (Ed.), *Clinical geropsychology* (pp. 307–326). New York: Pergamon.

Antonucci, T. C. (2001). Social relations: An examination of social networks, social support, and sense of control. In J. E. Birren & K. W. Schaie (Eds.), *Handbook of the psychology of aging* (5th ed., pp. 427–453). San Diego, CA: Academic Press.

Antonucci, T. C., & Akiyama, H. (1995). Convoys of social relations: Family and friendships within a life span context. In R. Blieszner & V. H. Bedford (Eds.), *Handbook of aging and the family* (pp. 355–372). Westport, CT: Greenwood Press.

Areán, P. A. (2003). Advances in psychotherapy for mental illness in late life. *American Journal of Geriatric Psychiatry, 11,* 4–6.

Areán, P. A., & Cook, B. L. (2002). Psychotherapy and combined psychotherapy/pharmacotherapy for late life depression. *Biological Psychiatry, 52,* 293–303.

Areán, P. A., Perri, M. G., Nezu, A. M., Schein, R. L., Christopher, F., & Joseph, T. X. (1993). Comparative effectiveness of social problem-solving therapy and reminiscence therapy as treatments for depression in older adults. *Journal of Consulting and Clinical Psychology, 61,* 1003–1010.

Assessment of competency and capacity of the older adult: A practice guideline forpsychologists. (1997). National Center for Cost Containment, U.S. Department of Veterans Affairs, Milwaukee, WI (NTIS # PB-97-147904).

Bachman, D. L., Wolf, P. A., Linn, R., Knoefel, J. E., Cobb, J., Belanger, A., et al. (1992). Prevalence of dementia and probable senile dementia of the Alzheimer type in the Framingham Study. *Neurology, 42,* 115–119.

Bäckman, L., Small, B. J., & Wahlin, Å. (2001) Aging and memory: Cognitive and biological perspectives. In J. E. Birren & K. W. Schiae (Eds.), *Handbook of the psychology of aging* (5th ed., pp. 349–377). San Diego, CA: Academic Press.

Ball, K. (1997). Attention problems in older drivers. *Alzheimer's Disease and Associated Disorders, 11*, 42–47.

Baltes, M. M. (1996). *The many faces of dependency in old age.* Cambridge, England: Cambridge University Press.

Baltes, P. B. (1997). On the incomplete architecture of human ontogeny: Selection, optimization, and compensation as foundation of developmental theory. *American Psychologist, 52*, 366–380.

Baltes, P. B., & Baltes, M. M. (1990). Psychological perspectives on successful aging: The model of selective optimization with compensation. In P. B. Baltes & M. M. Baltes (Eds.), *Successful aging: Perspectives from the behavioral sciences* (pp. 1–34). Cambridge, England: Cambridge University Press.

Baltes, P. B., & Lindenberger, U. (1997). Emergence of a powerful connection between sensory and cognitive functions across the adult life span: A new window to the study of cognitive aging? *Psychology and Aging, 12*, 12–21.

Baltes, P. B., & Staudinger, U. M. (2000). Wisdom: A metaheuristic (pragmatic) to orchestrate mind and virtue towards excellence. *American Psychologist, 55*, 122–136.

Banks, M. A., Ackerman, R. J., & Clark, E. O. (1986). Elderly women in family therapy. *Women & Therapy, 5*(2–3), 107–116.

Bengtson, V. L. (2001). Beyond the nuclear family: The increasing importance of multigenerational bonds (The Burgess Award Lecture). *Journal of Marriage and the Family, 63*, 1–16.

Bengtson, V. L., Rosenthal, C., & Burton, L. (1996). Paradoxes of families and aging. In R. H. Binstock & L. K. George (Eds.), *Handbook of aging and the social sciences* (4th ed., pp. 253–282). San Diego, CA: Academic Press.

Bengtson, V. L., & Schaie, K. W. (Eds.). (1999). *Handbook of theories of aging.* New York: Springer.

Birren, J. E., & Deutchman, D. E. (1991). *Guiding autobiography groups for older adults: Exploring the future of life.* Baltimore: Johns Hopkins University Press.

Birren, J. E., & Schaie, K. W. (Eds.). (1977). *Handbook of the psychology of aging.* New York: Van Nostrand Reinhold.

Birren, J. E., & Schaie, K. W. (Eds.). (1985). *Handbook of the psychology of aging* (2nd ed.). New York: Van Nostrand Reinhold.

Birren, J. E., & Schaie, K. W. (Eds.). (1990). *Handbook of the psychology of aging* (3rd ed.). San Diego, CA: Academic Press.

Birren, J. E., & Schaie, K. W. (Eds.). (1996). *Handbook of the psychology of aging* (4th ed.). San Diego, CA: Academic Press.

Birren, J. E., & Schaie, K. W. (Eds.). (2001). *Handbook of the psychology of aging* (5th ed.). San Diego, CA: Academic Press.

Blanchard-Fields, F., & Hess, T. M. (Eds.). (1996). *Perspectives on cognitive change in adulthood and aging*. New York: McGraw-Hill.

Blieszner, R., & Bedford, V. H. (Eds.). (1995). *Aging and the family: Theory and research*. Westport, CT: Praeger.

Blow, F. C. (2000). Treatment of older women with alcohol problems: Meeting the challenge for a special population. *Alcoholism, Clinical and Experimental Research, 24,* 1257–1266.

Blow, F. C., Oslin, D. W., & Barry, K. L. (2002). Misuse and abuse of alcohol, illicit drugs, and psychoactive medication among older people. *Generations: Journal of the American Society on Aging, 26,* 50–54.

Bonwick, R. J., & Morris, P. L. P. (1996). Post-traumatic stress disorders in elderly war veterans. *International Journal of Geriatric Psychiatry, 11,* 1071–1076.

Bootzin, R. R., Epstein, D., Engle-Friedman, M., & Salvio, M.-A. (1996). Sleep disturbances. In L. L. Carstensen, B. A. Edelstein, & L. Dornbrand (Eds.), *The practical handbook of clinical gerontology* (pp. 398–420). Thousand Oaks, CA: Sage.

Bortz, W. M., II, & Bortz, S. S. (1996). Prevention, nutrition, and exercise in the aged. In L. L. Carstensen, B. A. Edelstein, & L. Dornbrand (Eds.), *The practical handbook of clinical gerontology* (pp. 36–53). Thousand Oaks, CA: Sage.

Braithwaite, V. A. (1986). Old age stereotypes: Reconciling contradictions. *Journal of Gerontology, 41,* 353–360.

Burgio, K. L. (1998). Behavioral vs. drug treatment for urge urinary incontinence in older women: A randomized controlled trial. *Journal of the American Medical Association, 280,* 1995–2000.

Burgio, K. L., & Locher, J. L. (1996). Urinary incontinence. In L. L. Carstensen, B. A. Edelstein, & L. Dornbrand (Eds.), *The practical handbook of clinical gerontology* (pp. 349–373). Thousand Oaks, CA: Sage.

Burgio, L. (1996). Interventions for the behavioral complications of Alzheimer's disease: Behavioral approaches. *International Psychogeriatrics, 8*(Suppl. 1), 45–52.

Burns, B. J., Wagner, H. R., Taube, J. E., Magaziner, J., Permutt, T., & Landerman, L. R. (1993). Mental health service use by the elderly in nursing homes. *American Journal of Public Health, 83,* 331–337.

Burt, D. B., & Aylward, E. H. (1999). Assessment methods for diagnosis of dementia. In M. P. Janicki & A. J. Dalton (Eds.), *Dementia, aging, and intellectual disabilities: A handbook* (pp. 141–156). Philadelphia: Brunner-Routledge.

Buschmann, M. B. T., Hollinger-Smith, L. M., & Peterson-Kokkas, S. E. (1999). Implementation of expressive physical touch in depressed older adults. *Journal of Clinical Geropsychology, 5,* 291–300.

Butler, R. N. (1963). The life review: An interpretation of reminiscence in the aged. *Psychiatry, 119,* 721–728.

Butler, R. N. (1969). Ageism: Another form of bigotry. *Gerontologist, 9,* 243–246.

Butler, R. N., Lewis, M. I., & Sunderland, T. (1998). *Aging and mental health: Positive psychosocial and biomedical approaches* (5th ed.). Philadelphia: Allyn & Bacon.

Butters, M. A., Becker, J. T., Nebes, R. D., Zmuda, M. D., Mulsant, B. H., Pollock, B. G., & Reynolds, C. F., III. (2000). Changes in cognitive functioning following treatment of late-life depression. *American Journal of Psychiatry, 157*, 1912–1914.

Butters, M. A., Salmon, D. P., & Butters, N. (1994). Neuropsychological assessment of dementia. In M. Storandt & G. R. VandenBos (Eds.), *Neuropsychological assessment of dementia and depression in older adults: A clinician's guide* (pp. 33–60). Washington, DC: American Psychological Association.

Cacioppo, J. T., Poehlmann, K. M., Burleson, M. H., Kiecolt-Glaser, J. K., Malarkey, W. B., Bernston, G. G., & Glaser, R. (1998). Cellular immune responses to acute stress in female caregivers of dementia patients and matched controls. *Health Psychology, 17*, 182–189.

California State Senate Bill 953, Ch. 541, Statutes of 2002. Retrieved March 3, 2003, from http://www.psychboard.ca.gov/laws_regs/sb_953.pdf

Camp, C. J., & McKitrick, L. A. (1992). Memory interventions in DAT populations: Methodological and theoretical issues. In R. L. West & J. D. Sinnott (Eds.), *Everyday memory and aging: Current research and methodology* (pp. 155–172). New York: Springer-Verlag.

Carney, S. S., Rich, C. L., Burke, P. A., & Fowler, R. C. (1994). Suicide over 60: The San Diego study. *Journal of the American Geriatrics Society, 42*, 174–180.

Carstensen, L. L., Isaacowitz, D. M., & Charles, S. T. (1999). Taking time seriously: A theory of socioemotional selectivity. *American Psychologist, 54*, 165–181.

Cavanaugh, J. C., & Whitbourne, S. K. (Eds.). (1999). *Gerontology: An interdisciplinary perspective.* New York: Oxford University Press.

Coburn, A., & Bolda, E. (1999). The rural elderly and long-term care. In T. C. Ricketts (Ed.), *Rural health in the United States* (pp. 179–189). New York: Oxford University Press.

Cohen-Mansfield, J., Werner, P., Culpepper, W. J., II, Wolfson, M. A., & Bickel, E. (1996). Wandering and aggression. In L. L. Carstensen, B. A. Edelstein, & L. Dornbrand (Eds.), *The practical handbook of clinical gerontology* (pp. 374–397). Thousand Oaks, CA: Sage.

Congress triples funding for GPE program. (2003, February 20). Electronic notice posted on the APA Public Policy Office Web site. Retrieved February 28, 2003, from http://www.apa.org/ppo/issues/eappops03.html

Conwell, Y., & Duberstein, P. R. (2001). Suicide in elders. *Annals of the New York Academy of Sciences, 932*, 132–150.

Coon, D., Gallagher-Thompson, D., & Thompson, L. W. (Eds.). (2003). *Innovative interventions to reduce dementia caregiver distress.* New York: Springer.

Costa, P. T., Jr., & McCrae, R. R. (1988). Personality in adulthood: A six-year longitudinal study of self-reports and spouse ratings on the NEO Personality Inventory. *Journal of Personality and Social Psychology, 54*, 853–863.

Costa, P. T., Jr., Yang, J., & McCrae, R. R. (1998). Aging and personality traits: Generalizations and clinical implications. In I. H. Nordhus, G. R. VandenBos, S. Berg, & P. Fromholt (Eds.), *Clinical geropsychology.* Washington, DC: American Psychological Association.

Craik, F. I. M., & Salthouse, T. A. (Eds.). (2000). *The handbook of aging and cognition*. Mahwah, NJ: Erlbaum.

Crowther, M. R., & Zeiss, A. M. (2003). Aging and mental health. In J. S. Mio & G. Y. Iwamasa (Eds.), *Culturally diverse mental health: The challenge of research and resistance* (pp. 309–322). New York: Brunner-Routledge.

Curry, L. C., & Stone, J. G. (1995). Understanding elder abuse: The social problem of the 1990s. *Journal of Clinical Geropsychology, 1*(2), 147–156.

Depression and suicide in older adults resource guide. (2002). [electronic version] Retrieved February 6, 2003, from the APA Office on Aging Web site: http://www.apa.org/pi/aging/depression.html

Diehl, M. (1998) Everyday competence in later life: Current status and future directions. *Gerontologist, 38*, 422–433.

Diehl, M., Coyle, N., & Labouvie-Vief, G. (1996). Age and sex differences in strategies of coping and defense across the life span. *Psychology and Aging, 11*, 127–139.

Dolan, M. M., Hawkes, W. G., Zimmerman, S. I., Morrison, R. S., Gruber-Baldini, A. L., Hebel, J. R., & Magaziner, J. (2000). Delirium on hospital admission in aged hip fracture patients: Prediction of mortality and 2-year functional outcomes. *Journal of Gerontology: Medical Sciences, 55A*, M527–M534.

Duffy, M. (Ed.). (1999a). *Handbook of counseling and psychotherapy with older adults*. New York: John Wiley & Sons.

Duffy, M. (1999b). Reaching the person behind the dementia: Treating comorbid affective disorders through subvocal and nonverbal strategies. In M. Duffy (Ed.), *Handbook of counseling and psychotherapy with older adults* (pp. 577–589). New York: John Wiley & Sons.

Dupree, L. W., & Patterson, R. L. (1985). Assessing deficits and supports in the elderly. In M. Hersen & S. M. Turner (Eds.), *Diagnostic interviewing* (pp. 337–359). New York: Plenum.

Edelstein, B. A. (Ed.). (2001). *Clinical geropsychology*. New York: Pergamon.

Edelstein, B., & Kalish, K. (1999). Clinical assessment of older adults. In J. C. Cavanaugh & S. Whitbourne (Eds.), *Gerontology: An interdisciplinary perspective* (pp. 269–304). New York: Oxford University Press.

Edelstein, B. A., & Semenchuk, E. M. (1996). Interviewing older adults. In L. L. Carstensen, B. A. Edelstein, & L. Dornbrand (Eds.), *The practical handbook of clinical gerontology* (pp. 153–173). Thousand Oaks, CA: Sage.

Eisdorfer, C., & Lawton, M. P. (Eds.). (1973). *The psychology of adult development and aging*. Washington, DC: American Psychological Association.

Eizenman, D. R., Nesselroade, J. R., Featherman, D. L., & Rowe, J. W. (1997). Intraindividual variability in perceived control in an older sample: The MacArthur Successful Aging studies. *Psychology and Aging, 12*, 489–502.

Elder abuse and neglect: In search of solutions. (1999). Washington, DC: American Psychological Association. [electronic version] Retrieved February 6, 2003, from the APA Office on Aging Web site: http://www.apa.org/pi/aging/eldabuse.html

Elder, G. H., Jr. (1999). *Children of the Great Depression: Social change in life experience* (25th anniversary ed.). Boulder, CO: Westview Press.

Elder, G. H., Jr., & Hareven, T. K. (1994). Rising above life's disadvantage: From the Great Depression to war. In G. H. Elder, Jr., J. Modell, & R. D. Parke (Eds.), *Children in time and place: Developmental and historical insights* (pp. 47–72). New York: Cambridge University Press.

Erikson, E. H., Erikson, J. M., & Kivnick, H. (1986). *Vital involvement in old age: The experience of old age in our time.* New York: Norton.

Evans, D. A., Funkenstein, H. H., Albert, M. S., Scherr, P. A., Cook, N. R., Chown, M. J., et al. (1989). Prevalence of Alzheimer's disease in a community population of older persons: Higher than previously reported. *Journal of the American Medical Association, 262,* 2551–2556.

Federal Interagency Forum on Aging-Related Statistics. (2000). *Older Americans 2000: Key indicators of well-being.* Washington, DC: U.S. Government Printing Office.

Fees, B. S., Martin, P., & Poon, L. W. (1999). A model of loneliness in older adults. *Journal of Gerontology: Psychological Sciences, 54B,* P231–P239.

Femia, E. E., Zarit, S. H., & Johansson, B. (2001). The disablement process in very late life: A study of the oldest-old in Sweden. *Journal of Gerontology: Psychological Sciences, 56B,* P12–P23.

Fisher, J. E., & Carstensen, L. L. (1990). Behavior management of the dementias. *Clinical Psychology Review, 10,* 611–629.

Fisher, J. E., & Noll, J. P. (1996). Anxiety disorders. In L. L. Carstensen, B. A. Edelstein, & L. Dornbrand (Eds.), *The practical handbook of clinical gerontology* (pp. 304–323). Thousand Oaks, CA: Sage.

Fisher, J. E., Swingen, D. N., & Harsin, C. M. (2001). Agitated and aggressive behavior. In B. Edelstein (Ed.), *Clinical geropsychology.* New York: Pergamon.

Floyd, M., & Scogin, F. (1997). Effects of memory training on the subjective memory functioning and mental health of older adults: A meta analysis. *Psychology and Aging,12,* 150–161.

Frank, E., Prigerson, H. G., Shear, M. K., & Reynolds, C. F. (1997). Phenomenology and treatment of bereavement-related distress in the elderly. *International Clinical Psychopharmacology, 12,* S25–S29.

Frazer, D. W. (1995) The medical issues in geropsychology training and practice. In B. G. Knight, L. Teri, P. Wohlford, & J. Santos (Eds.), *Mental health services for older adults: Implications for training and practice in geropsychology* (pp. 63–71). Washington, DC: American Psychological Association.

Frazer, D. W., Leicht, M. L., & Baker, M. D. (1996). Psychological manifestations of physical disease in the elderly. In L. L. Carstensen, B. A. Edelstein, & L. Dornbrand (Eds.), *The practical handbook of clinical gerontology* (pp. 217–235). Thousand Oaks, CA: Sage.

Fuller-Thomson, E., Minkler, M., & Driver, D. (1997). A profile of grandparents raising grandchildren in the United States. *Gerontologist, 37,* 406–411.

Fuller-Thomson, E., & Minkler, M. (2003). Housing issues and realities facing grandparent caregivers who are renters. *Gerontologist, 43,* 92–98.

Gallagher-Thompson, D., & Devries, H. M. (1994). "Coping with frustration" classes: Development and preliminary outcomes with women who care for relatives with dementia. *Gerontologist, 34*, 548–552.

Gallagher-Thompson, D., & Steffen, A. M. (1994). Comparative effects of cognitive-behavioral and brief dynamic therapy for depressed family caregivers. *Journal of Consulting and Clinical Psychology, 62*, 543–549.

Gallagher-Thompson, D., & Thompson, L. W. (1996). Applying cognitive-behavioral therapy to the psychological problems of later life. In S. H. Zarit & B. G. Knight (Eds.), *A guide to psychotherapy and aging: Effective clinical interventions in a life-stage context* (pp. 61–82). Washington, DC: American Psychological Association.

Gallo, J. J., & Lebowitz, B. D. (1999). The epidemiology of common late-life mental disorders in the community: Themes for the new century. *Psychiatric Services, 50*, 1158–1166.

Gallo, J. J., & Rabins, P. V. (1999). Depression without sadness: Alternative presentations of depression in late life. *American Family Physician, 60*, 820–826.

Gatz, M. (1998). Towards a developmentally-informed theory of mental disorder in older adults. In J. Lomranz (Ed.), *Handbook of aging and mental health* (pp. 101–120). New York: Plenum.

Gatz, M., & Finkel, S. I. (1995). Education and training of mental health service providers. In M. Gatz (Ed.), *Emerging issues in mental health and aging* (pp. 282–302). Washington, DC: American Psychological Association.

Gatz, M., Fiske, A., Fox, L. S., Kaskie, B., Kasl-Godley, J. E., McCallum, T. J., & Wetherell, J. L. (1998). Empirically validated psychological treatments for older adults. *Journal of Mental Health and Aging, 4*, 9–46.

Gatz, M., & Pearson, C. G. (1988). Ageism revised and provision of psychological services. *American Psychologist, 43*, 184–189.

Gatz, M., & Smyer, M. A. (2001). Mental health and aging at the outset of the twenty-first century. In J. E. Birren & K. W. Schaie (Eds.), *Handbook of the psychology of aging* (5th ed., pp. 523–544). San Diego, CA: Academic Press.

Gelfand, D. E. (1999). *The aging network: Programs and services* (5th ed.). New York: Springer.

Gerontological Society of America Task Force on Minority Issues in Gerontology. (1994). *Minority elders: Five goals toward building a public policy base.* Washington, DC: Gerontological Society of America.

Geropsychology assessment resource guide. (1996). National Center for Cost Containment, U.S. Department of Veterans Affairs, Milwaukee, WI (NTIS # PB-96-144365).

Gilhooly, M. L. M. (1986). Legal and ethical issues in the management of the dementing elderly. In M. L. M. Gilhooly, S. H. Zarit, & J. E. Birren (Eds.), *The dementias: Policy and management* (pp. 131–160). Englewood Cliffs, NJ: Prentice-Hall.

Goodstein, R. K. (1985). Common clinical problems in the elderly: Camouflaged by ageism and atypical presentation. *Psychiatric Annals, 15*, 299–312.

Green, J. (2000). *Neuropsychological evaluation of the older adult: A clinician's guidebook*. San Diego, CA: Academic Press.

Greenberg, J. S., Seltzer, M. M., & Greenley, J. R. (1993). Aging parents of adults with disabilities: The gratifications and frustrations of later-life caregiving. *Gerontologist, 33*, 542–550.

Guidelines for psychotherapy with lesbian, gay, & bisexual clients. (2000). *American Psychologist, 55*, 1440–1451. [electronic version] Retrieved August 19, 2002, from http://www.apa.org/pi/lgbc/guideline.html

Guralnick, S., Kemel, K., Stamm, B. H., & Greving, A. M. (2003). Rural geriatrics and gerontology. In B. H. Stamm (Ed.), *Rural behavioral health care: An interdisciplinary guide*. Washington, DC: American Psychological Association.

Gutmann, D. (1994). *Reclaimed powers: Men and women in later life*. Evanston, IL: Northwestern University Press.

Haight, B. K. (1991). Reminiscing: The state of the art as a basis for practice. *International Journal of Aging and Human Development, 33*, 1–32.

Haight, B. K., & Webster, J. D. (Eds.). (1995). *The art and science of reminiscing: Theory, research methods, and applications*. Bristol, PA: Taylor & Francis.

Hartman-Stein, P. E. (1998). Hope amidst the behavioral healthcare crisis. In P. E. Hartman-Stein (Ed.), *Innovative behavioral healthcare for older adults* (pp. 201–214). San Francisco: Jossey-Bass Publishers.

Hersen, M., & Van Hasselt, V. B. (1992). Behavioral assessment and treatment of anxiety in older adults. *Clinical Psychology Review, 12*, 619–640.

Hinrichsen, G. A. (2000). Knowledge of and interest in geropsychology among psychology trainees. *Professional Psychology: Research and Practice, 31*, 442–445.

Hinrichsen, G. A., & Arnold, M. (2001). Directory of predoctoral internships with clinical geropsychology training opportunities and postdoctoral clinical geropsychology fellowships (2nd ed.) [electronic version]. Washington, DC: American Psychological Association, Division 12, Section II. Retrieved August 19, 2002, from APA Section on Clinical Geropsychology Web site: http://bama.ua.edu/~appgero/apa12_2/training/trainmain.html

Horvath, A. O., & Bedi, R. P. (2002). The alliance. In J. C. Norcross (Ed.), *Psychotherapy relationships that work* (pp. 37–70). New York: Oxford University Press.

Hunt, T., & Lindley, C. J. (Eds.). (1990). *Testing older adults: A reference guide for geropsychological assessments*. Austin, TX: Pro-ed.

Huyck, M. H. (1990). Gender differences in aging. In J. E. Birren & K. W. Schaie (Eds.), *Handbook of the psychology of aging* (3rd ed.; pp. 124–132). San Diego, CA: Academic Press.

Hyer, L. A., & Sohnle, S. J. (2001). *Trauma among older people: Issues and treatment*. Philadelphia: Bruner-Routledge.

Ivnik, R. J., Malec, J. F., Smith, G. E., Tangalos, E. G., et. al. (1992). Mayo's Older American Normative Studies: WMS-R norms for ages 56–94. *The Clinical Neuropsychologist, 6*, 49–82.

Jackson, J. S. (Ed). (1988). *The black American elderly: Research on physical and psychosocial health*. New York: Springer.

James, J. W., & Haley, W. E. (1995). Age and health bias in practicing clinical psychologists. *Psychology and Aging, 10*, 610–616.

Janicki, M. P., & Dalton, A. J. (Eds.). (1999). *Dementia, aging, and intellectual disabilities: A handbook.* Philadelphia: Brunner-Routledge.

Janicki, M. P., Dalton, A. J., Henderson, C. M., & Davidson, P. W. (1999). Mortality and morbidity among older adults with intellectual disability: Health services considerations. *Disability & Rehabilitation, 21*, 284–294.

Janicki, M. P., Heller, T., & Hogg, J. (1996). Practice guidelines for the clinical assessment and care management of Alzheimer's disease and other dementias among adults with intellectual disability. *Journal of Intellectual Disability Research, 40*, 374–382.

Jeste, D. V., Alexopoulos, G. S., Bartels, S. J., Cummings, J. L., Gallo, J. J., Gottlieb, G. L, et al. (1999). Consensus statement on the upcoming crisis in geriatric mental health: Research agenda for the next 2 decades. *Archives of General Psychiatry, 56*, 848–853.

Jongsma, A., & Frazer, D. (1998). *The older adult psychotherapy treatment planner.* New York: Wiley.

Kahana, E., Kahana, B., & Riley K. (1989). Person-environment transactions relevant to control and helplessness in institutional settings. In P. S. Fry (Ed.), *Psychological perspectives of helplessness and control in the elderly* (pp. 121–153). Advances in Psychology.

Karel, M. J., Ogland-Hand, S., & Gatz, M. (2002). *Assessing and treating late-life depression: A casebook and resource guide.* New York: Basic Books.

Kasl-Godley, J., & Gatz, M. (2000). Psychosocial intervention for individuals with dementia: An integration of theory, therapy, and a clinical understanding of dementia. *Clinical Psychology Review, 20*, 755–782.

Kastenbaum, R. (1999). Dying and bereavement. In J. C. Cavanaugh & S. K. Whitbourne (Eds.), *Gerontology: An interdisciplinary perspective* (pp. 155–185). New York: Oxford University Press.

Kastenbaum, R. (2000). Counseling the dying patient. In V. Molinari (Ed.), *Professional psychology in long term care: A comprehensive guide* (pp. 201–226). New York: Hatherleigh Press.

Kaszniak, A. W., & Christenson, G. D. (1994). Differential diagnosis of dementia and depression. In M. A. Storandt, & G. R. VandenBos (Eds.), *Neuropsychological assessment of dementia and depression in older adults: A clinician's guide* (pp. 81–117). Washington, DC: American Psychological Association.

Kennedy, G. (2000). *Geriatric mental health care.* New York: Guilford.

Kiecolt-Glaser, J. K., Dura, J. R., Speicher, C. E., Trask, J., & Glaser, R. (1991). Spousal caregivers of dementia victims: Longitudinal changes in immunity and health. *Psychosomatic Medicine, 53*, 345–362.

Kimerling, R. E., Zeiss, A. M., & Zeiss, R. A. (2000). Therapist emotional responses to patients: Building a learning based language. *Cognitive and Behavioral Practice, 7*, 312–321.

Kimmel, D. (1995). Lesbians and gay men also grow old. In L. Bond, S. Cutler, & A. Grams (Eds.), *Promoting successful and productive aging* (pp. 289–303). Thousand Oaks, CA: Sage.

Kite, M. E., & Wagner, L. S. (2002). Attitudes toward older adults. In T. D. Nelson (Ed.), *Ageism: Stereotyping and prejudice against older persons* (pp. 129–161). Cambridge, MA: The MIT Press.

Knight, B. G. (1992). *Older adults in psychotherapy: Case histories.* Newbury Park, CA: Sage.

Knight, B. G. (1996). *Psychotherapy with older adults* (2nd ed.). Thousand Oaks, CA: Sage.

Knight, B. G., & Kaskie, B. (1995). Models for mental health service delivery to older adults. In M. Gatz (Ed.), *Emerging issues in mental health and aging* (pp. 231–255). Washington, DC: American Psychological Association.

Knight, B. G., Kelly, M., & Gatz, M. (1992). Psychotherapy and the older adult: An historical review. In D. K. Freedheim (Ed.), *History of psychotherapy: A century of change* (pp. 528–551). Washington, DC: American Psychological Association.

Knight, B. G., Lutzky, S. M., & Macofsky-Urban, F. (1993). A meta-analytic review of interventions for caregiver distress: Recommendations for future research. *Gerontologist, 33,* 240–248.

Knight, B. G., & Satre, D. D. (1999). Cognitive behavioral psychotherapy with older adults. *Clinical Psychology: Science and Practice, 6,* 188–203.

Knight, B. G., Teri, L., Wohlford, P., & Santos, J. (Eds.). (1995). *Mental health services for older adults: Implications for training and practice in geropsychology.* Washington, DC: American Psychological Association.

Koenig, H. G., George, L. K., & Schneider, R. (1994). Mental health care for older adults in the year 2000: A dangerous and avoided topic. *Gerontologist, 34,* 674–679.

Kramer, N. A., & Smith, M. C. (2000). Training nursing assistants to care for nursing home residents with dementia. In V. Molinari (Ed.), *Professional psychology in long term care: A comprehensive guide* (pp. 227–256). New York: Hatherleigh Press.

Lamberty, G. J., & Bieliauskas, L. A. (1993). Distinguishing between depression and dementia in the elderly: A review of neuropsychological findings. *Archives of Clinical Neuropsychology, 8,* 149–170.

LaRue, A. (1992). *Aging and neuropsychological assessment.* New York: Plenum.

Lawton, M. P. (1989). Environmental proactivity and affect in older people. In S. Spacapan & S. Oskamp (Eds.), *The social psychology of aging* (pp. 135–163). Newbury Park, CA: Sage.

Lawton, M. P., & Salthouse, T. A. (Eds.). (1998). *Essential papers on the psychology of aging.* New York: New York University Press.

Lawton, M. P., & Teresi, J. A. (Eds.). (1994). *Focus on assessment techniques.* New York: Springer.

Lebowitz, B. D., & Niederehe, G. (1992). Concepts and issues in mental health and aging. In J. E. Birren, R. B. Sloane, & G. D. Cohen (Eds.), *Handbook of mental health and aging* (2nd ed., pp. 3–26). San Diego, CA: Academic Press.

Levenson, R. W., Carstensen, L. L., & Gottman, J. M. (1993). Long-term marriage: Age, gender, and satisfaction. *Psychology and Aging, 8,* 301–313.

Levy, M. L., & Uncapher, H. (2000). Basic psychopharmacology in the nursing home. In V. Molinari, (Ed.), *Professional psychology in long term care: A comprehensive guide* (pp. 279–297). New York: Hatherleigh Press.

Lichtenberg, P. A. (1994). *A guide to psychological practice in geriatric long term care.* New York: Haworth Press.

Lichtenberg, P. A. (Ed.). (1999). *Handbook of assessment in clinical gerontology.* New York: Wiley.

Lichtenberg, P. A., & Hartman-Stein, P. E. (1997). Effective geropsychology practice in nursing homes. In L. VandeCreek, S. Knapp, & T. L. Jackson (Eds.), *Innovations in clinical practice: A source book* (pp. 265–281). Sarasota, FL: Professional Resource Press.

Lichtenberg, P. A., Smith, M., Frazer, D., Molinari, V., Rosowsky, E., Crose, R., et al. (1998). Standards for psychological services in long-term care facilities. *Gerontologist, 38,* 122–127.

Light, E., & Lebowitz, B. D. (Eds.). (1991). *The elderly with chronic mental illness.* New York: Springer.

Lundervold, D. A., & Lewin, L. M. (1992). *Behavior analysis and therapy in nursing homes.* Springfield, IL: Charles C. Thomas.

Maercker, A. (2002). Life-review technique in the treatment of PTSD in elderly patients: Rationale and three single case studies. *Journal of Clinical Geropsychology, 8,* 239–249.

Magai, C. (2001). Emotions over the life span. In J. E. Birren & K. W. Schaie (Eds.), *Handbook of the psychology of aging* (5th ed., pp. 399–426). San Diego, CA: Academic Press.

Marson, D. (2002). Competency assessment and research in an aging society. *Generations: Journal of the American Society on Aging, 26,* 99–103.

Marson, D. C., Chatterjee, A., Ingram, K. K., & Harrell, L. E. (1996). Toward a neurologic model of competency: Cognitive predictors of capacity to consent in Alzheimer's disease using three different legal standards. *Neurology, 46,* 666–672.

McClearn, G. E., & Vogler, G. P. (2001). The genetics of behavioral aging. In J. E. Birren & K. W. Schaie (Eds.), *Handbook of the psychology of aging* (5th ed., pp. 109–131). San Diego, CA: Academic Press.

McCrae, R. R., & Costa, P. T., Jr. (1990). *Personality in adulthood.* New York: Guilford.

Medicare handbook: A guide for psychologists. (2003). Washington, DC: APA Practice Directorate. Retrieved from the APA Practice Directorate Web site: http://www.apa.org/practice/medtoc.html

Medicare Local Medical Review Policies Tool Kit. (2003, March). Retrieved from the APA Office on Aging Wed site: http://www.apa.org./pi/aging/lmrp/toolkit.pdf

Meeks, S., & Murrell, S. A. (1997). Mental illness in late life: Socioeconomic conditions, psychiatric symptoms, and adjustment of long-term sufferers. *Psychology and Aging, 12,* 296–308.

Miles, T. P. (Ed.). (1999). *Full-color aging: Facts, goals, and recommendations for America's diverse elders.* Washington, DC: Gerontological Society of America.

Miller, N. E., & Lipowski, Z. J. (Eds.). (1991). Delirium: Advances in research and clinical practice. *International Psychogeriatrics, 3*(2, Whole Issue), 97–414.

Mittelman, M. S., Ferris, S. H., Shulman, E., Steinberg, G., Ambinder, A., Mackell, J. A., & Cohen, J. (1995). A comprehensive support program: Effect on depression in spousecaregivers of AD patients. *Gerontologist, 35,* 792–802.

Mohlman, J., Gorenstein, E. E., Kleber, M., de Jesus, M., Gorman, J. M., & Papp L. A. (2003). Standard and enhanced cognitive-behavior therapy for late-life generalized anxiety disorder: Two pilot investigations. *American Journal of Geriatric Psychiatry, 11,* 24–32.

Molinari, V. (Ed.). (2000). *Professional psychology in long term care: A comprehensive guide.* New York: Hatherleigh Press.

Morin. C. M., Colecchi, C., Stone, J., Sood, R., & Brink, D. (1999). Behavioral and pharmacological treatments for late-life insomnia: A randomized controlled trial. *Journal of the American Medical Association, 281,* 991–999.

Morin, C. M., Kowatch, R. A., Barry, T., & Walton, E. (1993). Cognitive–behavior therapy for late-life insomnia. *Journal of Consulting and Clinical Psychology, 61,* 137–146.

Moye, J. (1999). Assessment of competency and decision making capacity. In P. Lichtenberg (Ed.), *Handbook of assessment in clinical gerontology* (pp. 488–528). New York: Wiley.

Moye, J. (2000). Ethical issues. In V. Molinari (Ed.), *Professional psychology in long term care: A comprehensive guide* (pp. 329–348). New York: Hatherleigh Press.

Mroczek, D. K., & Kolarz, C. M. (1998). The effect of age on positive and negative affect: A developmental perspective on happiness. *Journal of Personality and Social Psychology, 75,* 1333–1349.

Myers, J. E. (1999). Adjusting to role loss and leisure in later life. In M. F. Duffy (Ed.), *Handbook of counseling and psychotherapy with older adults.* New York: Wiley.

National Academy on an Aging Society. (1999). *Challenges for the 21st century: Chronic and disabling conditions* [electronic version]. Retrieved from the NAAS Web site: http://www.agingsociety.org/agingsociety/publications/chronic/index.html

Neely, A. S., & Bäckman, L. (1995). Effects of multifactorial memory training in old age: Generalizability across tasks and individuals. *Journal of Gerontology: Psychological Sciences, 50B,* P134–P140.

Newton, N. A., & Jacobowitz, J. (1999). Transferential and countertransferential processes in therapy with older adults. In M. Duffy (Ed.), *Handbook of counseling and psychotherapy with older adults.* New York: Wiley.

Nelson, E. A., & Dannefer, D. (1992). Aged heterogeneity: Fact or fiction? The fate of diversity in gerontological research. *Gerontologist, 32,* 17–23.

Nelson, T. D. (Ed.). (2002). *Stereotyping and prejudice against older persons*. Cambridge, MA: MIT Press.

Niederehe, G. (1998). The significance of memory complaints in later life: Methodologial and theoretical considerations. In J. Lomranz (Ed.), *Handbook of aging and mental health* (pp. 417–434). New York: Plenum.

Niederehe, G., & Schneider, L. S. (1998). Treatment of depression and anxiety in the aged. In P. E. Nathan & J. M. Gorman (Eds.), *A guide to treatments that work* (pp. 270–287). New York: Oxford Press.

Norris, M. P. (2000). Public policy and the delivery of mental health care to older adults. In V. Molinari (Ed.), *Professional psychology in long term care: A comprehensive guide* (pp. 425–443). New York: Hatherleigh Press.

Norris, M. P., Molinari, V., & Ogland-Hand, S. (Eds.). (2002). *Emerging trends in psychological practice in long-term care*. Binghamptom, NY: Haworth Press.

Norris, M. P., Molinari, V., & Rosowsky, E. (1998). Providing mental health care to older adults: Unraveling the maze of Medicare and managed care. *Psychotherapy, 35*, 490–497.

Nussbaum, P. D. (Ed.). (1996). *Handbook of neuropsychology and aging*. New York: Plenum.

Odenheimer, G., Beaudet, M., Jette, A. M., Albert, M. S., Grande, L., & Minaker, K. L. (1994). Performance based driving evaluation of the elderly driver: Safety, reliability, and validity. *Journal of Gerontology: Medical Sciences, 49*, M153–159.

Older adults and insomnia resource guide. (2001). Retrieved February 6, 2003, from the APA Office on Aging Web site: http://www.apa.org/pi/aging/insomnia.html

Omnibus Budget Reconciliation Act of 1987, PL 100-203.

Palmer, B. W., Folsom, D., Bartels, S., & Jeste, D. V. (2002). Psychotic disorders in late life: Implications for treatment and future directions for clinical services. *Generations: Journal of the American Society on Aging, 26*, 39–43.

Park, D. C., Morrell, R., & Shifren, K. (Eds.). (1999). *Aging patients and medical treatment: An information processing perspective*. Mahwah, NJ: Erlbaum.

Park, D. C., & Schwarz, N. (Eds.). (2000). *Cognitive aging: A primer*. Philadelphia: Psychology Press.

Park, R. W., Zec, R. F., & Wilson, R. S. (1993). *Neuropsychology of Alzheimer's disease and other dementias*. New York: Oxford University Press.

Peake, T. H. (1998). *Healthy aging, healthy treatment: The impact of telling stories*. Westport, CT: Praeger Publishers.

Pearson, J. L. (2002). Recent research on suicide in the elderly. *Current Psychiatry Reports, 4*, 59–63.

Pearson, J. L., & Brown, G. K. (2000). Suicide prevention in late life: Directions for science and practice. *Clinical Psychology Review, 20*, 685–705.

Perdue, C. W., & Gurtman, M. B. (1990). Evidence for the automaticity of ageism. *Journal of Experimental Social Psychology, 26*, 199–216.

Perlick, D., & Atkins, A. (1984). Variations in the reported age of a patient: A source of bias in the diagnosis of depression and dementia. *Journal of Consulting and Clinical Psychology, 52*, 812–820.

Phillips, M. A., & Murrell, S. A. (1994). Impact of psychological and physical health, stressful events, and social support on subsequent mental health help seeking among older adults. *Journal of Consulting and Clinical Psychology, 62,* 270–275.

Pinquart, M., & Soerensen, S. (2001). How effective are psychotherapeutic and other psychosocial interventions with older adults? A meta analysis. *Journal of Mental Health and Aging, 7,* 207–243.

Pollack, D., & Weiner, A. (1995). Clinical aspects of handling an elder abuse case: The legal and social work perspectives. *Journal of Clinical Geropsychology, 1*(4), 271–281.

Poon, L. W. (Ed.). (1980). *Aging in the 1980s: Psychological issues.* Washington, DC: American Psychological Association.

Poon, L. W., Crook, T., Davis, K. L., Eisdorfer, C., Gurland, B. J., Kaszniak, A. W., & Thompson, L. W. (Eds.). (1986). *Handbook for clinical memory assessment of older adults.* Washington, DC: American Psychological Association.

Psychological services for long term care resource guide. (2000). Retrieved on February 6, 2003, from the APA Office on Aging Web site: http://www.apa.org/pi/aging/longterm.html

Psychotherapy and older adults resource guide. (2003). Available March, 2003, from the APA Office on Aging Web site: http://www.apa.org/pi/aging/

Qualls, S. H. (1995). Clinical interventions with later-life families. In R. Blieszner & V. H. Bedford (Eds.), *Handbook of aging and the family* (pp. 474–487). Westport, CT: Greenwood Press.

Qualls, S. H. (1999). Realizing power in intergenerational family hierarchies: Family reorganization when older adults decline. In M. F. Duffy (Ed.), *Handbook of counseling and psychotherapy with older adults.* New York: Wiley.

Qualls, S. H., & Abeles, N. (Eds.). (2000). *Psychology and the aging revolution: How we adapt to longer life.* Washington, DC: American Psychological Association.

Qualls, S. H., Segal, D., Norman, S., Niederehe, G., & Gallagher-Thompson, D. (2002). Psychologists in practice with older adults: Current patterns, sources of training, and need for continuing education. *Professional Psychology: Research and Practice, 33,* 435–442.

Reid, J. (1995). Development in late life: Older lesbian and gay lives. In A. D'Augelli & C. Patterson (Eds.), *Lesbian, gay, and bisexual identities over the lifespan: Psychological perspectives* (pp. 215–240). New York: Oxford University Press.

Resource directory for older people. (2001). Joint effort of National Institute on Aging and Administration on Aging. [electronic version] Retrieved February 6, 2002, from http://www.aoa.gov/eldfam/How_To_Find/ResourceDirectory/ResourceDirectory.pdf

Reynolds, C. F., III., & Charney, D. S. (Eds.). (2002). Unmet needs in the diagnosis and treatment of mood disorders in later life. *Biological Psychiatry, 52*(3, Special Issue), 145–303.

Roberts, A. H. (1986). Excess disability in the elderly: Exercise management. In L. Teri & P. M. Lewinsohn (Eds.), *Geropsychological assessment and treatment: Selected topics* (pp. 87–120). New York: Springer.

Robertson, J. F. (1995). Grandparenting in an era of rapid change. In R. Blieszner & V. H. Bedford (Eds.), *Aging and the family: Theory and research* (pp. 243–260). Westport, CT: Praeger.

Rodeheaver, D. (1990). Ageism. In I. A. Parham, L.W. Poon, & I. C. Siegler (Eds.), *ACCESS: Aging curriculum content for education in the social and behavioral sciences* (pp. 7.1–7.43). New York: Springer.

Rogers, W. A., & Fisk, A. D. (2001). Understanding the role of attention in cognitive aging research. In J. E. Birren & K. W. Schaie (Eds.), *Handbook of the psychology of aging* (5th ed., pp. 267–287). San Diego, CA: Academic Press.

Rosowsky, E., Abrams, R. C., & Zweig, R. A. (Eds.). (1999). *Personality disorders in older adults: Emerging issues in diagnosis and treatment.* Mahwah, NJ: Erlbaum.

Rowe, J. W., & Kahn, R. L. (1998). *Successful aging.* New York: Pantheon Books.

Royall, D. R., Chiodo, L. K., & Polk, M. J. (2000). Correlates of disability among elderly retirees with "subclinical" cognitive impairment. *Journal of Gerontology: Medical Sciences, 55A,* M541–M546.

Russell, D. W., Cutrona, C. E., de la Mora, A., & Wallace, R. B. (1997). Loneliness and nursing home admission among rural older adults. *Psychology and Aging, 12,* 574–589.

Ryff, C. D., Kwan, C. M. L., & Singer, B. J. (2001). Personality and aging: Flourishing agendas and future challenges. In J. E. Birren & K.W. Schaie (Eds.), *Handbook of the psychology of aging* (5th ed., pp. 477–499). San Diego, CA: Academic Press.

Salthouse, T. A. (1996). The processing speed theory of adult age differences in cognition. *Psychological Review, 103,* 403–428.

Santos, J. F., & VandenBos, G. R. (Eds.). (1982). *Psychology and the older adult: Challenges for training in the 1980s.* Washington, DC: American Psychological Association.

Schaie, K. W. (1977). Quasi-experimental designs in the psychology of aging. In J. E. Birren & K. W. Schaie (Eds.), *Handbook of the psychology of aging* (pp. 1–19). New York: Van Nostrand Reinhold.

Schaie, K. W. (1993). Ageist language in psychological research. *American Psychologist, 48,* 49–51.

Schaie, K. W. (1994). The course of adult intellectual development. *American Psychologist, 49,* 304–313.

Scheidt, R. J., & Windley, P. G. (Eds.). (1998). *Environment and aging theory.* Westport, CT: Greenwood Press.

Schneider, J. (1996). Geriatric psychopharmacology. In L. L. Carstensen, B. A. Edelstein, & L. Dornbrand (Eds.), *The practical handbook of clinical gerontology* (pp. 481–542). Thousand Oaks, CA: Sage.

Schooler, C., Mulatu, M. S., & Oates, G. (1999). The continuing effect of substantively complex work on the intellectual functioning of older workers. *Psychology and Aging, 14,* 483–506.

Schulz, R., & Heckhausen, J. (1996). A life span model of successful aging. *American Psychologist, 51,* 702–714.

Schulz, R., Martire, L. M., Beach, S. R., & Scherer, M. F. (2000). Depression and mortality in the elderly. *Current Directions in Psychological Science, 9,* 204–208.

Schulz, R., O'Brien, A. T., Bookwala, J., & Fleissner, K. (1995). Psychiatric and physical morbidity effects of dementia caregiving: Prevalence, correlates, and causes. *Gerontologist, 35,* 771–791.

Scogin, F., & McElreath, L. (1994). Efficacy of psychosocial treatments for geriatric depression: A quantitative review. *Journal of Consulting and Clinical Psychology, 62,* 69–74.

Segal, E. S. (1996). Common medical problems in geriatric patients. In L. L. Carstensen, B. A. Edelstein, & L. Dornbrand (Eds.), *The practical handbook of clinical gerontology* (pp. 451–467). Thousand Oaks, CA: Sage.

Seltzer, M. M., Greenberg, J. S., Krauss, M. W., & Hong, J. (1997). Predictors and outcomes of the end of co-resident caregiving in aging families of adults with mental retardation or mental illness. *Family Relations: Journal of Applied Family & Child Studies, 46,* 13–22.

Settin, J. M. (1982). Clinical judgement in geropsychology practice. *Psychotherapy: Theory, Research,and Practice, 19,* 397–404.

Sherman, E. (1991). *Reminiscence and the self in old age.* New York: Springer.

Siegler, I. C., Bastian, L. A., Steffens, D. C., Bosworth, H. B., & Costa, P. T., Jr. (2002). Behavioral medicine and aging. *Journal of Consulting and Clinical Psychology, 70,* 843–851.

Sliwinski, M., & Buschke, H. (1999). Cross-sectional and longitudinal relationships among age, cognition, and processing speed. *Psychology and Aging, 14,* 18–33.

Smith, A. D. (1996). Memory. In J. E. Birren & K. W. Schaie (Eds.), *Handbook of the psychology of aging* (4th ed., pp. 236–250). San Diego, CA: Academic Press.

Smith, G. E., Petersen, R. C., Ivnik, R. J., Malec, J. F., & Tangalos, E. G. (1996). Subjective memory complaints, psychological distress, and longitudinal change in objective memory performance. *Psychology and Aging, 11,* 272–279.

Smyer, M. A. (1993). Aging and decision-making capacity. In M. A. Smyer (Ed.), *Mental health and aging* (pp. 101–114). New York: Springer.

Smyer, M. A., & Allen-Burge, R. (1999). Older adults' decision-making capacity: Institutional settings and individual choices. In J. C. Cavanaugh & S. K. Whitbourne (Eds.), *Gerontology: An interdisciplinary perspective* (pp. 391–413). New York: Oxford University Press.

Smyer, M. A., Cohn, M. D., & Brannon, D. (1988). *Mental health consultation in nursing homes.* New York: New York University Press.

Smyer, M. A., & Downs, M. G. (1995). Psychopharmacology: An essential element in educating clinical psychologists for working with older adults. In B. G. Knight, L. Teri, P. Wohlford, & J. Santos (Eds.), *Mental health services for older adults: Implications for training and practice in geropsychology* (pp. 73–83). Washington, DC: American Psychological Association.

Smyer, M. A., & Gatz, M. (1979). Aging and mental health: Business as usual? *American Psychologist, 34,* 240–246.

Smyer, M. A., & Qualls, S. H. (1999). *Aging and mental health.* Malden, MA: Blackwell Publishers.

Smyer, M., Schaie, K. W., & Kapp, M. B. (Eds.). (1996). *Older adults' decision-making and the law.* New York: Springer.

Spencer, K. A., Tompkins, C. A., & Schulz, R. (1997). Assessment of depression in patients with brain pathology: The case of stroke. *Psychological Bulletin, 122*(2), 132–152.

Sprenkel, D. G. (1999). Therapeutic issues and strategies in group therapy with older men. In M. Duffy (Ed.), *Handbook of counseling and psychotherapy with older adults* (pp. 214–227). New York: John Wiley & Sons.

Stanley, M. A., Beck, J. G., & Glassco, J. D. (1996). Treatment of generalized anxiety in older adults: A preliminary comparison of cognitive-behavioral and supportive approaches. *Behavior Therapy, 27,* 565–581.

Staudinger, U. M., Marsiske, M., & Baltes, P. B. (1995). Resilience and reserve capacity in later adulthood: Potentials and limits of development across the life span. In D. Cicchetti & D. J. Cohen (Eds.), *Developmental psychopathology. Vol. 2: Risk, disorder, and adaptation* (pp. 801–847). New York: Wiley.

Sternberg, R. J., & Lubart T. I. (2001). Wisdom and creativity. In J. E. Birren & K. W. Schaie (Eds.), *Handbook of the psychology of aging* (5th ed., pp. 500–522). San Diego, CA: Academic Press.

Sterns, H. L., & Gray, J. H. (1999). Work, leisure, and retirement. In J. C. Cavanaugh & S. K. Whitbourne (Eds.), *Gerontology: An interdisciplinary perspective* (pp. 355–389). New York: Oxford University Press.

Storandt, M., & VandenBos, G. R. (Eds.). (1994). *Neuropsychological assessment of dementia and depression in older adults: A clinician's guide.* Washington, DC: American Psychological Association.

Suominen, K., Henriksson, M., Suokas, J., Isometsä, E., Ostamo, A., & Lönnqvist, J. (1996). Mental disorders and comorbidity in attempted suicide. *Acta Psychiatrica Scandinavica, 94,* 234–240.

Surgeon General. (1999). *Mental health: A report of the Surgeon General* [electronic version]. Retrieved July 8, 2001, from http://surgeongeneral.gov/library/mentalhealth/index.html

Szinovacz, M. E. (1998). Grandparents today: A demographic profile. *The Gerontologist, 38,* 37–52.

Szinovacz, M. E., DeViney, S., & Atkinson, M. P. (1999). Effects of surrogate parenting on grandparents' well-being. *Journal of Gerontology: Social Sciences, 54B,* S376–S388.

Teri, L., Logsdon, R. G., Uomoto, J., & McCurry, S. M. (1997). Behavioral treatment of depression in dementia patients: A controlled clinical trial. *Journal of Gerontology: Psychological Sciences, 52B,* P159–P166.

Teri, L., & McCurry, S. M. (1994). Psychosocial therapies with older adults. In C. E. Coffey & J. L. Cummings (Eds.), *Textbook of geriatric neuropsychiatry* (pp. 662–682). Washington, DC: American Psychiatric Press.

Teri, L., Storandt, M., Gatz, M., Smyer, M., & Stricker, G. (1992). *Recommendations from a National Conference on Clinical Training in Psychology: Improving Psychological Services for Older Adults.* Unpublished manuscript. Washington, DC: American Psychological Association.

Teri, L., & Wagner, A. (1991). Assessment of depression in patients with Alzheimer's disease: Concordance between informants. *Psychology and Aging, 6,* 280–285.

Thompson, L.W., & Gallagher-Thompson, D. (1996). Practical issues related to maintenance of mental health and positive well-being in family caregivers. In L. L. Carstensen, B. A. Edelstein, & L. Dornbrand (Eds.), *The practical handbook of clinical gerontology* (pp. 129–150). Thousand Oaks, CA: Sage.

Tobin, S. S. (1999). *Preservation of the self in the oldest years: With implications for practice.* New York: Springer.

Trotman, F. K., & Brody, C. M. (2002). *Psychotherapy and counseling with older women: Cross-cultural, family, and end-of-life issues.* New York: Springer.

U.S. Bureau of the Census. (1993). *Population projections of the United States, by age, sex, race, and Hispanic origin: 1993–2050.* Current Population Reports. Washington, DC: U.S. Government Printing Office.

U.S. Bureau of the Census. (2001). *An aging world: 2001.* Retrieved from http://www.census.gov/prod/2001pubs/p95-01-1.pdf

Vasquez, C. I., & Clavigo, A. M. (1995). The special needs of elderly minorities: A profile of 63 Hispanics. In B. G. Knight, L. Teri, P. Wohlford, & J. Santos (Eds.), *Mental health services for older adults: Implications for training and practice in geropsychology* (pp. 93–99). Washington, DC: American Psychological Association.

Vernon, M. (1989). Assessment of persons with hearing disabilities. In T. Hunt & C. J. Lindley (Eds.), *Testing older adults: A reference guide for geropsychological assessments* (pp. 150–162). Austin, TX: PRO-ED, Inc.

Verwoerdt, A. (1976). *Clinical geropsychiatry.* Baltimore, MD: Williams & Wilkins.

Wahl, H.-W. (2001). Environmental influences in aging and behavior. In J. E. Birren & K. W. Schaie (Eds.), *Handbook of the psychology of aging* (5th ed., pp. 215–237). San Diego, CA: Academic Press.

Waldstein, S. R. (2000). Health effects on cognitive aging. In P. C. Stern & L. L. Carstensen (Eds.), *The aging mind: Opportunities in cognitive research* (report of Committee on Future Directions for Cognitive Research on Aging, National Resource Council [electronic version]) (pp. 189–217). Washington, DC: National Academy Press. Retrieved from http://www.nap.edu/books/309069408/html/

Watkins, K. W., Shifrin, K., Park, D. C., & Morrell, R. W. (1999). Age, pain, and coping with rheumatoid arthritis. *Pain, 82,* 217–228.

Webster, J. (1995). Adult age differences in reminiscence functions. In B. K. Haight & J. D. Webster (Eds.), *The art and science of reminiscing: Theory, research methods, and applications.* Bristol, PA: Taylor & Francis.

Weintraub, D., Furlan, P., & Katz, I. R. (2002). Depression and coexisting medical disorders in late life. *Generations: Journal of the American Society on Aging, 26*, 55–58.

Wetherell, J. L. (1998). Treatment of anxiety in older adults. *Psychotherapy, 35*, 444–458.

Wetherell, J. L. (2002). Behavior therapy for anxious older adults. *Behavior Therapist, 25*, 16–17.

Whitbourne, S. K. (1996). *The aging individual: Physical and psychological perspectives.* New York: Springer.

Whitbourne, S. K. (1998). Physical changes in the aging individual: Clinical implications. In I. H. Nordhus, G. R. VandenBos, S. Berg, & P. Fromholt (Eds.), *Clinical geropsychology.* Washington, DC: American Psychological Association.

Whitbourne, S. K. (Ed.). (2000). *Psychopathology in later adulthood.* New York: Wiley.

Wilber, K. H., & McNeilly, D. P. (2001). Elder abuse and victimization. In J. E. Birren & K. W. Schaie (Eds.), *Handbook of the psychology of aging* (5th ed., pp. 569–591). San Diego, CA: Academic Press.

Willis, S. L., Allen-Burge, R., Dolan, M. M., Bertrand, R. M., Yesavage, J., & Taylor, J. L. (1998). Everyday problem solving among individuals with Alzheimer's disease. *Gerontologist, 38*, 569–577.

Wisocki, P. A. (Ed.). (1991). *Handbook of clinical behavioral therapy with the elderly client.* New York: Plenum.

Wolf, R. A. (1998). Domestic elder abuse and neglect. In I. H. Nordhus, G. R. VandenBos, S. Berg, & P. Fromholt (Eds.), *Clinical geropsychology.* Washington, DC: American Psychological Association.

Woods, R. T. (Ed.). (1999). *Psychological problems of ageing: Assessment, treatment and care.* Chichester, UK and New York: Wiley.

Working Group for the Establishment of Criteria for the Diagnosis of Dementia. (2000). Test battery for the diagnosis of dementia in individuals with intellectual disability. *Journal of Intellectual Disability Research, 44*, 175–180.

Yarhouse, M. A., & DeVries, H. M. (1998). The general principles of ethical conduct: A framework for psychologists working with older adults. *Journal of Clinical Geropsychology, 4*, 141–152.

Yeo, G., & Hikoyeda, N. (1993). *Differential assessment and treatment of mental health problems: African American, Latino, Filipino, and Chinese American elders.* Stanford, CA: Stanford Geriatric Education Center Working Paper Series No. 13.

Zacks, R. T., Hasher, L., & Li, Z. H. (2000). Human memory. In F. I. M. Craik & T. A. Salthouse (Eds.), *Handbook of aging and cognition* (2nd ed.). Mahwah, NJ: Erlbaum.

Zarit, S. H. (1980). *Aging and mental disorders: Psychological approaches to assessment and treatment.* New York: The Free Press.

Zarit, S. H., & Knight, B. G. (Eds.). (1996). *A guide to psychotherapy and aging: Effective clinical interventions in a life-stage context.* Washington, DC: American Psychological Association.

Zarit, S. H., & Zarit, J. M. (1998). *Mental disorders in older adults: Fundamentals of assessment and treatment.* New York: Guilford.

Zeiss, A. M., & Steffen, A. M. (1996). Treatment issues in elderly clients. *Cognitive & Behavioral Practice, 3,* 371–389.

Zeiss, A. M., & Steffen, A. M. (1998). Interdisciplinary health care teams in geriatrics: An international model. In B. A. Edelstein (Ed.), *Clinical geropsychology* (pp. 551–570). London: Pergamon Press.

Zigman, W., Silverman, W., & Wisniewski, H. M. (1996). Aging and Alzheimer's disease in Down syndrome: Clinical and pathological changes. *Mental Retardation & Developmental Disabilities Research Reviews, 2*(2), 73–79.

APPENDIX H
APA Guidelines for the Evaluation of Dementia and Age-Related Cognitive Decline

APA Presidential Task Force on the Assessment of Age-Consistent Memory Decline and Dementia

APPROVED BY THE COUNCIL OF REPRESENTATIVES
AMERICAN PSYCHOLOGICAL ASSOCIATION
FEBRUARY 1998

APA Presidential Task Force on the Assessment of Age-Consistent Memory Decline and Dementia

Thomas H. Crook, III, Ph.D., Chair
Glenn J. Larrabee, Ph.D.
Asenath LaRue, Ph.D.
Barry D. Lebowitz, Ph.D.
Martha Storandt, Ph.D.
James Youngjohn, Pd.D.

GUIDELINES FOR THE EVALUATION OF DEMENTIA AND AGE-RELATED COGNITIVE DECLINE

Psychologists can play a leading role in the evaluation of the memory complaints and changes in cognitive functioning that frequently occur in the later decades of life. Although some healthy aging persons maintain very high cognitive performance levels throughout life, most older people will experience a decline in certain cognitive abilities. This decline is usually not

From *APA Guidelines for Evaluation of Dementia and Age-Related Cognitive Decline*, by the American Psychological Association, 1998, Washington, DC: American Psychological Association. Copyright 1998 by the American Psychological Association. Retrieved September 23, 2004, from PsychNET® Web site: http://www.apa.org/practice/dementia.html

Suggested citation: American Psychological Association, Presidential Task Force on the Assessment of Age-Consistent Memory Decline and Dementia (1998). *Guidelines for the evaluation of dementia and age-related cognitive decline*. Washington, DC: American Psychological Association.

279

pathological, but rather parallels a number of common decreases in physiological function that occur in conjunction with normal developmental processes. For some older persons, however, declines go beyond what may be considered "normal" and are relentlessly progressive, robbing them of their memories, intellect, and eventually their abilities to recognize spouses or children, maintain basic personal hygiene, or even utter comprehensible speech. These more malignant forms of cognitive deterioration are caused by a variety of neuropathological conditions and dementing diseases.

Psychologists are uniquely equipped by training, expertise, and the use of specialized neuropsychological tests to assess changes in memory and cognitive functioning and to distinguish normal changes from early signs of pathology. Although strenuous efforts are being exerted to identify the physiological causes of dementia, there are still no conclusive biological markers short of autopsy for the most common forms of dementia, including Alzheimer's disease. Neuropsychological evaluation and cognitive testing remain the most effective differential diagnostic methods in discriminating pathophysiological dementia from age-related cognitive decline, cognitive difficulties that are depression-related, and other related disorders. Even after reliable biological markers have been discovered, neuropsychological evaluation and cognitive testing will still be necessary to determine the onset of dementia, the functional expression of the disease process, the rate of decline, the functional capacities of the individual, and hopefully, response to therapies.

The following guidelines were developed for psychologists who perform evaluations of dementia and age-related cognitive decline. These guidelines conform to the American Psychological Association's *Ethical Principles of Psychologists and Code of Conduct* (APA, 1992).

Assessment of dementia and age-related cognitive decline in clinical practice is a core activity of the specialty of Clinical Neuropsychology. The recent Houston Conference on Specialty Education and Training in Clinical Neuropsychology (Hannay et al., 1998) has specified the appropriate integrated training model to attain that specialty. These guidelines, however, are intended to specify appropriate cautions and concerns for all clinicians which are specific to the assessment of dementia and age-related cognitive decline. These guidelines are aspirational in intent and are neither mandatory nor exhaustive. They are guidelines for practice and are not intended to represent standards for practice. The goal of the guidelines is to promote proficiency and expertise in assessing dementia and age-related cognitive decline in clinical practice. They may not be applicable in certain circumstances, such as some experimental or clinical research projects and/or some forensic evaluations.

GUIDELINES FOR THE EVALUATION OF DEMENTIA AND AGE-RELATED COGNITIVE DECLINE

I. General Guidelines: Familiarity With Nomenclature and Diagnostic Criteria

1. Psychologists performing evaluations of dementia and age-related cognitive decline should be familiar with the prevailing diagnostic nomenclature and specific diagnostic criteria.

A. Alzheimer's disease (AD) is the major cause for dementia in later life (Evans, Funkenstein, & Albert, 1989). The most widely accepted diagnostic criteria for probable AD are those offered by the National Institute of Neurological and Communicative Disorders and Stroke and by the Alzheimer's Disease and Related Disorders Association (NINCDS-ADRDA; McKhann et al., 1984). These criteria include the presence of dementia established by clinical examination and confirmed by neuropsychological testing. The dementia is described as involving multiple, progressive cognitive deficits in older persons in the absence of disturbances of consciousness, presence of psychoactive substances, or any other medical, neurological, or psychiatric conditions that might in and of themselves account for these progressive deficits. The *Diagnostic and Statistical Manual of Mental Disorders: 4th Edition* of the American Psychiatric Association (*DSM–IV*, 1994) also outlines diagnostic criteria for dementia of the Alzheimer's type that are generally consistent with the NINCDS-ADRDA criteria. *DSM–IV* also provides diagnostic criteria for vascular dementia, as well as dementia due to other general medical conditions including HIV disease, head trauma, Parkinson's disease, Huntington's disease, Pick's disease, Creutzfeldt-Jakob disease, and other general medical conditions and etiologies. New causes and varieties of dementia continue to be elucidated (e.g., dementia with Lewy bodies; McKeith et al., 1996) and diagnostic criteria for the dementing disorders continue to be refined (e.g., *International Classification of Diseases-10* and subsequent revisions).

B. Some older persons have memory and cognitive difficulties identified by neuropsychological testing that are greater than those typical of normal aging, but not so severe as to warrant a diagnosis of dementia. Some of these persons go on to develop frank dementia and some do not. There is not yet a clear consensus regarding nosology for this middle group. Proposed nomenclature includes mild neurocognitive disorder, mild cognitive impairment, late-life forgetfulness, possible dementia, incipient dementia, benign senescent forgetfulness, senescent forgetfulness, and provisional dementia (see Table 1). Terms such as incipient dementia, provisional dementia, and mild cognitive impairment refer to persons who are somewhat more severely impaired and have a relatively greater likelihood of eventually becoming demented (Flicker, Ferris, & Reisberg, 1991). Terms such as benign senescent forgetfulness or late-life forgetfulness refer to persons with milder cognitive difficulties relative to their age peers who are less likely to go on to develop dementia.

C. Declines in memory and cognitive abilities are a normal consequence of aging in humans (e.g., Craik & Salthouse, 1992). This is true across cultures and, indeed, in virtually all mammalian species. The nosological category of Age-Associated Memory Impairment was proposed by a National Institute of Mental Health (NIMH) work group to describe older persons with objective memory declines relative to their younger years, but cognitive functioning that is normal relative to their age peers (Crook et al., 1986). The group's recommendations contained explicit operational definitions and psychometric criteria to assist in identifying these persons. The more recent term, Age-Consistent Memory Decline, has been proposed as being a less pejorative label and to emphasize that these are normal developmental changes (Crook, 1993; Larrabee, 1996), are not pathophysiological (Smith et al., 1991), and rarely progress to overt dementia (Youngjohn & Crook, 1993). The DSM–IV (1994) has codified the diagnostic classification of Age-Related Cognitive Decline, which will be used throughout the body of these Guidelines. This nomenclature has the advantage of not limiting the focus solely to memory, but lacks the operational definitions and explicit psychometric criteria of age-associated memory impairment.

II. General Guidelines: Ethical Considerations

2. Psychologists attempt to obtain informed consent.

A. Psychologists recognize that there are special considerations regarding informed consent and competency, given the nature of these evaluations with some patients who may be suffering from advanced stages of dementia. Psychologists attempt when possible to educate patients regarding the nature of their services, financial arrangements, potential risks inherent in their services, and limits of confidentiality. When patients are clearly not competent to give their informed consent, psychologists attempt to discuss these issues with family members and/or legal guardians, as appropriate.

B. There may also be special considerations regarding the limits of confidentiality in these circumstances. Family members, other professionals, and state agencies may have to be involved under circumstances of potential harm to the patients or others, without patients' consent. In potential cases of abuse or neglect, there may be mandated reporting responsibilities for psychologists consistent with state statutes and/or other applicable laws.

3. Psychologists gain specialized competence.

A. Psychologists who propose to perform evaluations for dementia and age-related cognitive decline are aware that special competencies and knowledge are required for such evaluations. Competence in conducting clinical interviews and administering, scoring, and interpreting psychological and neuropsychological tests is necessary, but may not be sufficient. Education, training, experience, and/or supervision in the areas of gerontology, neuropsychology, rehabilitation psychology, neuropathology, psychopharmacology, and psychopathology in older adults may help to prepare the psychologist for performing evaluations of age-related cognitive decline and dementia.

B. Psychologists use current knowledge of scientific and professional developments, consistent with accepted clinical and scientific standards, in selecting data collection methods and procedures. The *Standards for Educational and Psychological Testing* (APA, 1985) are adhered to in the use of psychological tests and other assessment tools.

4. Psychologists seek and provide appropriate consultation.

A. Psychologists performing dementia and age-related cognitive decline evaluations communicate their findings to primary care physicians and/or other referring physicians, with sensitivity to issues of informed consent. When the psychologist is the first professional contact, the client is referred, when appropriate, for a thorough medical evaluation to discover any underlying medical disorder or any potentially reversible medical causes for dementia or cognitive decline. Given the prevalence of health problems in the elderly it is recommended that psychologists providing services to this population be particularly sensitive to these issues. A thorough dementia work-up is a multidisciplinary effort (Small et al., in press).

B. Psychologists help to educate health care professionals who may be administering mental status examinations or psychological screening tools regarding the psychometric properties of these instruments and their clinical utility for particular applications. Education is also provided about the differences between brief screening examinations and more comprehensive psychological or neuropsychological evaluation.

C. In the course of conducting evaluations for dementia and age-related cognitive decline, allegations of abuse, neglect, or family violence, issues regarding legal competence or guardianship, indications of other medical, neurological, or psychiatric conditions, or other issues may arise that are not necessarily within the scope of a particular evaluator's expertise. If this is so, the psychologist seeks additional consultation, supervision, and/or specialized knowledge, training, or experience to address these issues.

5. Psychologists are aware of personal and societal biases and engage in nondiscriminatory practice.

Psychologists are aware of how biases regarding age, gender, race, ethnicity, national origin, religion, sexual orientation, disability, language, culture, and socioeconomic status may interfere with an objective evaluation and recommendations. The psychologist strives to overcome any such biases or withdraws from the evaluation. Psychologists are alert and sensitive to differing roles, expectations, and normative standards within a sociocultural context.

III. Procedural Guidelines: Conducting Evaluations of Dementia and Age-Related Cognitive Decline

6. Psychologists conduct a clinical interview as part of the evaluation.

A. Psychologists obtain the client's self-report and subjective impressions regarding changes in memory and cognitive functioning. This information can be obtained through informal interview or through formal memory complaint questionnaires (Crook & Larrabee, 1990; Dixon, Hultsch, & Hertzog, 1988; Gilewski, Zelinski, & Schaie, 1990). Advantages of formal scales include the quantification of memory complaints and the ability to measure subsequent changes in perception of memory loss.

B. Psychologists are aware that self-reported memory problems often do not correspond to actual decreases in memory performance (Bolla, Lindgren, Bonaccorsy, & Bleecker, 1991). Frequently, persons with significant cognitive dysfunction are not aware of the problem. This lack of awareness of genuine impairment can be a component of the neurobehavioral syndrome or it can be the result of denial or other psychological defenses. Conversely, some persons who report severe memory deficits actually have normal, or even above average performance. Depression and other psychological factors can lead to over-reporting of cognitive disturbance. Additionally, clients performing in the average range may actually have experienced significant decreases in performance, relative to their premorbid functioning (Rubin et al., in press).

C. It is important, when possible, to obtain behavioral descriptions and subjective estimations of cognitive performance from collateral sources such as family and friends. This information can be obtained either through clinical interview or through memory complaint questionnaires. It is important to be particularly alert to discordance between self and family reports. When formal scales are used, discrepancies between self and family reports can be quantified (Feher, Larrabee, Sudilovsky, & Crook, 1994; Zelinski, Gilewski, & Anthony-Bergstone, 1990).

D. It is important to take a careful history. The time of onset and nature and rate of the course of the difficulties provide information important to differential diagnosis. The clinical interview provides an opportunity to assess for the presence of deleterious side effects of medication, substance abuse, previous head injury, or other medical, neurological, or psychiatric history relevant to diagnosis. Obtaining a family history of dementia is also important.

E. Depression in elderly persons can mimic the effects of dementia (Kaszniak & Christenson, 1994). Psychomotor retardation and decreased motivation can result in nondemented persons appearing to have pathophysiologically determined cognitive disturbances in both day-to-day functioning and on formal neuropsychological testing. Depression can also cause nondemented persons to over-report the severity of cognitive disturbance. Consequently, it is important to perform a careful assessment for depression when evaluating for dementia and age-related cognitive decline. Depression is best assessed during an interview, so that the clinician can obtain information regarding the client's body language and affective display. Formal mood scales (e.g., Beck et al., 1961; Yesavage et al., 1983) can also play an important role in assessing for depression and have the advantages of quantifying and facilitating the assessment of changes in mood over time. Psychologists are sensitive to sociocultural factors that might cause some older persons to underreport depressive symptoms. Psychologists are also aware that depression and dementia are not mutually exclusive. Depression and dementia and/or age-related cognitive decline frequently coexist in the same person. Depression can also be a feature of certain subcortical dementing conditions, such as Parkinson's disease (Cummings & Benson, 1983; Youngjohn, Beck, Jogerst, & Cain, 1992).

7. Psychologists are aware that standardized psychological and neuropsychological tests are important tools in the assessment of dementia and age-related cognitive decline.

A. The use of psychometric instruments may represent the most important and unique contribution of psychologists to the assessment of dementia and age-related cognitive decline. Tests used by psychologists should be standardized, reliable, valid, and have normative data directly referable to the older population. Discriminant, convergent, and/or ecological validity should all be considered in selecting tests. There are many tests and approaches that are useful for these evaluations, including but not limited to the Wechsler scales of intelligence and memory, tests from the Halstead-Reitan battery, and the Benton tests. Psychologists seeking more comprehensive compendiums of appropriate tests are referred to *The Buros Yearbooks of Mental Measurement, Neuropsychological Assessment* (3rd ed.) (Lezak, 1995), and *A Compendium of Neuropsychological Tests* (Spreen & Strauss, 1991). Many other excellent texts also provide lists of valuable neuropsychological instruments for use in these evaluations. For example, La Rue (*Aging and Neuropsychological Assessment*, 1992), Nussbaum (*Handbook of Neuropsychology* and *Aging*, 1997), and Storandt and VandenBos (*Neuropsychological Assessment of Dementia and Depression in Older Adults: A Clinician's Guide*, 1994) present a variety of useful psychological and neuropsychological methods and issues relevant to assessing older adults.

B. Brief mental status examinations and screening instruments are not adequate for diagnosis in most cases. Comprehensive neuropsychological evaluations for dementia and age-related cognitive decline include tests or assessments of a range of multiple cognitive domains, typically including memory, attention, perceptual and motor skills, language, visuospatial abilities, problem solving, and executive functions. It is recognized, however, that detection of profound dementia may not require a comprehensive neuropsychological test battery.

8. When measuring cognitive changes in individuals, psychologists attempt to estimate premorbid abilities.

A. Ideally, psychologists assessing for cognitive declines in older persons would have baseline test data from earlier years against which current performance could be compared. Unfortunately, this information rarely exists, so psychologists must try to estimate premorbid abilities by taking into consideration socioeconomic status, educational level, occupational history, and client and family reports. Clinical judgement can be an important part of this process. There are a number of systematic biases in human judgement that may lead to inaccurate clinical estimates of premorbid function (Kareken, 1997). Various techniques have been used to estimate cognitive abilities in earlier years (e.g., Barona, Reynolds, & Chastain, 1984; Blair & Spreen, 1989). Psychologists are aware, however, that any measure of current cognitive functioning can be affected by dementia (Larrabee, Largen, & Levin, 1985; Storandt, Stone, & LaBarge, 1995).

B. Once a person has been tested, these data can serve as a baseline against which to measure future changes in cognitive functions. Magnitudes and rates of cognitive change, as well as response to treatment, can also be determined by follow-up testing. In most cases a one year follow-up interval is adequate for monitoring changes in cognitive performance, unless the client, family, or other health care professional report a more rapid decline, emergence of new symptoms, or changes in life circumstances. Psychologists try to be knowledgeable of the test-retest reliability of tests that are used so that patterns and extent of change can be interpreted appropriately. Interim follow-up not involving formal testing may also be useful in many cases.

C. Because declines in average levels of performance with age are observed on some tests, it is important that tests selected for use in the evaluation of dementia and age-related cognitive decline have adequate age-adjusted norms. Until recently, the relative lack of older adult norms posed a problem for clinicians, but better and larger older adult standardization samples are now available for many commonly used clinical tests. Gaps still remain in the normative data for very old persons and for diverse linguistic and ethnic populations. Comparison of an individual's test performance against even age-adjusted norms can be misleading if the individual's earlier abilities fell outside of the population curve.

9. Psychologists are sensitive to the limitations and sources of variability and error in psychometric performance.

A. Psychologists are aware that practice effects can result when tests are readministered in close temporal proximity. Such effects are more likely to be observed in normally aging older persons than in patients with dementia or amnestic conditions. In cases of questionable cognitive decline, the presence of robust practice effects can help to establish that cognitive functions are intact. Repeated, closely spaced testings, however, can obscure cognitive changes or intervention effects. The use of alternate test forms of equivalent difficulty can help to attenuate practice effect artifact, but such forms may not be available for many otherwise appropriate tests.

B. Psychologists realize that persons can have significant declines in day-to-day functional abilities that are not demonstrated on psychometric instruments because of a relative lack of sensitivity of the tests used. Psychometric instruments are effective, but still imperfect, measures of real-life abilities.

C. Reasons why people may do poorly on tests when the ability being assessed is intact include, but are not limited to, sensory deficits, fatigue, medication side effects, physical illness and frailness, discomfort or disability, poor motivation, financial disincentives, depression, anxiety, not understanding the test instructions, and lack of interest. Psychologists attempt to assess these sources of error and to limit and control them to the extent that they are able.

10. Psychologists recognize that providing constructive feedback, support, and education, as well as maintaining a therapeutic alliance, can be important parts of the evaluation process.

A. In many instances, patients may benefit from feedback regarding the evaluation in language that they can understand. Psychologists should exercise clinical judgement and take into consideration the needs and capabilities of the particular client when feedback is provided.

B. Providing feedback, education, and support to the family, with clients' informed consent, are also important aspects of evaluations and enhance their value and applicability. Knowledge regarding levels of impairment, the expected course, and expected outcomes can help families to make adequate preparations. Working with families can provide them with effective and humane methods for managing persons with problematic behaviors.

Appropriately counseling families regarding known genetic components and the heritability of the various disorders can address their concerns, and in many cases, allay needless fears. Healthy older adults who have had concerns about their cognitive functions can benefit from reassurance based on results of testing (Youngjohn, Larrabee, & Crook, 1992) and from suggestions as to how they may enhance their everyday cognitive function.

C. Psychologists attempt to educate themselves regarding currently approved somatic and nonsomatic treatments of dementia and age-related cognitive decline. This is a rapidly evolving area and both families and healthcare professionals can benefit from education.

D. Psychologists offer or recommend appropriate treatment to persons with dementia and age-related cognitive decline for coexisting emotional and behavioral disturbances. Cognitive rehabilitation and memory training have limited effectiveness for persons with dementia, although environmental restructuring may be useful. By contrast, training in cognitive strategies, use of memory aids, and mnemonic techniques have proven effectiveness with nondemented persons, including those with age-related cognitive decline or those with focal brain disorders (Lapp, 1996; West & Crook, 1991). Clients and families can be educated about these treatments, which can be offered to clients as appropriate.

Summary

Assessment of cognitive function among older adults requires specialized training and refined psychometric tools. Psychologists conducting such assessments must learn current diagnostic nomenclature and criteria, gain specialized competence in the selection and use of psychological tests, and understand both the limitations of these tests and the context in which they may be used and interpreted. Assessment of cognitive issues in dementia and age-related cognitive decline is a core focus of the specialty of Clinical Neuropsychology. Therefore, these guidelines are not intended to suggest the development of an independent proficiency. Rather, they are intended to state explicitly some appropriate cautions and concerns for all psychologists who wish to assess cognitive abilities among older adults, particularly in distinguishing between normal and pathological processes.

References

American Psychiatric Association. (1994). *Diagnostic and statistical manual of mental disorders (4th ed.).* Washington, DC: Author.

American Psychological Association. (1985). *Standards for educational and psychological testing.* Washington DC: Author.

American Psychological Association. (1992). Ethical principles of psychologists and code of conduct. *American Psychologist, 47,* 1597–1611.

Barona, A., Reynolds, C. R., & Chastain, R. (1984). A demographically based index of premorbid intelligence for the WAIS-R. *Journal of Consulting and Clinical Psychology, 5*, 885–887.

Beck, A. T., Ward, C. H., Mendelson, M., Mock, J., & Erbaugh, J. K. (1961). An inventory for measuring depression. *Archives of General Psychiatry, 4*, 561–571.

Blackford, R. C., & La Rue, A. (1989). Criteria for diagnosing age-associated memory impairment: Proposed improvements from the field. *Developmental Neuropsychology, 5*, 295–306.

Blair, J. R., & Spreen, V. (1989). Predicting premorbid IQ: A revision of the National Adult Reading Test. *The Clinical Neuropsychologist, 3*, 129–136.

Bolla, K. I., Lindgren, K. N., Bonaccorsy, C., & Bleecker, M. L. (1991). Memory complaints in older adults: Fact or fiction? *Archives of Neurology, 48*, 61–64.

Buros Institute of Mental Measurements. *The mental measurements yearbooks.* Lincoln: The University of Nebraska Press.

Craik, F. I. M., & Salthouse, T. A. (1992). *Handbook of aging and cognition.* Hillsdale, NJ: Erlbaum.

Crook, T. H. (1993). Diagnosis and treatment of memory loss in older patients who are not demented. In R. Levy, R. Howard, & A. Burns (Eds.), *Treatment and care in old age psychiatry* (pp. 95–111). London: Wrightson Biomedical Publishing.

Crook, T. H., Bartus, R. T., Ferris, S. H., Whitehouse, P., Cohen, G. D., & Gershon, S. (1986). Age-associated memory impairment: Proposed diagnostic criteria and measures of clinical change—Report of a National Institute of Mental Health workgroup. *Developmental Neuropsychology, 2*, 261–276.

Crook, T. H., & Larrabee, G. J. (1990). A self-rating scale for evaluating memory in everyday life. *Psychology and Aging, 5*, 48–57.

Cummings, J. L., & Benson, D. F. (1992). *Dementia: A clinical approach.* Stoneham, MA: Butterworth-Heineman.

Dixon, R. A., Hultsch, D. F., & Hertzog, C. (1988). The Metamemory in Adulthood (MIA) Questionnaire. *Psychopharmacology Bulletin, 24*, 67–68.

Evans, D. A., Funkenstein, H. H., & Albert, M. S. (1989). Prevalence of Alzheimer's disease in a community population of older persons. *Journal of the American Medical Association, 262*, 2551–2556.

Feher, E. P., Larrabee, G. J., Sudilovsky, A., & Crook, T. H. (1994). Memory self-report in Alzheimer's disease and in age-associated memory impairment. *Journal of Geriatric Psychiatry and Neurology, 7*, 58–65.

Ferris, S. H., & Kluger, A. (1996). Commentary on age-associated memory impairment, age-related cognitive decline and mild cognitive impairment. *Aging, Neuropsychology, and Cognition, 3*, 148–153.

Flicker, C., Ferris, S. H., & Reisberg, B. (1991). Mild cognitive impairment in the elderly: Predictors of dementia. *Neurology, 41*, 1006–1009.

Gilewski, M. J., Zelinski, E. M., & Schaie, K. W. (1990). The memory functioning questionnaire for assessment of memory complaints in adulthood and old age. *Psychology and Aging, 5*, 482–490.

Hannay, H. J., Bieliauskas, L., Crosson, B. A., Hammeke, T. A., Hamsher, K. S., & Koffler, S. (Eds.). (1998). Proceedings of the Houston Conference on Specialty Education and Training in Clinical Neuropsychology. *Archives of Clinical Neuropsychology, 13,* 157–249.

Kareken, D. A. (1997). Judgment pitfalls in estimating premorbid intellectual function. *Archives of Clinical Neuropsychology, 12,* 701–709.

Kaszniak, A. W., & Christenson, G. D. (1994). Differential diagnosis of dementia and depression. In M. Storandt & G. R. VandenBos (Eds.), *Neuropsychological assessment of dementia and depression in older adults: A clinician's guide* (pp. 81–118). Washington, DC: American Psychological Association.

Kral, V. A. (1962). Senescent forgetfulness: Benign and malignant. *Journal of the Canadian Medical Association, 86,* 257–260.

Lapp, D. C. (1996). *Don't forget! Easy exercises for a better memory.* Reading, MA: Addison, Wesley, Longman.

Larrabee, G. J. (1996). Age-Associated Memory Impairment: Definition and psychometric characteristics. *Aging, Neuropsychology, and Cognition, 3,* 118–131.

Larrabee, G. J., Largen, J. W., & Levin, H. S. (1985). Sensitivity of age-decline resistant ("Hold") WAIS subtests to Alzheimer's disease. *Journal of Clinical and Experimental Neuropsychology, 7,* 497–504.

Larrabee, G. J., Levin, H. S., & High, W. M. (1986). Senescent forgetfulness: A quantitative study. *Developmental Neuropsychology, 2,* 373–385.

La Rue, A. (1992). *Aging and neuropsychological assessment.* New York: Plenum.

Lezak, M. (1995). *Neuropsychological assessment* (3rd ed.). New York: Oxford.

McKeith, G., Galasko, D., Kosaka, K., Perry, E., Dickson, D., Hansen, L., Salmon, D., Lowe, J., Mirra, S., Byrne, E., Lennox, G., Quinn, N., Edwardson, J., Ince, P., Bergeron, C., Burns, A., Miller, B., Lovestone, S., Collerton, D., Jansen, E., Ballard, C., de Vos, R., Wilcock, G., Jellinger, K., & Perry, R. (1996). Consensus guidelines for the clinical and pathologic diagnosis of dementia with Lewy bodies (DLB): Report of the consortium on DLB international workshop. *Neurology, 47,* 1113–1124.

McKhann, G., Drachman, D., Folstein, M., Katzman, R., Price, D., & Stadlan, E. M. (1984). Clinical diagnosis of Alzheimer's disease: Report of the NINCDS–ADRDA work group under the auspices of Department of Health and Human Services Task Force on Alzheimer's disease. *Neurology, 34,* 939–944.

Nussbaum, P. D. (Ed.). (1997). *Handbook of neuropsychology and aging.* New York: Plenum.

Rediess, S., & Caine, E. D. (1996). Aging, cognition, and DSM–IV. *Aging, Neuropsychology, and Cognition, 3,* 105–117.

Rubin, E. H., Storandt, M., Miller, J. P., Kincherf, D. A., Grant, E. A., Morris, J. C., & Berg, L. (in press). A prospective study of cognitive function and onset of dementia in cognitively healthy elders. *Archives of Neurology.*

Small, G. W., Rabins, P. V., Barry, P. P., Buckholtz, N. S., DeKosky, S. T., Ferris, S. H., Finkel, S. I., Gwyther, L. P., Khachaturian, Z. S., Lebowitz, B. D., McRae, T. D., Morris, J. C., Oakley, F., Schneider, L. S., Streim, J. E., Sunderland, T., Teri,

L. A., Tune, L. E. (in press). Diagnosis and treatment of Alzheimer's disease and related disorders: Consensus statement of the American Association for Geriatric Psychiatry, the Alzheimer's Association, and the American Geriatrics Society. *Journal of the American Medical Association.*

Smith, G., Ivnik, R. J., Peterson, R. C., Malec, J. F., Kokmen, E., & Tangalos, E. (1991). Age-Associated Memory Impairment diagnoses: Problems of reliability and concerns for terminology. *Psychology and Aging, 6,* 551–558.

Smith, G. E., Petersen, R. C., Parisi, J. E., Ivnik, R. J., Kokmem, E., Tangalos, E. G., Waring, S. (1996). Definition, course, and outcome of mild cognitive impairment. *Aging, Neuropsychology, and Cognition, 3,* 141–147.

Spreen, O., & Strauss, E. (1991). *A compendium of neuropsychological tests: Administration, norms, and commentary.* New York: Oxford.

Storandt, M., Stone, K., & LaBarge, E. (1995). Deficits in reading performance in very mild dementia of the Alzheimer type. *Neuropsychology, 9,* 174–176.

Storandt, M., & VandenBos, G. R. (Eds.). (1994). *Neuropsychological assessment of dementia and depression in older adults: A clinician's guide.* Washington, DC: American Psychological Association.

West, R. L., & Crook, T. H. (1991). Video training of imagery for mature adults. *Applied Cognitive Psychology, 6,* 307–320.

Yesavage, J., Brink, T., Rose, T., Lum, O., Huang, O., Adey, V., & Leier, V. (1983). Development and validation of a geriatric depression scale: A preliminary report. *Journal of Psychiatric Research, 17,* 37–49.

Youngjohn, J. R., Beck, J., Jogerst, J., & Cain, C. (1992). Neuropsychological impairment, depression, and Parkinson's disease. *Neuropsychology, 6,* 123–136.

Youngjohn, J. R., & Crook, T. H. (1993). Stability of everyday memory in age-associated memory impairment: A longitudinal study. *Neuropsychology, 7,* 406–416.

Youngjohn, J. R., Larrabee, G. J., & Crook, T. H. (1992). Discriminating age-associated memory impairment and Alzheimer's disease. *Psychological Assessment, 4,* 54–59.

Zelinski, E. M., Gilewski, M. J., & Anthony-Bergstone, C. R. (1990). Memory functioning questionnaire: Concurrent validity with memory performance and self-reported memory failures. *Psychology and Aging, 5,* 388–399.

APPENDIX I

APA Guidelines for Providers of Psychological Services to Ethnic, Linguistic, and Culturally Diverse Populations

INTRODUCTION

There is increasing motivation among psychologists to understand culture and ethnicity factors in order to provide appropriate psychological services. This increased motivation for improving quality of psychological services to ethnic and culturally diverse populations is attributable, in part, to the growing political and social presence of diverse cultural groups, both within APA and in the larger society. New sets of values, beliefs, and cultural expectations have been introduced into educational, political, business, and healthcare systems by the physical presence of these groups. The issues of language and culture do impact on the provision of appropriate psychological services.

Psychological service providers need a sociocultural framework to consider diversity of values, interactional styles, and cultural expectations in a systematic fashion. They need knowledge and skills for multicultural assessment and intervention, including abilities to:

1. recognize cultural diversity;
2. understand the role that culture and ethnicity/race play in the sociopsychological and economic development of ethnic and culturally diverse populations;
3. understand that socioeconomic and political factors significantly impact the psychosocial, political and economic development of ethnic and culturally diverse groups;
4. help clients to understand/maintain/resolve their own sociocultural identification; and understand the interaction of culture, gender, and sexual orientation on behavior and needs.

Likewise, there is a need to develop a conceptual framework that would enable psychologists to organize, access, and accurately assess the value and

These guidelines were approved by the Council of Representatives in August of 1990 during the 98th Annual Convention in Boston, Massachusetts. From *APA Guidelines for Providers of Psychological Services to Ethic, Linguistic, and Culturally Diverse Populations*, by the American Psychological Association, 2003, Washington, DC: American Psychological Association. Copyright 2003 by the American Psychological Association. Retrieved September 23, 2004, from PsychNET® Web site: http://www.apa.org/pi/oema/guide.html

utility of existing and future research involving ethnic and culturally diverse populations.

Research has addressed issues regarding responsiveness of psychological services to the needs of ethnic minority populations. The focus of mental health research issues has included:

1. the impact of ethnic/racial similarity in the counseling process (Acosta & Sheenan, 1976; Atkinson, 1983; Parham & Helms, 1981);

2. minority utilization of mental health services (Cheung & Snowden, 1990; Everett, Proctor, & Cartmell, 1983; Rosado, 1986; Snowden & Cheung, 1990);

3. relative effectiveness of directed versus nondirected styles of therapy (Acosta, Yamamoto, & Evans, 1982: Dauphinais, Dauphinais, & Rowe, 1981; Lorion, 1974);

4. the role of cultural values in treatment (Juarez, 1985; Padilla & Ruiz, 1973; Padilla, Ruiz, & Alvarez, 1975; Sue & Sue, 1987);

5. appropriate counseling and therapy models (Comas-Diaz & Griffith, 1988; McGoldrick, Pearce, & Giordino, 1982; Nishio & Blimes, 1987);

6. competency in skills for working with specific ethnic populations (Malgady, Rogler, & Constantino, 1987; Root, 1985; Zuniga, 1988).

The APA's Board of Ethnic Minority Affairs (BEMA) established a Task Force on the Delivery of Services to Ethnic Minority Populations in 1988 in response to the increased awareness about psychological service needs associated with ethnic and cultural diversity. The populations of concern include, but are not limited to the following groups: American Indians/Alaska Natives, Asian Americans, and Hispanics/Latinos. For example, the populations also include recently arrived refugee and immigrant groups and established U.S. subcultures such as Amish, Hasidic Jewish, and rural Appalachian people.

The Task Force established as its first priority development of the Guidelines for Providers of Psychological Services to Ethnic, Linguistic, and Culturally Diverse Populations. The guidelines that follow are intended to enlighten all areas of service delivery, not simply clinical or counseling endeavors. The clients referred to may be clients, organizations, government and/or community agencies.

GUIDELINES

Preamble: The Guidelines represent general principles that are intended to be aspirational in nature and are designed to provide suggestions to psychologists in working with ethnic, linguistic, and culturally diverse populations.

1. Psychologists educate their clients to the processes of psychological intervention, such as goals and expectations; the scope and, where appropriate, legal limits of confidentiality; and the psychologists' orientations.
   a. Whenever possible, psychologists provide information in writing along with oral explanations.
   b. Whenever possible, the written information is provided in the language understandable to the client.
2. Psychologists are cognizant of relevant research and practice issues as related to the population being served.
   a. Psychologists acknowledge that ethnicity and culture impact on behavior and take those factors into account when working with various ethnic/racial groups.
   b. Psychologists seek out educational and training experiences to enhance their understanding to address the needs of these populations more appropriately and effectively. These experiences include cultural, social, psychological, political, economic, and historical material specific to the particular ethnic group being served.
   c. Psychologists recognize the limits of their competencies and expertise. Psychologists who do not possess knowledge and training about an ethnic group seek consultation with, and/or make referrals to, appropriate experts as necessary.
   d. Psychologists consider the validity of a given instrument or procedure and interpret resulting data, keeping in mind the cultural and linguistic characteristics of the person being assessed. Psychologists are aware of the test's reference population and possible limitations of such instruments with other populations.
3. Psychologists recognize ethnicity and culture as significant parameters in understanding psychological processes.
   a. Psychologists, regardless of ethnic/racial background, are aware of how their own cultural background/experiences, attitudes, values, and biases influence psychological processes. They make efforts to correct any prejudices and biases.
   Illustrative Statement: Psychologists might routinely ask themselves, 'Is it appropriate for me to view this client or organization any differently than I would if they were from my own ethnic or cultural group?'

b. Psychologists' practice incorporates an understanding of the client's ethnic and cultural background. This includes the client's familiarity and comfort with the majority culture as well as ways in which the client's culture may add to or improve various aspects of the majority culture and/or of society at large.

Illustrative Statement: The kinds of mainstream social activities in which families participate may offer information about the level and quality of acculturation to American society. It is important to distinguish acculturation from length of stay in the United States, and not to assume that these issues are relevant only for new immigrants and refugees.

c. Psychologists help clients increase their awareness of their own cultural values and norms, and they facilitate discovery of ways clients can apply this awareness to their own lives and to society at large.

Illustrative Statement: Psychologists may be able to help parents distinguish between generational conflict and culture gaps when problems arise between them and their children. In the process, psychologists could help both parents and children to appreciate their own distinguishing cultural values.

d. Psychologists seek to help a client determine whether a 'problem' stems from racism or bias in others so that the client does not inappropriately personalize problems.

Illustrative Statement: The concept of 'healthy paranoia,' whereby ethnic minorities may develop defensive behaviors in response to discrimination, illustrates this principle.

e. Psychologists consider not only differential diagnostic issues but also cultural beliefs and values of the clients and his/her community in providing intervention.

Illustrative Statement: There is a disorder among the traditional Navajo called 'Moth Madness.' Symptoms include seizure-like behaviors. The disorder is believed by the Navajo to be the supernatural result of incestuous thoughts or behaviors. Both differential diagnosis and intervention should take into consideration the traditional values of Moth Madness.

4. Psychologists respect the roles of family members and community structures, hierarchies, values, and beliefs within the client's culture.

a. Psychologists identify resources in the family and the larger community.

b. Clarification of the role of the psychologist and the expectations of the client precede intervention. Psychologists seek to ensure that both the psychologist and client have a clear understanding of what services and roles are reasonable.

   Illustrative Statement: It is not uncommon for an entire American Indian family to come into the clinic to provide support to the person in distress. Many of the healing practices found in American Indian communities are centered in the family and the whole community.

5. Psychologists respect clients' religious and/or spiritual beliefs and values, including attributions and taboos, since they affect world view, psychosocial functioning, and expressions of distress.

   a. Part of working in minority communities is to become familiar with indigenous beliefs and practices and to respect them.

      Illustrative Statement: Traditional healers (e.g., shamans, curanderos, espiritistas) have an important place in minority communities.

   b. Effective psychological intervention may be aided by consultation with and/or inclusion of religious/spiritual leaders/practitioners relevant to the client's cultural and belief systems.

6. Psychologists interact in the language requested by the client and, if this is not feasible, make an appropriate referral.

   a. Problems may arise when the linguistic skills of the psychologist do not match the language of the client. In such a case, psychologists refer the client to a mental health professional who is competent to interact in the language of the client. If this is not possible, psychologists offer the client a translator with cultural knowledge and an appropriate professional background. When no translator is available, then a trained paraprofessional from the client's culture is used as a translator/culture broker.

   b. If translation is necessary, psychologists do not retain the services of translators/paraprofessionals that may have a dual role with the client to avoid jeopardizing the validity of evaluation or the effectiveness of intervention.

   c. Psychologists interpret and relate test data in terms understandable and relevant to the needs of those assessed.

7. Psychologists consider the impact of adverse social, environmental, and political factors in assessing problems and designing interventions.

a. Types of intervention strategies to be used match to the client's level of need (e.g., Maslow's hierarchy of needs).

Illustrative Statement: Low income may be associated with such stressors as malnutrition, substandard housing, and poor medical care; and rural residency may mean inaccessibility of services. Clients may resist treatment at government agencies because of previous experience (e.g., refugees' status may be associated with violent treatments by government officials and agencies).

b. Psychologists work within the cultural setting to improve the welfare of all persons concerned, if there is a conflict between cultural values and human rights.

8. Psychologists attend to as well as work to eliminate biases, prejudices, and discriminatory practices.

a. Psychologists acknowledge relevant discriminatory practices at the social and community level that may be affecting the psychological welfare of the population being served.

Illustrated Statement: Depression may be associated with frustrated attempts to climb the corporate ladder in an organization that is dominated by a top echelon of White males.

b. Psychologists are cognizant of sociopolitical contexts in conducting evaluations and providing interventions; they develop sensitivity to issues of oppression, sexism, elitism, and racism.

Illustrative Statement: An upsurge in the public expression of rancor or even violence between two ethnic or cultural groups may increase anxiety baselines in any member of these groups. This baseline of anxiety would interact with prevailing symptomatology. At the organizational level, the community conflict may interfere with open communication among staff.

9. Psychologists working with culturally diverse populations should document culturally and sociopolitically relevant factors in the records.

a. number of generations in the country
b. number of years in the country
c. fluency in English
d. extent of family support (or disintegration of family)
e. community resources
f. level of education
g. change in social status as a result of coming to this country (for immigrant or refugee)
h. intimate relationship with people of different backgrounds
i. level of stress related to acculturation

REFERENCES

Acosta, F. X., & Sheehan, J. G. (1976). Preference towards Mexican American andAnglo American psychotherapists. *Journal of Consulting and Clinical Psychology, 44*(2), 272–279.

Acosta, F., Yamamoto, J., & Evans, L. (1982). *Effective psychotherapy for low income and minority patients.* New York: Plenum Press.

Atkinson, D. R. (1983). Ethnic similarity in counseling psychology: A review of research. *The Counseling Psychologists, 11,* 79–92.

Cheung, F. K., & Snowden, L. R. (1990). Community mental health and ethnic minority populations. *Community Mental Health Journal, 26,* 277–291.

Comas-Diaz, L., & Griffith, E. H. (1988). *Clinical guidelines in cross-cultural mental-health.* John Wiley.

Dauphinais, P., Dauphinais, L., & Rowe, W. (1981). Effects of race and communication style on Indian perceptions of counselor effectiveness. *Counselor Education and Supervision, 20,* 37–46.

Everett, F., Proctor, N., & Cartmell, B. (1983). Providing psychological services toAmerican Indian children and families. *Professional Psychology: Research and Practice, 14*(5), 588–603.

Juarez, R. (1985). Core issues in psychotherapy with the Hispanic child. *Psychotherapy, 22*(25), 441–448.

Lorion, R. P. (1974). Patient and therapist variables in the treatment of low incomepatients. *Psychological Bulletin, 81,* 344–354.

Malgady, R. G., Rogler, L. H., & Constantino, G. (1987). Ethnocultural and linguistic bias in mental health evaluation of Hispanics. *American Psychologist, 42*(3), 228–234.

McGoldrick, M., Pearce, J. K., & Giordano, J. (1982). *Ethnicity and family therapy.* New York: Guilford Press.

Nishio, K., & Bilmes, M. (1987). Psychotherapy with Southeast Asian American clients. *Professional Psychology: Research and Practice, 18*(4), 342–346.

Padilla, A. M., & Ruiz, R. A. (1973). *Latino mental health: A review of literature* (DHEW publication No. HSM 73-9143). Washington, DC: U.S. Government Printing Office.

Padilla, A. M., Ruiz., R. A., & Alvarez, R. (1975). Community mental health for the Spanish-speaking/surnamed population. *American Psychologist, 30,* 892–905.

Parham, T. A., & Helms, J. E. (1981). The influence of Black students racial identity attitudes on preferences for counselor's race. *Journal of Counseling Psychology, 28,* 250–257.

Root, Maria P. P. (1985). Guidelines for facilitating therapy with Asian American clients. *Psychotherapy, 22*(2s), 349–356.

Rosado, J. W. (1986). Toward an interfacing of Hispanic cultural variables with school psychology service delivery systems. *Professional Psychology: Research and Practice, 17*(3), 191–199.

Snowden, L. R., & Cheung, F. K. (1990). Use of inpatient mental health services by members of ethnic minority groups. *American Psychologist, 45,* 347–355.

Sue, D., & Sue, S. (1987). Cultural factors in the clinical assessment of Asian American. *Journal of Consulting and Clinical Psychology, 55*(4), 479–487.

Zuniga, M. E. (1988). Assessment issues with Chicanas: practical implications. *Psychotherapy, 25*(2), 288–293.

Task Force on the Delivery of Services to Ethnic Minority Populations:

Charles Joseph Pine, PhD, Chair
Jose Cervantes, PhD
Freda Cheung, PhD
Christine C. Iijima Hall, PhD
Jean Holroyd, PhD
Robin LaDue, PhD
LaVome Robinson, PhD
Maria P. P. Root, PhD

APPENDIX J

APA Guidelines on Multicultural Education, Training, Research, Practice, and Organizational Change for Psychologists (Abridged Version[1])

AMERICAN PSYCHOLOGICAL ASSOCIATION

This document was approved as policy of the American Psychological Association (APA) by the APA Council of Representatives in August 2002. This document was drafted by a joint task force of APA Divisions 17 (Counseling Psychology) and 45 (The Society for the Psychological Study of Ethnic Minority Issues). These guidelines have been in the process of development for 22 years, so many individuals and groups require acknowledgment. The Divisions 17/45 writing team for the present document included Nadya Fouad, PhD (co-chair); Patricia Arredondo, EdD (co-chair); Michael D'Andrea, EdD; and Allen Ivey, EdD. These guidelines build on work related to multicultural counseling competencies by Division 17 (D. W. Sue et al., 1982) and the Association of Multicultural Counseling and Development (Arredondo et al., 1996; D. W. Sue, Arredondo, & McDavis, 1992). The task force acknowledges Allen Ivey, EdD; Thomas Parham, PhD; and Derald Wing Sue, PhD, for their leadership related to the work on competencies. The Divisions 17/45 writing team for these guidelines was assisted in reviewing the relevant literature by Rod Goodyear, PhD; Jeffrey S. Mio, PhD; Ruperto (Toti) Perez, PhD; William Parham, PhD; and Derald Wing Sue, PhD. Additional writing contributions came from Gail Hackett, PhD; Jeanne Manese, PhD; Louise Douce, PhD; James Croteau, PhD; Janet Helms, PhD; Sally Horwatt, PhD; Kathleen Boggs, PhD; Gerald Stone, PhD; and Kathleen Bieschke, PhD. Editorial contributions were provided by Nancy Downing

From "Guidelines on Multicultural Education, Training, Research, Practice, and Organizational Change for Psychologists," by the American Psychological Association, 2003, *American Psychologist*, 58, 377–402. Copyright 2003 by the American Psychological Association. Retrieved September 23, 2004, from PsychNET® Web site: http://www.apa.org/pi/multiculturalguidelines.pdf

Correspondence concerning this article should be directed to the Public Interest Directorate, American Psychological Association, 750 First Street, NE, Washington, DC, 20002-4242.

1. Because of space limitations, only Guidelines 1 and 2, relating to commitment to cultural awareness/knowledge of self and others, and Guideline 5, relating to practice, are reproduced here. Guidelines 3 and 4, relating to education and research respectively, and Guideline 6, relating to organizational change, are not reproduced here, although they are referred to in the introductory material. Readers are strongly encouraged to consult the full guidelines at www.apa.org/pi/multiculturalguidelines.pdf.

Hansen, PhD; Patricia Perez; Tiffany Rice; and Dan Rosen. The task force is grateful for the active support and contributions of a series of presidents of APA Divisions 17, 35, and 45, including Rosie Bingham, PhD; Jean Carter, PhD; Lisa Porche Burke, PhD; Gerald Stone, PhD; Joseph Trimble, PhD; Melba Vasquez, PhD; and Jan Yoder, PhD. Other individuals who contributed through their advocacy include Guillermo Bernal, PhD; Robert Carter, PhD; J. Manuel Casas, PhD; Don Pope-Davis, PhD; Linda Forrest, PhD; Margaret Jensen, PhD; Teresa LaFromboise, PhD; Joseph G. Ponterotto, PhD; and Ena Vazquez Nuttall, EdD.

The final version of this document was strongly influenced by the contributions of a working group jointly convened by the APA Board for the Advancement of Psychology in the Public Interest (BAPPI) and the APA Board of Professional Affairs (BPA). In addition to Nadya Fouad, PhD, and Patricia Arredondo, EdD, from the Divisions 17/45 task force, members of the working group included Maria Root, PhD, BAPPI (working group co-chair); Sandra L. Shullman, PhD, BPA (working group co-chair); Toy Caldwell-Colbert, PhD, APA Board of Educational Affairs; Jessica Henderson Daniels, PhD, APA Committee for the Advancement of Professional Practice; Janet Swim, PhD, representing the APA Board of Scientific Affairs; Kristin Hancock, PhD, BPA Committee on Professional Practice and Standards; and Laura Barbanel, PhD, APA Board of Directors. This working group was assisted in its efforts by APA staff members Shirlene A. Archer, JD, Public Interest Directorate; and Geoffrey M. Reed, PhD, Practice Directorate, who also jointly shepherded the document through the final approval process. The task force also acknowledges APA staff members Paul Donnelly; Alberto Figueroa; Bertha Holliday, PhD; Sarah Jordan; Joan White; and Henry Tomes, PhD, for their support.

This document is scheduled to expire as APA policy by 2009. After this date, users are encouraged to contact the APA Public Interest Directorate to confirm the status of the document.

APPENDIX OUTLINE

Preface

Scope of Guidelines

Racial/Ethnic Diversity in the United States and Psychology

Definitions
- Culture
- Race
- Ethnicity
- Multiculturalism and Diversity
- Culture-Centered

PREFACE

All individuals exist in social, political, historical, and economic contexts, and psychologists are increasingly called upon to understand the influence of these contexts on individuals' behavior. The "Guidelines on Multicultural Education, Training, Research, Practice, and Organizational Change for Psychologists" reflect the continuing evolution of the study of psychology, changes in society at large, and emerging data about the different needs of particular individuals and groups historically marginalized or disenfranchised within and by psychology based on their ethnic/racial heritage and social group identity or membership. These "Guidelines on Multicultural Education, Training, Research, Practice, and Organizational Change for Psychologists" reflect knowledge and skills needed for the profession in the midst of dramatic historic sociopolitical changes in U.S. society, as well as needs of new constituencies, markets, and clients.

The specific goals of these guidelines are to provide psychologists with (a) the rationale and needs for addressing multiculturalism and diversity in education, training, research, practice, and organizational change; (b) basic information, relevant terminology, current empirical research from psychology and related disciplines, and other data that support the proposed guidelines and underscore their importance; (c) references to enhance ongoing education, training, research, practice, and organizational change methodologies; and (d) paradigms that broaden the purview of psychology as a profession.

In these guidelines, education refers to the psychological education of students in all areas of psychology, while training refers more specifically to the application of that education to the development of applied and research skills. We refer to research that involves human participants, rather than research using animals or mathematical simulations. Practice refers to interventions with children, adolescents, adults, families, and organizations typically conducted by clinical, consulting, counseling, organizational, and school psychologists. Finally, we focus on the work of psychologists as administrators, as consultants, and in other organizational management roles positioned to promote organizational change and policy development.

These guidelines address U.S. ethnic and racial minority[2] groups as well as individuals, children, and families from biracial, multiethnic, and multiracial backgrounds. Thus, we are defining multicultural in these guidelines narrowly to refer to interactions between individuals from minority ethnic and racial groups in the United States and the dominant European-American culture. Ethnic and racial minority group membership includes individuals of Asian and Pacific Islander, sub-Saharan Black African, Latino/Hispanic, and Native American/American Indian descent, although there is great heterogeneity within each of these groups. The guidelines also address psychologists' work and interactions with individuals from other nations, including international students, immigrants, and temporary workers in this country.

The term guidelines refers to pronouncements, statements, or declarations that suggest or recommend specific professional behavior, endeavors, or conduct for psychologists (American Psychological Association [APA], 1992). Guidelines differ from standards in that standards are mandatory and may be accompanied by an enforcement mechanism (APA, 2001). Guidelines are intended to facilitate the continued systematic development of the profession and to help assure a high level of professional practice by psychologists. Guidelines are not intended to be mandatory or exhaustive and may not be applicable to every professional and clinical situation. They are not definitive and they are not intended to take precedence over the judgment of psychologists. In addition, federal or state laws may supercede these guidelines.

---

2. The term person/s of color is preferred by some instead of minority because of the technical definition the latter term connotes.

SCOPE OF GUIDELINES

This document is comprehensive but not exhaustive. We intend to reflect the context and rationale for these guidelines in multiple settings and situations, but we also acknowledge that we expect the document to evolve over time with more illustrative examples and references. In the current document, we initially provide evidence for the need for multicultural guidelines with an overview of the most recent demographic data on racial/ethnic diversity in the United States and the representation of racial/ethnic minorities in education and psychology. We then discuss the social and political developments in the United States and the profession of psychology that provide a context for the development of the guidelines and the fundamental principles on which we base the guidelines. Each guideline is then presented, with the first two guidelines designed to apply to all psychologists from two primary perspectives: (a) knowledge of self with a cultural heritage and varying social identities and (b) knowledge of other cultures. Guidelines 3–6 address the application of multiculturalism in education, training, research, practice, and organizational change.

While these guidelines have attempted to incorporate empirical studies of intergroup relations and ethnic identity, professional consensus, and other perceptions and experiences of ethnic and racial minority groups, it is beyond the scope of this document to provide a thorough and comprehensive review of all literature related to race, ethnicity, intergroup processes, and organizational development strategies to address multiculturalism in employment and professional education contexts. Rather, we have attempted to provide examples of empirical and conceptual literature relevant to the guidelines where possible.

RACIAL/ETHNIC DIVERSITY IN THE UNITED STATES AND PSYCHOLOGY

Individuals of ethnic and racial minority and/or with a biracial/multiethnic/multiracial heritage represent an increasingly large percentage of the population in the United States (Judy & D'Amico, 1997; U.S. Census Bureau, 2001; Wehrly, Kenney, & Kenney, 1999). While these demographic trends have been discussed since the previous census of 1990, educational institutions, employers, government agencies, and professional and accrediting bodies are now beginning to engage in systematic efforts to become more knowledgeable, proficient, and multiculturally responsive. Census 2000 data clarify the changes in U.S. diversity (U.S. Census Bureau, 2001). Overall, about 67% of the population identified as White, either alone or with another race. Of the remaining 33%, approximately 13% indicated they were African American, 1.5% American Indian or Alaskan Native, 4.5%

Asian/Pacific Islander, 13% Hispanic, and about 7% some other race. These categories overlap since individuals were able to choose more than one racial affiliation. Racial/ethnic diversity varies greatly by state. Summarized in a series of maps by C. A. Brewer and Suchan (2001) from the Census 2000 data, high-diversity states (those with counties that are 60%–77% racial/ ethnic groups) tend to be on the coast or Mexican border and include California, Texas, Arizona, New Mexico, and Virginia. In addition to these, however, medium-high-diversity states (those with counties that are 49%–59% racial/ethnic minority groups) are found across the country and include Maryland, New York, Illinois, Washington state, Nevada, Colorado, Montana, Alaska, North Dakota, South Dakota, Minnesota, Wisconsin, Michigan, Arkansas, Louisiana, Alabama, North Carolina, and South Carolina.

In the past 10 years, percentage-wise, the greatest increases have been reported for Asian American/Pacific Islanders and Latinos/Hispanics, and in some parts of the country, White European Americans are no longer a clear majority of the population. C. A. Brewer and Suchan (2001) found that diversity increased in all states in the country and, in parts of some states, increased as much as 34%. States that had the most growth in diversity varied geographically, including the Midwest (Nebraska, Iowa, Kansas, Colorado), South (Georgia, Florida, Texas, and Oklahoma), and Northwest (Idaho, Oregon). In addition, for the first time, Census 2000 allowed individuals to check more than one racial/ethnic affiliation (U.S. Census Bureau, 2001). While only 2.4% of the U.S. population checked more than one racial affiliation, 42% of those who checked two or more races were under 18, indicating an increase in the birthrate of biracial individuals. Certainly, the United States is becoming more racially and ethnically diverse, increasing the urgency for culturally responsive practices and services.

Ethnic, racial, and multiracial diversity in the population is reflected in higher education. This is important to psychologists because it reflects changes in the ethnic composition of students they teach and train. College enrollment increased 62% for students of color between 1988 and 1998 (the latest data available), although college-completion rates differed among Whites and racial/ethnic minority students. College-completion rates in 2000 (U.S. Census Bureau, 2001) for White individuals between 25–29 years was 29.6%, compared to 17.8% for African Americans, 53.9% for Asian/ Pacific Islander Americans, and 9.7% for Hispanics. Corresponding statistics for 1991 versus 1974 were 24.6% versus 22% for Whites, 11% versus 7.9% for African Americans/Blacks, and 9.2% versus 5.7% for Hispanics. Data for Hispanics were first collected in 1974; data for Asian/Pacific Islanders were not collected until the mid-1990s. Clearly, these data indicate that racial/ ethnic minority students are graduating at a lower rate than White students, but the data also show that they are making educational gains.

Completion of a psychology degree is particularly germane to these guidelines since obtaining a college degree is the first step in the pipeline to becoming a psychologist. The National Center for Education Statistics (NCES) collects information on degrees conferred by area, reported by race/ethnicity. Its latest report (NCES, 2001) indicated that 74,060 bachelor's degrees were awarded in psychology in 2001, 14,465 master's degrees were awarded in psychology, and 4,310 doctoral degrees were awarded in psychology. Of those degrees, the majority were awarded to Whites (72% of bachelor's and master's degrees and 77% of doctoral degrees). African Americans received 10% of both bachelor's and master's degrees and 5% of doctoral degrees; Hispanics received 10% of bachelor's degrees and 5% of both master's and doctoral degrees; Asian/Pacific Islanders received 6% of bachelor's degrees, 3% of master's, and 4% of doctoral degrees in psychology. American Indians received less than 1% of all the degrees in psychology. Compared to the percentage of the population for each of these minority groups noted above, racial/ethnic minority students are underrepresented at all levels of psychology but most particularly at the doctoral level, the primary entry point for becoming a psychologist.

Thus, racial/ethnic minority students, either because of personal or because of environmental reasons (e.g., discrimination and barriers due to external constraints), progressively drop out of the pipeline to become psychologists. The racial representation within the profession of psychology is similarly small. Kite et al. (2001) reported that the numbers of ethnic minority psychologists were too small to break down by ethnicity. Indeed, in 2002, APA membership data indicated that 0.3% of the membership was American Indian, 1.7% was Asian, 2.1% was Hispanic, and 1.7% was African American (APA Research Office, 2002a), clearly delineating the serious underrepresentation of psychologists of color within the organization. Representation was slightly better within APA governance in 2002—1.7% of those in APA governance were American Indian, 3.6% were Asian, 5.1% were Black, and 4.8% were Hispanic (APA Research Office, 2002b).

These guidelines are based on the central premise that the population of the United States is racially/ethnically diverse and that students, research participants, clients, and the workforce will be increasingly likely to come from racially/ethnically diverse cultures. Moreover, educators, trainers of psychologists, psychological researchers, providers of service, and those psychologists implementing organizational change are encouraged to gain skills to work effectively with individuals and groups of varying cultural backgrounds. We base our premise on psychologists' ethical principles to be competent to work with a variety of populations (Principle A), to respect others' rights (Principle D), to be concerned to not harm others (Principle E), and to contribute to social justice (Principle F; APA, 1992). We believe these guidelines will assist psychologists in seeking and using appropriate culturally centered education, training, research, practice, and organizational change.

Also informing these guidelines are research, professional consensus, and literature addressing perceptions of ethnic minority groups and intergroup relationships (Dovidio & Gaertner, 1998; Dovidio, Gaertner, & Validzic, 1998; Gaertner & Dovidio, 2000), experiences of ethnic and racial minority groups (S. Sue, 1999; Swim & Stangor, 1998; U.S. Department of Health and Human Services [USDHHS], 2001), multidisciplinary theoretical models about worldviews and identity (Arredondo & Glauner, 1992; Helms, 1990; Hofstede, 1980; Kluckhohn & Strodbeck, 1961; Markus & Kitayama, 2001; D. W. Sue & Sue, 1977), and the work on cross-cultural and multicultural guidelines and competencies developed over the past 20 years (Arredondo et al., 1996; D. W. Sue, Arredondo, & McDavis, 1992; D. W. Sue et al., 1982). Although we acknowledge that the issues addressed in these guidelines are increasingly important to consider in a global context, the guidelines focus on the context within the United States and its commonwealths or territories such as Puerto Rico and Guam.

DEFINITIONS

There is considerable controversy and overlap in terms used to connote race, culture, and ethnicity (Helms & Talleyrand, 1997; Phinney, 1996). In this section, we define the following terms that are used throughout these guidelines.

Culture

Culture is defined as the belief systems and value orientations that influence customs, norms, practices, and social institutions, including psychological processes (language, caretaking practices, media, educational systems) and organizations (media, educational systems; A. P. Fiske, Kitayama, Markus, & Nisbett, 1998). Inherent in this definition is the acknowledgment that all individuals are cultural beings and have a cultural, ethnic, and racial heritage. Culture has been described as the embodiment of a worldview through learned and transmitted beliefs, values, and practices, including religious and spiritual traditions. It also encompasses a way of living informed by the historical, economic, ecological, and political forces on a group. These definitions suggest that culture is fluid and dynamic and that there are both cultural universal phenomena and culturally specific or relative constructs.

Race

The biological basis of race has, at times, been the source of fairly heated debates in psychology (Fish, 1995; Helms & Talleyrand, 1997; Jensen, 1995; Levin, 1995; Phinney, 1996; Rushton, 1995; Sun, 1995; Yee, Fairchild, Weizmann, & Wyatt, 1993). Helms and Cook (1999) noted that race has no consensual definition and that, in fact, biological racial categories and phenotypic characteristics have more within-group variation than between-groups variation. In these guidelines, the definition of race is considered to be socially constructed rather than biologically determined. Race, then, is the category to which others assign individuals on the basis of physical characteristics, such as skin color or hair type, and the generalizations and stereotypes made as a result. Thus, "people are treated or studied as though they belong to biologically defined racial groups on the basis of such characteristics" (Helms & Talleyrand, 1997, p. 1247).

Ethnicity

Similar to the concepts of race and culture, the term ethnicity does not have a commonly agreed-upon definition; in these guidelines, we refer to ethnicity as the acceptance of the group mores and practices of one's culture of origin and the concomitant sense of belonging. We also note that, consistent with M. B. Brewer (1999), Sedikides and Brewer (2001), and Hornsey and Hogg (2000), individuals may have multiple ethnic identities that operate with different salience at different times.

Multiculturalism and Diversity

The terms multiculturalism and diversity have been used interchangeably to include aspects of identity stemming from gender, sexual orientation, disability, socioeconomic status, or age. Multiculturalism, in an absolute sense, recognizes the broad scope of dimensions of race, ethnicity, language, sexual orientation, gender, age, disability, class status, education, religious/spiritual orientation, and other cultural dimensions. All of these are critical aspects of an individual's ethnic/racial and personal identity, and psychologists are encouraged to be cognizant of issues related to all of these dimensions of culture. In addition, each cultural dimension has unique issues and concerns. As noted by the "Guidelines for Psychotherapy With Lesbian, Gay, and Bisexual Clients" (APA, 2000), each individual belongs to/identifies with a number of identities, and some of those identities interact with each other. To effectively help clients, to effectively train students, to be most effective as agents of change and as scientists, psychologists are encouraged to be familiar with issues of these multiple identities within and between individuals. However, as we noted earlier, in these guidelines, we use the term multicultural rather narrowly to connote interactions between racial/ethnic groups in the United States and the implications for education, training, research, practice, and organizational change.

The concept of diversity has been widely used in employment settings, with the term given greater visibility through research by the Hudson Institute reported in Workforce 2000 (Johnson & Packer, 1987) and Workforce

2020 (Judy & D'Amico, 1997). The application of the term began with reference to women and persons of color, underrepresented in the workplace, particularly in decision-making roles. It has since evolved to be more encompassing in its intent and application by referring to individuals' social identities, including age, sexual orientation, physical disability, socioeconomic status, race/ethnicity, workplace role/position, religious and spiritual orientation, and work/family concerns (Loden, 1996).

Culture-Centered

We use the term culture-centered throughout the guidelines to encourage psychologists to use a "cultural lens" as a central focus of professional behavior. In culture-centered practices, psychologists recognize that all individuals, including themselves, are influenced by different contexts, including the historical, ecological, sociopolitical, and disciplinary. "If culture is part of the environment, and all behavior is shaped by culture, then culture-centered counseling is responsive to all culturally learned patterns" (Pedersen, 1997, p. 256). For example, a culture-centered focus suggests to the psychologist the consideration that behavior may be shaped by culture, the groups to which one belongs, and cultural stereotypes including those about stigmatized group members (Gaertner & Dovidio, 2000; Major, Quinton, & McCoy, in press; Markus & Kitayama, 1991; Steele, 1997).

HISTORICAL AND SOCIOPOLITICAL DEVELOPMENTS FOR GUIDELINES

There are a number of national events, APA-specific developments, and initiatives of other related professional associations that provide a historical context for the development of multicultural and culture-specific guidelines, with a focus on racial/ethnic minority groups. Nationally, in 1954, the Supreme Court struck down the "separate but equal" doctrine of segregated education (Brown v. Board of Education, 1954). Benjamin and Crouse (2002) noted that in addition to setting the stage for greater social equity in education, Brown v. Board of Education was an important turning point for psychology because it was the "first time that psychological research was cited in a Supreme Court decision" (p. 38). A decade later, the 1964 passage of the Civil Rights Act set the stage for sociopolitical movements and the development of additional legislation to protect individual and group rights at national, state, and local levels. These movements and resulting legislation have specifically addressed the rights of equity and access based on gender, age, disability, national origin, religion, sexual orientation, and, of course, ethnicity and race. However, it is also important to note that movements to dismantle affirmative action in California, Michigan, and Texas are sociopolitical efforts that threaten the advancement of the rights of individuals and groups historically marginalized.

National issues regarding health care and mental health disparities for ethnic/racial minority groups culminated in psychologists playing a role in President Clinton's dialogue in the mid 1990s about race and racism and in the U.S. Surgeon General's report in 2001 (USDHHS, 2001). The national debates also led to noteworthy organizational structural changes. For example, the National Institute of Mental Health established an office of minority research in 1971 and reorganized to incorporate ethnic minority-focused research in all areas in 1985, including justifications for diversity of research populations. Findings from this funded research have been instrumental in setting policies specific to racial/ethnic minority groups.

Psychologists' perspective on the role of race in education has been addressed for nearly a century (a historical perspective is provided by Suzuki & Valencia, 1997). Indeed the constructs of race, culture, and intergroup relationships have been areas of research for psychologists since nearly the beginning of psychology, including Clark and Clark (1940), Allport (1954), and Lewin (1945; see Duckitt, 1992, for a historical review).

Within the profession of psychology, attention to culture as a variable in clinical practice was first mentioned at the Vail Conference of 1973 (Korman, 1974). One of the recommendations from this conference was to include training in cultural diversity in all doctoral programs and through continuing education workshops. Attention to appropriate training based on multicultural and culture-specific constructs and contexts continued through the next two decades. The APA Committee on Accreditation's Accreditation Handbook (APA Committee on Accreditation & Accreditation Office, 1986) included cultural diversity as a component of effective training in 1986, and this continued in the 2002 guidelines (APA, 2002). These efforts recognized the importance of cultural and individual differences and diversity in the training of clinical, counseling, and school psychologists. Subsequently, the training councils of these disciplines began to incorporate cultural diversity into their model programs, including the Council of Counseling Psychology's model training program in counseling psychology (Murdock, Alcorn, Heesacker, & Stoltenberg, 1998) and the standards of the National Council of Schools of Professional Psychology (Peterson, Peterson, & Abrams, 1999).

Concomitantly, changes to reflect greater attention to cultural diversity were occurring through structural and functional changes within the APA organization. The Office of Ethnic Minority Affairs was established in 1979. A year later, the Board of Ethnic Minority Affairs (BEMA) was established. BEMA was charged with promoting the scientific underpinning of the influence and impact of culture, race, and ethnicity on individuals' behavior, as well as with advancing the participation of ethnic minority psychologists within the organization. BEMA established a Task Force on Minority Education and Training in 1981, and a second Task Force on Communication

With Minority Constituents was formed in 1984. In 1990, the Board for the Advancement of Psychology in the Public Interest was formed, as was the Committee on Ethnic Minority Affairs. These entities replaced BEMA within APA's governance structure. The Commission on Ethnic Minority Recruitment, Retention, and Training was formed in 1994 and published a report and five-year plan to increase the number of students in psychology. These multiple efforts of APA and the divisions began to culminate in the production of policy. The "General Guidelines for Providers of Psychological Services" were "developed with the understanding that psychological services must be planned and implemented so that they are sensitive to factors related to life in a pluralistic society such as age, gender, affectional orientation, culture, and ethnicity" (APA, 1987, p. 713).

In 1990, APA published the Guidelines for Providers of Psychological Services to Ethnic, Linguistic, and Culturally Diverse Populations (APA, 1990). Following this, the 1992 revision of the Ethics Code included Principle D: Respect of People's Rights and Dignity, which stated in part, "Psychologists are aware of cultural, individual, and role differences, including those related to age, gender, race, ethnicity, national origin" (APA, 1992, p. 1598). The Ethics Code also contained ethical standards related to cultural diversity related to competence (Standard 1.08), assessment (Standard 2.04), and research (Standards 6.07 & 6.11).

The current "Guidelines on Multicultural Education, Training, Research, Practice, and Organizational Change for Psychologists" have developed as a result of the sociopolitical environment within the United States and the resulting work of psychologists within the professional organization. While there have been a variety of organizational initiatives that have focused on race and ethnicity, these guidelines are the first to address the implications of race and ethnicity in psychological education, training, research, practice, and organizational change. These guidelines are the latest step in an ongoing effort to provide psychologists in the United States with a framework for services to an increasingly diverse population and to assist psychologists in the provision of those services. In effect, there is a societal and guild/organizational history steadily indicating a rationale for attending to a multicultural and culture-specific agenda more formally.

INTRODUCTION TO THE GUIDELINES: ASSUMPTIONS AND PRINCIPLES

These guidelines, as noted earlier, pertain to the role of psychologists of both racial/ethnic minority and nonminority status in education, training, research, practice, and organizations, as well as to students, research participants, and clients of racial/ethnic heritage or minority heritage. In psychological education, training, research, and practice, all transactions occur between members of two or more cultures. As identity constructs and dynamic forces, race and ethnicity can impact psychological practice and interventions at all levels. These tenets articulate respect and inclusiveness for the national heritage of all cultural groups, recognition of cultural contexts as defining forces for individuals' and groups' lived experiences, and the role of external forces such as historical, economic, and sociopolitical events.

This philosophical grounding serves to influence the planning and implementation of culturally and scientifically sound education, research, practice, and organizational change and policy development in the larger society. To have a profession of psychology that is culturally informed in theory and practice calls for psychologists, as primary transmitters of the culture of the profession, to assume the responsibility for contributing to the advancement of cultural knowledge, sensitivity, and understanding. In other words, psychologists are in a position to provide leadership as agents of prosocial change, advocacy, and social justice, thereby promoting societal understanding, affirmation, and appreciation of multiculturalism against the damaging effects of individual, institutional, and societal racism, prejudice, and all forms of oppression based on stereotyping and discrimination.

The "Guidelines on Multicultural Education, Training, Research, Practice, and Organizational Change for Psychologists" are founded upon the following principles:

1. Ethical conduct of psychologists is enhanced by knowledge of differences in beliefs and practices that emerge from socialization through racial and ethnic group affiliation and membership and how those beliefs and practices will necessarily affect the education, training, research, and practice of psychology (Principles D & F of the APA [1992] Ethics Code; Council of National Psychological Associations for the Advancement of Ethnic Minority Interests [CNPAAEMI], 2000).

2. Understanding and recognizing the interface between individuals' socialization experiences based on ethnic and racial heritage can enhance the quality of education, training, practice, and research in the field of psychology (American Council on Education, 2000; American Council on Education & American Association of University Professors, 2000; Biddle, Bank, & Slavings, 1990).

3. Recognition of the ways in which the intersection of racial and ethnic group membership with other dimensions of identity (e.g., gender, age, sexual orientation, disability, religion/spiritual orientation, educational attainment/experiences, and socioeconomic status) enhances the understanding and treatment of all people (Berberich, 1998; Greene, 2000; Jackson-Triche et al., 2000; Wu, 2000).

4. Knowledge of historically derived approaches that have viewed cultural differences as deficits and have not valued certain social identities helps psychologists to understand the under-representation of ethnic minorities in the profession and affirms and values the role of ethnicity and race in developing personal identity (Coll, Akerman, & Cicchetti, 2000; Medved et al., 2001; Mosley-Howard & Burgan Evans, 2000; S. Sue, 1999; Witte & Morrison, 1995).
5. Psychologists are uniquely able to promote racial equity and social justice. This is aided by their awareness of their impact on others and the influence of their personal and professional roles in society (Comas-Díaz, 2000).
6. Psychologists' knowledge about the roles of organizations, including employers and professional psychological associations, is a potential source of behavioral practices that encourage discourse, education and training, institutional change, and research and policy development that reflect, rather than neglect, cultural differences. Psychologists recognize that organizations can be gatekeepers or agents of the status quo, rather than leaders in a changing society, with respect to multiculturalism.

COMMITMENT TO CULTURAL AWARENESS AND KNOWLEDGE OF SELF AND OTHERS

Guideline 1: Psychologists are encouraged to recognize that, as cultural beings, they may hold attitudes and beliefs that can detrimentally influence their perceptions of and interactions with individuals who are ethnically and racially different from themselves.

Psychologists, like all people, are shaped and influenced by many factors. These include, but are not limited to, their cultural heritage(s), various dimensions of identity including ethnic and racial identity development, gender socialization, socioeconomic experiences, and other dimensions of identity that predispose individual psychologists to certain biases and assumptions about themselves and others. Psychologists approach interpersonal interactions with a set of attitudes, or worldview, that helps shape their perceptions of others. This worldview is shaped in part by their cultural experiences. Indeed, cross-cultural and multicultural literature consistently indicates that all people are multicultural beings, that all interactions are cross-cultural, and that all of our life experiences are perceived and shaped from within our own cultural perspectives (Arredondo et al., 1996; M. B. Brewer & Brown, 1998; A. P. Fiske et al., 1998; Fouad & Brown, 2000;

Markus & Kitayama, 1991; Pedersen, 2000; D. W. Sue et al., 1982, 1992; D. W. Sue, Ivey, & Pedersen, 1996).

Psychologists are encouraged to learn how cultures differ in basic premises that shape worldview. For example, it may be important to understand that a cultural facet of mainstream culture in the United States is a preference for individuals who are independent, who are focused on achieving and success, who have determined (and are in control of) their own personal goals, and who value rational decision making (A. P. Fiske et al., 1998; Markus & Kitayama, 1991; Oyserman, Coon, & Kemmelmeier, 2002). By contrast, individuals with origins in cultures of East Asia may prefer interdependence with others, orientation toward harmony with others, conformity with social norms, and subordination of personal goals and objectives to the will of the group (A. P. Fiske et al., 1998). A preference for an independent orientation may shape attitudes toward those with preferences for same or other orientations. This preference is a concern when a different orientation is unconsciously and automatically judged negatively (Greenwald & Banaji, 1995).

The perceiver in an interaction integrates not only the content of the interaction but also information about the target person, including personality traits, physical appearance, age, sex, ascribed race, ability/disability, among other characteristics (Kunda & Thagard, 1996). All of these perceptions are shaped by the perceiver's worldview and organized in some coherent whole to make sense of the other person's behavior. The psychological process that helps to organize the often overwhelming amount of information in perceiving others is to place people in categories, thereby reducing the information into manageable chunks that go together (S. T. Fiske, 1998). This normal process leads to associating various traits and behaviors with particular groups (e.g., all athletes are more brawn than brain, all women like to shop) even if they are inaccurate for particular, many, or even most individuals.

The most often used theoretical framework for understanding approaches that emphasize attention to categories has been social categorization theory, originally conceptualized by Allport (1954). In this framework, people make sense of their social world by creating categories of the individuals around them, a process that includes separating the categories into ingroups and out-groups (M. B. Brewer & Brown, 1998; S. T. Fiske, 1998; Hornsey & Hogg, 2000; Tajfel & Turner, 1986; Turner, Brown, & Tajfel, 1979). Categorization has a number of uses, including speed of processing and efficiency in use of cognitive resources, in part because it appears to happen fairly automatically (S. T. Fiske, 1998).

Relevant to these guidelines are factors that influence categorization and its effect on attitudes toward individuals who are racially or ethnically different from self. These include a tendency to exaggerate differences between groups and similarities within one group and a tendency to favor one's in-group over the out-group; this, too, is done outside conscious processing (S. T. Fiske, 1998). In-groups are more highly valued, are more trusted, and engender greater cooperation as opposed to competition (M. B. Brewer & Brown, 1998; Hewstone, Rubin, & Willis, 2002), and those with strongest in-group affiliation also show the most prejudice (Swim & Mallett, 2002). This becomes problematic when one group holds much more power than the other group or when resources among in-groups are not distributed equitably, as is currently the case in the United States.

Thus, it is quite common to have automatic biases and stereotypic attitudes about people in the out-group, and for most psychologists, individuals in racial/ethnic minority groups are in an out-group. The stereotype or the traits associated with the category become the predominant aspect of the category, even when disconfirming information is provided (Kunda & Thagard, 1996) and particularly when there is some motivation to confirm the stereotype (Kunda & Sinclair, 1999). These can influence interpretations of behavior and influence people's judgments about that behavior (S. T. Fiske, 1998; Kunda & Thagard, 1996). Automatic biases and attitudes may also lead to miscommunication since normative behavior in one context may not necessarily be understood or valued in another. For example, addressing peers, clients, students, or research participants by their first names may be acceptable for some individuals but may be considered a sign of disrespect for many racial/ethnic minority individuals who are accustomed to more formal interpersonal relations with individuals in an authority role.

Although the associations between particular stereotypic attitudes and resulting behaviors have not been consistently found, group categorization has been shown to influence intergroup behavior including behavioral confirmation (Stukas & Snyder, 2002), in-group favoritism (Hewstone et al., 2002), and subtle forms of behaviors (Crosby, Bromley, & Saxe, 1980). Psychologists are urged to become more aware of and sensitive to their own attitudes toward others as these attitudes may be more biased and culturally limiting then they think. It is sobering to note that even those who consciously hold egalitarian beliefs have shown unconscious endorsement of negative attitudes toward and stereotypes about groups (Greenwald & Banaji, 1995). Thus, psychologists who describe themselves as holding egalitarian values and/or as professionals who promote social justice may also unconsciously hold negative attitudes or stereotypes.

Given these findings, many have advocated that improvements in intergroup relationships would occur if there was a de-emphasis on group membership. One way that this has been done is that those who have desired to improve intergroup relationships have taken a "color-blind" approach to interactions with individuals who are racially or ethnically different from them. In this approach, racial or ethnic differences are minimized, and emphasis is on the universal or "human" aspects of behavior. This has been the traditional focus in the United States on assimilation, with its melting pot metaphor that this is a nation of immigrants that together make one whole, without a focus on any one individual cultural group. Proponents of this approach suggest that alternative approaches that attend to differences can result in inequity by promoting, for instance, categorical thinking including preferences for in-groups and use of stereotypes when perceiving out-groups. In contrast, opponents to the color-blind approach have noted the differential power among racial/ethnic groups in the United States and have noted that ignoring group differences can lead to the maintenance of the status quo and assumptions that racial/ethnic minority groups share the same perspective as dominant group members (Schofield, 1986; Sidanius & Pratto, 1999; Wolsko, Park, Judd, & Wittenbrink, 2000).

While the color-blind approach is based on an attempt to reduce inequities, social psychologists have provided evidence that a color-blind approach does not, in fact, lead to equitable treatment across groups. M. B. Brewer and Brown (1998), in their review of the literature, noted, "ignoring group differences often means that, by default, existing intergroup inequalities are perpetuated" (p. 583). For example, Schofield (1986) found that disregarding cultural differences in a school led to reestablishing segregation by ethnicity. Color-blind policies have also been documented as playing a role in differential employment practices (M. B. Brewer & Brown, 1998). In these cases, the color-blind approach may have the effect of maintaining a status quo in which Whites have more power than do people of color. There is also some evidence that a color-blind approach is less accurate in perception of others than a multicultural approach. Wolsko et al. (2000), for example, found that when White students were instructed to adopt either a color-blind or a multicultural approach, those with a multicultural approach had stronger stereotypes of other ethnic groups as well as more positive regard for other groups. White students in a multicultural approach also had more accurate perceptions of differences due to race/ethnicity and used category information about both ethnicity and individual characteristics more than those in the color-blind condition. Wolsko et al. concluded,

> When operating under a color-blind set of assumptions, social categories are viewed as negative information to be avoided, or suppressed . . . . In contrast, when operating under a multicultural set of assumptions, social categories are viewed as simply a consequence of cultural diversity. Failing to recognize and appreciate group similarities and differences is considered to inhibit more harmonious interactions between people from different backgrounds. (Wolsko et al., 2000, p. 649)

Consistent with the multicultural approach used by Wolsko et al. (2000), culture-centered training and interventions acknowledge cultural differences and differing worldviews among cultures, as well as experiences of being stigmatized (Crocker, Major, & Steele, 1998). This perspective is discussed more fully in Guideline 2. However, mere knowledge of a person's ethnic and racial background is not sufficient to be effective unless psychologists are cognizant of their positions as individuals with a worldview and that this worldview is brought to bear on interactions they have with others. As noted earlier, the worldviews of the client, student, or research participant and of the psychologist may be quite different, leading to communication problems or premature relationship termination. This does not argue that psychologists should shape their worldviews to be consistent with those of clients and students but rather that they have awareness of their own worldview, thereby enabling them to understand others' frame of cultural reference (Ibrahim, 1999; Sodowsky & Kuo, 2001; Triandis & Singelis, 1998).

The literature on social categorization places all human interaction within a cultural context and encourages an understanding of the various factors that influence our perceptions of others. These premises suggest that the psychologist is a part of the multicultural equation; therefore, ongoing development of one's personal and cross-cultural awareness, knowledge, and skills is recommended. S. T. Fiske (1998) noted that automatic biases can be controlled with motivation, information, and appropriate mood. Given the above research, psychologists are encouraged to explore their worldview—beliefs, values, and attitudes—from a personal and professional perspective. They are encouraged to examine their potential preferences for within-group similarity and to realize that, once impressions are formed, these impressions are often resistant to disconfirmation (Gilbert, 1998). Moreover, psychologists are encouraged to understand their own assumptions about ways to improve multicultural interactions and the potential issues associated with different approaches. Psychologists' self-awareness and appreciation of cultural, ethnic, and racial heritage may serve as a bridge in cross-cultural interactions, not necessarily highlighting but certainly not minimizing these factors as they attempt to build understanding (Arredondo et al., 1996; Hofstede, 1980; Ibrahim, 1985; Jones, Lynch, Tenglund, & Gaertner, 2000; Locke, 1992; D. W. Sue, 1978; D. W. Sue & Sue, 1999; Triandis & Singelis, 1998).

The research on reducing stereotypic attitudes and biases suggests a number of strategies (Hewstone et al., 2002) that psychologists may use. The first and most critical is awareness of those attitudes and values (Devine, Plant, & Buswell, 2000; Gaertner & Dovidio, 2000). The second and third strategies, respectively, are effort and practice in changing the automatically favorable perceptions of in-group and negative perceptions of out-group. How this change occurs has been the subject of many years of empirical effort, with varying degrees of support (Hewstone et al., 2002). It appears, though, that increased contact with other groups (Pettigrew, 1998) is helpful, particularly if, in this contact, the individuals are of equal status and the psychologist is able to take the other's perspective (Galinsky & Moskowitz, 2000) and has empathy for him or her (Finlay & Stephan, 2000). Some strategies to do this have included actively seeing individuals as individuals rather than as members of a group, in effect decategorizing (M. B. Brewer & Miller, 1988).

Another strategy is to change the perception of us versus them to we or to recategorize the out-group as members of the in-group (Gaertner & Dovidio, 2000). Both of these models have been shown to be effective, particularly under low-prejudice conditions and when the focus is on interpersonal communication (M. B. Brewer & Brown, 1998; Hewstone et al., 2002). In addition, psychologists may want to actively increase their tolerance (Greenberg et al., 1992) and trust of racial/ethnic groups (Kramer, 1999).

Thus, psychologists are encouraged to be aware of their attitudes and to work to increase their contact with members of other racial/ethnic groups, building trust in others and increasing their tolerance for others. Since covert attempts to suppress automatic associations can backfire, with attempts at suppression resulting in increased use of stereotypes (Macrae & Bodenhausen, 2000), psychologists are urged to become overtly aware of their attitudes toward others. It has been shown, though, that repeated attempts at suppression lead to improvements in automatic biases (Plant & Devine, 1998). Such findings suggest that psychologists' efforts to change their attitudes and biases help to prevent those attitudes from detrimentally affecting their relationships with students, research participants, and clients who are racially/ethnically different from them.

Guideline 2: Psychologists are encouraged to recognize the importance of multicultural sensitivity/responsiveness to, knowledge of, and understanding about ethnically and racially different individuals.

As noted in Guideline 1, membership in one group helps to shape perceptions of not only one's own group but also other groups. The links between those perceptions and attitudes are loyalty to and valuing of one's own group and devaluing the other group. The Minority Identity Development model (Atkinson, Morten, & Sue, 1998) is one such example, applying to ethnic/racial minority individuals but also to others who have experienced historical oppression and marginalization. The devaluing of the other group occurs in a variety of ways, including the "ultimate attributional error" (Pettigrew, 1979), the tendency to attribute positive behaviors to internal traits within one's own group but negative behaviors to the internal traits of the out-group (although Gilbert [1998] suggested that the ultimate attributional error may be culturally specific to individually oriented cultures, such as the United States). In the United States, then, the result may be positive, such as ensuring greater cooperation within one's group, or negative, such as the development of prejudice and stereotyping of other groups. Decades of research have been conducted and multiple theories have been developed to reduce prejudice toward other groups, most developing around the central premise that greater knowledge of and contact with the other groups will result in greater intercultural communication and less prejudice and stereotyping (M. B. Brewer & Miller, 1988; Gaertner & Dovidio, 2000). M. B. Brewer and Miller (1988) delineated the factors that have been found to be successful in facilitating prejudice reduction through contact among groups:

social and institutional support, sufficient frequency and duration for relationships to occur, equal status among participants, and cooperation. It appears, as discussed in Guideline 1, that attention to out-group stereotyping reduces prejudice (K. J. Reynolds & Oakes, 2000), as does overt training to reduce stereotyping (Kawakami, Dovidio, Moll, Hermsen, & Russin, 2000).

It is within this framework that psychologists are urged to gain a better understanding and appreciation of the worldview and perspectives of those racially and ethnically different from themselves. Psychologists are also encouraged to understand the stigmatizing aspects of being a member of a culturally devalued other group (Crocker et al., 1998; Major et al., in press). This includes experience, sometimes daily, with overt experiences of prejudice and discrimination, awareness of the negative value of one's own group in the cultural hierarchy, the threat of one's behavior being found consistent with a racial/ethnic stereotype (stereotype threat), and the uncertainty (e.g., due to prejudice or individual behavior) of the attribution of stigmatizing comments and outcomes.

Understanding a client's or student's or research participant's worldview, including the effect of being in a stigmatized group, helps to understand his or her perspectives and behaviors. Racial and ethnic heritage, worldview, and life experiences as a result of this identity may affect such factors as the ways students present themselves in class, their learning style, their willingness to seek and trust the advice from and consultation with faculty, and their ability and interest in working with others on class projects (Neville & Mobley, 2001). In the clinical realm, worldview and life experiences may affect how clients present symptoms to therapists, the meaning that illness has in their lives, their motivation and willingness to seek treatment and social support networks, and their perseverance in treatment (Anderson, 1995; USDHHS, 2001). People of color are underrepresented in mental health services in large part because they are less likely to seek services (Kessler et al., 1996; Zhang, Snowden, & Sue, 1998). The Surgeon General's report on culture and mental health (USDHHS, 2001) strongly suggested, "cultural misunderstanding or communication problems between clients and therapists may prevent minority group members from using services and receiving appropriate care" (p. 42). One way to address this problem is for psychologists to gain greater knowledge and understanding of the cultural practices of clients.

Psychologists are encouraged to increase their knowledge of the multicultural bases of general psychological theories and information from a variety of cultures and cultural/racial perspectives and theories, such as Mestizo psychology (Ramirez, 1998), psychology of Nigrescence (W. E. Cross, 1978; Helms, 1990; Parham, 1989, 2001; Vandiver, Fhagen-Smith, Cokley, Cross, & Worrell, 2001; Worrell, Cross, & Vandiver, 2001), Latino/Hispanic frameworks (Padilla, 1995; Ruiz, 1990; Santiago-Rivera, Arredondo, & Gallardo-Cooper, 2002), Native American models (Cameron, in press; LaFromboise & Jackson, 1996), and biracial/multiracial models (Root, 1992; Wehrly et al., 1999) specific to racial/ethnic minority groups in the United States. In addition, psychologists are encouraged to become knowledgeable about how history has been different for the major U.S. cultural groups. Past experiences in relation to the dominant culture, including slavery, Asian concentration camps, the American Indian holocaust, and the colonization of the major Latino groups on their previous Southwest homelands, contribute to some of the sociopolitical dynamics influencing worldview. Psychologists may also become knowledgeable about the psychological issues and gender-related concerns related to immigration and refugee status (Cienfuegos & Monelli, 1983; Comas-Díaz & Jansen, 1995; Espin, 1997, 1999; Fullilove, 1996).

As noted in Guideline 1, one of the premises underlying these guidelines is that all interpersonal interactions occur within a multicultural context. To enhance sensitivity and understanding further, psychologists are encouraged to become knowledgeable about federal legislation including the Civil Rights Act (1964), affirmative action, and equal employment opportunity that were enacted to protect groups marginalized due to ethnicity, race, national origin, religion, age, and gender (Crosby & Cordova, 1996). Concomitantly, psychologists are encouraged to understand the impact of the dismantling of affirmative action and of antibilingual education legislation on the lives of ethnic and racial minority groups (Fine, Weis, Powell, & Wong, 1997; Glasser, 1988).

Built on variations of the social categorization models described in Guideline 1, ethnic and racial identity models, such as the Minority Identity Development model (Atkinson et al., 1998) noted earlier, have also been developed for specific racial/ethnic minority groups (W. E. Cross, 1978; Helms, 1990; Parham, 1989, 2001; Ruiz, 1990; Vandiver et al., 2001; Worrell et al., 2001). These models propose that members of racial/ethnic minority groups initially value the other group (dominant culture) and devalue their own culture, move to valuing their own group and devaluing the dominant culture, and integrate a value for both groups in a final stage. These models are key constructs in the cross-cultural domain, and psychologists are encouraged to understand how the individual's ethnic and racial identity status and development affect beliefs, emotions, behavior, and interaction styles (M. B. Brewer & Brown, 1998; A. P. Fiske et al., 1998; Hays, 1995; Helms & Cook, 1999). This information will help psychologists to communicate more effectively with clients, peers, students, research participants, and organizations and to understand their coping responses (Crocker et al., 1998; Major et al., in press; Swim & Mallet, 2002). Psychologists are encouraged to become knowledgeable about ethnic and racial identity research including research on Asian, Black, White, Mexican, Mestizo, minority, Native American, and biracial identity models (Atkinson et al., 1998; W. E. Cross, 1991; Fouad & Brown, 2000; Helms, 1990; Hong & Ham, 2001; Phinney, 1991; Ramirez,

1998; Root, 1992; Ruiz, 1990; Sodowsky, Kuo-Jackson, & Loya, 1997; Wehrly et al., 1999). Additionally, psychologists may also learn about other theories of identity development that are not stage models, as well as other models that demonstrate the multidimensionality of individual identity across different historical contexts (Oetting & Beauvais, 1990–1991; Oyserman, Gant, & Ager, 1995; Robinson & Howard-Hamilton, 2000; Root, 1999; Santiago-Rivera et al., 2002; Sellers, Smith, Shelton, Rowley, & Chavous, 1998; Thompson & Carter, 1997).

PRACTICE

Guideline 5: Psychologists are encouraged to apply culturally appropriate skills in clinical and other applied psychological practices.

Consistent with previous discussions in Guidelines 1 and 2, culturally appropriate psychological applications assume awareness and knowledge about one's worldview as a cultural being and as a professional psychologist and about the worldview of others, particularly as influenced by ethnic/racial heritage. This guideline refers to applying that awareness and knowledge in psychological practice. It is not necessary to develop an entirely new repertoire of psychological skills to practice in a culture-centered manner. Rather, it is helpful for psychologists to realize that there will likely be situations where culture-centered adaptations in interventions and practices will be more effective. Psychological practice is defined here as the use of psychological skills in a variety of settings and for a variety of purposes, encompassing counseling, clinical, school, consulting, and organizational psychology. This guideline further suggests that regardless of their practice site and purview of practice, psychologists are responsive to the Ethics Code (APA, 1992). In the Preamble of the Ethics Code is language that advocates behavior that values human welfare and basic human rights.

Psychologists are likely to find themselves increasingly engaged with others ethnically, linguistically, and racially different from and similar to themselves as human-resource specialists, school psychologists, consultants, agency administrators, and clinicians. Moreover, visible group membership differences (Atkinson & Hackett, 1995; Carter, 1995; W. E. Cross, 1991; Helms, 1990; Herring, 1999; Hong & Ham, 2001; Niemann, 2001; Padilla, 1995; Santiago-Rivera et al., 2002; D. W. Sue & Sue, 1999) may belie other identity factors also at work and strong forces in individuals' socialization process and life experiences. These include language, gender, biracial/multiracial heritage, spiritual/religious orientations, sexual orientation, age, disability, socioeconomic situation, and historical life experience, for example, immigration and refugee status (Arredondo & Glauner, 1992; Davenport &

Yurich, 1991; Espin, 1997; Hong & Ham, 2001; Lowe & Mascher, 2001; Prendes-Lintel, 2001). Projections regarding the increasing numbers of individuals categorized as ethnic and racial minorities have been discussed earlier in these guidelines. The result of these changes is that in urban, rural, and other contexts, psychologists will interface regularly with culturally pluralistic populations (Ellis, Arredondo, & D'Andrea, 2000; Lewis, Lewis, Daniels, & D'Andrea, 1998; Middleton, Arredondo, & D'Andrea, 2000).

However, while Census 2000 showed that the population of the United States is more culturally and linguistically diverse than it has ever been (U.S. Census Bureau, 2001), individuals seeking and utilizing psychological services continue to underrepresent those populations. With respect to clinical/counseling services, D. W. Sue and Sue (1999) highlighted some of the reasons for the underutilization of services, including lack of cultural sensitivity of therapists, distrust of services by racial/ethnic clients, and the perspective that therapy "can be used as an oppressive instrument by those in power to ... mistreat large groups of people" (p. 7). A number of authors (Arroyo, Westerberg, & Tonigan, 1998; Dana, 1998; Flaskerud & Liu, 1991; McGoldrick, Giordano, & Pearce, 1996; Ridley, 1995; Santiago-Rivera et al., 2002; D. W. Sue, Bingham, Porche-Burke, & Vasquez, 1999; D. W. Sue et al., 1998; D. W. Sue & Sue, 1999) have outlined the urgent need for clinicians to develop multicultural sensitivity and understanding.

Essentially, the concern of the authors noted above is that the traditional Eurocentric therapeutic and interventions models in which most therapists have been trained are based on and designed to meet the needs of a small proportion of the population (White, male, and middle-class persons). Ironically, the typical dyad in psychotherapy historically was a White middle-class woman treated by a White middle-class therapist. These authors have noted that Eurocentric models may not be effective in working with other populations as well and, indeed, may do harm by mislabeling or misdiagnosing problems and treatments.

Psychologists are encouraged to develop cultural sensitivity and understanding to be the most effective practitioners (therapists) for all clients. The discussion that follows, however, primarily relates to therapeutic settings where individual, family, and group psychotherapy interventions are likely to take place. The discussion addresses three areas: focusing on the client within his or her cultural context, using culturally appropriate assessment tools, and having a broad repertoire of interventions (Arredondo, 1998, 1999; Arredondo et al., 1996; Arredondo & Glauner, 1992; Costantino et al., 1994; Dana, 1998; Duclos et al., 1998; Flores & Carey, 2000; Fouad & Brown, 2000; Hays, 1995; Ivey & Ivey, 1999; Kopelowicz, 1997; López, 1989; Lukasiewicz & Harvey, 1991; Parham, White, & Ajamu, 1999; Pedersen, 1999; Ponterotto & Pedersen, 1993; Prieto, McNeill, Walls, & Gomez, 2001; Rodriguez

& Walls, 2000; Root, 1992; Santiago-Rivera et al., 2002; Seeley, 2000; D. W. Sue et al., 1996; S. Sue, 1998).

Client in Context

Clients might have socialization experiences, health and mental health issues, and workplace concerns associated with discrimination and oppression (e.g., ethnocentrism, racism, sexism, ableism, and homophobia). Thus, psychologists are encouraged to acquire an understanding of the ways in which these experiences relate to presenting psychological concerns (Byars & McCubbin, 2001; Fischer, Jome, & Atkinson, 1998; Flores & Carey, 2000; Fuertes & Gretchen, 2001; Helms & Cook, 1999; Herring, 1999; Hong & Ham, 2001; Lowe & Mascher, 2001; Middleton, Rollins, & Harley, 1999; Sanchez, 2001; D. W. Sue & Sue, 1999). This may include how the client's worldview and cultural background(s) interact with individual, family, or group concerns.

Thus, in client treatment situations, culturally and sociopolitically relevant factors in a client's history may include relevant generational history (e.g., number of generations in the country, manner of coming to the country), citizenship or residency status (e.g., number of years in the country, parental history of migration, refugee flight, or immigration), fluency in standard English (and other languages or dialects), extent of family support or disintegration of family, availability of community resources, level of education, change in social status as a result of coming to this country (for immigrant or refugee), work history, and level of stress related to acculturation (Arredondo, 2002; Ruiz, 1990; Saldana, 1995; Smart & Smart, 1995). When the client is a group or organization in an employment context, another set of factors may apply. Recognizing these factors, culturally centered practitioners are encouraged to take into account how contextual factors may affect the client worldview (behavior, thoughts, or feelings).

Historical experiences for various populations differ. This may be manifested in the expression of different belief systems and value sets among clients and across age cohorts. For example, therapists are strongly encouraged to be aware of the ways that enslavement has shaped the worldviews of African Americans (W. E. Cross, 1991; Parham et al., 1999). At the same time, the within-group differences among African Americans and others of African descent also suggest the importance of not assuming that all persons of African descent share this perspective. Thus, knowledge about sociopolitical viewpoints and ethnic/racial identity literature would be important and extremely helpful when working with individuals of ethnic minority descent. Culturally centered practitioners assist clients in determining whether a problem stems from institutional or societal racism (or other prejudice) or individual bias in others so that the client does not inappropriately personalize problems (Helms & Cook, 1999; Ridley, 1995; D. W. Sue et al., 1992).

Consistent with the discussion in Guideline 2 about the effects of stigmatizing, psychologists are urged to help clients recognize the cognitive and affective motivational processes involved in determining whether they are targets of prejudice (Crocker et al., 1998). Psychologists are also encouraged to be aware of the environment (neighborhood, building, and specific office) and how this may appear to clients or employees. For example, bilingual phone service, receptionists, magazines in the waiting room, and other signage can demonstrate cultural and linguistic sensitivity (Arredondo, 1996; Arredondo et al., 1996; Grieger & Ponterotto, 1998).

Psychologists are also encouraged to be aware of the role that culture may play in the establishment and maintenance of a relationship between the client and therapist. Culture, ethnicity, race, and gender are among the factors that may play a role in the perception of and expectations for therapy and the role the therapist plays (American Psychiatric Association, 1994; Carter, 1995; Comas-Díaz & Jacobsen, 1991; Cooper-Patrick et al., 1999; Seeley, 2000).

Assessment

Consistent with Standard 2.04 of the APA Ethics Code (APA, 1992), multiculturally sensitive practitioners are encouraged to be aware of the limitations of assessment practices, from intakes to the use of standardized assessment instruments (Constantine, 1998; Helms, 2002; Ridley, Hill, & Li, 1998), diagnostic methods (Ivey & Ivey, 1998; S. Sue, 1998), and instruments used for employment screening and personality assessments in work settings. Clients unfamiliar with mental health services and who hold worldviews that value relationship over task may experience disrespect if procedures are not fully explained. Thus, if such a client does not feel that the therapist is valuing the relationship between the therapist and client enough, the client may not adhere to the suggestions of the therapist. Psychologists are encouraged to know and consider the validity of a given instrument or procedure. This includes interpreting resulting data appropriately and keeping in mind the cultural and linguistic characteristics of the person being assessed. Culture-centered psychologists are also encouraged to have knowledge of a test's reference population and possible limitations of the instrument with other populations. When using standardized assessment tools and methods, multicultural practitioners should exercise critical judgment (Sandoval, Frisby, Geisinger, Scheuneman, & Ramos-Grenier, 1998). Multiculturally sensitive practitioners are encouraged to attend to the effects on the validity of measures of issues related to test bias, test fairness, and cultural equivalence (APA, 1990, 1992; Arredondo, 1999; Arredondo et al., 1996; Dana, 1998; Grieger & Ponterotto, 1995; López, 1989; Paniagua, 1994, 1998; Ponterotto, Casas, Suzuki, & Alexander, 1995; Samuda, 1998).

Interventions

Cross-culturally sensitive practitioners are encouraged to develop skills and practices that are attuned to the unique worldviews and cultural backgrounds of clients by striving to incorporate understanding of a client's ethnic, linguistic, racial, and cultural background into therapy (American Psychiatric Association, 1994; Falicov, 1998; Flores & Carey, 2000; Fukuyama & Ferguson, 2000; Helms & Cook, 1999; Hong & Ham, 2001; Langman, 1998; Middleton et al., 1999; Santiago-Rivera et al., 2002). They are encouraged to become knowledgeable about the Guidelines for Providers of Psychological Services to Ethnic, Linguistic, and Culturally Diverse Populations (APA, 1990) and the Guidelines for Research in Ethnic Minority Communities (CNPAAEMI, 2000). They are encouraged to learn about helping practices used in non-Western cultures within as well as outside the North American and Northern European context that may be appropriately included as part of psychological practice. Multiculturally sensitive psychologists should recognize that culture-specific therapy (individual, family, and group) may require nontraditional interventions and should strive to apply this knowledge in practice (Alexander & Sussman, 1995; Fukuyama & Sevig, 1999; Ridley, 1995; Santiago-Rivera et al., 2002; Sciarra, 1999; Society for the Psychological Study of Ethnic Minority Issues, Division 45 of the American Psychological Association & Microtraining Associates, Inc., 2000; D. W. Sue et al., 1998; D. W. Sue & Sue, 1999). This may include inviting recognized helpers to assist with assessment and intervention plans. Psychologists are encouraged to participate in culturally diverse and culture-specific activities. They are also encouraged to seek out community leaders, change agents, and influential individuals (ministers, store owners, nontraditional healers, natural helpers) when appropriate, enlisting their assistance with clients as part of a total family or community-centered (healing) approach (Arredondo et al., 1996; Grieger & Ponterotto, 1998; Lewis et al., 1998).

Multiculturally sensitive and effective therapists are encouraged to examine traditional psychotherapy practice interventions for their cultural appropriateness, for example, person-centered, cognitive-behavioral, psychodynamic forms of therapy (Bernal & Scharoo-del-Rio, 2001). They are urged to expand these interventions to include multicultural awareness and culture-specific strategies. This may include respecting the language preference of the client and ensuring that the accurate translation of documents occurs by providing informed consent about the language in which therapy, assessments, or other procedures will be conducted. Psychologists are also encouraged to respect the client's boundaries by not using interpreters who are family members, authorities in the community, or unskilled in the area of mental health practice.

CONCLUSION

Psychology has been traditionally defined by and based upon Western, Eurocentric, and biological perspectives and assumptions. These traditional premises in psychological education, research, practice, and organizational change have not always considered the influence and impact of racial and cultural socialization. They also have not considered that the effects of related biases have, at times, been detrimental to the increasingly complex needs of clients and the public interest. These guidelines have been designed to aid psychologists as they increase their knowledge and skills in multicultural education, training, research, practice, and organizational change.

Readers will note that these guidelines are scheduled to expire in 2009. This document is intended as a living document. The empirical research on which the rationales for the various guidelines are based will continue to expand, as will legislation and practices related to an increasingly diverse population. The integration of the psychological constructs of racial and ethnic identity into psychological theory, research, and therapy has only just begun. Psychologists are starting to investigate the differential impact of historical, economic, and sociopolitical forces on individuals' behavior and perceptions. Psychology will continue to develop a deeper knowledge and awareness of race and ethnicity in psychological constructs and to actively respond by integrating the psychological aspects of race and ethnicity into the various areas of application in psychology. It is anticipated that, with this increased knowledge base and effectiveness of applications, the guidelines will continue to evolve over the next several years.

REFERENCES

Alexander, C. M., & Sussman, L. (1995). Creative approaches to multicultural counseling. In J. G. Ponterotto, J. M. Casas, L. A. Suzuki, & C. M. Alexander (Eds.), *Handbook of multicultural counseling* (pp. 375–384). Thousand Oaks, CA: Sage.

Allport, G. W. (1954). *The nature of prejudice.* Cambridge, MA: Addison-Wesley.

American Council on Education. (2000). *18th annual status report on minorities in higher education.* Washington, DC: Author.

American Council on Education & American Association of University Professors. (2000). *Does diversity make a difference? Three research studies on diversity in college classrooms.* Washington, DC: Authors.

American Psychiatric Association. (1994). *Diagnostic and statistical manual of mental disorders* (4th ed.). Washington, DC: Author.

American Psychological Association. (1987). General guidelines for providers of psychological services. *American Psychologist, 42,* 712–723.

American Psychological Association. (1990). *Guidelines for providers of psychological services to ethnic, linguistic, and culturally diverse populations*. Washington, DC: Author.

American Psychological Association. (1992). Ethical principles and code of conduct. *American Psychologist, 48*, 1597–1611.

American Psychological Association. (2000). Guidelines for psychotherapy with lesbian, gay, and bisexual clients. *American Psychologist, 55*, 1440–1451.

American Psychological Association. (2001). *Criteria for practice guideline development and evaluation*. Washington, DC: Author.

American Psychological Association. (2002). *Guidelines and principles for accreditation*. Washington, DC: Author.

American Psychological Association Committee on Accreditation & Accreditation Office. (1986). *Accreditation handbook*. Washington, DC: American Psychological Association.

American Psychological Association Research Office. (2002a). *Demographic characteristics of APA members by race/ethnicity, analyses of APA directory survey: 2000*. Washington, DC: American Psychological Association.

American Psychological Association Research Office. (2002b). *Race/ethnicity of APA members and APA governance members: Analyses of APA governance survey*. Washington, DC: American Psychological Association.

Anderson, N. B. (1995). Behavioral and sociological perspectives on ethnicity and health: Introduction to the special issue. *Health Psychology, 14*, 589–591.

Arredondo, P. (1996). *Successful diversity management initiatives: A blueprint for planning and implementation*. Thousand Oaks, CA: Sage.

Arredondo, P. (1998). Integrating multicultural counseling competencies and universal helping conditions in culture-specific contexts. *Counseling Psychologist, 26*, 592–601.

Arredondo, P. (1999). Multicultural counseling competencies as tools to address oppression and racism. *Journal of Counseling and Development, 77*, 102–108.

Arredondo, P. (2000, November/December). Suggested "best practices" for increasing diversity in APA divisions. *APA/Division Dialogue*, pp. 1–3.

Arredondo, P. (2002). Counseling individuals from specialized, marginalized and underserved groups. In P. Pedersen, J. G. Draguns, W. J. Lonner, & J. E. Trimble (Eds.), *Counseling across cultures* (5th ed., pp. 241–250). Thousand Oaks, CA: Sage.

Arredondo, P., & D'Andrea, M. (2000, July). Assessing multicultural competence: A professional issue of relevance. *Counseling Today, 43*(1), 30–35.

Arredondo, P., & Glauner, T. (1992). *Personal dimensions of identity model*. Boston: Empowerment Workshops.

Arroyo, J. A., Westerberg, V. S., & Tonigan, J. S. (1998). Comparison of treatment utilization and outcome for Hispanics and non-Hispanic Whites. *Journal of Studies on Alcohol, 59*, 286–291.

Atkinson, D. R., & Hackett, G. (1995). *Counseling diverse populations* (2nd ed.). Boston: McGraw-Hill.

Atkinson, D. R., Morten, G., & Sue, D. W. (1998). *Counseling American minorities* (5th ed.). New York: McGraw-Hill.

Benjamin, L. T., Jr., & Crouse, E. M. (2002). The American Psychological Association's response to Brown v. Board of Education: The case of Kenneth B. Clark. *American Psychologist, 57*, 38–50.

Berberich, D. A. (1998). Posttraumatic stress disorder: Gender and cross-cultural clinical issues. *Psychotherapy in Private Practice, 17*, 29–41.

Bernal, G., & Scharro-del-Rio, M. R. (2001). Are empirically supported treatments valid for ethnic minorities? Toward an alternative approach for treatment research. *Cultural Diversity and Ethnic Minority Psychology, 7*, 328–342.

Biddle, B. J., Bank, B. J., & Slavings, R. L. (1990). Modality of thought, campus experiences, and the development of values. *Journal of Educational Psychology, 82*, 671–682.

Brewer, C. A., & Suchan, T. A. (2001). *Mapping Census 2000: The geography of U.S. diversity.* Washington, DC: U.S. Government Printing Office.

Brewer, M. B. (1999). The psychology of prejudice: Ingroup love or outgroup hate? Journal of *Social Issues, 55*, 429–444.

Brewer, M. B., & Brown, R. J. (1998). Intergroup relations. In D. T. Gilbert & S. T. Fiske (Eds.), *The handbook of social psychology* (4th ed., Vol. 2, pp. 554–594). New York: McGraw-Hill.

Brewer, M. B., & Miller, N. (1988). Contact and cooperation: When do they work? In P. A. Katz & D. A. Taylor (Eds.), *Eliminating racism: Profiles in controversy* (pp. 315–326). New York: Plenum Press.

Brown, S. P., Parham, T. A., & Yonker, R. (1996). Influence of a cross-cultural training on racial identity attitudes of White women and men. *Journal of Counseling and Development, 74*, 510–516.

Brown v. Board of Education 347 U.S. 483 (1954).

Byars, A. M., & McCubbin, L. D. (2001). Trends in career development research with racial/ethnic minorities: Prospects and challenges. In J. G. Ponterotto, J. M. Casas, L. A. Suzuki, & C. M. Alexander (Eds.), *Handbook of multicultural counseling* (2nd ed., pp. 633–654). Thousand Oaks, CA: Sage.

Cameron, S. (in press). American Indian mental health: An examination of resiliency in the face of overwhelming odds. In F. D. Harper & J. McFadden (Eds.), *Culture and counseling: New approaches.* Boston: Allyn/Bacon.

Carter, R. T. (1995). *The influence of race and racial identity in psychotherapy.* New York: Wiley.

Cienfuegos, A. J., & Monelli, C. (1983). The testimony of political repression as a therapeutic instrument. *American Journal of Orthopsychiatry, 53*, 43–51.

Civil Rights Act 42 U.S.C. §S2000D et seq. (1964).

Clark, K. B., & Clark, M. K. (1940). Skin color as a factor in racial identification of Negro preschool children. *Journal of Social Psychology, 11*, 159–169.

Coll, C. G., Akerman, A., & Cicchetti, D. (2000). Cultural influences on developmental processes and outcomes: Implications for the study of development and psychopathology. *Development and Psychopathology, 12*, 333–356.

Comas-Díaz, L. (2000). An ethnopolitical approach to working with People of Color. *American Psychologist, 55,* 1319–1325.

Comas-Díaz, L., & Jacobsen, F. M. (1991). Ethnocultural transference and counter-transference in the therapeutic dyad. *American Journal of Orthopsychiatry, 61,* 392–402.

Comas-Díaz, L., & Jansen, M. A. (1995). Global conflict and violence against women. *Peace and Conflict: Journal of Peace Psychology, 1,* 315–331.

Constantine, M. G. (1998). Developing competence in multicultural assessment: Implications for counseling psychology training and practice. *Counseling Psychologist, 6,* 922–929.

Cooper-Patrick, L., Gallo, J. J., Gonzales, J. J., Vu, H. T., Powe, N. R., Nelson, C., & Ford, D. E. (1999). Race, gender, and partnership in the patient-physician relationship. *JAMA, 282,* 583–589.

Council of National Psychological Associations for the Advancement of Ethnic Minority Interests. (2000). *Guidelines for research in ethnic minority communities.* Washington, DC: American Psychological Association.

Crocker, J., Major, B., & Steele, C. (1998). Social stigma. In D. T. Gilbert & S. T. Fiske (Eds.), *The handbook of social psychology* (4th ed., Vol. 2, pp. 504–553). New York: McGraw-Hill.

Crosby, F. J., Bromley, S., & Saxe, L. (1980). Recent unobtrusive studies of Black and White discrimination and prejudice: A literature review. *Psychological Bulletin, 87,* 546–563.

Crosby, F. J., & Cordova, D. I. (1996). Words worth of wisdom: Toward an understanding of affirmative action. *Journal of Social Issues, 52,* 33–49.

Cross, W. E., Jr. (1978). The Thomas and Cross models of psychological nigrescence: A review. *Journal of Black Psychologist, 5,* 15–31.

Cross, W. E., Jr. (1991). *Shades of Black: Diversity in African American identity.* Philadelphia: Temple University Press.

Dana, R. H. (1998). *Understanding cultural identity in intervention and assessment.* Thousand Oaks, CA: Sage.

D'Andrea, M., Daniels, J., & Heck, R. (1991). Evaluating the impact of multicultural counseling training. *Journal of Counseling and Development, 70,* 143–150.

Davenport, D. S., & Yurich, J. M. (1991). Multicultural gender issues. *Journal of Counseling and Development, 70,* 64–71.

Devine, P. G., Plant, E. A., & Buswell, B. N. (2000). Breaking the prejudice habit: Progress and obstacles. In S. Oskamp (Ed.), *Reducing prejudice and discrimination* (pp. 185–208). Mahwah, NJ: Erlbaum.

Dovidio, J. F., & Gaertner, S. L. (1998). On the nature of contemporary prejudice: The causes, consequences, and challenges of aversive racism. In J. L. Eberhardt & S. T. Fiske (Eds.), *Confronting racism: The problem and the response* (pp. 3–32). Thousand Oaks, CA: Sage.

Dovidio, J. F., Gaertner, S. L., & Validzic, A. (1998). Intergroup bias: Status, differentiation, and a common in-group identity. *Journal of Personality and Social Psychology, 75,* 109–120.

Duckitt, J. H. (1992). Psychology and prejudice: A historical analysis and integrative framework. *American Psychologist, 47*, 1182–1193.

Duclos, C. W., Beals, J., Novins, D. K., Martin, C., Jewett, C. S., & Manson, S. M. (1998). Prevalence of common psychiatric disorders among American Indian adolescent detainees. *Journal of the American Academy of Child and Adolescent Psychiatry, 37*, 866–873.

Ellis, C., Arredondo, P., & D'Andrea, M. (2000, November). How cultural diversity affects predominantly White towns. *Counseling Today, 43*(5), 25.

Espin, O. M. (1997). *Latina realities: Essays on healing, migration, and sexuality*. Boulder, CO: Westview.

Espin, O. M. (1999). *Women crossing boundaries: A psychology of immigration and transformation of sexuality*. New York: Routledge.

Falicov, C. J. (1998). *Latino families in therapy: A guide to multicultural practice*. New York: Guilford Press.

Fine, M., Weis, L., Powell, L. C., & Wong, L. M. (Eds.). (1997). *Off white: Readings on race, power, and society*. Florence, KY: Taylor & Francis/Routledge.

Finlay, K. A., & Stephan, W. G. (2000). Improving intergroup relations: The effects of empathy on racial attitudes. *Journal of Applied Social Psychology, 30*, 1720–1737.

Fischer, A. R., Jome, L. M., & Atkinson, D. R. (1998). Reconceptualizing multicultural counseling: Universal healing conditions in a culturally specific context. *Counseling Psychologist, 26*, 525–588.

Fish, J. M. (1995). Why psychologists should learn some anthropology. *American Psychologist, 50*, 44–45.

Fiske, A. P., Kitayama, S., Markus, H. R., & Nisbett, R. E. (1998). The cultural matrix of social psychology. In D. T. Gilbert & S. T. Fiske (Eds.), *The handbook of social psychology* (4th ed., Vol. 2, pp. 915–981). New York: McGraw-Hill.

Fiske, S. T. (1998). Stereotyping, prejudice, and discrimination. In D. T. Gilbert & S. T. Fiske (Eds.), *The handbook of social psychology* (4th ed., Vol. 2, pp. 357–411). New York: McGraw-Hill.

Flaskerud, J. H., & Liu, P. Y. (1991). Effects of an Asian client-therapist language, ethnicity, and gender match on utilization and outcome of therapy. *Community Mental Health Journal, 27*, 31–41.

Flores, M. T., & Carey, G. (Eds.). (2000). *Family therapy with Hispanics*. Needham Heights, MA: Allyn & Bacon.

Fouad, N. A., & Brown, M. (2000). Race, ethnicity, culture, class and human development. In S. D. Brown & R. W. Lent (Eds.), *Handbook of counseling psychology* (3rd. ed., pp. 379–410). New York: Wiley.

Fuertes, J. N., Bartolomeo, M., & Nichols, C. M. (2001). Future research directions in the study of counselor multicultural competency. *Journal of Multicultural Counseling and Development, 29*, 3–12.

Fuertes, J. N., & Gretchen, D. (2001). Emerging theories of multicultural counseling. In J. G. Ponterotto, J. M. Casas, L. A. Suzuki, & C. M. Alexander (Eds.), *Handbook of multicultural counseling* (2nd ed., pp. 509–541). Thousand Oaks, CA: Sage.

Fukuyama, M. A., & Ferguson, A. D. (2000). Lesbian, gay, and bisexual People of Color: Understanding cultural complexity and managing multiple oppressions. In R. M. Perez, K. A. DeBord, & K. J. Bieschke (Eds.), *Handbook of counseling and psychotherapy with lesbian, gay, and bisexual clients* (pp. 81–106). Washington, DC: American Psychological Association.

Fukuyama, M. A., & Sevig, T. D. (1999). *Integrating spirituality into multicultural counseling*. Thousand Oaks, CA: Sage.

Fullilove, M. T. (1996). Psychiatric implications of displacement: Contributions from the psychology of place. *American Journal of Psychiatry, 153,* 1516–1523.

Gaertner, S. L., & Dovidio, J. F. (2000). *Reducing intergroup bias: The common ingroup identity model*. Philadelphia: Brunner/Mazel.

Galinsky, A. D., & Moskowitz, G. B. (2000). Perspective-taking: Decreasing stereotype expression, stereotype accessibility, and in-group favoritism. *Journal of Personality and Social Psychology, 78,* 708–724.

Gilbert, D. T. (1998). Ordinary personalogy. In. D. T. Gilbert & S. T. Fiske (Eds.), *The handbook of social psychology* (4th ed., Vol. 2, pp. 89–150). New York: McGraw-Hill.

Glasser, I. (1988). Affirmative action and the legacy of racial injustice. In P. A. Katz & D. A. Taylor (Eds.), *Eliminating racism: Profiles in controversy* (pp. 341–357). New York: Plenum Press.

Grady, K. E. (1981). Sex bias in research design. *Psychology of Women Quarterly, 5,* 628–636.

Greenberg, J., Solomon, S., Pyszczynski, T., Rosenblatt, A., Burling, J., & Lyon, D. (1992). Why do people need self-esteem? Converging evidence that self-esteem serves an anxiety-buffering function. *Journal of Personality & Social Psychology, 63,* 913–922.

Greene, B. (2000). African American lesbian and bisexual women. *Journal of Social Issues, 56,* 239–249.

Greenleaf, R. K. (1998). *The power of servant-leadership: Essays*. San Francisco: Berrett-Koehler.

Greenwald, A. G., & Banaji, M. R. (1995). Implicit social cognition: Attitudes, self-esteem, and stereotypes. *Psychological Review, 102,* 4–27.

Grieger, I., & Ponterotto, J. G. (1995). A framework for assessment in multicultural counseling. In J. G. Ponterotto, J. M. Casas, L. A. Suzuki, & C. M. Alexander (Eds.), *Handbook of multicultural counseling* (pp. 357–374). Thousand Oaks, CA: Sage.

Grieger, I., & Ponterotto, J. G. (1998). Challenging intolerance. In C. L. Lee & G. R. Walz (Eds.), *Social action: A mandate for counselors* (pp. 17–50). Alexandria, VA: American Counseling Association & Greensboro, NC: ERIC Counseling & Student Services Clearinghouse.

Hays, P. A. (1995). Multicultural applications of cognitive-behavior therapy. *Professional Psychology: Research and Practice, 26,* 309–315.

Helms, J. E. (1990). *Black and White racial identity: Theory, research, and practice*. Westport, CT: Greenwood.

Helms, J. E. (1992). Why is there no study of cultural equivalence in standardized cognitive ability testing? *American Psychologist, 47*, 1083–1101.

Helms, J. E. (2002). A remedy for the Black-White test-score disparity. *American Psychologist, 57*, 303–304.

Helms, J. E., & Cook, D. A. (1999). *Using race and culture in counseling and psychotherapy: Theory and process*. Boston: Allyn & Bacon.

Helms, J. E., & Talleyrand, R. M. (1997). Race is not ethnicity. *American Psychologist, 52*, 1246–1247.

Herring, R. D. (1999). *Counseling with Native American Indians and Alaska Natives: Strategies for helping professionals*. Thousand Oaks, CA: Sage.

Hewstone, M., Rubin, M., & Willis, H. (2002). Intergroup bias. *Annual Review of Psychology, 53*, 575–604.

Hofstede, G. (1980). *Culture's consequences*. London: Sage.

Hong, G. K., & Ham, M. D. C. (2001). *Psychotherapy and counseling with Asian American clients*. Thousand Oaks, CA: Sage.

Hornsey, M. J., & Hogg, M. A. (2000). Assimilation and diversity: An integrative model of subgroup relations. *Personality and Social Psychology Review, 4*, 143–156

Ibrahim, F. A. (1985). Effective cross cultural counseling and psychotherapy: A framework. *Counseling Psychologist, 13*, 625–638.

Ibrahim, F. A. (1999). Transcultural counseling: Existential worldview theory and cultural identity. In J. McFadden (Ed.), *Transcultural counseling* (2nd ed., pp. 23–58). Alexandria, VA: American Counseling Association.

Ivey, A., & Ivey, M. (1998). Reframing DSM–IV: Positive strategies from developmental counseling and therapy. *Journal of Counseling and Development, 76*, 334–350.

Ivey, A., & Ivey, M. (1999). *Intentional interviewing and counseling: Facilitating multicultural development*. Pacific Grove, CA: Brooks/Cole.

Jackson-Triche, M. E., Sullivan, J. G., Wells, K. B., Rogers, W., Camp, P., & Mazel, R. (2000). Depression and health-related quality of life in ethnic minorities seeking care in general medical settings. *Journal of Affective Disorders, 58*, 89–97.

Jensen, A. R. (1995). Psychological research on race differences. *American Psychologist, 50*, 41–42.

Johnson, W. B., & Packer, A. H. (1987). *Workforce 2000*. Indianapolis, IN: Hudson Institute.

Jones, J. M., Lynch, P. D., Tenglund, A. A., & Gaertner, S. L. (2000). Toward a diversity hypothesis multidimensional effects of intergroup contact. *Applied & Preventive Psychology, 9*, 53–62.

Judy, R. W., & D'Amico, C. (1997). *Workforce 2020*. Indianapolis, IN: Hudson Institute.

Kawakami, K., Dovidio, J. F., Moll, J., Hermsen, S., & Russin, A. (2000). Just say no (to stereotyping): Effects of training in the negation of stereotypic associations on stereotype activation. *Journal of Personality and Social Psychology, 78*, 871–888.

Kessler, R. C., Berglund, P. A., Zhao, S., Leaf, P. I., Kouzis, A. C., & Bruce, M. L. (1996). The 12-month prevalence and correlates of serious mental illness. In R. W. Manderscheid & M. A. Sonnenschein (Eds.), *Mental health, United States* (Pub. No. [SMA] 96-3098, pp. 59–70). Rockville, MD: Center for Mental Health Services.

Kite, M. E., Russo, N. F., Brehm, S. S., Fouad, N. A., Hall, C. C., Hyde, J. S., & Keita, G. P. (2001). Women psychologists in academe: Mixed progress, unwarranted complacency. *American Psychologist, 56,* 1080–1098.

Kluckhohn, F. R., & Strodbeck, F. L. (1961). *Variations in value orientations.* Evanston, IL: Row, Patterson.

Kopelowicz, A. (1997). Social skills training: The moderating influence of culture in the treatment of Latinos with schizophrenia. *Journal of Psychopathology and Behavioral Assessment, 19,* 101–108.

Korman, M. (1974). National conference on levels and patterns of professional training in psychology. *American Psychologist, 29,* 441–449.

Kramer, R. M. (1999). Trust and distrust in organizations: Emerging perspectives, enduring questions. *Annual Review of Psychology, 50,* 569–598.

Kunda, Z., & Sinclair, L. (1999). Motivated reasoning with stereotypes: Activation, application, and inhibition. *Psychological Inquiry, 10,* 12–22.

Kunda, Z., & Thagard, P. (1996). Forming impressions from stereotypes, traits, and behaviors: A parallel-constraint-satisfaction theory. *Psychological Review, 103,* 284–308.

LaFromboise, T. D., & Jackson, M. (1996). MCT theory and Native-American populations. In D. W. Sue, A. E. Ivey, & P. B. Pedersen (Eds.), *A theory of multicultural counseling and therapy* (pp. 192–203). Pacific Grove, CA: Brooks/Cole.

Langman, P. F. (1998). *Jewish issues in multiculturalism: A handbook for educators and clinicians.* Northvale, NJ: Jason Aronson.

Lee, W. M. L. (1999). *An introduction to multicultural counseling.* Philadelphia: Accelerated Development.

Levin, M. (1995). Does race matter? *American Psychologist, 50,* 45–46.

Lewin, K. (1945). The Research Center for Group Dynamics at Massachusetts Institute of Technology. *Sociometry, 8,* 126–136.

Lewis, J. A., Lewis, M. D., Daniels, J. A., & D'Andrea, M. J. (1998). *Community counseling: Empowerment strategies for a diverse society.* San Francisco: Brooks/Cole.

Locke, D. C. (1992). *Increasing multicultural understanding.* Newbury Park, CA: Sage.

Loden, M. (1996). *Implementing diversity.* Chicago: Irwin.

López, S. R. (1989). Patient variable biases in clinical judgment: Conceptual overview and methodological consideration. *Psychological Bulletin, 106,* 184–203.

Lowe, S. M., & Mascher, J. (2001). The role of sexual orientation in multicultural counseling: Integrating bodies of knowledge. In J. G. Ponterotto, J. M. Casas, L. A. Suzuki, & C. M. Alexander (Eds.), *Handbook of multicultural counseling* (2nd ed., pp. 755–778). Thousand Oaks, CA: Sage.

Lukasiewicz, M., & Harvey, E. (Producers). (1991, September 26). *True Colors on 20/20: Primetime Live*. New York: ABC.

Macrae, C. N., & Bodenhausen, G. V. (2000). Social cognition: Thinking categorically about others. *Annual Review of Psychology, 51,* 93–120.

Major, B., Quinton, W. J., & McCoy, S. K. (in press). Antecedents and consequences of attributions to discrimination: Theoretical and empirical advances. In M. P. Zanna (Ed.), *Advances in experimental social psychology* (Vol. 34). New York: Academic Press.

Markus, H. R., & Kitayama, S. (1991). Culture and the self: Implications for cognition, emotion, and motivation. *Psychological Review, 98,* 224–253.

Markus, H. R., & Kitayama, S. (2001). The cultural construction of self and emotion: Implications for social behavior. In W. G. Perrod (Ed.), *Emotions in social psychology: Essential reading* (pp 119–137). Philadelphia: Brunner-Routledge.

McGoldrick, M., Giordano, J., & Pearce, J. K. (Eds.). (1996). *Ethnicity and family therapy* (2nd ed.). New York: Guilford Press.

Medved, C. E., Morrison, K., Dearing, J. E., Larson, R. S., Cline, G., & Brummans, B. H. (2001). Tensions in community health improvement initiatives: Communication and collaboration in a managed care environment. *Journal of Applied Communication Research, 29,* 137–151.

Middleton, R. A., Arredondo, P., & D'Andrea, M. (2000, December). The impact of Spanish-speaking newcomers in Alabama towns. *Counseling Today, 43*(6), 24.

Middleton, R. A., Rollins, C. W., & Harley, D. A. (1999). The historical and political context of the civil rights of persons with disabilities: A multicultural perspective for counselors. *Journal of Multicultural Counseling and Development, 27,* 105–120.

Mio, J. S., & Awakuni, G. I. (2000). *Resistance to multiculturalism: Issues and interventions*. Philadelphia: Brunner/Mazel.

Mosley-Howard, G. S., & Burgan Evans, C. (2000). Relationships and contemporary experiences of the African American family: An ethnographic case study. *Journal of Black Studies, 30,* 428–452.

Murdock, N. L., Alcorn, J., Heesacker, M., & Stoltenberg, C. (1998). Model training program in counseling psychology. *Counseling Psychologist, 26,* 658–672.

Nanus, B. (1992). *Visionary leadership: Creating a compelling sense of direction for your organization*. San Francisco: Jossey-Bass.

National Center for Education Statistics. (2001). *The condition of education*. Washington, DC: U.S. Department of Education.

Neville, H. A., & Mobley, M. (2001). Social identities in contexts: An ecological model of multicultural counseling psychology processes. *Counseling Psychologist, 29,* 471–486.

Niemann, Y. F. (2001). Stereotypes about Chicanas and Chicanos: Implications for counseling. *Counseling Psychologist, 29,* 55–90.

Oetting, G. R., & Beauvais, F. (1990–1991). Orthogonal cultural identification theory: The cultural identification of minority adolescents. *International Journal of the Addictions, 25,* 655–685.

Oyserman, D., Coon, H. M., & Kemmelmeier, M. (2002). Rethinking individualism and collectivism: Evaluation of theoretical assumptions and meta-analyses. *Psychological Bulletin, 128,* 3–72.

Oyserman, D., Gant, L., & Ager, J. (1995). A socially contextualized model of African American identity: Possible selves and school persistence. *Journal of Personality and Social Psychology, 69,* 1216–1232.

Padilla, A. M. (Ed.). (1995). *Hispanic psychology: Critical issues in theory and research.* Thousand Oaks, CA: Sage.

Paniagua, F. (1994). *Assessing and treating culturally different clients.* Newbury Park, CA: Sage.

Paniagua, F. (1998). *Assessing and treating culturally diverse clients* (2nd ed.). Thousand Oaks, CA: Sage.

Parham, T. A. (1989). Cycles of psychological nigrescence. *Counseling Psychologist, 17,* 187–226.

Parham, T. A. (2001). Psychological nigrescence revisited: A foreword. *Journal of Multicultural Counseling and Development, 29,* 162–164.

Parham, T. A., White, J. L., & Ajamu, A. (1999). *The psychology of Blacks: An African centered perspective* (3rd ed.). Upper Saddle River, NJ: Prentice Hall.

Pedersen, P. (1997). *Culture-centered counseling interventions: Striving for accuracy.* Thousand Oaks, CA: Sage.

Pedersen, P. (1999). *Multiculturalism as a fourth force.* Philadelphia: Brunner/Mazel.

Pedersen, P. (2000). *Hidden messages in culture-centered counseling: A triad training model.* Thousand Oaks, CA: Sage.

Peterson, R. L., Peterson, D. R., & Abrams, J. C. (Eds.). (1999). *Standards for education in professional psychology.* Washington, DC: American Psychological Association & National Council of Schools of Professional Psychology.

Pettigrew, T. F. (1979). The ultimate attribution error: Extending Allport's cognitive analysis of prejudice. *Personality and Social Psychology Bulletin, 5,* 461–476.

Pettigrew, T. F. (1998). Applying social psychology to international social issues. *Journal of Social Issues, 54,* 663–675.

Phinney, J. S. (1991). Ethnic identity and self-esteem: A review and integration. *Hispanic Journal of Behavioral Sciences, 13,* 193–208.

Phinney, J. S. (1996). When we talk about American ethnic groups, what do we mean? *American Psychologist, 51,* 918–927.

Plant, E. A., & Devine, P. G. (1998). Internal and external motivation to respond without prejudice. *Journal of Personality and Social Psychology, 75,* 811–832.

Ponterotto, J. G., Casas, J. M., Suzuki, L. A., & Alexander, C. M. (Eds.). (1995). *Handbook of multicultural counseling.* Thousand Oaks, CA: Sage.

Ponterotto, J. G., & Pedersen, P. B. (1993). *Preventing prejudice: A guide for counselors and educators.* Newbury Park, CA: Sage.

Prendes-Lintel, M. (2001). A working model in counseling recent refugees. In J. G. Ponterotto, J. M. Casas, L. A. Suzuki, & C. M. Alexander (Eds.), *Handbook of multicultural counseling* (2nd ed., pp. 729–752). Thousand Oaks, CA: Sage.

Prieto, L. R., McNeill, B. W., Walls, R. G., & Gomez, S. P. (2001). Chicanas/os and mental health services: An overview of utilization, counselor preference and assessment issues. *Counseling Psychologist, 29*, 18–54.

Ramirez, M. (1998). *Multicultural/multiracial psychology: Mestizo perspectives in personality and mental health*. Northvale, NJ: Jason Aronson.

Reynolds, A. L. (1995). Challenges and strategies for teaching multicultural counseling courses. In J. G. Ponterotto, J. M. Casas, L. A. Suzuki, & C. M. Alexander (Eds.), *Handbook of multicultural counseling* (pp. 312–330). Thousand Oaks, CA: Sage.

Reynolds, K. J., & Oakes, P. J. (2000). Variability in impression formation: Investigating the role of motivation, capacity, and the categorization process. *Personality and Social Psychology Bulletin, 26*, 355–373.

Ridley, C. R. (1995). *Overcoming unintentional racism in counseling and therapy: A practitioner's guide to intentional intervention*. Thousand Oaks, CA: Sage.

Ridley, C. R., Hill, C., & Li, L. (1998). Revisiting and refining the multicultural assessment procedure. *Counseling Psychologist, 6*, 939–947.

Robinson, T. L., & Howard-Hamilton, M. (2000). *The convergence of race, ethnicity, and gender*. Upper Saddle River, NJ: Prentice Hall.

Rodriguez, R., & Walls, N. (2000). Culturally educated questioning: Toward a skill-based approach in multicultural counselor training. *Applied and Preventive Psychology, 2*, 89–99.

Root, M. P. P. (Ed.). (1992). *Racially mixed people in America*. Newbury Park, CA: Sage.

Root, M. P. P. (1999). The biracial baby boom: Understanding ecological constructions of racial identity in the 21st century. In R. H. Sheets & E. R. Hollins (Eds.), *Racial and ethnic identity in school practices: Aspects of human development* (pp. 67–89). Mahwah, NJ: Erlbaum.

Ruiz, A. S. (1990). Ethnic identity: Crisis and resolution. *Journal of Multicultural Counseling and Development, 18*, 29–40.

Rules of State Board of Examiners of Psychologists, Ga. Comp. R. & Regs. r. 510-8-01 (2001).

Rushton, J. P. (1995). Construct validity, censorship, and the genetics of race. *American Psychologist, 50*, 40–41.

Saldana, D. (1995). Acculturative stress: Minority status and distress. In A. M. Padilla (Ed.), *Hispanic psychology* (pp. 43–56). Thousand Oaks, CA: Sage.

Samuda, R. J. (1998). *Psychological testing of American minorities*. Thousand Oaks, CA: Sage.

Sanchez, A. R. (2001). Multicultural family counseling: Toward cultural sensibility. In J. G. Ponterotto, J. M. Casas, L. A. Suzuki, & C. M. Alexander (Eds.), *Handbook of multicultural counseling* (2nd ed., pp. 672–700). Thousand Oaks, CA: Sage.

Sandoval, J., Frisby, C. L., Geisinger, K. F., Scheuneman, J. D., & Grenier, J. R. (Eds.). (1998). *Test interpretation and diversity: Achieving equity in assessment*. Washington, DC: American Psychological Association.

Santiago-Rivera, A., Arredondo, P., & Gallardo-Cooper, M. (2002). *Counseling Latinos and la familia: A practitioner's guide*. Thousand Oaks, CA: Sage.

Schofield, J. W. (1986). Causes and consequences of the colorblind perspective. In J. F. Dovidio & S. L. Gaertner (Eds.), *Prejudice, discrimination, and racism* (pp. 231–253). San Diego, CA: Academic Press.

Sciarra, D. T. (1999). *Multiculturalism in counseling*. Itasca, IL: Peacock.

Sedikides, C., & Brewer, M. B. (2001). *Individual self, relational self, collective self*. Philadelphia: Brunner-Routledge.

Seeley, K. M. (2000). *Cultural psychotherapy*. Northvale, NJ: Jason Aronson.

Sellers, R. M., Smith, M. A., Shelton, J. N., Rowley, S. A., & Chavous, T. M. (1998). Multidimensional model of racial identity: A reconceptualization of African American racial identity. *Personality and Social Psychology Review, 2*, 18–39.

Sidanius, J., & Pratto, F. (1999). *Social dominance: An intergroup theory of social hierarchy and oppression*. New York: Cambridge University Press.

Smart, J., & Smart, D. W. (1995). Acculturative stress of Hispanics: Loss and challenge. *Journal of Counseling and Development, 73*, 390–396.

Society for the Psychological Study of Ethnic Minority Issues, Division 45 of the American Psychological Association & Microtraining Associates, Inc. (Sponsors/Producers). (2000). *Culturally-competent counseling and therapy: Live demonstrations of innovative approaches* [Motion picture]. (Available from Microtraining Associates, Inc., P.O. Box 9641, North Amherst, MA 01059-9641)

Sodowsky, G. R., & Kuo, P. Y. (2001). Determining cultural validity of personality assessment: Some guidelines. In D. B. Pope-Davis & H. L. K. Coleman (Eds.), *The intersection of race, class, and gender: Implications for multicultural counseling* (pp. 213–240). Thousand Oaks, CA: Sage.

Sodowsky, G. R., Kuo-Jackson, P. Y., & Loya, G. (1997). Outcome of training in the philosophy of assessment: Multicultural counseling competencies. In D. B. Pope-Davis & H. L. K. Coleman (Eds.), *Multicultural counseling competencies: Assessment education and training, and supervision* (pp. 3–42). Thousand Oaks, CA: Sage.

Steele, C. M. (1997). A threat in the air: How stereotypes shape intellectual identity and performance. *American Psychologist, 52*, 613–629.

Stukas, A. A., Jr., & Snyder, M. (2002). Targets' awareness of expectations and behavioral confirmation in ongoing interactions. *Journal of Experimental Social Psychology, 38*, 31–40.

Sue, D. W. (1978). Eliminating cultural oppression in counseling: Toward a general theory. *Journal of Counseling Psychology, 25*, 419–428.

Sue, D. W. (2001). Multidimensional facets of cultural competence. *Counseling Psychologist, 29*, 790–821.

Sue, D. W., Arredondo, P., & McDavis, R. J. (1992). Multicultural counseling competencies and standards: A call to the profession. *Journal of Counseling and Development, 70*, 477–483.

Sue, D. W., Bernier, J., Durran, M., Feinberg, L., Pedersen, P., Smith, E., & Vasquez-Nuttall, E. (1982). Position paper: Cross-cultural counseling competencies. *Counseling Psychologist, 10*, 45–52.

Sue, D. W., Bingham, R. P., Porche-Burke, L., & Vasquez, M. (1999). The diversification of psychology: A multicultural revolution. *American Psychologist, 54*, 1061–1069.

Sue, D. W., Carter, R. T., Casas, J. M., Fouad, N. A., Ivey, A. E., & Jensen, M. (1998). *Multicultural counseling competencies: Individual and organizational development.* Thousand Oaks, CA: Sage.

Sue, D. W., Ivey, A. E., & Pedersen, P. B. (1996). *A theory of multicultural counseling and therapy.* Pacific Grove, CA: Brooks/Cole.

Sue, D. W., & Sue, D. (1977). Ethnic minorities: Failures and responsibilities of the social sciences. *Journal of Non-White Concerns in Personnel and Guidance, 5*, 99–106.

Sue, D. W., & Sue, D. (1999). *Counseling the culturally different: Theory and practice* (3rd ed.). New York: Wiley.

Sue, S. (1998). In search of cultural competence in psychotherapy and counseling. *American Psychologist, 53*, 440–448.

Sue, S. (1999). Science, ethnicity, and bias: Where have we gone wrong? *American Psychologist, 54*, 1070–1077.

Sun, K. (1995). The definition of race. *American Psychologist, 50*, 43–44.

Suzuki, L. A., & Valencia, R. R. (1997). Race-ethnicity and measured intelligence: Educational implications. *American Psychologist, 52*, 1103–1114.

Swim, J., & Mallett, R. (2002). *Pride and prejudice: A multi-group model of identity and its association with intergroup and intragroup attitudes.* Manuscript submitted for publication.

Swim, J., & Stangor, C. (1998). *Prejudice: The target's perspective.* San Diego, CA: Academic Press.

Tajfel, H., & Turner, J. C. (1986). The social identity theory of intergroup behavior. In S. Worchel & W. G. Austin (Eds.), *Psychology of intergroup relations* (pp. 7–24). Chicago: Nelson-Hall.

Thompson, C. E., & Carter, R. T. (1997). *Racial identity theory: Applications to individual, group, and organizational interventions.* Mahwah, NJ: Erlbaum.

Triandis, H. C., & Singelis, T. M. (1998). Training to recognize individual differences in collectivism and individualism within culture. *International Journal of Intercultural Relations, 22*, 35–47.

Turner, J. C., Brown, R. J., & Tajfel, H. (1979). Social comparison and group interest in ingroup favouritism. *European Journal of Social Psychology, 9*, 187–204.

U.S. Census Bureau. (2001). U.S. Census 2000, Summary Files 1 and 2. Retrieved May 13, 2003, from http://www.census.gov/main/www/cen2000.html

U.S. Department of Health and Human Services. (2001). *Mental health: Culture, race and ethnicity-A supplement to Mental Health: A Report of the Surgeon General.* Rockville, MD: U.S. Department of Health and Human Services, Public Health Office, Office of the Surgeon General.

Vandiver, B. J., Fhagen-Smith, P. E., Cokley, K. O., Cross, W. E., Jr., & Worrell, F. C. (2001). Cross' nigrescence model: From theory to scale to theory. *Journal of Multicultural Counseling and Development, 29*, 174–200.

Wehrly, B., Kenney, K. R., & Kenney, M. E. (1999). *Counseling multiracial families*. Thousand Oaks, CA: Sage.

Witte, K., & Morrison, K. (1995). Intercultural and cross-cultural health communication: Understanding people and motivating healthy behaviors. In R. L. Wiseman (Ed.), *Intercultural communication theory* (pp. 216–246). Thousand Oaks, CA: Sage.

Wolsko, C., Park, B., Judd, C. M., & Wittenbrink, B. (2000). Framing interethnic ideology: Effects of multicultural and color-blind perspectives on judgments of groups and individuals. *Journal of Personality and Social Psychology, 78*, 635–654.

Worrell, F. C., Cross, W. E., Jr., & Vandiver, B. J. (2001). Nigrescence theory: Current status and challenges for the future. *Journal of Counseling and Development, 29*, 201–213.

Wu, A. W. (2000). Quality-of-life assessment in clinical research: Application in diverse populations. *Medical Care, 38*, II130–II135.

Yee, A. H., Fairchild, H. H., Weizmann, F., & Wyatt, G. E. (1993). Addressing psychology's problem with race. *American Psychologist, 48*, 1132–1140.

Zhang, A. Y., Snowden, L. R., & Sue, S. (1998). Differences between Asian and White-Americans' help-seeking and utilization patterns for the Los Angeles area. *Journal of Community Psychology, 26*, 317–326.

APPENDIX K
APA Guidelines for Psychotherapy With Lesbian, Gay, & Bisexual Clients

Introduction

Attitudes Toward Homosexuality and Bisexuality

- **Guideline 1.** Psychologists understand that homosexuality and bisexuality are not indicative of mental illness.
- **Guideline 2.** Psychologists are encouraged to recognize how their attitudes and knowledge about lesbian, gay, and bisexual issues may be relevant to assessment and treatment and seek consultation or make appropriate referrals when indicated.
- **Guideline 3.** Psychologists strive to understand the ways in which social stigmatization (i.e., prejudice, discrimination, and violence) poses risks to the mental health and well-being of lesbian, gay, and bisexual clients.
- **Guideline 4.** Psychologists strive to understand how inaccurate or prejudicial views of homosexuality or bisexuality may affect the client's presentation in treatment and the therapeutic process.

Relationships and Families

- **Guideline 5.** Psychologists strive to be knowledgeable about and respect the importance of lesbian, gay, and bisexual relationships.
- **Guideline 6.** Psychologists strive to understand the particular circumstances and challenges facing lesbian, gay, and bisexual parents.
- **Guideline 7.** Psychologists recognize that the families of lesbian, gay, and bisexual people may include people who are not legally or biologically related.
- **Guideline 8.** Psychologists strive to understand how a person's homosexual or bisexual orientation may have an impact on his or her family of origin and the relationship to that family of origin.

From *APA Guidelines for Psychotherapy With Lesbian, Gay, & Bisexual Clients*, by the American Psychological Association, 2003, Washington, DC: American Psychological Association. Copyright 2003 by the American Psychological Association. Retrieved September 23, 2004, from PsychNET® Web site: http://www.apa.org/pi/lgbc/guidelines.html

Issues of Diversity

- **Guideline 9.** Psychologists are encouraged to recognize the particular life issues or challenges experienced by lesbian, gay, and bisexual members of racial and ethnic minorities that are related to multiple and often conflicting cultural norms, values, and beliefs.
- **Guideline 10.** Psychologists are encouraged to recognize the particular challenges experienced by bisexual individuals.
- **Guideline 11.** Psychologists strive to understand the special problems and risks that exist for lesbian, gay, and bisexual youth.
- **Guideline 12.** Psychologists consider generational differences within lesbian, gay, and bisexual populations, and the particular challenges that may be experienced by lesbian, gay, and bisexual older adults.
- **Guideline 13.** Psychologists are encouraged to recognize the particular challenges experienced by lesbian, gay, and bisexual individuals with physical, sensory, and/or cognitive/emotional disabilities.

Education

- **Guideline 14.** Psychologists support the provision of professional education and training on lesbian, gay, and bisexual issues.
- **Guideline 15.** Psychologists are encouraged to increase their knowledge and understanding of homosexuality and bisexuality through continuing education, training, supervision, and consultation.
- **Guideline 16.** Psychologists make reasonable efforts to familiarize themselves with relevant mental health, educational, and community resources for lesbian, gay, and bisexual people.

Acknowledgements

Endnotes

References

INTRODUCTION

In 1975, the American Psychological Association (APA) adopted a resolution stating that "Homosexuality per se implies no impairment in judgment, stability, reliability, or general social or vocational capabilities" (Conger, 1975, p. 633) following a rigorous discussion of the 1973 decision of the American Psychiatric Association to remove homosexuality from its list of mental disorders (American Psychiatric Association, 1974). Over 25 years later the implications of this resolution have yet to be fully implemented in practice (Garnets, Hancock, Cochran, Goodchilds, & Peplau, 1991; Dworkin, 1992; Firestein, 1996; Fox, 1996; Greene, 1994a; Iasenza, 1989; Markowitz, 1991, 1995; Nystrom, 1997). Many of these authors suggest that there is a need for better education and training of mental health practitioners in this area. This document is intended to assist psychologists in seeking and utilizing appropriate education and training in their treatment of lesbian, gay, and bisexual clients.[1]

The specific goals of these guidelines are to provide practitioners with (1) a frame of reference for the treatment of lesbian, gay, and bisexual clients, and (2) basic information and further references in the areas of assessment, intervention, identity, relationships, and the education and training of psychologists. These guidelines build on the American Psychological Association's Ethical Principles of Psychologists and Code of Conduct (APA, 1992),[2] other policies of the APA, and policies of other mental health organizations.

The term "guidelines" refers to pronouncements, statements, or declarations that suggest or recommend specific professional behavior, endeavor, or conduct for psychologists. Guidelines differ from standards in that standards are mandatory and may be accompanied by an enforcement mechanism. Thus, these guidelines are aspirational in intent. They are intended to facilitate the continued systematic development of the profession and to help assure a high level of professional practice by psychologists. These guidelines are not intended to be mandatory or exhaustive and may not be applicable to every clinical situation. They should not be construed as definitive and are not intended to take precedence over the judgment of psychologists.

These guidelines are organized in four sections: (1) Attitudes toward Homosexuality and Bisexuality, (2) Relationships and Families, (3) Issues of Diversity, and (4) Education.

ATTITUDES TOWARD HOMOSEXUALITY AND BISEXUALITY

Guideline 1. Psychologists understand that homosexuality and bisexuality are not indicative of mental illness.

For over a century, homosexuality and bisexuality were assumed to be mental illnesses. Hooker's (1957) study was the first to question this assumption. She found no difference between nonclinical samples of heterosexual

---

1. Throughout this document, the term "client" refers to individuals across the lifespan. This includes youth, adult, and older adult lesbian, gay, and bisexual clients. There may be issues that are specific to a given age range, and where appropriate, the document will identify those groups.

2. Hereafter this document will be referred to as the Ethics Code.

and homosexual men on projective test responses. Subsequent studies have shown no difference between heterosexual and homosexual groups on measures of cognitive abilities (Tuttle & Pillard, 1991) and psychological well-being and self-esteem (Coyle, 1993; Herek, 1990; Savin-Williams, 1990). Fox (1996) found no evidence of psychopathology in nonclinical studies of bisexual men and women. Further, an extensive body of literature has emerged that identifies few significant differences between heterosexual, homosexual, and bisexual people on a wide range of variables associated with overall psychological functioning (Pillard, 1988; Rothblum, 1994; Gonsiorek, 1991). When studies have noted differences between homosexual and heterosexual subjects with regard to psychological functioning (DiPlacido, 1998; Ross, 1990; Rotheram-Borus, Hunter, & Rosario, 1994; Savin-Williams, 1994), these differences have been attributed to the effects of stress related to stigmatization based on sexual orientation. This stress may lead to increased risk for suicide attempts, substance abuse, and emotional distress.

The literature that classifies homosexuality and bisexuality as mental illness has been found to be methodologically unsound. Gonsiorek (1991) reviewed this literature and found serious methodological flaws including unclear definition of terms, inaccurate classification of subjects, inappropriate comparison of groups, discrepant sampling procedures, an ignorance of confounding social factors, and questionable outcome measures. The results from these flawed studies have been used to support theories of homosexuality as mental illness and/or arrested psychosexual development. Although these studies concluded that homosexuality is a mental illness, they have no valid empirical support and serve as the foundation for beliefs that lead to inaccurate representations of lesbian, gay, and bisexual people.

All major American mental health associations have affirmed that homosexuality is not a mental illness. In 1975, the American Psychological Association (APA) urged all psychologists to "take the lead in removing the stigma long associated with homosexual orientations" (Conger, 1975, p. 633). Subsequently, the APA and all other major mental health associations adopted a number of resolutions and policy statements founded on this basic principle, which has also been embodied in their ethical codes (cf. American Association for Marriage & Family Therapy, 1991; American Counseling Association, 1996; Canadian Psychological Association, 1995: National Association of Social Workers, 1996). In addition, this principle has informed a number of APA *amicus curiae* briefs (Bersoff & Ogden, 1987).

Thus, psychologists affirm that a homosexual or bisexual orientation is not a mental illness (APA, 1998). "In their work-related activities, psychologists do not engage in unfair discrimination based on . . . sexual orientation . . . " (APA, 1992). Furthermore, psychologists assist clients in overcoming the effects of stigmatization that may lead to emotional distress.

Guideline 2. Psychologists are encouraged to recognize how their attitudes and knowledge about lesbian, gay, and bisexual issues may be relevant to assessment and treatment and seek consultation or make appropriate referrals when indicated.

The Ethics Code calls upon psychologists to " . . . strive to be aware of their own belief systems, values, needs, and limitations and the effect of these on their work" (APA, 1992, p. 1599). This principle is reflected in training programs and educational material for psychologists. The Ethics Code further urges psychologists to evaluate their competencies and the limitations of their expertise—especially when treating groups of people who share distinctive characteristics. Without a high level of awareness about their own beliefs, values, needs, and limitations, psychologists may impede the progress of a client in psychotherapy (Corey, Schneider-Corey, & Callanan, 1993).

The assessment and treatment of lesbian, gay, and bisexual clients can be adversely affected by therapists' explicit or implicit negative attitudes. For example, when homosexuality and bisexuality are consciously regarded as evidence of mental illness, a client's homosexual or bisexual orientation is apt to be viewed as a major source of the client's psychological difficulties even when sexual orientation has not been presented as a problem (Garnets, Hancock, Cochran, Goodchilds, & Peplau, 1991; Liddle, 1996; Nystrom, 1997). When psychologists are unaware of their negative attitudes, the effectiveness of psychotherapy can be compromised by heterosexist bias. Herek (1995) defined heterosexism as "the ideological system that denies, denigrates, and stigmatizes any nonheterosexual form of behavior, identity, relationship or community" (p. 321). Heterosexism pervades the language, theories, and psychotherapeutic interventions of psychology (Anderson, 1996; Brown, 1989). When heterosexual norms for identity, behavior, and relationships are applied to lesbian, gay, or bisexual clients, their thoughts, feelings, and behaviors may be misinterpreted as abnormal, deviant, and undesirable. Psychologists strive to avoid making assumptions that a client is heterosexual even in the presence of apparent markers of heterosexuality (e.g., marital status, since lesbian, gay, and bisexual people can be heterosexually married) (Glenn & Russell, 1986; Greene, 1994).

Another manifestation of heterosexism in psychotherapy is approaching treatment with a "sexual-orientation-blind" perspective. Like "color-blind" models, such a perspective denies the culturally unique experiences of a population—in this case lesbian, gay, and bisexual populations—as a strategy for avoiding a pathologizing stance. However, when psychologists deny the culture-specific experiences in the lives of lesbian, gay, and bisexual people, heterosexist bias is also likely to pervade that work in a manner unhelpful to clients (Garnets et al., 1991; Winegarten, Cassie, Markowski, Kozlowski, & Yoder, 1994). When psychologists are uninformed about the unique issues of lesbian, gay, and bisexual people, they may not understand the effects of stigmatization on individuals and their intimate relationships.

Because many psychologists have not received sufficient current information regarding lesbian, gay, and bisexual clients (Buhrke, 1989; Pilkington & Cantor, 1996), psychologists are strongly encouraged to seek training, experience, consultation and/or supervision to ensure competent practice with these populations when necessary. Key issues for practice include an understanding of human sexuality; the "coming out" process and how variables such as age, gender, ethnicity, race, disability, and religion may influence this process; same-sex relationship dynamics; family of origin relationships; struggles with spirituality and religious group membership; career issues and workplace discrimination; and coping strategies for successful functioning.

According to the Ethics Code, psychologists "are aware of culture, individual, and role differences, including those due to . . . sexual orientation . . . and try to eliminate the effect on their work of biases based on [such] factors" (APA, 1992, pp. 1599–1600). Hence, psychologists are encouraged to use appropriate methods of self-exploration and self-education (e.g., consultation, study, and formal continuing education) to identify and ameliorate preconceived biases about homosexuality and bisexuality.

Guideline 3. Psychologists strive to understand the ways in which social stigmatization (i.e., prejudice, discrimination, and violence) poses risks to the mental health and well-being of lesbian, gay, and bisexual clients.

Many lesbian, gay, and bisexual people face social stigmatization, violence, and discrimination (Herek, 1991). Living in a heterosexist society may precipitate a significant degree of stress for lesbian, gay, and bisexual people, many of whom may be tolerated only when they are "closeted" (DiPlacido, 1998). Sexual minority status increases risk for stress related to "chronic daily hassles (e.g., hearing anti-gay jokes, always being on guard)" to more serious "negative life events, especially gay-relevant events (e.g., loss of employment, home, custody of children, anti-gay violence and discrimination due to sexual orientation)" (DiPlacido, 1998, p. 140). Greene (1994b) noted that the cumulative effects of heterosexism, sexism, and racism may put lesbian, gay, and bisexual racial/ethnic minorities at special risk for social stressors.

Research has shown that gay men are at risk for mental health problems (Meyer, 1995) and emotional distress (Ross, 1990) as a direct result of discrimination and negative experiences in society. DiPlacido (1998) reported that research on psychosocial stress factors for lesbian and bisexual women is virtually nonexistent. She suggested that "some lesbians and bisexual women may be coping with stressors resulting from their multiple minority status in maladaptive and unhealthy ways" (p. 141). Social stressors affecting lesbian, gay, and bisexual older adults, such as a lack of legal rights and protection in medical emergencies and lack of acknowledgment of couples' relationships, particularly following the loss of a partner, have been associated with feelings of helplessness, depression, and disruption of normative grief processes (Berger & Kelly, 1996; Slater, 1995). Stress factors have been examined in lesbian, gay, and bisexual youth, for whom social vulnerability and isolation have been identified as prominent concerns. Social stressors affecting lesbian, gay, and bisexual youth, such as verbal and physical abuse, have been associated with academic problems, running away, prostitution, substance abuse, and suicide (Savin-Williams, 1994, 1998). Anti-gay verbal and physical harassment have been found to be significantly more common among adolescent gay and bisexual males who had attempted suicide compared with those who had not (Rotheram-Borus, Hunter, & Rosario, 1994). These stressors have also been associated with high-risk sexual behavior (Rotheram-Borus, Rosario, Van-Rossem, Reid, & Gillis, 1995).

Lesbian, gay, and bisexual people who live in rural communities may experience stress related to the risk of disclosure because anonymity about their sexual orientation may be more difficult to maintain. Fears about the loss of employment and housing may be more significant because of the limited opportunities within a small community. Less visibility and fewer lesbian, gay, and bisexual support organizations may intensify feelings of social isolation. Furthermore, lesbian, gay, and bisexual people may feel more vulnerable to acts of violence and harassment because rural communities may provide fewer legal protections (D'Augelli & Garnets, 1995).

Given the real and perceived social and physical dangers faced by many lesbian, gay, and bisexual clients, developing a sense of safety is of primary importance. Societal stigmatization, prejudice, and discrimination (e.g., anti-gay ballot initiatives or the murders of lesbian, gay, and bisexual individuals) can be sources of stress and create concerns about workplace and personal security for these clients (Rothblum & Bond, 1996; Fassinger, 1995; Prince, 1995). Physical safety and social and emotional support have been identified as central to stress reduction (Hershberger & D'Augelli, 1995; Levy, 1992) among lesbian, gay, and bisexual people.

In addition to external stressors, Gonsiorek (1993) described the process by which many lesbian, gay, and bisexual people internalize negative societal attitudes. This internalization may result in self-image problems ranging from a lack of self-confidence to overt self-hatred (Gonsiorek, 1993), depression (Meyer, 1995; Shidlo, 1994), and/or alcoholism and other substance abuse (Glaus, 1988). Meyer and Dean (1998) showed that gay men scoring high on a measure of internalized homophobia were significantly more likely than less homophobic gay men to experience sexual dysfunction, relationship instability, and to blame themselves for anti-gay victimization.

Psychologists working with lesbian, gay, and bisexual people are encouraged to assess the client's history of victimization as a result of harassment, discrimination, and violence. This enables the psychologist to understand the extent to which the client's world view has been affected by these abuses and whether any post-traumatic concerns need to be addressed. Further, the psychological consequences of internalized negative attitudes toward homosexuality and bisexuality are not always obvious or conscious (Shidlo, 1994). Therefore, in planning and conducting treatment, psychologists are encouraged to consider more subtle manifestations of these consequences, such as shame, anxiety and/or low self-esteem, and to consider the differential diagnostic implications of such stressors, both historically and in a client's ongoing psychosocial context.

Guideline 4. Psychologists strive to understand how inaccurate or prejudicial views of homosexuality or bisexuality may affect the client's presentation in treatment and the therapeutic process.

Bias and misinformation about homosexuality and bisexuality continue to be widespread in our society (APA, 1998; Haldeman, 1994). Due to the stigmatization of homosexuality and bisexuality, it is to be expected that many lesbian, gay, and bisexual people will feel conflicted or have significant questions about aspects or consequences of their sexual orientation (see Guideline 3). Fear of multiple personal losses including family, friends, career, and spiritual community, as well as vulnerability to harassment, discrimination, and violence, may contribute to an individual's fear of self-identifying as lesbian, gay, or bisexual. These factors have been considered central in creating a lesbian, gay, or bisexual person's discomfort with his or her sexual orientation (Davison, 1991; Haldeman, 1994). Many clients who are conflicted about or are questioning the implications of their sexual orientation seek psychotherapy to resolve their concerns. A psychologist who harbors prejudice or is misinformed about sexual orientation may offer responses to the questioning or conflicted client that may exacerbate the client's distress (see Guideline 2). Such an uncritical stance would consist of a psychologist's agreement with the notion that the only effective strategy for coping with such conflict or discrimination is to seek to change the lesbian, gay, or bisexual person's sexual orientation.

APA's policy, "Appropriate Therapeutic Responses to Sexual Orientation" (1998), offers a framework for psychologists working with clients who are concerned about the implications of their sexual orientation. The policy highlights those sections of the Ethics Code that apply to all psychologists working with lesbian, gay, and bisexual clients. These sections include prohibitions against discriminatory practices (e.g., basing treatment upon pathology-based views of homosexuality or bisexuality); a prohibition against the misrepresentation of scientific or clinical data (e.g., the unsubstantiated claim that sexual orientation can be changed); and a requirement for informed consent (APA, 1992). Based upon the Ethics Code, the policy "Appropriate Therapeutic Responses to Sexual Orientation" calls upon psychologists to discuss the treatment, its theoretical basis, reasonable outcomes, and alternative treatment approaches. In providing the client with accurate information about the social stressors that may lead to discomfort with sexual orientation, psychologists may help neutralize the effects of prejudice and inoculate the client against further harm. If psychologists are unable to provide this or other relevant information due to lack of knowledge or contravening personal beliefs, they should obtain the requisite information or make appropriate referrals (see Section 1.08, Ethics Code). Further, when a client presents with discomfort about sexual orientation, it is important for psychologists to assess the psychological and social context in which this discomfort occurs. Such an assessment might include an examination of internal and external pressures on clients to change their sexual orientation, the presence or absence of social support and models of positive lesbian, gay, or bisexual life, and the extent to which clients associate homosexuality or bisexuality with negative stereotypes and experiences. These and other dimensions of sexual orientation discomfort are important for psychologists to explore as the meanings associated with them are invariably complex. The role of psychologists, regardless of therapeutic orientation, is not to impose their beliefs on clients but to examine thoughtfully the clients' experiences and motives. Psychologists may also serve as a resource for accurate information about sexual orientation (e.g., by providing clients with access to empirical data on such questions as the development of sexual orientation or the relationship between mental health and sexual orientation).

RELATIONSHIPS AND FAMILIES

Guideline 5. Psychologists strive to be knowledgeable about and respect the importance of lesbian, gay, and bisexual relationships.

Lesbian, gay, and bisexual couples are both similar to and different from heterosexual couples (Peplau, Veniegas, & Campbell, 1996). They form relationships for similar reasons (Klinger, 1996) and express similar satisfactions with their relationships (Kurdek, 1995). The differences derive from several factors, including different patterns of sexual behavior, gender role socialization, and the stigmatization of their relationships (Garnets & Kimmel, 1993). Lesbian, gay, or bisexual people in relationships may seek therapy for reasons common to many couples or for reasons that are unique to those in same-sex relationships (Cabaj & Klinger, 1996; Matteson, 1996; Murphy, 1994). Common relationship problems such as communication difficulties, sexual problems, dual career issues, and commitment decisions can be affected by societal and internalized negative attitudes toward same-sex relationships. Problems presented in therapy specific to lesbian, gay, and bisexual couples include disclosure of sexual orientation as a couple to family, work colleagues; health professionals and caregivers; differences between partners in the disclosure process; issues derived from the effects of gender socialization in same-sex couples; and HIV status (Cabaj & Klinger, 1996; Slater, 1995). External issues such as pressure from families of origin and/or current or former heterosexual partners may also arise. Parenting may present unique issues for lesbian, gay, and bisexual people (e.g., possible risks to child custody from previous heterosexual partners or grandparents; lack of legal right for one of the parents). Changes in physical health may present unique issues, especially to older lesbian, gay, and bisexual couples (e.g., possible separation and loss of contact for partners in nursing homes and other in-patient settings).

Psychologists are encouraged to consider the negative effects of societal prejudice and discrimination on lesbian, gay, and bisexual relationships. It is important for psychologists to understand that, in the absence of socially sanctioned forms and supports for their relationships, lesbian, gay, and bisexual people may create their own relationship models and support systems. Therefore, psychologists strive to be knowledgeable about the diverse nature of lesbian, gay, and bisexual relationships and value and respect the meaning of these relationships.

Guideline 6. Psychologists strive to understand the particular circumstances and challenges facing lesbian, gay, and bisexual parents.

Research has indicated no significant differences between the capabilities of lesbian, gay, and bisexual parents when compared to heterosexual parents (Allen & Burrell, 1996; Bigner & Bozett, 1990; Bozett, 1989; Cramer, 1986; Falk, 1989; Gibbs, 1988; Kweskin & Cook, 1982; Patterson, 1996a). However, lesbian, gay, and bisexual parents face challenges not encountered by most heterosexual parents because of the stigma associated with homosexuality and bisexuality. Prejudice has led to institutional discrimination by the legal, educational, and social welfare systems. In a number of instances, lesbian, gay, and bisexual parents have lost custody of their children, have been restricted in visiting their children, have been prohibited from living with their domestic partners, and/or have been prevented from adopting or being foster parents, on the basis of their sexual orientation (Editors of the Harvard Law Review, 1990; Falk, 1989; Patterson, 1996).

The primary difficulties facing children of lesbian, gay, and bisexual parents are associated with misconceptions about their parents that are held by society at large. Three areas of concern have been raised by those in the legal and social welfare systems about the impact a parent's lesbian, gay, or bisexual orientation may have on children. These concerns include the influence of a lesbian, gay, or bisexual parent on a child's gender identity, gender role conformity, and sexual orientation. The body of research on lesbian mothers is currently considerably larger than that on gay fathers. In her comprehensive review of the literature, Patterson (1996b) concluded that there was no evidence of gender identity difficulties among children of lesbian mothers. She also reported studies indicating that gender role behavior among children of lesbian mothers was within normal ranges. Furthermore, children of lesbian, gay, and bisexual parents appear to be no different than peers raised by heterosexual parents in their emotional development and their likelihood of becoming homosexual (Bailey, Bobrow, Wolfe, & Mikach, 1995; Golombok & Tasker, 1994).

Psychologists rely on scientifically and professionally derived knowledge and avoid discriminatory practices when conducting assessments for suitability for child custody, adoption, and/or foster parenting. Psychologists provide accurate information and correct misinformation in their work with parents, children, community organizations and institutions (e.g., educational, legal, and social welfare systems).

Guideline 7. Psychologists recognize that the families of lesbian, gay, and bisexual people may include people who are not legally or biologically related.

The recognition of diverse family forms, including extended and blended families, is central to effective psychotherapy with ethnically and culturally diverse clients (Ho, 1987; Thomas & Dansby, 1985). For many lesbian, gay, and bisexual people, the primary partner and/or a network of close friends constitute an alternative family structure. In the absence of legal or institutional recognition, and in the face of societal, workplace, and familial discrimination, these alternative family structures may be more significant than the individual's family of origin (Kurdek, 1988; Weston, 1992). The importance of alternative family structures to lesbian, gay, and bisexual adults and youth is not always understood. Further, these relationships have been devalued or denied by some psychologists (Garnets, Hancock, Cochran, Goodchilds, & Peplau, 1991; Laird & Green, 1996).

Social support is an important resource in a heterosexual couple's capacity to handle relationship distress (Sarason, Pierce, & Sarason, 1990). People in same-sex relationships tend to derive less support in adulthood and old age from their families of origin than do their heterosexual counterparts (Kurdek, 1991; Laird & Green, 1996). Close relationships with a network of supportive friends also are considered by lesbian, gay, and bisexual youth to be extremely important. A strong friendship network has been viewed as pivotal in sexual identity exploration and development (D'Augelli, 1991).

Given the importance of social support in overall relationship satisfaction and longevity, psychologists are encouraged to consider the importance of lesbian, gay, or bisexual alternative family relationships. Psychologists are also aware of the stress that clients may experience when their family of origin, employers, or others do not recognize their family structure. Therefore, when conducting an assessment, psychologists are encouraged to ask clients who they consider to be part of their family.

Guideline 8. Psychologists strive to understand how a person's homosexual or bisexual orientation may have an impact on his or her family of origin and the relationship to that family of origin.

Families of origin may be unprepared to accept a lesbian, gay, or bisexual child or family member because of familial, ethnic, or cultural norms and/or religious beliefs or negative stereotypes (Chan, 1995; Greene, 1994a; Matteson, 1996). The awareness of a family member's homosexuality or bisexuality may precipitate a family crisis that can result in the expulsion of the homosexual or bisexual member, rejection of the parents and siblings by the homosexual or bisexual member, parental guilt and self-incrimination, or conflicts within the parents' relationship (Griffin, Wirth, & Wirth, 1996; Savin-Williams & Dube, 1998; Strommen, 1993). Even when reactions are more positive, adjustments may be necessary to accommodate a new understanding of the lesbian, gay, or bisexual family member (Laird, 1996). Many families are faced with their own "coming out" process when a family member discloses his or her homosexuality or bisexuality (Bass & Kaufman, 1996; Savin-Williams & Dube, 1998).

Families may need to adjust to the loss of hopes, perceptions, or expectations associated with the presumption of heterosexuality (Savin-Williams, 1996). Families may also need assistance in developing new understandings of sexual orientation, in confronting the ways in which negative societal attitudes about homosexuality and bisexuality are manifested within the family, and in addressing difficulties related to societal stigmatization. Psychologists also are sensitive to the cultural variations in a family's reaction and ways of adapting to a lesbian, gay, or bisexual member. Local and national resources are available that can provide information, assistance, and support to family members (e.g., Parents, Family, and Friends of Lesbians and Gays; Children of Lesbians and Gays Everywhere).

ISSUES OF DIVERSITY

Guideline 9. Psychologists are encouraged to recognize the particular life issues or challenges experienced by lesbian, gay, and bisexual members of racial and ethnic minorities that are related to multiple and often conflicting cultural norms, values, and beliefs.

Racial/ethnic minority lesbian, gay, and bisexual people must negotiate the norms, values, and beliefs regarding homosexuality and bisexuality of both mainstream and minority cultures (Chan, 1992, 1995; Greene, 1994a; Manalansan, 1996; Rust, 1996). Cultural variation in these norms, values, and beliefs can be a major source of psychological stress. There may be no one group or community to which a racial/ethnic minority lesbian, gay, or bisexual person can anchor his or her identity and receive full acceptance. This problem may be an even greater challenge for racial/ethnic minority youth who are exploring their sexual identity and orientation.

In offering psychological services to racially and ethnically diverse lesbian, gay, and bisexual populations, it is not sufficient that psychologists simply recognize the racial and ethnic backgrounds of their clients. Multiple minority status may complicate and exacerbate the difficulties experienced by these clients. Clients may be affected by the ways in which their cultures view homosexuality and bisexuality (Gock, 1992; Greene, 1994c). The effects of racism within lesbian, gay, and bisexual communities are also critical factors to consider (Gock, 1992; Greene, 1994b; Morales, 1996; Rust, 1996). A sensitivity to the complex dynamics associated with factors such as cultural values about gender roles, religious and procreative beliefs, degree of individual and family acculturation, and the personal and cultural history of discrimination or oppression is also important. All of these factors may have a significant impact on identity integration and psychological and social functioning (Chan, 1995; Greene, 1994b; Rust, 1996).

Guideline 10. Psychologists are encouraged to recognize the particular challenges experienced by bisexual individuals.

Bisexual adults and youth may experience a variety of stressors in addition to the societal prejudice due to same-sex attractions. One such stressor is that the polarization of sexual orientation into heterosexual and homosexual categories invalidates bisexuality. (Elliason, 1997; Fox, 1996; Markowitz, 1995; Matteson, 1996; Ochs, 1996; Paul, 1996; Shuster, 1987). This view has influenced psychological theory and practice as well as societal attitudes and institutions. Consequently, bisexuality may be inaccurately represented as a transitional state. Although no evidence of psychological maladjustment or psychopathology has been found, bisexual individuals who do not adopt an exclusively heterosexual or homosexual identity may nevertheless be viewed as developmentally arrested or in other ways psychologically impaired (Fox, 1996).

Negative individual and societal attitudes toward bisexuality in both the heterosexual and homosexual communities adversely affect bisexual individuals (Fox, 1996; Ochs, 1996). Such attitudes may be due to a lack of information about or access to a visible and supportive community of other bisexual individuals (Hutchins, 1996). According to Hutchins (1996) and Matteson (1996), information on community resources can facilitate the development and maintenance of positive bisexual identities.

Psychotherapy with bisexual clients involves respect for the diversity of their experiences and relationships (Fox, 1996; Klein, Sepekoff, & Wolf, 1985; Matteson, 1996). Psychologists are encouraged to adopt a more complex understanding of sexual orientation rather than a dichotomous model in their approach to treatment (Matteson, 1996).

Guideline 11. Psychologists strive to understand the special problems and risks that exist for lesbian, gay, and bisexual youth.

It is important for psychologists to understand the unique difficulties and risks faced by lesbian, gay, and bisexual adolescents (D'Augelli, 1998). Lesbian, gay, and bisexual youth may experience estrangement from their parents when revealing their sexual orientation (Cramer & Roach, 1988). When lesbian, gay, or bisexual youth have been rejected by their parents, they are at increased risk of becoming homeless (Kruks, 1991), may resort to prostitution (Coleman, 1989), and increase their risk for HIV infection (Gold & Skinner, 1992) and stress (Hershberger & D'Augelli, 1995; Savin-Williams, 1994). Youth who identify as lesbian, gay, or bisexual at an early age are also at increased risk to become victims of violence (Hunter, 1990), even within their families (Harry, 1989), to abuse substances (Garofalo, Wolf, Kessel, Palfrey, & DuRant, 1998), and to attempt suicide (Remafedi, French, Story, Resnick, & Blum, 1998).

Such difficulties may also complicate the developmental tasks of adolescence (Gonsiorek, 1991). The social stigma associated with lesbian, gay, and bisexual identity may also complicate career development and choice issues (Prince, 1995). Perceived parental and peer acceptance has an important impact on lesbian, gay, and bisexual youths' adjustment (Savin-Williams, 1989). Although peers and educators may be helpful in improving the psychosocial environment for these youth (Anderson, 1994; Caywood, 1993; Lipkin, 1992; Woog, 1995), they may not be useful if they lack the appropriate information and experience. When these potential sources of support are heterosexist, they may cause additional conflict and distress (Martin & Hetrick, 1988; Telljohann & Price, 1993).

Appropriate therapeutic strategies for work with lesbian, gay, and bisexual youth have been described in the professional literature (Browning, 1987; Coleman & Remafedi, 1989; Gonsiorek, 1988; Ryan & Futterman, 1998). Psychologists strive to create a safe therapeutic context for youth to explore sexual orientation issues. Psychologists should be aware of the ways in which psychological, ethical, and legal issues involved in working with minors are made even more complex when working with lesbian, gay, and bisexual youth.[3]

---

3. Psychologists should be aware of relevant federal and state laws, regulations, and professional standards that address these treatment issues, such as confidentiality and informed consent.

Guideline 12. Psychologists consider generational differences within lesbian, gay, and bisexual populations, and the particular challenges that may be experienced by lesbian, gay, and bisexual older adults.

Psychologists are encouraged to recognize that (1) lesbian, gay, and bisexual people of different generations may have had significantly different developmental experiences; and (2) older lesbian, gay, and bisexual people grew into adulthood with peers who share characteristics that may make them distinct as a generation (Kimmel, 1995). Examples of factors influencing generational differences include changing societal attitudes toward homosexuality, the AIDS epidemic, and the women's and civil rights movements. These cohort effects may significantly influence gay identity development, as well as psychological and social functioning (McDougal, 1993; Fassinger, 1997; Frost, 1997).

Psychologists are encouraged to be aware of the special transitions and life tasks facing lesbian, gay, and bisexual older adults, such as normative changes in health, retirement, finances, and social support (Slater, 1995; Berger, 1994). In many respects, these issues are the same as those of heterosexual older adults (Kimmel, 1990; Kirkpatrick, 1989; Reid, 1995; Slater, 1995). However, clients' multiple minority status may exacerbate problems, and gender may create different issues (see Guideline 9; Quam & Whitford, 1992; Turk-Charles, Rose, & Gatz, 1996). Moreover, end of life span tasks for lesbian, gay, and bisexual older adults are often complex and can develop into crises due to psychosocial stressors and heterosexism (Adelman, 1990; Berger & Kelly, 1996). Older lesbian, gay, and bisexual couples present potential issues, particularly because they lack legal rights and protection afforded to older heterosexual couples (see Guideline 5). Psychologists are encouraged to (1) be aware that state laws and regulations may affect the rights of their clients, and (2) support clients in seeking legal consultation related to medical crises, financial crises, and death.

Older adults are a diverse group, and normative changes in aging may be positive as well as negative and are not necessarily related to pathology or a client's sexual orientation. There are several descriptions of positive adaptation to aging among lesbian, gay, and bisexual older adults (Friend, 1990; Lee, 1987) that may be helpful to psychologists treating these clients. Having already addressed issues of being a stigmatized minority may help older gay men, lesbians, and bisexual people to address ageism and transitions in old age (Kimmel, 1995; Fassinger, 1997).

Guideline 13. Psychologists are encouraged to recognize the particular challenges experienced by lesbian, gay, and bisexual individuals with physical, sensory, and/or cognitive/emotional disabilities.

Lesbian, gay, and bisexual individuals with physical and/or sensory disabilities may experience a wide range of challenges related to the social stigmas associated with both disability and sexual orientation (Saad, 1997). One concern is the extent to which the individual's self concept is affected by social stigmas, which in turn may affect the individual's sense of autonomy and personal agency, sexuality, and self-confidence (Shapiro, 1993). For example, people with disabilities may be particularly vulnerable to the effects of "looksism" (i.e., basing social value on physical appearance and marginalizing those who do not conform, for reasons of age, ability, or appearance, to socially constructed standards). Another area of concern relates to how physical disability affects the person's relationship with partners, family, caregivers, and health care professionals. Within partner relationships, there may be issues related to life management, including mobility, sexuality, and medical and legal decision making. Family support may not be available due to negative reactions to the person's sexual orientation (Rolland, 1994; McDaniel, 1995). There may also be stress associated with a lesbian, gay, or bisexual person's need to "come out" to caregivers and health care professionals (O'Toole & Bregante, 1992).

Lesbian, gay, and bisexual people with disabilities may not have access to information, support, and services available to non-disabled lesbian, gay, and bisexual people (O'Toole & Bregante, 1992). Lack of societal recognition for lesbian, gay, and bisexual people in relationships affects those with ongoing medical concerns such as medical insurance coverage for domestic partners, family medical leave policies, hospital visitation, medical decision making by partners, and survivorship issues (Laird, 1993).

Saad (1997) recommends that psychologists inquire about the person's sexual history and current sexual functioning and provide information and facilitate problem-solving in this area. Studies have reported that many lesbians and gay men with disabilities have experienced coercive sexual encounters (Swartz, 1995; Thompson, 1994). It may be important for psychologists to assess the extent to which the person may have experienced sexual or physical victimization. Lastly, given the prejudice, discrimination, and lack of social support both within and beyond the lesbian, gay, and bisexual communities, it also may be important that psychologists recognize that when physical, sensory, and/or cognitive/emotional disabilities are present, social barriers and negative attitudes may limit life choices (Shapiro, 1993).

EDUCATION

Guideline 14. Psychologists support the provision of professional education and training on lesbian, gay, and bisexual issues.

There remains a gap between policy and practice in the psychotherapeutic treatment of lesbian, gay, and bisexual clients (Dworkin, 1992; Fox, 1996; Garnets, Hancock, Cochran, Goodchilds, & Peplau, 1991; Greene,

1994a; Iasenza, 1989: Markowitz, 1991, 1995; Nystrom, 1997). Despite the recent addition of diversity training during graduate education and internship, studies have shown that graduate students in psychology often report inadequate education and training in lesbian, gay, and bisexual issues (Buhrke, 1989; Glenn & Russell, 1986; Pilkington & Cantor, 1996) and that graduate students and novice therapists feel unprepared to work effectively with lesbian, gay, and bisexual clients (Allison, Crawford, Echemendia, Robinson, & Knepp, 1994; Buhrke, 1989; Graham, Rawlings, Halpern, & Hermes, 1984). The gap between policy and practice can be addressed by including information regarding these populations in all training programs.

Faculty, supervisors, and consultants are encouraged to integrate current information about lesbian, gay, and bisexual issues throughout training for professional practice. Resources are available to assist faculty in including lesbian, gay, and bisexual content in their curricula (e.g., APA, 1995; Buhrke & Douce, 1991; Cabaj & Stein, 1996; Croteau & Bieschke, 1996; Greene & Croom, in press; Hancock, 1995; Pope, 1995; Savin-Williams & Cohen, 1996). Psychologists who have expertise in lesbian, gay, and bisexual psychology may be utilized on a full-time or part-time basis to provide training and consultation to faculty as well as course and clinical supervision to students. Faculty and supervisors may be encouraged to seek continuing education course work in lesbian, gay, and bisexual issues.

Guideline 15. Psychologists are encouraged to increase their knowledge and understanding of homosexuality and bisexuality through continuing education, training, supervision, and consultation.

The Ethics Code urges psychologists to " . . . maintain a reasonable level of awareness of current scientific and professional information . . . and undertake ongoing efforts to maintain competence in the skills they use" (APA, 1992, p. 1600). Unfortunately, the education, training, practice experience, consultation, and/or supervision psychologists receive regarding lesbian, gay, and bisexual issues have often been inadequate, outdated, or unavailable (Buhrke, 1989; Glenn & Russell, 1986; Graham, Rawlings, Halpern, & Hermes, 1984; Pilkington & Cantor, 1996). Studies have revealed psychotherapist prejudice and insensitivity in working with lesbian, gay, and bisexual people (Garnets, Hancock, Cochran, Goodchilds, & Peplau, 1991; Liddle, 1996; Nystrom, 1997, Winegarten, Cassie, Markowski, Kozlowski, & Yoder, 1994).

Preparation for the provision of psychotherapy to lesbian, gay, and bisexual clients may include additional education, training, experience, consultation, or supervision in such areas as (a) human sexuality; (b) lesbian, gay, and bisexual identity development; (c) the effects of stigmatization upon lesbian, gay, and bisexual individuals, couples, and families; (d) ethnic and cultural factors affecting identity; and (e) unique career development and workplace issues experienced by lesbian, gay, and bisexual individuals.

ACKNOWLEDGEMENTS

These guidelines were developed by the Division 44/Committee on Lesbian, Gay, and Bisexual Concerns Joint Task Force on Guidelines for Psychotherapy with Lesbian, Gay, and Bisexual Clients (JTF). They were adopted by the Council of Representatives on February 26, 2000. The JTF co-chairs were Kristin Hancock, PhD (John F. Kennedy University, Orinda, California) and Armand Cerbone, PhD (independent practice, Chicago, Illinois). The JTF members included Christine Browning, PhD (University of California, Irvine); Douglas Haldeman, PhD (independent practice, Seattle, Washington); Ronald Fox, PhD (independent practice, San Francisco, California); Terry Gock, PhD (Asian Pacific Family Center, Rosemead, California); Steven James, PhD (Goddard College, Plainfield, Vermont); Scott Pytluk, PhD (private practice, Chicago, Illinois); Ariel Shidlo, PhD (Columbia Universiy, New York). The JTF wishes to acknowledge Alan Malyon, PhD for his foresight regarding the need for guidelines and for initiating their careful development. In addition, the JTF is grateful to Catherine Acuff, PhD (Board of Directors) for her vision, support, and skillful guidance; to Ron Rozensky, PhD (BPA), Lisa Grossman, PhD/JD (COPPS), and Dan Abrahamson, PhD (BPA) for their thorough and thoughtful review and editorial suggestions; to Kate Hays, PhD, Harriette Kaley, PhD, and Bianca Murphy, PhD (BAPPI) for their assistance in providing important feedback on several earlier drafts of the guidelines; to Ruth Paige, PhD (Board of Directors), Jean Carter, PhD (CAPP), and the many other APA colleagues for the consultation and assistance they gave to this project; to the Board for the Advancement of Psychology in the Public Interest, the Board of Professional Affairs, the Committee on Lesbian, Gay, and Bisexual Concerns, and especially Division 44 for their kind support; to Clinton Anderson (CLGBC Staff Officer) for all the hard work, patience, and counsel he provided to the JTF throughout this project; and to CLGBC's Task Force on Bias whose work (published in the September, 1991 issue of the American Psychologist) formed the basis for the development of these guidelines.

REFERENCES

Adelman, M. (1990). Stigma, gay lifestyles, and adjustment to aging: A study of later-life gay men and lesbians. *Journal of Homosexuality, 20*(3–4), 7–32.

Allen, M., & Burrell, N. (1996). Comparing the impact of homosexual and heterosexual parents on children: Meta-analysis of existing research. *Journal of Homosexuality, 32*(2), 19–35.

Allison, K., Crawford, I., Echemendia, R., Robinson, L., & Knepp, D. (1994). Human diversity and professional competence: Training in clinical and counseling psychology revisited. *American Psychologist, 49*, 792–796.

American Association for Marriage and Family Therapy. (1991). *AAMFT code of ethics*. Washington, DC: AAMFT.

American Counseling Association. (1996). ACA code of ethics and standards of practice. In B. Herlihy & G. Corey (Eds.), *ACA ethical standards casebook* (5th ed., pp. 26–59). Alexandria, VA: American Counseling Association.

American Psychiatric Association. (1974). Position statement on homosexuality and civil rights. *American Journal of Psychiatry, 131,* 497.

American Psychological Association. (1998). Appropriate therapeutic responses to sexual orientation in the proceedings of the American Psychological Association, Incorporated, for the legislative year 1997. *American Psychologist, 53*(8), 882–939.

American Psychological Association. (1995). *Lesbian and gay parenting: A resource for psychologists*. Washington, DC: Author.

American Psychological Association. (1992). Ethical principles and code of conduct. *American Psychologist, 48*(12), 1597–1611.

American Psychological Association. (1990). *Graduate training in psychology and associated fields*. Washington, DC: Author.

Anderson, J. (1994). School climate for gay and lesbian students and staff members. *Phi Delta Kappan, 76*(2), 151–154.

Anderson, S. (1996). Addressing heterosexist bias in the treatment of lesbian couples with chemical dependency. In J. Laird & R. Green (Eds.), *Lesbians and gays in couples and families* (pp. 316–340). San Francisco: Jossey-Bass.

Bailey, J., Bobrow, D., Wolfe, M., & Mikach, S. (1995). Sexual orientation of adult sons of gay fathers. Special Issue: Sexual orientation and human development. *Developmental Psychology, 31*(1), 124–129.

Bass, E., & Kaufman, K. (1996). *Free your mind: The book for gay, lesbian, and bisexual youth and their allies*. New York: Harper Collins.

Berger, R. (1984). *Gay and gray: The older homosexual man*. Boston: Alyson Press.

Berger, R., & Kelly, J. (1996). Gay men and lesbians grown older. In R. Cabaj & T. Stein (Eds.), *Textbook of homosexuality and mental health* (pp. 305–316). Washington, DC: American Psychiatric Press.

Bersoff, D., & Ogden, D. (1991). APA *Amicus curiae* briefs: Furthering lesbian and gay male civil rights. *American Psychologist, 46,* 950–956.

Bigner, J., & Bozett, F. (1990). Parenting by gay fathers. In F. Bozett & M. Sussman (Eds.), *Homosexuality and family relations* (pp. 155–176). New York: Harrington Park Press.

Bozett, F. (1989). Gay fathers: A review of the literature. In F. Bozett (Ed.), *Homosexuality and the family* (pp. 137–162). New York: Harrington Park Press.

Brown, L. (1989). Lesbians, gay men, and their families: Common clinical issues. *Journal of Gay and Lesbian Psychotherapy, 1*(1), 65–77.

Browning, C. (1987). Therapeutic issues and intervention strategies with young adult lesbian clients: A developmental approach. *Journal of Homosexuality, 14*(1/2), 45–52.

Buhrke, R. (1989). Female student perspectives on training in lesbian and gay issues. *Counseling Psychologist, 17*, 629–636.

Cabaj, R., & Klinger, R. (1996). Psychotherapeutic interventions with lesbian and gay couples. In R. Cabaj & T. Stein (Eds.), *Textbook of homosexuality and mental health* (pp. 485–502). Washington, DC: American Psychiatric Press.

Canadian Psychological Association. (1995). *Canadian code of ethics for psychologists.* [On-line]. Available: http://www.cycor.ca/Psych/ethics/html

Caywood, C. (1993). Reaching out to gay teens. *School Library Journal, 39*(4), 50.

Chan, C. (1995). Issues of sexual identity in an ethnic minority: The case of Chinese American lesbians, gay men, and bisexual people. In A. DiAugelli & C. Patterson (Eds.), *Lesbian, gay, and bisexual identities over the life span* (pp. 87–101). New York: Oxford University Press.

Chan, C. (1992). Asian-American lesbians and gay men. In S. Dworkin & F. Gutierrez (Eds.), *Counseling gay men and lesbians: Journey to the end of the rainbow* (pp. 115–124). Alexandria, VA: American Association for Counseling and Development.

Coleman, E. (1989). The development of male prostitution activity among gay and bisexual adolescents. In G. Herdt (Ed.), *Gay and lesbian youth* (pp. 131–149). New York: Haworth Press.

Coleman, E., & Remafedi, G. (1989). Gay, lesbian, and bisexual adolescents: A critical challenge to counselors. *Journal of Homosexuality, 18*(3/4), 70–81.

Conger, J. (1975). Proceedings of the American Psychological Association for the year 1974: Minutes of the annual meeting of the council of representatives. *American Psychologist, 30*, 620–651.

Corey, G., Schneider-Corey, M., & Callanan, P. (1993). *Issues and ethics in the helping professions* (4th ed.) Belmont, CA: Brooks/Cole.

Coyle, A. (1993). A study of psychological well-being among gay men using the GHQ-30. *British Journal of Clinical Psychology, 32*(2), 218–220.

Cramer, D. (1986). Gay parents and their children: A review of research and practical implications. *Journal of Counseling and Development, 64*, 504–507.

Cramer, D., & Roach, A. (1988). Coming out to mom and dad: A study of gay males and their relationships with their parents. *Journal of Homosexuality, 15*, 79–91.

Croteau, J., & Bieschke, K. (1996). Beyond pioneering: An introduction to the special issue on the vocational issues of lesbian women and gay men. *Journal of Vocational Behavior, 48*, 119–124.

D'Augelli, A. (1998). Developmental implications of victimization of lesbian, gay, and bisexual youth. In G. Herek (Ed.), *Psychological perspectives on lesbian and gay issues: Vol. 4. Stigma and sexual orientation* (pp. 187–210). Thousand Oaks, CA: Sage.

D'Augelli, A. (1991). Gay men in college: Identity processes and adaptations. *Journal of College Student Development, 32*(2), 140–146.

D'Augelli, A., & Garnets, L. (1995). Lesbian, gay, and bisexual communities. In A. D'Augelli & C. Patterson (Eds.), *Lesbian, gay, and bisexual identities over the life-*

span: Psychological perspectives (pp. 293–320). New York: Oxford University Press.

Davison, G. (1991). Constructionism and morality in therapy for homosexuality. In J. Gonsiorek & J. Weinrich (Eds.), *Homosexuality: Research implications for pubic policy* (pp. 137–148). Thousand Oaks, CA: Sage Publications.

DiPlacido, J. (1998). Minority stress among lesbians, gay men and bisexuals: A consequence of heterosexism, homophobia, and stigmatization. In G. Herek (Ed.), *Psychological perspectives on lesbian and gay issues: Vol. 4. Stigma and sexual orientation: Understanding prejudice against lesbians, gay men, and bisexuals* (pp. 138–159). Thousand Oaks, CA: Sage Publications.

Dworkin, S. (1992). Some ethical considerations when counseling gay, lesbian, and bisexual clients. In S. Dworkin & F. Gutierrez (Eds.), *Counseling gay men and lesbians: Journey to the end of the rainbow* (pp. 325–334). Alexandria, VA: American Association for Counseling and Development.

Editors of the Harvard Law Review. (1990). *Sexual orientation and the law.* Cambridge, MA: Harvard University Press.

Eliason, M. (1997). The prevalence and nature of biphobia in heterosexual undergraduate students. *Archives of Sexual Behavior, 26*(3), 317–325.

Esterberg, K. (1996). Gay cultures, gay communities: The social organization of lesbians, gay men, and bisexuals. In R. Savin-Williams & K. Cohen (Eds.), *The lives of lesbians, gay, and bisexual: Children to adults* (pp. 337–392). New York: Oxford University Press.

Falk, P. (1989). Lesbian mothers: Psychosocial assumptions in family law. *American Psychologist 44*, 941–947.

Fassinger, R. (1997). Issues in group work with older lesbians, *Group, 21*(2), 191–210.

Fassinger, R. (1995). From invisibility to integration: Lesbian identity in the workplace. *Career Development Quarterly, 14*, 148–167.

Firestein, B. (1996). Bisexuality as a paradigm shift: Transforming our disciplines. In B. Firestein (Ed.), *Bisexuality: The psychology and politics of an invisible minority* (pp. 263–291). Newbury Park, CA: Sage Publications.

Fox, R. (1996). Bisexuality in perspective: A review of theory and research. In B. Firestein (Ed.), *Bisexuality: The psychology and politics of an invisible minority* (pp. 3–50). Newbury Park, CA: Sage Publications.

Friend, R. (1990). Older lesbian and gay people: A theory of successful aging. *Journal of Homosexuality, 20*, 99–118.

Frost, J. (1997). Group psychotherapy with the gay male: Treatment of choice. *Group, 21*(3), 267–285.

Garnets, L., Hancock, K., Cochran, S., Goodchilds, J., & Peplau, L. (1991). Issues in psychotherapy with lesbians and gay men: A survey of psychologists. *American Psychologist, 46*(9), 964–972.

Garnets, L., & Kimmel, D. (1993). Lesbian and gay male dimensions in the psychological study of human diversity. In L. Garnets & D. Kimmel (Eds.), *Psycholog-*

ical perspectives on lesbian and gay male experiences (pp. 1–51). New York: Columbia University Press.

Garofalo, R., Wolf, R., Kessel, S., Palfrey, S., & DuRant, (1998). The association between health risk behaviors and sexual orientation among a school-based sample of adolescents. *Pediatrics, 101*(5), 895–902.

Gibbs, E. (1988). Psychosocial development of children raised by lesbian mothers: A review of research. *Women and Therapy, 8,* 65–75.

Glaus, O. (1988). Alcoholism, chemical dependency, and the lesbian client. *Women and Therapy, 8,* 131–144.

Glenn, A., & Russell, R. (1986). Heterosexual bias among counselor trainees. *Counselor Education and Supervision, 25*(3), 222–229.

Gock, T. (1992). The challenges of being gay, Asian, and proud. In B. Berzon (Ed.), *Positively gay.* Millbrae, CA: Celestial Arts.

Gold, R., & Skinner, M. (1992). Situational factors and thought processes associated with unprotected intercourse in young gay men. *AIDS, 6*(9), 1021–1030.

Golombok, S., & Tasker, F. (1996). Do parents influence the sexual orientation of their children? Findings from a longitudinal study of lesbian families. *Developmental Psychology, 32*(1), 3–11.

Golombok, S., & Tasker, F. (1994). Children in lesbian and gay families: Theories and evidence. *Annual Review of Sex Research, 5,* 73–100.

Gonsiorek, J. (1993). Mental health issues of gay and lesbian adolescents. In L. Garnets & D. Kimmel (Eds.), *Psychological perspectives on lesbian and gay male experiences* (pp. 469–485). New York: Columbia University Press.

Gonsiorek, J. (1991). The empirical basis for the demise of the illness model of homosexuality. In J. Gonsiorek & J. Weinrich (Eds.), *Homosexuality: Research implications for public policy* (pp. 115–136). Newbury Park, CA: Sage.

Gonsiorek, J. (1988). Mental health issues of gay and lesbian adolescents. *Journal of Adolescent Health Care, 9*(2), 114–121.

Gonsiorek, J., & Rudolph, J. (1991). Homosexual identity: Coming out and other developmental events. In J. Gonsiorek & J. Weinrich (Eds.), *Homosexuality: Research implications for public policy* (pp. 161–176). Newbury Park, CA: Sage.

Graham, D., Rawlings, E., Halpern, H., & Hermes, J. (1984). Therapists' needs for training in counseling lesbians and gay men. *Professional Psychology: Research and Practice, 15*(4), 482–496.

Greene, B. (1994a). Lesbian and gay sexual orientations: Implications for clinical training, practice, and research. In B. Greene & G. Herek (Eds.), *Psychological perspectives on lesbian and gay issues: Vol. 1. Lesbian and gay psychology: Theory, research, and clinical applications* (pp. 1–24). Thousand Oaks, CA: Sage.

Greene, B. (1994b). Ethnic minority lesbians and gay men: Mental health and treatment issues. *Journal of Consulting and Clinical Psychology, 62*(2), 243–251.

Greene, B. (1994c). Lesbian women of color: Triple jeopardy. In L. Comas-Diaz & B. Greene (Eds.), *Women of color: Integrating ethnic and gender identities in psychotherapy* (pp. 389–427). New York: Guilford.

Greene, B., & Croom, G. (Eds.). (in press). *Psychological perspectives on lesbian and gay issues: Vol. 5. Education, research and practice in lesbian, gay, bisexual, and transgendered psychology: A resource manual.* Thousand Oaks, CA: Sage.

Griffin, C., Wirth, M., & Wirth, A. (1996). *Beyond acceptance: Parents of lesbians and gays talk about their experiences.* New York: St. Martin's Press.

Haldeman, D. (1994). The practice and ethics of sexual orientation conversion therapy. *Journal of Consulting and Clinical Psychology, 62*(2), 221–227.

Harry, J. (1989). Parental physical abuse and sexual orientation in males. *Archives of Sexual Behavior, 18*(3), 251–261.

Herek, G. (1995). Psychological heterosexism in the United States. In A. D'Augelli & C. Patterson (Eds.), *Lesbian, gay, and bisexual identities over the lifespan: Psychological perspectives.* New York: Oxford University Press.

Herek, G. (1991). Stigma, prejudice and violence against lesbians and gay men. In J. Gonsiorek & J. Weinrich (Eds.), *Homosexuality: Research implications for public policy* (pp. 60–80). Newbury Park, CA: Sage.

Herek, G. (1990). Gay people and government security clearance: A social perspective. *American Psychologist, 45,* 1035–1042.

Hershberger, S., & D'Augelli, A. (1995). The impact of victimization on the mental health and suicidality of lesbian, gay and bisexual youths. *Developmental Psychology, 31,* 65–74.

Ho, M. (1987). *Family therapy with ethnic minorities.* Newbury Park, CA: Sage.

Hooker, E. (1957). The adjustment of the male over homosexual. *Journal of Projective Techniques, 21,* 18–31.

Hunter, J. (1990). Violence against lesbian and gay male youths. *Journal of Interpersonal Violence, 5,* 295–300.

Hutchins, L. (1996). Bisexuality: Politics and community. In B. Firestein (Ed.), *Bisexuality: The psychology and politics of an invisible minority* (pp. 240–259). Thousand Oaks, CA: Sage.

Iasenza, S. (1989). Some challenges of integrating sexual orientations into counselor training and research. [Special Issue: Gay, lesbian, and bisexual issues in counseling]. *Journal of Counseling and Development, 68*(1), 73–76.

Kimmel, D. (1995). Lesbians and gay men also grow old. In L. Bond, S. Cutler, & A. Grams (Eds.), *Promoting successful and productive aging* (pp. 289–303). Thousand Oaks, CA: Sage.

Klein, F., Sepekoff, B., & Wolf, T. (1985). Sexual orientation: A multi-variable dynamic process. Journal of Homosexuality, 11(1/2), 35–49.

Klinger, R. (1996). Lesbian couples. In R. Cabaj & T. Stein (Eds.), *Textbook of homosexuality and mental health* (pp. 339–352). Washington, DC: American Psychiatric Press.

Kruks, G. (1991). Gay and lesbian homeless/street youth: Special issues and concerns. *Journal of Adolescent Health, 12,* 515–518.

Kurdek, L. (1995). Lesbian and gay couples. In A. D'Augelli & C. Patterson (Eds.), *Lesbian, gay, and bisexual lives over the lifespan* (pp. 243–261). New York: Oxford University Press.

Kurdek, L. (1991). Correlates of relationship satisfaction in cohabiting gay and lesbian couples: Integration of contextual, investment, and problem-solving models. *Journal of Personality and Social Psychology, 61*, 910–922.

Kurdek, L. (1988). Perceived social support in gays and lesbians in cohabiting relationships. *Journal of Personality and Social Psychology, 54*, 504–509.

Kweskin, S., & Cook, A. (1982). Heterosexual and homosexual mothers self-described sex-role behavior and ideal sex-role behavior in children. *Sex Roles, 8*, 967–975.

Laird, J. (1996). Invisible ties: Lesbians and their families of origin. In J. Laird & R. Green (Eds.), *Lesbians and gays in couples and families: A handbook for therapists* (pp. 89–122). San Francisco: Jossey-Bass.

Laird, J. (1993). Lesbian and gay families. In F. Walsh (Ed.), *Normal family practices.* (2nd ed.). New York: W. W. Norton.

Laird, J., & Green, R. J. (1996). Lesbians and gays in couples and families: Central issues. In J. Laird & R. J. Green (Eds.), *Lesbians and gays in couples and families* (pp. 1–12). San Francisco: Jossey-Bass.

Lee. J. (1987). What can homosexual aging studies contribute to theories of aging? *Journal of Homosexuality, 13*(4), 43–71.

Levy, E. (1992). Strengthening the coping resources of lesbian families. *Families in Society, 73*, 23–31.

Liddle, B. (1997). Gay and lesbian client's selection of therapists and utilization of therapy. *Psychotherapy, 34*(1), 11–18.

Liddle, B. (1996). Therapist sexual orientation, gender, and counseling practices as they relate to ratings of helpfulness by gay and lesbian clients. *Journal of Counseling Psychology, 43*(4), 394–401.

Lipkin, A. (1992). Project 10: Gay and lesbian students find acceptance in their school community. *Teaching Tolerance, 1*(2), 25–27.

Manalansan, M. (1996). Double minorities: Latino, Black, and Asian men who have sex with men. In R. Savin-Williams & K. Cohen (Eds.), *The lives of lesbians, gays, and bisexuals: Children to adults* (pp. 393–415). Fort Worth, TX: Harcourt Brace.

Markowitz, L. (1995, July). Bisexuality: Challenging our either/or thinking. *In the Family, 1*, 6–11, 23.

Markowitz, L. (1991, January/February). Homosexuality: Are we still in the dark? *The Family Therapy Networker*, 26–29, & 31–35.

Martin, A., & Hetrick, E. (1988). The stigmatization of the gay and lesbian adolescent. *Journal of Homosexuality, 15*(1/2), 163–183.

Matteson, D. (1996). Counseling and psychotherapy with bisexual and exploring clients. In B. Firestein (Ed.), *Bisexuality: The psychology and politics of an invisible minority* (pp. 185–213). Newbury Park, CA: Sage.

McDaniel, J. (1995). *The lesbian couples' guide: Finding the right woman and creating a life together.* New York: Harper Collins.

McDougal, G. (1993). Therapeutic issues with gay and lesbian elders. *Clinical Gerontologist, 14*, 45–57.

Morales, E. (1996). Gender roles among Latino gay and bisexual men: Implications for family and couple relationships. In J. Laird & R. Green (Eds.), *Lesbians and gays in couples and families: A handbook for therapists* (pp. 272–297). San Francisco: Jossey Bass.

Murphy, B. (1994). Difference and diversity: Gay and lesbian couples. *Journal of Gay and Lesbian Social Services, 1*(2), 5–31.

Meyer, I. (1995). Minority stress and mental health in gay men. *Journal of Health and Social Behavior, 7,* 9–25.

Meyer, I., & Dean, L. (1998). Internalized homophobia, intimacy, and sexual behavior among gay and bisexual men. In G. Herek (Ed.), *Psychological perspectives on lesbian and gay issues: Vol. 4. Stigma and sexual orientation: Understanding prejudice against lesbians, gay men, and bisexuals* (pp. 160–186). Thousand Oaks, CA: Sage.

Morin, S. (1977). Heterosexual bias in psychological research on lesbianism and male homosexuality. *American Psychologist, 32,* 629–637.

National Association of Social Workers. (1996). *Code of ethics of the National Association of Social Workers.* [On-line] Available: http://www.ss.msu.edu/~sw/nasweth.html (4/19/97).

Nystrom, N. (1997, February). *Mental health experiences of gay men and lesbians.* Paper presented at the American Association for the Advancement of Science, Houston, TX.

Ochs, R. (1996). Biphobia: It goes more than two ways. In B. Firestein (Ed.), *Bisexuality: The psychology and politics of an invisible minority* (pp. 185–213). Thousand Oaks, CA: Sage.

O'Toole, C. J., & Bregante, J. (1992). Lesbians with disabilities. *Sexuality and Disability, 10*(3), 163–172.

Paul, J. (1996). Bisexuality: Exploring/exploding the boundaries. In R. Savin-Williams & K. Cohen (Eds.), *The lives of lesbians, gays, and bisexuals: Children to adults* (pp. 436–461). Fort Worth, TX: Harcourt Brace.

Patterson, C. (1996a). Lesbian and gay parenthood. In M. Bornstein (Ed.), *Handbook of parenting* (pp. 255–274). Hillsdale, NJ: Lawrence Erlbaum Associates.

Patterson, C. (1996b). Lesbian and gay parents and their children. In R. Savin-Williams & K. Cohen (Eds.), *The lives of lesbians, gays, and bisexuals: Children to adults* (pp. 274–304). Fort Worth, TX: Harcourt Brace.

Peplau, L., Veniegas, R., & Campbell, S. (1996). Gay and lesbian relationships. In R. Savin-Williams & K. Cohen (Eds.), *The lives of lesbians, gays, and bisexuals: Children to adults* (pp. 250–273). Fort Worth, TX: Harcourt Brace.

Phillips, J., & Fischer, A. (1998). Graduate students; training experiences with lesbian, gay, and bisexual issues. *The Counseling Psychologist, 26*(5), 712–734.

Pilkington, N., & Cantor, J. (1996). Perceptions of heterosexual bias in professional psychology programs: A survey of graduate students. *Professional Psychology: Research and Practice, 27*(6), 604–612.

Pillard, R. (1988). Sexual orientation and mental disorder. *Psychiatric Annals, 18*(1), 51–56.

Pope, K., Tabachnik, B. & Keith-Speigel, P. (1987). Ethics of practice: The beliefs and behaviors of psychologists as therapists. *American Psychologist, 42*(11), 993–1006.

Pope, M. (1995). Career interventions for gay and lesbian clients: A synopsis of practice, knowledge and research needs. *Career Development Quarterly, 44,* 191–203.

Prince, J. (1995). Influences on the career development of gay men. *Career Development Quarterly, 44,* 168–177.

Quam, J., & Whitford, G. (1992). Adaptation and age-related expectations of older gay and lesbian adults. *The Gerontologist, 32*(3), 367–374.

Reid, J. (1995). Development in late life: Older lesbian and gay lives. In A. D'Augelli & C. Patterson (Eds.), *Lesbian, gay, and bisexual identities over the lifespan: Psychological perspectives* (pp. 215–240). New York: Oxford University.

Remafedi, G., French, S., Story, M., Resnick, M., Michael, D., & Blum, R. (1998). The relationship between suicide risk and sexual orientation: Results of a population-based study. *American Journal of Public Health, 88*(1), 57–60.

Rolland, J. (1994). In sickness and in health: The impact of illness on couples' relationships. *Journal of Marital and Family Therapy, 20*(4), 327–347.

Ross, M. (1990). The relationship between life events and mental health in homosexual men. *Journal of Clinical Psychology, 46,* 402–411.

Rothblum, E., & Bond, L. (Eds.), (1996). *Preventing heterosexism and homophobia.* Thousand Oaks, CA: Sage.

Rothblum, E. (1994). "I only read about myself on bathroom walls": The need for research on the mental health of lesbians and gay men. *Journal of Consulting and Clinical Psychology, 62*(2), 213–220.

Rotheram-Borus, M., Hunter, J., & Rosario, M. (1994). Suicidal behavior and gay-related stress among gay and bisexual male adolescents. *Journal of Adolescent Research, 9,* 498–508.

Rotheram-Borus, M., Rosario, M., Van-Rossem, R., Reid, H., & Gillis, R. (1995). Prevalence, course, and predictors of multiple problem behaviors among gay and bisexual male adolescents. *Developmental Psychology, 31,* 75–85.

Rust, P. (1996). Managing multiple identities: Diversity among bisexual women and men. In B. Firestein (Ed.), *Bisexuality: The psychology and politics of an invisible minority* (pp. 53–83). Thousand Oaks, CA: Sage.

Ryan, C., & Futterman, D. (1998). *Counseling gay and lesbian youth.* New York: Columbia University Press.

Saad, C. (1997). Disability and the lesbian, gay man, or bisexual individual. In M. Sipski & C. Alexander (Eds.), *Sexual function in people with disability and chronic illness: A health professionals guide.* Gaithersburg, MD: Aspen Publications.

Sarason, I., Pierce, G., & Sarason, B. (1990). Social support and interactional processes: A triadic hypothesis. *Journal of Social and Personal Relationships, 7,* 495–506.

Savin-Williams, R. (1998). " . . . and then I became gay": Young men's stories. New York: Routledge.

Savin-Williams, R. (1996). Self-labeling and disclosure among lesbian, gay, and bisexual youths. In J. Laird & R. Green (Eds.), *Lesbians and gays in couples and families: A handbook for therapists* (pp. 153–182). San Francisco: Jossey-Bass.

Savin-Williams, R. (1994). Verbal and physical abuse as stressors in the lives of lesbian, gay male, and bisexual youths: Associations with school problems, running away, substance abuse, prostitution, and suicide. *Journal of Consulting and Clinical Psychology, 62,* 261–269.

Savin-Williams, R. (1990). *Gay and lesbian youth: Expressions of identity.* New York: Hemisphere.

Savin-Williams, R. (1989). Parental influences on the self-esteem of gay and lesbian youths: A reflected appraisals model. In G. Herdt (Ed.), *Gay and lesbian youth* (pp. 93–109). New York: Haworth Press.

Savin-Williams, R., & Dube, E. (1998). Parental reactions to their child's disclosure of gay/lesbian identity. *Family Relations, 47,* 1–7.

Shapiro, J. P. (1993). *No pity.* New York: Times Books.

Shidlo, A. (1994). Internalized homophobia: Conceptual and empirical issues in measurement. In B. Greene & G. Herek (Eds.), *Psychological perspectives on lesbian and gay issues: Vol. 1. Lesbian and gay psychology: Theory, research, and clinical applications* (pp. 176–205). Thousand Oaks, CA: Sage.

Shuster, R. (1987). Sexuality as a continuum: The bisexual identity. In Boston Lesbian Psychologies Collective (Eds.), *Lesbian psychologies: Explorations and challenges* (pp. 56–71). Urbana: University of Illinois Press.

Slater, S. (1995). *The lesbian family life cycle.* New York: Free Press.

Strommen, E. (1993). "You're a what": Family member reactions to the disclosure of homosexuality. In L. Garnets & D. Kimmel (Eds.), *Psychological perspectives on lesbian and gay male experiences* (pp. 248–266). New York: Columbia University Press.

Swartz, D. B. (1995). Cultural implications of audiological deficits on the homosexual male. *Sexuality and Disability, 13*(2), 159–181.

Task Force on Sex Bias and Sex Role Stereotyping in Psychotherapeutic Practices. (1978). Guidelines for therapy with women. *American Psychologist, 33*(12), 1122–1123.

Telljohann, S., & Price, J. (1993). A qualitative examination of adolescent homosexuals' life experiences: Ramifications for secondary school personnel. *Journal of Homosexuality, 26*(1), 41–56.

Thomas, M., & Dansby, P. (1985). Black clients: Family structures, therapeutic issues, and strengths. *Psychotherapy, 22*(2), 398–407.

Thompson, D. (1994). The sexual experiences of men with learning disabilities having sex with men: Issues for HIV prevention. *Sexuality and Disabilities, 12*(3), 221–242.

Turk-Charles, S., Rose, T., & Gatz, M. (1996). The significance of gender in the treatment of older adults. In L. Carstensen, B. Adelstein, & L. Dornbrand (Eds.), *The handbook of clinical gerontology* (pp. 107–128). Thousand Oaks, CA: Sage.

Tuttle, G., & Pillard, R. (1991). Sexual orientation and cognitive abilities. *Archives of Sexual Behavior, 20*(3), 307–318.

Weston, K. (1992). *Families we choose.* New York: Columbia University Press.

Winegarten, B., Cassie, N., Markowski, K., Kozlowski, J., & Yoder, J. (1994, August). *Aversive heterosexism: Exploring unconscious bias toward lesbian psychotherapy clients.* Paper presented at the annual meeting of the American Psychological Association, Los Angeles, CA.

Woog, D. (1995). *School's out: The impact of gay and lesbian issues on America's schools.* Boston: Alyson Publications.

APPENDIX L

APA Rights and Responsibilities of Test Takers: Guidelines and Expectations

PREAMBLE

The intent of this statement is to enumerate and clarify the expectations that test takers may reasonably have about the testing process, and the expectations that those who develop, administer, and use tests may have of test takers.

Tests are defined broadly here as psychological and educational instruments developed and used by testing professionals in organizations such as schools, industries, clinical practice, counseling settings and human service and other agencies, including those assessment procedures and devices that are used for making inferences about people in the above-named settings.

The purpose of the statement is to inform and to help educate not only test takers, but also others involved in the testing enterprise so that measurements may be most validly and appropriately used. This document is intended as an effort to inspire improvements in the testing process and does not have the force of law. Its orientation is to encourage positive and high quality interactions between testing professionals and test takers.

The rights and responsibilities listed in this document are neither legally based nor inalienable rights and responsibilities such as those listed in the United States of America's Bill of Rights. Rather, they represent the best judgments of testing professionals about the reasonable expectations that those involved in the testing enterprise (test producers, test users, and test takers) should have of each other.

Testing professionals include developers of assessment products and services, those who market and sell them, persons who select them, test administrators and scorers, those who interpret test results, and trained users of the information. Persons who engage in each of these activities have significant responsibilities that are described elsewhere, in documents such as those that follow (American Association for Counseling and Development, 1988; American Speech-Language-Hearing Association, 1994; Joint Committee on Testing Practices, 1988; National Association of School Psychologists, 1992; National Council on Measurement in Education, 1995).

In some circumstances, the test developer and the test user may not be the same person, group of persons, or organization. In such situations, the professionals involved in the testing should clarify, for the test taker as well as for themselves, who is responsible for each aspect of the testing process. For example, when an individual chooses to take a college admissions test, at least three parties are involved in addition to the test taker: the test developer and publisher, the individuals who administer the test to the test taker, and the institutions of higher education who will eventually use the information. In such cases a test taker may need to request clarifications about their rights and responsibilities. When test takers are young children (e.g., those taking standardized tests in the schools) or are persons who spend some or all their time in institutions or are incapacitated, parents or guardians may be granted some of the rights and responsibilities, rather than, or in addition to, the individual.

Perhaps the most fundamental right test takers have is to be able to take tests that meet high professional standards, such as those described in Standards for Educational and Psychological Testing (American Educational Research Association, American Psychological Association, & National Council on Measurement in Education, 1999) as well as those of other appropriate professional associations. This statement should be used as an adjunct, or supplement, to those standards. State and federal laws, of course, supersede any rights and responsibilities that are stated here.

References

American Association for Counseling and Development (now American Counseling Association) & Association for Measurement and Evaluation in Counseling and Development (now Association for Assessment in Counseling). (1989). *Responsibilities of users of standardized tests: RUST statement revised*. Alexandria, VA: Author.

American Educational Research Association, American Psychological Association, & National Council on Measurement in Education. (1999). *Standards for educational and psychological testing*. Washington, DC: American Educational Research Association.

American Speech-Language-Hearing Association. (1994). Protection of rights of people receiving audiology or speech-language pathology services. *ASHA, 36,* 60–63.

Joint Committee on Testing Practices. (1988). *Code of fair testing practices in education*. Washington, DC: American Psychological Association.

National Association of School Psychologists. (1992). *Standards for the provision of school psychological services*. Springs, MD: Author.

National Council on Measurement in Education. (1995). *Code of professional responsibilities in educational measurement*. Washington, DC: Author.

THE RIGHTS AND RESPONSIBILITIES OF TEST TAKERS: GUIDELINES AND EXPECTATIONS

Test Taker Rights and Responsibilities
Working Group of the Joint Committee on Testing Practices
August, 1998

As a test taker, you have the right to:

1. Be informed of your rights and responsibilities as a test taker.
2. Be treated with courtesy, respect, and impartiality, regardless of your age, disability, ethnicity, gender, national origin, religion, sexual orientation or other personal characteristics.
3. Be tested with measures that meet professional standards and that are appropriate, given the manner in which the test results will be used.
4. Receive a brief oral or written explanation prior to testing about the purpose(s) for testing, the kind(s) of tests to be used, if the results will be reported to you or to others, and the planned use(s) of the results. If you have a disability, you have the right to inquire and receive information about testing accommodations. If you have difficulty in comprehending the language of the test, you have a right to know in advance of testing whether any accommodations may be available to you.
5. Know in advance of testing when the test will be administered, if and when test results will be available to you, and if there is a fee for testing services that you are expected to pay.
6. Have your test administered and your test results interpreted by appropriately trained individuals who follow professional codes of ethics.
7. Know if a test is optional and learn of the consequences of taking or not taking the test, fully completing the test, or canceling the scores. You may need to ask questions to learn these consequences.
8. Receive a written or oral explanation of your test results within a reasonable amount of time after testing and in commonly understood terms.
9. Have your test results kept confidential to the extent allowed by law.
10. Present concerns about the testing process or your results and receive information about procedures that will be used to address such concerns.

As a test taker, you have the responsibility to:

1. Read and/or listen to your rights and responsibilities as a test taker.
2. Treat others with courtesy and respect during the testing process.
3. Ask questions prior to testing if you are uncertain about why the test is being given, how it will be given, what you will be asked to do, and what will be done with the results.
4. Read or listen to descriptive information in advance of testing and listen carefully to all test instructions. You should inform an examiner in advance of testing if you wish to receive a testing accommodation or if you have a physical condition or illness that may interfere with your performance on the test. If you have difficulty comprehending the language of the test, it is your responsibility to inform an examiner.
5. Know when and where the test will be given, pay for the test if required, appear on time with any required materials, and be ready to be tested.
6. Follow the test instructions you are given and represent yourself honestly during the testing.
7. Be familiar with and accept the consequences of not taking the test, should you choose not to take the test.
8. Inform appropriate person(s), as specified to you by the organization responsible for testing, if you believe that testing conditions affected your results.
9. Ask about the confidentiality of your test results, if this aspect concerns you.
10. Present concerns about the testing process or results in a timely, respectful way, if you have any.

The Rights of Test Takers: Guidelines for Testing Professionals

Test takers have the rights described below. It is the responsibility of the professionals involved in the testing process to ensure that test takers receive these rights.

1. Because test takers have the right to be informed of their rights and responsibilities as test takers, it is normally the responsibility of the individual who administers a test (or the organization that prepared the test) to inform test takers of these rights and responsibilities.
2. Because test takers have the right to be treated with courtesy, respect, and impartiality, regardless of their age, disability,

ethnicity, gender, national origin, race, religion, sexual orientation, or other personal characteristics, testing professionals should:

a. Make test takers aware of any materials that are available to assist them in test preparation. These materials should be clearly described in test registration and/or test familiarization materials.

b. See that test takers are provided with reasonable access to testing services.

3. Because test takers have the right to be tested with measures that meet professional standards that are appropriate for the test use and the test taker, given the manner in which the results will be used, testing professionals should:

a. Take steps to utilize measures that meet professional standards and are reliable, relevant, useful given the intended purpose and are fair for test takers from varying societal groups.

b. Advise test takers that they are entitled to request reasonable accommodations in test administration that are likely to increase the validity of their test scores if they have a disability recognized under the Americans with Disabilities Act or other relevant legislation.

4. Because test takers have the right to be informed, prior to testing, about the test's purposes, the nature of the test, whether test results will be reported to the test takers, and the planned use of the results (when not in conflict with the testing purposes), testing professionals should:

a. Give or provide test takers with access to a brief description about the test purpose (e.g., diagnosis, placement, selection, etc.) and the kind(s) of tests and formats that will be used (e.g., individual/group, multiple-choice/free response/performance, timed/untimed, etc.), unless such information might be detrimental to the objectives of the test.

b. Tell test takers, prior to testing, about the planned use(s) of the test results. Upon request, the test taker should be given information about how long such test scores are typically kept on file and remain available.

c. Provide test takers, if requested, with information about any preventative measures that have been instituted to safeguard the accuracy of test scores. Such information would include any quality control procedures that are employed and some of the steps taken to prevent dishonesty in test performance.

d. Inform test takers, in advance of the testing, about required materials that must be brought to the test site (e.g., pencil, paper) and about any rules that allow or prohibit use of other materials (e.g., calculators).

e. Provide test takers, upon request, with general information about the appropriateness of the test for its intended purpose, to the extent that such information does not involve the release of proprietary information. (For example, the test taker might be told, "Scores on this test are useful in predicting how successful people will be in this kind of work" or "Scores on this test, along with other information, help us to determine if students are likely to benefit from this program.")

f. Provide test takers, upon request, with information about re-testing, including if it is possible to re-take the test or another version of it, and if so, how often, how soon, and under what conditions.

g. Provide test takers, upon request, with information about how the test will be scored and in what detail. On multiple-choice tests, this information might include suggestions for test taking and about the use of a correction for guessing. On tests scored using professional judgment (e.g., essay tests or projective techniques), a general description of the scoring procedures might be provided except when such information is proprietary or would tend to influence test performance inappropriately.

h. Inform test takers about the type of feedback and interpretation that is routinely provided, as well as what is available for a fee. Test takers have the right to request and receive information regarding whether or not they can obtain copies of their test answer sheets or their test materials, if they can have their scores verified, and if they may cancel their test results.

i. Provide test takers, prior to testing, either in the written instructions, in other written documents or orally, with answers to questions that test takers may have about basic test administration procedures.

j. Inform test takers, prior to testing, if questions from test takers will not be permitted during the testing process.

k. Provide test takers with information about the use of computers, calculators, or other equipment, if any, used in the testing and give them an opportunity to practice using such equipment, unless its unpracticed use is part of the test purpose, or practice would compromise the validity of the results, and to provide a testing accommodation for the use of such equipment, if needed.

    l. Inform test takers that, if they have a disability, they have the right to request and receive accommodations or modifications in accordance with the provisions of the Americans with Disabilities Act and other relevant legislation.

    m. Provide test takers with information that will be of use in making decisions if test takers have options regarding which tests, test forms or test formats to take.

5. Because that test takers have a right to be informed in advance when the test will be administered, if and when test results will be available, and if there is a fee for testing services that the test takers are expected to pay, test professionals should:

    a. Notify test takers of the alteration in a timely manner if a previously announced testing schedule changes, provide a reasonable explanation for the change, and inform test takers of the new schedule. If there is a change, reasonable alternatives to the original schedule should be provided.

    b. Inform test takers prior to testing about any anticipated fee for the testing process, as well as the fees associated with each component of the process, if the components can be separated.

6. Because test takers have the right to have their tests administered and interpreted by appropriately trained individuals, testing professionals should:

    a. Know how to select the appropriate test for the intended purposes.

    b. When testing persons with documented disabilities and other special characteristics that require special testing conditions and/or interpretation of results, have the skills and knowledge for such testing and interpretation.

    c. Provide reasonable information regarding their qualifications, upon request.

    d. Insure that test conditions, especially if unusual, do not unduly interfere with test performance. Test conditions will normally be similar to those used to standardize the test.

    e. Provide candidates with a reasonable amount of time to complete the test, unless a test has a time limit.

    f. Take reasonable actions to safeguard against fraudulent actions (e.g., cheating) that could place honest test takers at a disadvantage.

7. Because test takers have the right to be informed about why they are being asked to take particular tests, if a test is

optional, and what the consequences are should they choose not to complete the test, testing professionals should:

a. Normally only engage in testing activities with test takers after the test takers have provided their informed consent to take a test, except when testing without consent has been mandated by law or governmental regulation, or when consent is implied by an action the test takers have already taken (e.g., such as when applying for employment and a personnel examination is mandated).

b. Explain to test takers why they should consider taking voluntary tests.

c. Explain, if a test taker refuses to take or complete a voluntary test, either orally or in writing, what the negative consequences may be to them for their decision to do so.

d. Promptly inform the test taker if a testing professional decides that there is a need to deviate from the testing services to which the test taker initially agreed (e.g., should the testing professional believe it would be wise to administer an additional test or an alternative test), and provide an explanation for the change.

8. Because test takers have a right to receive a written or oral explanation of their test results within a reasonable amount of time after testing and in commonly understood terms, testing professionals should:

a. Interpret test results in light of one or more additional considerations (e.g., disability, language proficiency), if those considerations are relevant to the purposes of the test and performance on the test, and are in accordance with current laws.

b. Provide, upon request, information to test takers about the sources used in interpreting their test results, including technical manuals, technical reports, norms, and a description of the comparison group, or additional information about the test taker(s).

c. Provide, upon request, recommendations to test takers about how they could improve their performance on the test, should they choose or be required to take the test again.

d. Provide, upon request, information to test takers about their options for obtaining a second interpretation of their results. Test takers may select an appropriately trained professional to provide this second opinion.

e. Provide test takers with the criteria used to determine a passing score, when individual test scores are reported and related to a pass-fail standard.

f. Inform test takers, upon request, how much their scores might change, should they elect to take the test again. Such information would include variation in test performance due to measurement error (e.g., the appropriate standard errors of measurement) and changes in performance over time with or without intervention (e.g., additional training or treatment).

g. Communicate test results to test takers in an appropriate and sensitive manner, without use of negative labels or comments likely to inflame or stigmatize the test taker.

h. Provide corrected test scores to test takers as rapidly as possible, should an error occur in the processing or reporting of scores. The length of time is often dictated by individuals responsible for processing or reporting the scores, rather than the individuals responsible for testing, should the two parties indeed differ.

i. Correct any errors as rapidly as possible if there are errors in the process of developing scores.

9. Because test takers have the right to have the results of tests kept confidential to the extent allowed by law, testing professionals should:

a. Insure that records of test results (in paper or electronic form) are safeguarded and maintained so that only individuals who have a legitimate right to access them will be able to do so.

b. Should provide test takers, upon request, with information regarding who has a legitimate right to access their test results (when individually identified) and in what form. Testing professionals should respond appropriately to questions regarding the reasons why such individuals may have access to test results and how they may use the results.

c. Advise test takers that they are entitled to limit access to their results (when individually identified) to those persons or institutions, and for those purposes, revealed to them prior to testing. Exceptions may occur when test takers, or their guardians, consent to release the test results to others or when testing professionals are authorized by law to release test results.

d. Keep confidential any requests for testing accommodations and the documentation supporting the request.

10. Because test takers have the right to present concerns about the testing process and to receive information about procedures that will be used to address such concerns, testing professionals should:

a. Inform test takers how they can question the results of the testing if they do not believe that the test was administered properly or scored correctly, or other such concerns.

b. Inform test takers of the procedures for appealing decisions that they believe are based in whole or in part on erroneous test results.

c. Inform test takers, if their test results are under investigation and may be canceled, invalidated, or not released for normal use. In such an event, that investigation should be performed in a timely manner. The investigation should use all available information that addresses the reason(s) for the investigation, and the test taker should also be informed of the information that he/she may need to provide to assist with the investigation.

d. Inform the test taker, if that test taker's test results are canceled or not released for normal use, why that action was taken. The test taker is entitled to request and receive information on the types of evidence and procedures that have been used to make that determination.

The Responsibilities of Test Takers: Guidelines for Testing Professionals

Testing professionals should take steps to ensure that test takers know that they have specific responsibilities in addition to their rights described above.

1. Testing professionals need to inform test takers that they should listen to and/or read their rights and responsibilities as a test taker and ask questions about issues they do not understand.

2. Testing professionals should take steps, as appropriate, to ensure that test takers know that they:

   a. Are responsible for their behavior throughout the entire testing process.

   b. Should not interfere with the rights of others involved in the testing process.

   c. Should not compromise the integrity of the test and its interpretation in any manner.

3. Testing professionals should remind test takers that it is their responsibility to ask questions prior to testing if they are uncertain about why the test is being given, how it will be given, what they will be asked to do, and what will be done with the results. Testing professionals should:

a. Advise test takers that it is their responsibility to review materials supplied by test publishers and others as part of the testing process and to ask questions about areas that they feel they should understand better prior to the start of testing.

b. Inform test takers that it is their responsibility to request more information if they are not satisfied with what they know about how their test results will be used and what will be done with them.

4. Testing professionals should inform test takers that it is their responsibility to read descriptive material they receive in advance of a test and to listen carefully to test instructions. Testing professionals should inform test takers that it is their responsibility to inform an examiner in advance of testing if they wish to receive a testing accommodation or if they have a physical condition or illness that may interfere with their performance. Testing professionals should inform test takers that it is their responsibility to inform an examiner if they have difficulty comprehending the language in which the test is given. Testing professionals should:

a. Inform test takers that, if they need special testing arrangements, it is their responsibility to request appropriate accommodations and to provide any requested documentation as far in advance of the testing date as possible. Testing professionals should inform test takers about the documentation needed to receive a requested testing accommodation.

b. Inform test takers that, if they request but do not receive a testing accommodation, they could request information about why their request was denied.

5. Testing professionals should inform test takers when and where the test will be given, and whether payment for the testing is required. Having been so informed, it is the responsibility of the test taker to appear on time with any required materials, pay for testing services and be ready to be tested. Testing professionals should:

a. Inform test takers that they are responsible for familiarizing themselves with the appropriate materials needed for testing and for requesting information about these materials, if needed.

b. Inform the test taker, if the testing situation requires that test takers bring materials (e.g., personal identification, pencils, calculators, etc.) to the testing site, of this responsibility to do so.

6. Testing professionals should advise test takers, prior to testing, that it is their responsibility to:
   a. Listen to and/or read the directions given to them.
   b. Follow instructions given by testing professionals.
   c. Complete the test as directed.
   d. Perform to the best of their ability if they want their score to be a reflection of their best effort.
   e. Behave honestly (e.g., not cheating or assisting others who cheat).
7. Testing professionals should inform test takers about the consequences of not taking a test, should they choose not to take the test. Once so informed, it is the responsibility of the test taker to accept such consequences, and the testing professional should so inform the test takers. If test takers have questions regarding these consequences, it is their responsibility to ask questions of the testing professional, and the testing professional should so inform the test takers.
8. Testing professionals should inform test takers that it is their responsibility to notify appropriate persons, as specified by the testing organization, if they do not understand their results, or if they believe that testing conditions affected the results. Testing professionals should:
   a. Provide information to test takers, upon request, about appropriate procedures for questioning or canceling their test scores or results, if relevant to the purposes of testing.
   b. Provide to test takers, upon request, the procedures for reviewing, re-testing, or canceling their scores or test results, if they believe that testing conditions affected their results and if relevant to the purposes of testing.
   c. Provide documentation to the test taker about known testing conditions that might have affected the results of the testing, if relevant to the purposes of testing.
9. Testing professionals should advise test takers that it is their responsibility to ask questions about the confidentiality of their test results, if this aspect concerns them.
10. Testing professionals should advise test takers that it is their responsibility to present concerns about the testing process in a timely, respectful manner.

Members of the JCTP Working Group on Test Taker Rights and Responsibilities:

- Kurt F. Geisinger, PhD (Co-Chair); William Schafer, EdD (Co-Chair); Gwyneth Boodoo, PhD; Ruth Ekstrom, EdD; Tom

Fitzgibbon, PhD; John Fremer, PhD; Joanne Lenke, PhD; Sharon Goldsmith, PhD; Kevin Moreland, PhD; Julie Noble, PhD; James Sampson Jr., PhD; Douglas Smith, PhD; Nicholas Vacc, EdD; Janet Wall, EdD.
Staff liaisons: Heather Fox, PhD, and Lara Frumkin, PhD

APPENDIX M

APA Statement on Services by Telephone, Teleconferencing, and Internet

A STATEMENT BY THE ETHICS COMMITTEE OF THE AMERICAN PSYCHOLOGICAL ASSOCIATION

The American Psychological Association's Ethics Committee issued the following statement on November 5, 1997, based on its 1995 statement on the same topic.

The Ethics Committee can only address the relevance of and enforce the "Ethical Principles of Psychologists and Code of Conduct" and cannot say whether there may be other APA Guidelines that might provide guidance. The Ethics Code is not specific with regard to telephone therapy or teleconferencing or any electronically provided services as such and has no rules prohibiting such services. Complaints regarding such matters would be addressed on a case by case basis.

Delivery of services by such media as telephone, teleconferencing and internet is a rapidly evolving area. This will be the subject of APA task forces and will be considered in future revision of the Ethics Code. Until such time as a more definitive judgment is available, the Ethics Committee recommends that psychologists follow Standard 1.04c, Boundaries of Competence, which indicates that "In those emerging areas in which generally recognized standards for preparatory training do not yet exist, psychologists nevertheless take reasonable steps to ensure the competence of their work and to protect patients, clients, students, research participants, and others from harm." Other relevant standards include Assessment (Standards 2.01–2.10), Therapy (4.01–4.09, especially 4.01 Structuring the Relationship and 4.02 Informed Consent to Therapy), and Confidentiality (5.01–5.11). Within the General Standards section, standards with particular relevance are 1.03, Professional and Scientific Relationship; 1.04 (a, b, and c), Boundaries of Competence; 1.06, Basis for Scientific and Professional Judgments; 1.07a, Describing the Nature and Results of Psychological Services; 1.14, Avoiding Harm; and 1.25, Fees and Financial Arrangements. Standards under Advertising, particularly 3.01–3.03 are also relevant.

Psychologists considering such services must review the characteristics of the services, the service delivery method, and the provisions for confidentiality. Psychologists must then consider the relevant ethical standards and other requirements, such as licensure board rules.

APPENDIX N

Specialty Guidelines for Forensic Psychologists[1]

AMERICAN BOARD OF FORENSIC PSYCHOLOGY
COMMITTEE ON ETHICAL GUIDELINES FOR
FORENSIC PSYCHOLOGISTS[2]

The *Specialty Guidelines for Forensic Psychologists*, while informed by the *Ethical Principles of Psychologists* (APA, 1990) and meant to be consistent with them, are designed to provide more specific guidance to forensic psychologists in monitoring their professional conduct when acting in assistance to courts, parties to legal proceedings, correctional and forensic mental health facilities, and legislative agencies. The primary goal of the Guidelines is to improve the quality of forensic psychological services offered to individual clients and the legal system and thereby to enhance forensic psychology as a discipline and profession. The *Specialty Guidelines for Forensic Psychologists* represent a joint statement of the American Psychology-Law Society and Division 41 of the American Psychological Association and are endorsed by the American Academy of Forensic Psychology. The *Guidelines* do not represent an official statement of the American Psychological Association.

From "The Specialty Guidelines for Forensic Psychologists," by the Committee on Ethical Guidelines for Forensic Psychologists, 1991, *Law and Human Behavior*, 15, pp. 655–665. Copyright 1991 by Springer. Reprinted with permission. Retrieved September 24, 2004 from American Academy of Forensic Psychology Web site: http://www.abfp.com/careers.asp

1. The *Specialty Guidelines for Forensic Psychologists* were adopted by majority vote of the members of Division 41 and the American Psychology-Law Society. They have also been endorsed by majority vote by the American Academy of Forensic Psychology. The Executive Committee of Division 41 and the American Psychology Law Society formally approved these *Guidelines* on March 9, 1991. The Executive Committee also voted to continue the Committee on Ethical Guidelines in order to disseminate the *Guidelines* and to monitor their implementation and suggestions for revision. Individuals wishing to reprint these *Guidelines* or who have queries about them should contact either Stephen L. Golding, PhD, Department of Psychology, University of Utah, Salt Lake City, UT84 1 J. 2,80 1-58 1-8028 (voice) or 80 1-58 1-584 1 (FAX) or other members of the Committee listed below. Reprint requests should be sent to Cathy Oslzly, Department of Psychology, University of Nebraska-Lincoln, Lincoln, NE 68588-0308.

2. These *Guidelines* were prepared and principally authored by a joint Committee on Ethical Guidelines of Division 41 and the American Academy of Forensic-Psychology (Stephen L. Golding, [Chair], Thomas Grisso, David Shapiro, and Herbert Weissman [Co-chairs]). Other members of the Committee included Robert Fein, Kirk Heiibrun, Judith McKenna, Norman Poythress, and Daniel Schuman. Their hard work and willingness to tackle difficult conceptual and pragmatic issues is gratefully acknowledged. The Committee would also like to acknowledge specifically the assistance and guidance provided by Dort Bigg, Larry Cowan, Eric Harris, Arthur Lemer, Michael Miller, Russell Newman, Melvin Rudov, and Ray Fowler. Many other individuals also contributed by their thoughtful critique and suggestions for improvement of earlier drafts which were widely circulated.

The *Guidelines* provide an aspirational model of desirable professional practice by psychologists, within any subdiscipline of psychology (e.g., clinical, developmental, social, experimental), when they are engaged regularly as experts and represent themselves as such, in an activity primarily intended to provide professional psychological expertise to the judicial system. This would include, for example, clinical forensic examiners; psychologists employed by correctional or forensic mental health systems; researchers who offer direct testimony about the relevance of scientific data to a psycholegal issue; trial behavior consultants; psychologists engaged in preparation of *amicus* briefs; or psychologists, appearing as forensic experts, who consult with, or testify before, judicial, legislative, or administrative agencies acting in an adjudicative capacity. Individuals who provide only occasional service to the legal system and who do so without representing themselves as *forensic experts* may find these *Guidelines* helpful, particularly in conjunction with consultation with colleagues who are forensic experts.

While the *Guidelines* are concerned with a model of desirable professional practice, to the extent that they may be construed as being applicable to the advertisement of services or the solicitation of clients, they are intended to prevent false or deceptive advertisement or solicitation, and should be construed in a manner consistent with that intent.

I. PURPOSE AND SCOPE

A. Purpose

1. While the professional standards for the ethical practice of psychology, as a general discipline, are addressed in the American Psychological Association's *Ethical Principles of Psychologists*, these ethical principles do not relate, in sufficient detail, to current aspirations of desirable professional conduct for forensic psychologists. By design, none of the *Guidelines* contradicts any of the *Ethical Principles of Psychologists*; rather, they amplify those *Principles* in the context of the practice of forensic psychology, as herein defined.

2. The *Guidelines* have been designed to be national in scope and are intended to conform with state and Federal law. In situations where the forensic psychologist believes that the requirements of law are in conflict with the *Guidelines*, attempts to resolve the conflict should be made in accordance with the procedures set forth in these *Guidelines* [IV(G)] and in the *Ethical Principles of Psychologists*.

B. Scope

1. The *Guidelines* specify the nature of desirable professional practice by forensic psychologists, within any

subdiscipline of psychology (e.g., clinical, developmental, social, experimental), when engaged regularly as forensic psychologists.

    a. "Psychologist" means any individual whose professional activities are defined by the American Psychological Association or by regulation of title by state registration or licensure, as the practice of psychology.

    b. "Forensic psychology" means all forms of professional psychological conduct when acting, with definable foreknowledge, as a psychological expert on explicitly psycholegal issues, in direct assistance to courts, parties to legal proceedings, correctional and forensic mental health facilities, and administrative, judicial, and legislative agencies acting in an adjudicative capacity.

    c. "Forensic psychologist" means psychologists who regularly engage in the practice of forensic psychology as defined in I(B)(1)(b).

2. The *Guidelines* do not apply to a psychologist who is asked to provide professional psychological serpvices when the psychologist was not informed at the time of delivery of the services that they were to be used as forensic psychological services as defined above. The *Guidelines* may be helpful, however, in preparing the psychologist for the experience of communicating psychological data in a forensic context.

3. Psychologists who are not forensic psychologists as defined in I(B)(1)(c), but occasionally provide limited forensic psychological services, may find the *Guidelines* useful in the preparation and presentation of their professional services.

C. Related Standards

1. Forensic psychologists also conduct their professional activites in accord with the *Ethical Principles of Psychologists* and the various other statements of the American Psychological Association that may apply to particular subdisciplines or areas of practice that are relevant to their professional activities.

2. The standards of practice and ethical guidelines of other relevant "expert professional organizations" contain useful guidance and should be consulted even though the present *Guidelines* take precedence for forensic psychologists.

II. RESPONSIBILITY

A. Forensic psychologists have an obligation to provide services in a manner consistent with the highest standards of their profession. They are responsible for their own conduct and the conduct of those individuals under their direct supervision.

B. Forensic psychologists make a reasonable effort to ensure that their services and the products of their services are used in a forthright and responsible manner.

III. COMPETENCE

A. Forensic psychologists provide services only in areas of psychology in which they have specialized knowledge, skill, experience, and education.

B. Forensic psychologists have an obligation to present to the court, regarding the specific matters to which they will testify, the boundaries of their competence, the factual bases (knowledge, skill, experience, training, and education) for their qualification as an expert, and the relevance of those factual bases to their qualification as an expert on the specific matters at issue.

C. Forensic psychologists are responsible for a fundamental and reasonable level of knowledge and understanding of the legal and professional standards that govern their participation as experts in legal proceedings.

D. Forensic psychologists have an obligation to understand the civil rights of parties in legal proceedings in which they participate, and manage their professional conduct in a manner that does not diminish or threaten those rights.

E. Forensic psychologists recognize that their own personal values, moral beliefs, or personal and professional relationships with parties to a legal proceeding may interfere with their ability to practice competently. Under such circumstances, forensic psychologists are obligated to decline participation or to limit their assistance in a manner consistent with professional obligations.

IV. RELATIONSHIPS

A. During initial consultation with the legal representative of the party seeking services, forensic psychologists have an obligation to inform the party of factors that might reasonably affect the decision to contract with the forensic psychologist. These factors include, but are not limited to

1. the fee structure for anticipated professional services;
2. prior and current personal or professional activities, obligations, and relationships that might produce a conflict of interests;
3. their areas of competence and the limits of their competence; and
4. the known scientific bases and limitations of the methods and procedures that they employ and their qualifications to employ such methods and procedures.

B. Forensic psychologists do not provide professional services to parties to a legal proceeding on the basis of "contingent fees," when those services involve the offering of expert testimony to a court or administrative body, or when they call upon the psychologist to make affirmations or representations intended to be relied upon by third parties.

C. Forensic psychologists who derive a substantial portion of their income from fee-for-service arrangements should offer some portion of their professional services on a pro bono or reduced fee basis where the public interest or the welfare of clients may be inhibited by insufficient financial resources.

D. Forensic psychologists recognize potential conflicts of interest in dual relationships with parties to a legal proceeding, and they seek to minimize their effects.
   1. Forensic psychologists avoid providing professional services to parties in a legal proceeding with whom they have personal or professional relationships that are inconsistent with the anticipated relationship.
   2. When it is necessary to provide both evaluation and treatment services to a party in a legal proceeding (as may be the case in small forensic hospital settings or small communities), the forensic psychologist takes reasonable steps to minimize the potential negative effects of these circumstances on the rights of the party, confidentiality, and the process of treatment and evaluation.

E. Forensic psychologists have an obligation to ensure that prospective clients are informed of their legal rights with respect to the anticipated forensic service, of the purposes of any evaluation, of the nature of procedures to be employed, of the intended uses of any product of their services, and of the party who has employed the forensic psychologist.

1. Unless court ordered, forensic psychologists obtain the informed consent of the client or party, or their legal representative, before proceeding with such evaluations and procedures. If the client appears unwilling to proceed after receiving a thorough notification of the purposes, methods, and intended uses of the forensic evaluation, the evaluation should be postponed and the psychologist should take steps to place the client in contact with his/her attorney for the purpose of legal advice on the issue of participation.

2. In situations where the client or party may not have the capacity to provide informed consent to services or the evaluation is pursuant to court order, the forensic psychologist provides reasonable notice to the client's legal representative of the nature of the anticipated forensic service before proceeding. If the client's legal representative objects to the evaluation, the forensic psychologist notifies the court issuing the order and responds as directed.

3. After a psychologist has advised the subject of a clinical forensic evaluation of the intended uses of the evaluation and its work product, the psychologist may not use the evaluation work product for other purposes without explicit waiver to do so by the client or the client's legal representative.

F. When forensic psychologists engage in research or scholarly activities that are compensated financially by a client or party to a legal proceeding, or when the psychologist provides those services on a pro *bono* basis, the psychologist clarifies any anticipated further use of such research or scholarly product, discloses the psychologist's role in the resulting research or scholarly products, and obtains whatever consent or agreement is required by law or professional standards.

G. When conflicts arise between the forensic psychologist's professional standards and the requirements of legal standards, a particular court, or a directive by an officer of the court or legal authorities, the forensic psychologist has an obligation to make those legal authorities aware of the source of the conflict and to take reasonable steps to resolve it. Such steps may include, but are not limited to, obtaining the consultation of fellow forensic professionals, obtaining the advice of independent counsel, and conferring directly with the legal representatives involved.

V. CONFIDENTIALITY AND PRIVILEGE
A. Forensic psychologists have an obligation to be aware of the legal standards that may affect or limit the confidentiality or privilege that may attach to their services or their products, and they conduct their professional activities in a manner that respects those known rights and privileges.
    1. Forensic psychologists establish and maintain a system of record keeping and professional communication that safeguards a client's privilege.
    2. Forensic psychologists maintain active control over records and information. They only release information pursuant to statutory requirements, court order, or the consent of the client.
B. Forensic psychologists inform their clients of the limitations to the confidentiality of their services and their products (see also Guideline IV E) by providing them with an understandable statement of their rights, privileges, and the limitations of confidentiality.
C. In situations where the right of the client or party to cofidentiality is limited, the forensic psychologist makes every effort to maintain confidentiality with regard to any information that does not bear directly upon the legal purpose of the evaluation.
D. Forensic psychologists provide clients or their authorized legal representatives with access to the information in their records and a meaningful explanation of that information, consistent with existing Federal and state statutes, the *Ethical Principles of Psychologists*, the *Standards for Educational and Psychological Testing*, and institutional rules and regulations.

VI. METHODS AND PROCEDURES
A. Because of their special status as persons qualified as experts to the court, forensic psychologists have an obligation to maintain current knowledge of scientific, professional and legal developments within their area of claimed competence. They are obligated also to use that knowledge, consistent with accepted clinical and scientific standards, in selecting data collection methods and

procedures for an evaluation, treatment, consultation or scholarly/empirical investigation.

B. Forensic psychologists have an obligation to document and be prepared to make available, subject to court order or the rules of evidence, all data that form the basis for their evidence or services. The standard to be applied to such documentation or recording *anticipates* that the detail and quality of such documentation will be subject to reasonable judicial scrutiny; this standard is higher than the normative standard for general clinical practice. When forensic psychologists conduct an examination or engage in the treatment of a party to a legal proceeding, with foreknowledge that their professional services will be used in an adjudicative forum, they incur a special responsibility to provide the best documentation possible under the circumstances.

1. Documentation of the data upon which one's evidence is based is subject to the normal rules of discovery, disclosure, confidentiality, and privilege that operate in the jurisdiction in which the data were obtained. Forensic psychologists have an obligation to be aware of those rules and to regulate their conduct in accordance with them.

2. The duties and obligations of forensic psychologists with respect to documentation of data that form the basis for their evidence apply from the moment they know or have a reasonable basis for knowing that their data and evidence derived from it are likely to enter into legally relevant decisions.

C. In providing forensic psychological services, forensic psychologists take special care to avoid undue influence upon their methods, procedures, and products, such as might emanate from the party to a legal proceeding by financial compensation or other gains. As an expert conducting an evaluation, treatment, consultation, or scholarly/empirical investigation, the forensic psychologist maintains professional integrity by examining the issue at hand from all reasonable perspectives, actively seeking information that will differentially test plausible rival hypotheses.

D. Forensic psychologists do not provide professional forensic services to a defendant or to any party in, or in contemplation of, a legal proceeding prior to that individual's representation by counsel, except for persons judicially determined, where appropriate, to be handling their representation *pro se*. When the forensic services are pursuant to court order and the client is not represented by counsel, the forensic psychologist makes reasonable efforts to inform the court prior to providing the services.

1. A forensic psychologist may provide emergency mental health services to a pretrial defendant prior to court order or the appointment of counsel where there are reasonable grounds to believe that such emergency services are needed for the protection and improvement of the defendant's mental health and where failure to provide such mental health services would constitute a substantial risk of imminent harm to the defendant or to others. In providing such services the forensic psychologist nevertheless seeks to inform the defendant's counsel in a manner consistent with the requirements of the emergency situation.

2. Forensic psychologists who provide such emergency mental health services should attempt to avoid providing further professional forensic services to that defendant unless that relationship is reasonably unavoidable [see IV(D)(2)].

E. When forensic psychologists seek data from third parties, prior records, or other sources, they do so only with the prior approval of the relevant legal party or as a consequence of an order of a court to conduct the forensic evaluation.

F. Forensic psychologists are aware that hearsay exceptions and other rules governing expert testimony place a special ethical burden upon them. When hearsay or otherwise inadmissible evidence forms the basis of their opinion, evidence, or professional product, they seek to minimize sole reliance upon such evidence. Where circumstances reasonably permit, forensic psychologists seek to obtain independent and personal verification of data relied upon as part of their professional services to the court or to a party to a legal proceeding.

1. While many forms of data used by forensic psychologists are hearsay, forensic psychologists attempt to corroborate critical data that form the basis for their professional product. When using hearsay data that have not been corroborated, but are nevertheless utilized, forensic psychologists have an affirmative

responsibility to acknowledge the uncorroborated status of those data and the reasons for relying upon such data.

2. With respect to evidence of any type, forensic psychologists avoid offering information from their investigations or evaluations that does not bear directly upon the legal purpose of their professional services and that is not critical as support for their product, evidence or testimony, except where such disclosure is required by law.

3. When a forensic psychologist relies upon data or information gathered by others, the origins of those data are clarified in any professional product. In addition, the forensic psychologist bears a special responsibility to ensure that such data, if relied upon, were gathered in a manner standard for the profession.

G. Unless otherwise stipulated by the parties, forensic psychologists are aware that no statements made by a defendant, in the course of any (forensic) examination, no testimony by the expert based upon such statements, nor any other fruits of the statements can be admitted into evidence against the defendant in any criminal proceeding, except on an issue respecting mental condition on which the defendant has introduced testimony. Forensic psychologists have an affirmative duty to ensure that their written products and oral testimony conform to this Federal Rule of Procedure (12.2[c]), or its state equivalent.

1. Because forensic psychologists are often not in a position to know what evidence, documentation, or element of a written product may be or may lend to a "fruit of the statement," they exercise extreme caution in preparing reports or offering testimony prior to the defendant's assertion of a mental state claim or the defendant's introduction of testimony regarding a mental condition. Consistent with the reporting requirements of state or federal law, forensic psychologists avoid including statements from the defendant relating to the time period of the alleged offense.

2. Once a defendant has proceeded to the trial stage, and all pretrial mental health issues such as competency have been resolved, forensic psychologists may include in their reports or testimony any statements made by the defendant that are directly relevant to supporting their expert evidence, providing that the

defendant has "introduced" mental state evidence or testimony within the meaning of Federal Rule of Procedure 12.2(c), or its state equivalent.

H. Forensic psychologists avoid giving written or oral evidence about the psychological characteristics of particular individuals when they have not had an opportunity to conduct an examination of the individual adequate to the scope of the statements, opinions, or conclusions to be issued. Forensic psychologists make every reasonable effort to conduct such examinations. When it is not possible or feasible to do so, they make clear the impact of such limitations on the reliability and validity of their professional products, evidence, or testimony.

VII. PUBLIC AND PROFESSIONAL COMMUNICATIONS

A. Forensic psychologists make reasonable efforts to ensure that the products of their services, as well as their own public statements and professional testimony, are communicated in ways that will promote understanding and avoid deception, given the particular characteristics, roles, and abilities of various recipients of the communications.

1. Forensic psychologists take reasonable steps to correct misuse or misrepresentation of their professional products, evidence, and testimony.

2. Forensic psychologists provide information about professional work to clients in a manner consistent with professional and legal standards for the disclosure of test results, interpretations of data, and the factual bases for conclusions. A full explanation of the results of tests and the bases for conclusions should be given in language that the client can understand.

   a. When disclosing information about a client to third parties who are not qualified to interpret test results and data, the forensic psychologist complies with Principle 16 of the *Standards for Educational and Psychological Testing*. When required to disclose results to a nonpsychologist, every attempt is made to ensure that test security is maintained and access to information is restricted to individuals with a legitimate and professional interest in the data. Other qualified mental health professionals who make a request for information pursuant to a lawful order are, by definition, "individuals with a legitimate and professional interest."

b. In providing records and raw data, the forensic psychologist takes reasonable steps to ensure that the receiving party is informed that raw scores must be interpreted by a qualified professional in order to provide reliable and valid information.

B. Forensic psychologists realize that their public role as "expert to the court" or as "expert representing the profession" confers upon them a special responsibility for fairness and accuracy in their public statements. When evaluating or commenting upon the professional work product or qualifications of another expert or party to a legal proceeding, forensic psychologists represent their professional disagreements with reference to a fair and accurate evaluation of the data, theories, standards, and opinions of the other expert or party.

C. Ordinarily, forensic psychologists avoid making detailed public (out-of-court) statements about particular legal proceedings in which they have been involved. When there is a strong justification to do so, such public statements are designed to assure accurate representation of their role or their evidence, not to advocate the positions of parties in the legal proceeding. Forensic psychologists address particular legal proceedings in publications or communications only to the extent that the information relied upon is part of a public record, or consent for that use has been properly obtained from the party holding any privilege.

D. When testifying, forensic psychologists have an obligation to all parties to a legal proceeding to present their findings, conclusions, evidence, or other professional products in a fair manner. This principle does not preclude forceful representation of the data and reasoning upon which a conclusion or professional product is based. It does, however, preclude an attempt, whether active or passive, to engage in partisan distortion or misrepresentation. Forensic psychologists do not, by either commission or omission, participate in a misrepresentation of their evidence, nor do they participate in partisan attempts to avoid, deny, or subvert the presentation of evidence contrary to their own position.

E. Forensic psychologists, by virtue of their competence and rules of discovery, actively disclose all sources of information obtained in the course of their professional services; they actively disclose which information from which source was used in formulating a particular written product or oral testimony.

F. Forensic psychologists are aware that their essential role as expert to the court is to assist the trier of fact to understand the evidence or to determine a fact in issue. In offering expert evidence, they are aware that their own professional observations, inferences, and conclusions must be distinguished from legal facts, opinions, and conclusions. Forensic psychologists are prepared to explain the relationship between their expert testimony and the legal issues and facts of an instant case.

APPENDIX O

APA Strategies for Private Practitioners Coping With Subpoenas or Compelled Testimony for Client Records or Test Data

AMERICAN PSYCHOLOGICAL ASSOCIATION
COMMITTEE ON LEGAL ISSUES

ABSTRACT

Psychologists have numerous ethical, professional, and legal obligations regarding the release of client records, test data, and other information in the legal context. The demands of the legal system sometimes conflict with psychologists' ethical obligations to maintain confidentiality of client records, to protect the integrity and security of test materials, and to avoid misuse of assessment techniques and data. This article identifies legal issues that may arise when private practitioners are faced with subpoenas or compelled court testimony for client records or test data and suggests strategies that might be considered in the event such a subpoena or demand is received.

In response to a large number of inquiries by psychologists faced with subpoenas or compelled court testimony concerning client records or test data,

Correspondence concerning this article should be addressed to COLI Staff Liaison, Executive Office, Sixth Floor, American Psychological Association, 750 First Street, NE, Washington, DC 20002-4242. From "Strategies for Private Practitioners Coping With Subpoenas or Compelled Testimony for Client Records or Test Data," by the American Psychological Association, Committee on Legal Issues, 1996, *Professional Psychology: Research and Practice, 27*, pp. 245–251. Copyright 1996 by the American Psychological Association.

Editor's Note. This document does not provide legal advice, nor is it intended to be or to substitute for the advice of an attorney. Relevant law varies substantially from state to state and context to context. Psychologists receiving a subpoena or other legal process that requires or is likely to require revelation of client records or test data, manuals, protocols, or other test information are encouraged to consult legal counsel, who can review the pertinent law and facts and provide appropriate legal assistance.

This document is the product of over 3 years of American Psychological Association (APA) volunteer and staff effort. The Committee on Legal Issues (COLI) and the Office of General Counsel wish to thank current and former members of COLI and central office staff for their efforts in conceiving, drafting, and producing this document. In addition, COLI and the Office of General Counsel wish to extend special appreciation to the APA's Committee on Professional Practice Standards, the Board of Professional Affairs, the Committee for the Advancement of Professional Practice, and the Ethics Committee for their valuable input and encouragement. Many other APA governance groups and individuals contributed by their thoughtful critique and suggestions for improvement of earlier drafts, which were widely circulated.

Received Date: August 2, 1995; Accepted Date: January 19, 1996.

manuals, protocols, and other test information, the American Psychological Association's Committee on Legal Issues prepared this article. It identifies legal issues that may arise from such subpoenas and similar legal demands, and it suggests strategies that might be considered in the event such a subpoena or demand is received. This document is not intended to establish any standards of care or conduct for practitioners; rather, it addresses the general question, What strategies may be available to psychologists in private practice for responding to subpoenas or compelled court testimony concerning client records, test data, test manuals, test protocols, or other test information?

As a general principle of law, all citizens are required to provide information necessary for deciding issues before a court. From the perspective of the legal system, the more relevant information available to the trier of fact (i.e., judge or jury), the fairer the decision. Statutes, rules of civil and criminal procedure, and rules of evidence have established the procedures for the transmittal of such information. In order to obtain this material, subpoenas (legal commands to appear to provide testimony) or subpoenas duces tecum (legal commands to appear and bring along specific documents) may be issued. Alternatively, the court may issue a court order to provide testimony or produce documents. A subpoena requesting testimony or documents, even if not signed by a judge, requires a timely response, but it may be modified or quashed (i.e., made void or invalid). However, once a court order for testimony or documents is issued and any attempt (made in a timely manner) to have the court vacate or modify its order has been unsuccessful, a psychologist may be held in contempt of court if he or she fails to comply.

The demands of the legal system sometimes conflict with the responsibility of psychologists to maintain the confidentiality of client records. This responsibility arises from tenets of good clinical practice, ethical standards, professional licensing laws, statutes, and other applicable laws. In many contexts, the client material generated in the course of a professional relationship may also fall under an evidentiary privilege, which protects such information from judicial scrutiny. Most state and federal jurisdictions recognize a psychotherapist-patient privilege that allows the client to prevent confidential material conveyed to a psychotherapist from being communicated to others in legal settings. In most jurisdictions, the privilege belongs to the client, not to the therapist. The psychologist has a responsibility to maintain confidentiality and to assert the psychotherapist-patient privilege unless the client has explicitly waived privilege, unless a legally recognized exception to privilege exists, or unless the court orders the psychologist to turn over the client's information. Therapy notes, process notes, client information forms, billing records, and other such information usually may be turned over to the court with an appropriate release by the client or with a court order. Psychological test material presents a more complicated situation because inappropriate disclosure may seriously impair the security and threaten the validity of the test and its value as a measurement tool.

Psychologists have numerous ethical, professional, and legal obligations that touch on the release of client records, test data, and other information in the legal context. Many such obligations may favor disclosure, including, in particular, the general obligation of all citizens to give truthful and complete testimony in courts of law when subpoenaed to do so. But there are often conflicting duties and principles that favor withholding such information. These may include obligations to (a) clients or other individuals who are administered psychological tests (e.g., privileged or confidential communications that may include client responses to test items); (b) the public (e.g., to avoid public dissemination of test items, questions, protocols, or other test information that could adversely affect the integrity and continued validity of tests); (c) test publishers (e.g., contractual obligations between the psychologist and test publishers not to disclose test information; obligations under the copyright laws); and (d) other third parties (e.g., employers). Such obligations may, at times, conflict with one another. Psychologists must identify and seek to reconcile their obligations. For more on these obligations, see the American Psychological Association's (APA's) "Ethical Principles of Psychologists and Code of Conduct" (APA, 1992/2002), hereinafter referred to as the APA Ethics Code.[a]

There are specific settings (e.g., educational, institutional, employment) in which the legal or ethical obligations of psychologists as they relate to disclosure of client records or test information present special problems. This document does not purport to address disclosure issues in these special contexts, nor does it attempt to resolve dilemmas faced by psychologists in reconciling legal and ethical obligations.

STRATEGIES FOR DEALING WITH SUBPOENAS

Determine Whether the Request for Information Carries the Force of Law

It must first be determined whether a psychologist has, in fact, received a legally valid demand for disclosure of sensitive test data and client records. If a demand is not legally enforceable for any reason, then the psychologist has no legal obligation to comply with it and may have no legal obligation even to respond. Even a demand that claims to be legally enforceable may not be. For example, the court issuing the subpoena may not have jurisdiction over the psychologist or his or her records (e.g., a subpoena issued in one state may not be legally binding on a psychologist residing and working in a different

---

a. Readers should note that the 2002 revision of the APA Ethics Code can be found in Appendix B of this book.

state). Or, the subpoena may not have been properly served on the psychologist (e.g., some states may require service in person or by certified mail or that a subpoena for such records be accompanied by a special court order). It is advisable that a psychologist consult with an attorney in making such a determination.[1] If the psychologist concludes that the demand is legally valid, then some formal response to the court will be required—either compliance with or opposition to the demand, in whole or in part. A psychologist's obligations in responding to a valid subpoena are not necessarily the same as those under a court order (see section titled File a Motion to Quash the Subpoena or File a Protective Order below). The next step, in most cases, will involve contacting the psychologist's client. However, the psychologist may wish to consider grounds for opposing or limiting production of the demanded information before contacting the client so that the client can more fully understand his or her options (see section titled Possible Grounds for Opposing or Limiting Production of Client Records or Test Data below).

Contact the Client

The client to whom requested records pertain often has a legally protected interest in preserving the confidentiality of the records. If, therefore, a psychologist receives a subpoena or advance notice that he or she may be required to divulge client records or test data, the psychologist should discuss the implications of the demand with the client (or his or her legal guardian). When appropriate, the psychologist may consult with the client's attorney. This discussion will inform the client which information has been demanded, the purpose of the demand, the entities or individuals to whom the information is to be provided, and the possible scope of further disclosure by those entities or individuals. Following such a discussion, a legally competent client or the client's legal guardian may choose to consent in writing to production of the data. Written consent may avoid future conflicts or legal entanglements with the client over the release of confidential tests or other records pertaining to the client. The client's consent may not, however, resolve the potential confidentiality claims of third parties (such as test publishers) and the obligations of psychologists to withhold test data or protocols. For more information, see APA Ethics Code, Ethical Standards Section 5 (APA, 1992/2002)[b], and Standards for Educational and Psychological Testing (1985).

Negotiate With the Requester

If a client does not consent to release of the requested information, the psychologist (often through counsel) may seek to prevent disclosure through

---

b. This Ethical Standard is Section 4 in the newly revised (2002) APA Ethics Code, which is reproduced in Appendix B of this book.

discussions with legal counsel for the requesting party. The psychologist's position in such discussions may be bolstered by legal arguments against disclosure. (Some possible arguments are outlined in the section titled Possible Grounds for Opposing or Limiting Production of Client Records or Test Data below.) Such negotiations may explore whether there are ways to achieve the requesting party's objectives without divulging confidential information, for example, through disclosure of nonconfidential materials or submission of an affidavit by the psychologist disclosing nonconfidential information. Negotiation may also be used as a strategy to avoid compelled testimony in court or by deposition. In short, negotiation can be explored as a possible means of avoiding the wholesale release of confidential test or client information—release that may not be in the best interests of the client, the public, or the profession, and that may not even be relevant to the issues before the court. Such an option could be explored in consultation with the psychologist's attorney or the client's attorney.

Seek Guidance From the Court

If, despite such discussions, the requesting party insists that confidential information or test data be produced, the safest course for the psychologist may be to seek a ruling from the court on whether disclosure is required. The simplest way of proceeding, and perhaps the least costly, may be for the psychologist (or his or her attorney) to write a letter to the court, with a copy to the attorneys for both parties, stating that the psychologist wishes to comply with the law but that he or she is ethically obligated not to produce the confidential records or test data or to testify about them unless compelled to do so by the court or with the consent of the client. In writing such a letter, the psychologist (or his or her lawyer) may request that the court consider the psychologist's obligations to protect the interests of the client, the interests of third parties (e.g., test publishers or others), and the interests of the public in preserving the integrity and continued validity of the tests themselves. This letter may help sensitize the court about the potential adverse effects of dissemination. The letter might also attempt to provide suggestions, such as the following, to the court on ways to minimize the adverse consequences of disclosure if the court is inclined to require production at all:

1. Suggest that, at most, the court direct the psychologist to provide test data only to another appropriately qualified psychologist designated by the court or by the party seeking such information.
2. Suggest that the court limit the use of client records or test data to prevent wide dissemination. For example, the court might order that the information be delivered, be kept under seal, and be used solely for the purposes of the litigation and that all

copies of the data be returned to the psychologist under seal after the litigation is terminated. The order might also provide that the requester may not provide the information to any third parties.

3. Suggest that the court limit the categories of information that must be produced. For example, client records may contain confidential information about a third party, such as a spouse, who may have independent interests in maintaining confidentiality, and such data may be of minimal or no relevance to the issues before the court. The court should limit its production order to exclude such information.

4. Suggest that the court determine for itself, through in camera proceedings (i.e., a nonpublic hearing or a review by the judge in chambers), whether the use of the client records or test data is relevant to the issues before the court or whether it might be insulated from disclosure, in whole or in part, by the therapist-client privilege or another privilege.

File a Motion to Quash the Subpoena or File a Protective Order

If, because of local procedure or other considerations, guidance cannot be sought through the informal means of a letter to the court, it may be necessary to file a motion seeking to be relieved of the obligations imposed by the demand for production of the confidential records. In many jurisdictions, the possible motions include a motion to quash the subpoena, in whole or in part, or a motion for a protective order. Filing such a motion may require the assistance of counsel, representing either the psychologist or the psychologist's client.

Courts are generally more receptive to a motion to quash or a motion for a protective order if it is filed by the client about whom information is sought (who would be defending his or her own interests) rather than by a psychologist who, in essence, would be seeking to protect the rights of the client or other third parties. The psychologist may wish to determine initially whether the client's lawyer is inclined to seek to quash a subpoena or to seek a protective order and, if so, may wish to provide assistance to the client's attorney in this regard. If the client has refused to consent to disclosure of the information, his or her attorney may be willing to take the lead in opposing the subpoena.

A motion to quash is a formal application made to a court or judge for purposes of having a subpoena vacated or declared invalid. Grounds may exist for asserting that the subpoena or request for testimony should be quashed, in whole or in part. For example, the information sought may be protected by the therapist-client privilege and therefore may not be subject to discovery, or it may not be relevant to the issues before the court (see section titled Possible Grounds for Opposing or Limiting Production of Client Records or Test Data below). This strategy may be used alone or in combination with a motion for a protective order.

A motion for a protective order seeks an order or decree from the court that protects against the untoward consequences of disclosing information. A protective order can be tailored to meet the legitimate interests of the client and of third parties such as test publishers and the public. The focus of this strategy first and foremost is to prevent or limit disclosure and the use of sensitive client and test information. The protective order—and the motion—may include any of the elements listed in the preceding section.

PSYCHOLOGISTS' TESTIMONY

If a psychologist is asked to disclose confidential information during questioning at a deposition, he or she may refuse to answer the question only if the information is privileged. If there is a reasonable basis for asserting a privilege, the psychologist may refuse to provide test data or client records until so ordered by the court. A psychologist who refuses to answer questions without a reasonable basis may be penalized by the court, including the obligation to pay the requesting parties' costs and fees in obtaining answers. For these reasons, it is advisable that a psychologist be represented by counsel at the deposition if he or she expects that questions concerning confidential information may be asked. A lawyer may advise the psychologist, on the record, when a question seeks confidential information; such on-the-record advice will help protect the psychologist from the adverse legal consequences of erroneous disclosures or erroneous refusals to disclose.

Similarly, if the request for confidential information arises for the first time during courtroom testimony, the psychologist may assert a privilege and refuse to answer unless directed to do so by the court. The law in this area is somewhat unsettled. Thus, if a psychologist anticipates that confidential materials may be elicited through testimony, it may be advisable for him or her to consult an attorney before testifying.

POSSIBLE GROUNDS FOR OPPOSING OR LIMITING PRODUCTION OF CLIENT RECORDS OR TEST DATA

The following theories may or may not be available under the facts of a particular case and jurisdiction for resisting a demand to produce confidential information, records, or test data (see Figure 1):

1. The court does not have jurisdiction over the psychologist, the client records, or the test data, or the psychologist did not

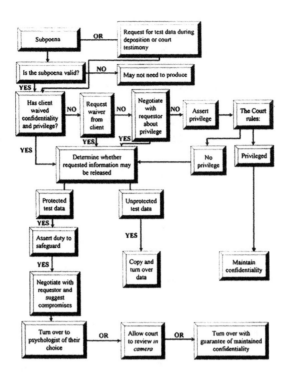

Figure 1. Disclosure Issues Diagram.

receive a legally sufficient demand (e.g., improper service) for production of records or test data testimony.

2. The psychologist does not have custody or control of the records or test data that are sought, because, for example, they belong not to the psychologist but to his or her employer.

3. The therapist-client privilege insulates the records or test data from disclosure. The rationale for the privilege, recognized in many states, is that the openness necessary for effective therapy requires that clients have an expectation that all records of therapy, contents of therapeutic disclosures, and test data will remain confidential. Disclosure would be a serious invasion of the client's privacy. The psychologist is under an ethical obligation to protect the client's reasonable expectations of confidentiality. See APA Ethics Code, Ethical Standards, Section 5 (APA, 1992/2002)[c].

---

c. This Ethical Standard is Section 4 in the newly revised (2002) APA Ethics Code, which is reproduced in Appendix B of this book.

4. The information sought is not relevant to the issues before the court, or the scope of the demand for information is over-broad in reaching information not relevant to the issues before the court, including irrelevant information pertaining to third parties such as a spouse.

5. Public dissemination of test information such as manuals, protocols, and so forth may harm the public interest because it may affect responses of future test populations. This effect could result in the loss of valuable assessment tools to the detriment of both the public and the profession of psychology.

6. Test publishers have an interest in the protection of test information, and the psychologist may have a contractual or other legal obligation (e.g., copyright laws) not to disclose such information. Such contractual claims, coupled with concerns about test data devolving into the public domain, may justify issuance of a protective order against dissemination of a test instrument or protocols (see Addendum).

7. Psychologists have an ethical obligation to protect the integrity and security of test information and data and to avoid misuse of assessment techniques and data. Psychologists are also ethically obligated to take reasonable steps to prevent others from misusing such information. In particular, psychologists are ethically obligated to refrain from releasing raw test results or raw data to persons other than the client, as appropriate, who are not qualified to use such information. See APA Ethics Code, Ethical Standards, Section 2 (APA, 1992/2002)[d]. This prohibition has the force of law in many jurisdictions where state boards of psychology or boards with similar responsibilities have either adopted the APA Ethics Code or a code of ethics with similar provisions.

8. Refer to ethical and legal obligations of psychologists as provided for under ethics codes; professional standards; state, federal, or local laws; or regulatory agencies.

ADDENDUM

Test publishers consistently incorporate provisions into test purchase or lease (hereinafter purchase) contracts to protect test security and integrity

---

d. This Ethical Standard is Standard 9 in the newly revised (2002) APA Ethics Code, which is reproduced in Appendix B of this book.

and to ensure competence in their use. The following describe the types of use restrictions that are often addressed in these contracts.

Competency of Purchaser

Publishers often require documentation, as a condition of purchase or lease, that test purchasers or licensees (hereinafter purchasers) are appropriately trained and qualified to use the tests. Some publishers will only sell certain categories of tests to purchasers on the basis of their degree of documented skill and knowledge. Skill and knowledge is assessed in the form of applications that purchasers must submit to the publisher with the purchase order. In these applications, purchasers list their degrees and training with tests and represent to the publisher that they are familiar with and will comply with the appropriate professional standards governing test use, administration and security (e.g., Standards for Educational and Psychological Testing, 1985). Many such publisher contracts, applications, and marketing literature indicate that the publisher retains sole discretion to deny sales or licenses of test products on the basis of this information or to withdraw approval to use them if the purchaser violates commonly acceptable practices or the conditions of the purchase contract.

Copyright Statement

Virtually all test publisher purchase contracts contain clear copyright statements indicating that all rights in and to the tests, protocols, manuals, and the like are reserved by the publisher. Such materials are considered trade secrets of and proprietary to the publisher. The copyright statements thus contain strong restrictions on reproduction, distribution, database storage, and other specified forms of use without the publisher's prior written approval.

Test Security

Virtually all publisher contracts contain stringent provisions governing test security. In addition to those provisions noted above, examples include the following:

1. Purchasers are required to hold in strict confidence all information and know-how, technical or otherwise, that is related to the test products and to take effective measures to ensure that their employees do likewise.
2. Purchasers must agree to protect the security of test products (e.g., tests, scoring keys, protocols) by retaining them in

locked files or storage cabinets accessible only to authorized personnel.

3. Neither purchasers nor their employees may divulge, furnish, use for the benefit of any third party, or make accessible the test products in any form, in whole or in part, without the publisher's prior written approval.

4. Purchasers and their employees may only divulge test materials and scores to those who are qualified to interpret and use them properly.

5. Purchasers may not assign, sublicense, or convey any rights or privileges granted to them under the contract.

6. Purchasers may not modify or alter the physical or electronic characteristics of the test products or attempt to "reverse engineer" same.

7. Some publishers even tailor contracts to govern security of test products provided to university or college bookstores for sale or for graduate student research purposes, and these publishers retain the discretion to withhold sales or withdraw permission to sell or use the test product if the publisher deems the security procedures inadequate.

Seeking Publisher Permissions in Subpoena or Mandated Disclosure Context

As noted above, many contracts require that psychologists and other test purchasers seek permission from the test publisher before providing test materials to any third parties. Psychologists thus have a contractual obligation to seek such permission.

Even if test purchase or leasing provisions do not explicitly require permission from the publisher before providing test materials sought through subpoena or other legal process, it is often a good strategy to consult with the test publisher and to request a letter outlining the publisher's position on the release of test information. Such a letter could be of assistance to the psychologist in advising the court or attorney who is seeking the test information of the need to protect test materials. Such letters often specify a proposed process for protecting test information, such as the following: (a) a psychologist should not turn over test materials to anyone other than a qualified psychologist (e.g., material could be turned over to a psychologist designated by the party seeking test information); (b) if the court, nonetheless, requires a psychologist to provide test materials to nonpsychologists, the publishers often request that the psychologist seek a protective order from the court that prohibits copying or disseminating the material, requires return of the test material to the psychologist once the court proceedings are concluded, and prohibits the material from becoming part of the public record of the case.

NOTES

1. Fees for consultation with or representation by an attorney may be substantial. If consultation with an attorney becomes necessary to protect the interests and privileges of the client, then the practitioner may wish to clarify with his or her client who will be responsible for such legal fees.

2. A psychologist's obligation to maintain confidentiality may not apply under certain legally recognized exceptions to the therapist-patient privilege, including, but not limited to, situations such as the following: when child abuse is involved; cases involving involuntary commitment evaluations; court-ordered evaluations; when clients raise their emotional condition as a basis for a legal claim or defense; or when the client presents an imminent danger to himself or herself or the community. Exceptions may depend on jurisdiction and the facts of a particular situation. Thus, the most prudent course of action may be for the psychologist to consult with an attorney.

REFERENCES

American Psychological Association. (1992). Ethical principles of psychologists and code of conduct. *American Psychologist, 47,* 1597–1611.

Standards for educational and psychological testing. (1985). Washington, DC: American Psychological Association.

INDEX

Tenants. *See* other tenants
Therapists
    anxiety, 15
    disrespecting work, 14
    energy, 14
    errors, 14
    interest, loss of, 15
    mistakes, 70, 90
Therapy, 147–149
Training, 140–141
    self-care strategies, 18
Transportation access, offices, 25, 31
Treatment plan, 52, 65, 95
Trojans. *See* malicious code

United States licensing boards, 116–122

Vacations, policies and procedures, 54–55
Validity, complaints, 89–90
Values, 3–4
Ventilation, offices, 27
Violation. *See* ethical violation
Viruses. *See* malicious code

Waiting room, 6, 23, 25–27, 30, 68, 72
Weapon, therapist obtaining, 20
Web sites
    accessibility, offices, 26
    clients finding, 73
    encryption, 79
    firewalls, 79
    practice management, 82
    viruses, 79–80
Weekday use offices, 26
What if situations, attorneys, 37
Wheelchair, accessibility, 26, 31, 102
White noise. *See* soundproofing
Worms. *See* malicious code
Work room, 23
Workload, fatigue and self-care
    strategies, 17
Written policies and procedures, 39,
    47–48

You too fallacy, 105

Zoning home offices, 30

ABOUT THE AUTHORS

Kenneth S. Pope, PhD, ABPP, received graduate degrees from Harvard and Yale and has been in independent practice as a licensed psychologist since the mid-1980s. A diplomate in clinical psychology, he has authored or coauthored over 100 articles and chapters in peer-reviewed scientific and professional journals and books. He is a charter fellow of the American Psychological Society (APS) and was elected fellow of American Psychological Association (APA) Divisions 1, 2, 12, 29, 35, 41, 42, 44, and 51.

Based on his research in the 1970s on therapist–patient sex, he cofounded the UCLA Post-Therapy Support Program, the first center offering services, conducting research, and providing university-based training for graduate students and therapists seeking to work with people who had been sexually exploited by therapists. Dr. Pope taught courses in psychological and neuropsychological assessment, abnormal psychology, and professional standards of care at the University of California, Los Angeles, where he served as a psychotherapy supervisor. He also chaired the Ethics Committees of the APA and the American Board of Professional Psychology.

In the early 1980s, Dr. Pope was the director of clinical programs for a consortium of community mental health centers and hospitals. He worked with the community and the consortium's staff to meet community needs in accordance with community cultures and ecology. By the end of his work with the consortium, their programs included homebound services (in which therapists and others went to the homes of people unable to travel), legal services for the indigent and people with mental disabilities, Manos de Esperanza (serving Spanish-speaking clients), a 24-hour crisis service, peer-support services, and group homes so that those who were mentally disabled could live independently.

His publications include 10 articles in the *American Psychologist* and 10 books. The books include *Ethics in Psychotherapy and Counseling* (2nd ed.), with Melba Vasquez; *The MMPI, MMPI-2 and MMPI-A in Court: A Practical Guide for Expert Witnesses and Attorneys* (2nd ed.), with Jim Butcher and Joyce Seelen; *Sexual Feelings in Psychotherapy: Explorations for Therapists and Therapists-in-Training*, with Janet Sonne and Jean Holroyd (APA, 1993); *Sexual Involvement With Therapists: Patient Assessment, Subsequent Therapy, Forensics* (APA, 1994); *On Love and Loving: Psychological Perspectives on the Nature and Experience of Romantic Love*; and *The Stream of Consciousness: Scientific Investigations into the Flow of Human Experience*, with Jerome Singer.

Dr. Pope received the Belle Mayer Bromberg Award for Literature; the Frances Mosseker Award for Fiction; the APA Division 42 Presidential Citation "In Recognition of his Voluntary Contributions, his Generosity of Time, the Sharing of his Caring Spirit [and] his Personal Resources;" the APA Division 44 Citation of Appreciation; the APA Division 12 Award for Distinguished Professional Contributions to Clinical Psychology; and the APA Award for Distinguished Contributions to Public Service.

Melba J. T. Vasquez, PhD, ABPP, has been in full-time independent practice in Austin, Texas, since 1991. She holds a diplomate in counseling psychology from the American Board of Professional Psychology. She is a fellow of APA Divisions 1, 9, 17, 35, 42, 45, and 49 and a member of Divisions 31 and 44.

Dr. Vasquez chaired the APA Board of Professional Affairs and the APA Board for the Advancement of Psychology in the Public Interest. She has also served on the APA Committee for the Advancement of Professional Practice.

She served as president of both APA Division 35, the Society for the Psychology of Women, and APA Division 17, the Society of Counseling Psychology. She has been elected to serve as president of the Texas Psychological Association in 2006.

Dr. Vasquez coauthored with Dr. Pope, *Ethics in Psychotherapy and Counseling: A Practical Guide for Psychologists* (2nd ed.). She also served on the APA Ethics Committee and on the Ethics Committee Task Force for Revision of the 1981 and the 1992 Ethics Codes.

Dr. Vasquez was chosen in 2003 to serve on the APA Board of Educational Affairs Advisory Council on Accreditation, and she has been elected to represent APA Division 42 (Psychologists in Independent Practice) on the APA Council of Representatives for 2004–2007.

Prior to beginning her full-time independent practice, Dr. Vasquez worked in university counseling center settings for 13 years, serving as a university counseling center psychologist at Colorado State University and at the Counseling and Mental Health Center of the University of Texas at Austin. She served as training director at both training centers. She has also taught various courses and published in the areas of professional ethics, psychology of women, supervision and training, and ethnic minority psychology. Recognition of her work includes the following:

- James M. Jones Lifetime Achievement Award, APA Minority Fellowship Program (2004)
- Psychologist of the Year, Texas Psychological Association (2003)
- Foremother Award, Section on Women, Society of Counseling Psychology, Division 17, American Psychological Association (2003)
- Senior Career Award for Distinguished Contributions to Psychology in the Public Interest, American Psychological Association (2002)
- Columbia University Janet E. Helms Award for Mentoring and Scholarship, Winter Roundtable on Cross-Cultural Psychology and Education (2002)
- Distinguished Leadership Award, APA Committee of Women in Psychology (2000)
- John Black Award for Contributions to Professional Practice in Counseling Psychology (2000)
- Distinguished Career Contributions to Service Award, Society for the Study of Ethnic Minority Issues, APA Division 45 (1999)
- Outstanding Contributions to Public Service Award, Texas Psychological Association (1999)